ENLIGHTENMENT CROSSINGS

pre- and post-modern discourses

anthropological

uniform with this volume

PERILOUS ENLIGHTENMENT
pre- and post-modern discourses
sexual, historical

ENLIGHTENMENT BORDERS
pre- and post-modern discourses
medical, scientific

ENLIGHTENMENT CROSSINGS

---

pre- and post-modern discourses

anthropological

G. S. Rousseau

**MANCHESTER
UNIVERSITY PRESS**

Manchester and New York

distributed exclusively in the USA and Canada
by St Martin's Press, New York

Copyright © Manchester University Press 1991

Published by Manchester University Press
Oxford Road, Manchester M13 9PL, UK
and Room 400, 175 Fifth Avenue,
New York, NY 10010, USA

Distributed exclusively in the USA and Canada
by St. Martin's Press, Inc.,
175 Fifth Avenue, New York, NY 10010, USA

British Library cataloging in publication data
Rousseau, G. S.
  Enlightment crossings: pre- and post-modern
  discourses, anthropological.
  1. Anthropology
  I. Title
  301

Library of Congress cataloging in publication data
Rousseau. G. S. (George Sebastian)
    Pre- and post-modern discourses / G.S. Rousseau
      p. cm
    Includes bibliographical references and index.
    Contents: v. 1. Enlightenment crossings — v. 2. Enlightenment
borders — v. 3. Perilous enlightenment.
    ISBN 0–7190–3072–2 (v. 1). — ISBN 0–7190–3506–6 (v. 2). — ISBN
0–7190–3301–2 (v. 3)
    1. Social history—18th century.   2. Civilization, Modern—18th
century. I. Title
  HN13.R68   1991
  306'.09'033 — dc20   90–19452

ISBN for complete set of 3 volumes 0–7190–3549–X
ISBN for this volume 0–7190–3072–2 *hardback*

Phototypeset by Input Typesetting Ltd, London

Printed in Great Britain
by Bell & Bain Limited, Glasgow

CONTENTS

ACKNOWLEDGEMENTS

Given the perilous disciplinary borders these essays traverse, it is not surprising that the extended essay (and sometimes not so extended) should have proved my métier. The essay form affords the probing but still unsettled mind, often hankering to make up its mind but plagued by uncertainty, the leisure to ponder alternatives and take roads not trodden. Essays of book length consume so much time and energy on single topics, and are put through such monolithic scrutiny, that they rarely permit their authors the possibility of breaking out of accepted moulds. This is all the more true when disciplinary boundaries are crossed.

For this reason I have relied on the essay form – diverse, dialogical and problematic as it is – to find my own bearings. All of these essays have been published before, but not in this form and not collected in this way. Indeed, the gathering of these essays into this collection and the process of deciding which essays to include has helped me to probe even further.

But I could not have done this alone, or without the sustained dialogues I have held with my friends and colleagues over the years. Chief among these have been ongoing discussions – written and oral – with Richard D. Lehan and Maximillian E. Novak, my colleagues at UCLA, and Roy Porter, my collaborator at the Wellcome Institute for the History of Medicine, whose academic post across an ocean and a continent has not prevented us from debating these matters. To them, as well as to the memory of my teacher and mentor, the late Marjorie Hope Nicolson, these essays are dedicated, partly in the hope that they may eventually serve as a type of record of our own crossing over many perilous borders. The last of these scholars cannot read them, but if the others discover the essays in *Enlightenment Crossings, Perilous Enlightenment* and *Enlightenment Borders* to be a useful reminder of their own important role in activating these debates over two decades, I shall be satisfied.

Others too numerous to name also played a crucial role in the formation of thought represented here by offering encouragement and agreement, as well as disagreement and sharp criticism. They included but are not limited to: Michael Allen, Joanne Trautman Banks, Gillian Beer, P.-G Boucé, Leila Brownfield, Mario Baggioli, Robert Adams Day, Philippa Foot, Clifford Geertz, Ruth Graham, Donald Greene, Roger Hahn, John Heilbron, Gert Hekma, Wallace Jackson, Carolyn Lyle Williams, David Morris, John Neubauer, James Paradis, Ronald Paulson, Richard Popkin, Pat Rogers, Elinor Shaffer, Simon Shaffer, Jean Starobinski, Lawrence Stone, Randolph Trumbach, Richard Zeimacki. I also owe a debt of thanks to my editor John Banks. He has read every one of these chapters with the care of a first-time reader, and prompted me to reconsider their form and content long after I thought I could doctor them no more. These essays could not have made their way through the various stages of publication at a large university press without his experienced editorial eye. My gratitude to him is therefore like that of a son to a father: as time passes the younger knows how much he owes to the older.

These essays appear in their original versions (some with changed titles) except that works originally cited as forthcoming and some of the scholarship have been brought up to date, chapters have been cross-referenced to each other for the reader's convenience, references have been standardised in part, and minor corrections have been made. While assembling the chapters and organising them in the three volumes I thought it particularly important that they be cross-referenced to each other. But there has been no attempt to rewrite the essays in order for them to appear more unified than they are, or to suggest that they now have a common audience. Disguise plays no role in the act of collecting and presenting them here, and the fact is that these essays were written over the span of a quarter of a century for different audiences on different occasions. It insults the reader's intelligence to pretend that this had not been the case, or to glaze over this plain fact by artificially recasting or reshaping them here. The place of all publications is London where not otherwise cited.

The original places of publication of the essays in this volume are as follows: (1) 'Science and the Discovery of the Imagination in Enlightened England', *Eighteenth-Century Studies*, III (fall 1969), 108–35; (2) 'Le Cat and the Physiology of Negroes', in Harold Pagliaro (ed.), *Racism in the Eighteenth Century* (Cleveland, 1973), 369–87; (3) 'Whose Enlightenment? Not Man's: The Case of Michel Foucault', *Eighteenth-Century Studies*, VI (1972), 238–56; (4) 'Psychology', in G. S. Rousseau and Roy Porter (eds.), *The Ferment of Knowledge: Studies in the Historiography of Science* (Cambridge, 1980), 143–209; (5) 'Nerves, Spirits and Fibres: Toward the Origins of Sensibility', in R. F. Brissenden (ed.), *Studies in the Eighteenth Century* (Canberra, 1975), 137–57. Reprinted 'with a Postscript 1976' in Angela Giannitrapani (ed.), *The Blue Guitar* (Rome, 1976), 125–6; (6) 'Threshold and Explanation: the Social Anthropologist and the Critic of Eighteenth-Century Literature', *The Eighteenth Century: Theory and Interpretation*, XXII (spring, 1981), 127–52; (7) 'Old or New Historical Injunctions?: Critical Theory, Referentiality and Academic Migration', *The Eighteenth Century*, XXVIII (1987), 250–8; (8) 'The Debate about the New Historicism and the Status of the History of Science', *Literature and History*, XI (autumn,1985), 159–75; (9) 'Madame Chimpanzee', *The Clark Newsletter*, X (1986), 1–4 (part one); XII (spring 1987), 4–7 (part two); (10) From *The Languages of Psyche: Mind and Body in Enlightenment Thought* (Berkeley, Los Angeles and Oxford; 1990), 1–47 (with Roy Porter).

UCLA, AUGUST 1990

FOR DICK, MAX AND ROY
with friendship and admiration

and to the memory of
MARJORIE HOPE NICOLSON
who would have applauded the attempt

INTRODUCTION

For as long as I can remember I have been writing essays in the borderlands between academic disciplines and crossing over their perilous boundaries. It has been an act of intellectual will as much as a temperamental proclivity prompting me to break away from the traditional boundaries dictated by university faculties and from the conventional departments academic disciplines designate. There are many implications – personal and professional, theoretical and practical – in crossing boundaries; and the role played by borders in cultural and social differences should not be minimised, either in my own development or in the intellectual life of the times in which I live. These chapters typify those crossings over two decades and constitute the first volumes of my collected essays since I published, almost ten years ago, an anthology of my essays about an eighteenth-century novelist now barely read (Tobias Smollett).

Throughout my writing career – now encompassing the best part of a quarter of a century – I have always looked beyond my immediate academic discipline – English literature of the eighteenth century – to frontiers where different disciplines come together. Some have called me a pioneer in this activity; others, who have felt unduly challenged and discomforted by the resulting dialogue, have claimed that the energy has been misspent and somewhat unintelligible. I would have done better, they have claimed, to remain at home, as it were, and cultivate my own garden.

My response is that I cannot. For many reasons, including ethical ones compelling persons to strive to leave the world better off than they found it, I must always be travelling to another country: to see its territory with an alien, sceptical eye; to taste its exotic and remote realms for myself; to bring my own local knowledge, the knowledge of my own discipline, to its distant borders. This matter of 'borders' penetrates to the essential tension displayed in these essays. The borders between disciplines, like those strange borderlands between countries, have always engendered hybrid cultures (think of the Swiss borders, for example) and bilingual discourses, and it is in these domains that I have elected to study the Enlightenment, about which I care so much.

Nor is the metaphor of countries and borders excessive to describe these disciplinary territories. The humanities and sciences are now practised in such diversity that even those who work in the same field (here is the metaphor under different stress) often discover they do not speak the same language. The theorisation of the academy in our time – to echo the phrases of Quentin Skinner and Frederick Crews – has intensified the disparity. Yet, in my own case, I was crossing these boundaries before the advent of poststructuralism, postmodernism, deconstruction, 'difference' – *différance* – and now postdisciplinary discourse. The trope that troubled me throughout the 1960s and early 1970s when some of these essays were written, was that of the 'Renaissance man': a creature with wide-ranging interests in diverse fields who refused to succumb to specialisation.

Enlightenment culture boasted many such figures, of which Franklin and Goethe are perhaps the best known. I did not think of myself as one under any circumstances; nevertheless the 'Renaissance man' represented the ideal for us (then green and young) academics to cultivate in the age of rampant technology and specialisation, when all broad knowledge was threatened with extinction. The Renaissance man did not, of course, have a chance of survival in our specialised universities endorsed by the post-industrial information state. Our research centres mandated just the opposite gaze: narrow, specialised, small pieces of knowledge; isolated practices and specialised discourses performed by technicians who resembled those poor souls toiling away in solitude in Leibniz's imaginary cells.

This ferment of knowledge, as I attempt to document briefly in the head notes to the essays, occurred during the 1970s when various social movements (e.g. the response to the liberalism of the 1960s, the revolt against many forms of authority) and intellectual currents (the first wave of poststructuralism) were palpably felt. It was then, I think, that the academy became theorised and was transformed into the institution we know it to be today. In that long decade extending from about 1968 to the early 1980s, a majestic transformation in the status of knowledge occurred throughout the western world, as it altered from an age of hierarchy and principle to one in which the processes of gathering and classifying information were themselves representative of the highest goal: from modernism to postmodernism; from a structural habit of mind to poststructuralist; from one set of technologies and its attendant practices to a quite different one labouring under the force of the microelectronic revolution. This transformation, about which the historians of the future shall fill many books, was bound to take its toll on the academy – among the most vulnerable of contemporary institutions anyway – and its conventional academic disciplines. Bluntly put, by the end of the 1970s it was clear within the universities that a whole repertoire of buzz words (interdisciplinary, transdisciplinary, crossdisciplinary) had become the signs – the real semiotics – of an oncoming postdisciplinary era in which the traditional disciplines would be hurled to the margins of civilised discourse. Having flown in the face of authority in this way, *post*disciplinary activity institutionalised itself at the centre – in the core – of academic dialogue and discourse.

The transformation posed significant challenges to me personally and professionally. To a certain extent I had been engaged in these encounters among disciplines for some time; crossing the borders, so to speak, before the challenges of the transformation; traversing discourses before the ideology of interdisciplinarity set in; so there was really no question about the novelty of the activity. By the time 'interdisciplinarity' became the favoured code word of administrators and all those seeking funding, I had been (to invoke another neologism) 'interdisciplinating' for some time. The disclosure may seem pungent but it was the methodological consequence of interdisciplinarity in the postdisciplinary age that consumed me rather than any search for novelty: especially the degree to which such a perilous approach could actually produce a more valid historicism by virtue of the broader contexts it created. If the crossing of disciplinary borders could locate previous cultures more accurately, then the risk was worth the effort.

This constellation of categories – culture, context, historicism – is the one this volume explores. It does so through a reconsideration of the ways in which that crucial transformation in twentieth-century cultures was conducted. The fact that the European Enlightenment has always been my preferred chronological period is of little consequence here: it could have been the Middle Ages, the Renaissance, or the Victorian Age, for history is always a dialogue of the present with the past as much as a perception of turning entirely to the past. The matter then is not my own diachronic period, the Enlightenment, but the ways in which that era and its culture have been related to the inescapable present; more explicitly, the ways in which the traditional academic disciplines become the abettors or detractors of that dialogue.

If the borders of these essays, which include critiques and metacritiques and which were written over two decades, are anthropological, scientific, medical, and sexual, their common boundary remains the zone explored in these essays. I make no claim that any *one* method has been invoked, or that an interdisciplinary methodology has emerged after such a long time. On the contrary all my fear and trembling arises from the knowledge that no single method has suggested itself *despite* a constant search for one. This resolution and the process it has entailed represents, I think, my own claim *against* theory and its grand edifice. Put otherwise, interdisciplinarity itself represents a set of curiosities, a range of possibilities, rather than the beginnings of any method or logic that can be codified and then applied.

The lack of recognised method is, of course, precisely what is held up against it by its detractors who profess that whatever their defects may be, the *traditional* disciplines at least have a methodology (i.e. craft, *kraft*), without which significant inquiry cannot begin, let alone be resolved. But this junction marks the very point complicating these perilous crossings. For we are not merely crossing disciplinary boundaries here but are doing so at a moment when the traditional disciplines themselves have ceased to exist in any organised way. At least this position is the one currently held by almost all those who have pondered these matters, and they themselves come from such a variety of disciplines and diversity of backgrounds that it is inconceivable there could be any collusion or consensus in this position: Kuhn, Weber, Habermas, Latour, Lyotard, Derrida, *et al.*

Something more elaborate must be said, even in a brief space, about this disciplinary-postdisciplinary milieu in which we find ourselves – teachers and students alike – today. The disciplinary still exists – of course – in the institutional sense. Colleges and universities everywhere have faculties, or departments, of history, philosophy, literature, mathematics, physics, and so forth. But – and it is the salient but – the concerns of those faculties and departments have been so remarkably transformed that their designating name signifies little and certainly does not indicate that its current members are asking any of the questions that were being asked a decade or two ago. It is as if these faculties are just the ruins – the shells – of their former selves. They remain vital because they are asking the important new questions, which often are interdisciplinary, not because they each embody a hard won craft or methodology. The semiotics of this state of affairs is that our contemporary institutional arrangements have much to do to catch up with the discourses and practices activated by their members.

These discourses and practices remain at the heart of the matter, and will eventually have to be addressed on a global scale. The essays in these three volumes – *Enlightenment Crossings*, *Perilous Enlightenment* and *Enlightenment Borders* – suggest that such a forum is actually overdue. But there are other concerns perhaps as crucial as the institutional aspect of the various disciplines. Why, some readers will shrewdly ask, are the disciplines so important? Why cannot scholars and critics merely explore wherever their curiosity takes them without concern or regard for disciplinary boundaries? The answer may appear unassailably positive to these questions, but the reality is quite otherwise. Disciplines since the eighteenth century have established their own vocabularies, even code words, and procedures, which function as union cards for admission to the guild. More consequential, disciplines have for two centuries now set the agenda – the kinds of questions – that could be asked by its practitioners. Given that the agenda always determines the conclusions that can be reached in any discussion, whether academic or not, this matter of programmatic agenda is essential if one contemplates traversing disciplinary boundaries in the way I have done here.

But for every reader who interrogates the disciplinary status of these essays, there will be three, I suspect, who want to penetrate to the essays themselves and who will ask questions about the broad range of the essays – will enquire into the background of the author. Here one thinks of Foucault's question, *What is an author?* How can someone whose 'field' is literature range so widely in the borderlands between topics anthropological, scientific, medical, sexual, etc? Is there not some polymorphous perversity here that should be curbed and eradicated? This is the point where postdisciplinary knowledge must be consulted, for – as I have been suggesting – at some point in the 1970s or early 1980s, knowledge ceased being local and disciplinary and became global and interdisciplinary, or – as others called it – discourse thriving on the margins of traditional discourse. Coeval with the movement away from local national structures was a turn to the world economy, world ecology, world environment, world debt crisis – in the vernacular, to one global village. Perhaps this is why Habermas's current project remains the investment in a 'philosophical discourse of modernism' without regard to the disciplinary at all. Others – Feyerabend, Kuhn, Deleuze, Derrida, Bordieu – have never been willing to label themselves historian, philosopher, critic, etc. in the first place. And still others have claimed that the boundaries drawn today are those of class, gender, and race, not of disciplines, institution, or nation.

If this is so, and there is reason to believe it is so, then these essays also serve as the personal chronicle of a scholar who found himself working between the two worlds of the local and the disciplinary versus the global and interdisciplinary. When I was starting out in the 1960s, I had little inkling that the traditional disciplines would soon become transformed as they have been; still less notion that within just a few years, I would soon find myself constricted by the conventional subjects and desperately trying to break out of them. It is as if a physicist were trying to become an interphysicist, or a historian a cultural-anthropological historian. Once she or he starts, the old disciplines appear increasingly constraining in the postdisciplinary age.

By the 1970s, I was self-reflectively searching for a whole series of ways to escape from the tyranny of the disciplines, often without knowing it. And the toll this frustration took is evident in many of the essays, whose genuine subject is the transformation of the traditional agenda of the disciplines in question, whether one discipline or another is now irrelevant.

This progression from disciplinary to postdisciplinary organisation also took a toll on my equilibrium. There were long intervals in which I did not feel as if I belonged to *any* disciplines. Some of my opponents called me a defector from the fold who had developed a sharp and polemical style to ward off the sceptics;

others claimed that my wide-ranging work in Enlightenment studies was suspicious by dint of not being the product of someone trained in the specific disciplines from which it emerged. But others latched on to these approaches and seemed to applaud the wide gaze. A distinguished historian of literature asked for how long I could expect to get away with not admitting that I had now become a professional historian of science. Yet another claimed that I would have little difficulty if I now called myself a professional historian of medicine. To these and others there is only one response it seems to me: that they are all correct because the traditional disciplines themselves had lost their former vitality. The chaos and confusion lay not in my individual development – as if it had been unique – but rather in the transforming disciplines which had grown miserably out of touch with the reality of the discourses and practices their members were writing and following.

The reader will also see that history remains an *arrière pensée* of these essays. No matter which border I perfidiously cross at this time, I keep returning to history and its vexations. If the purpose of theory is indeed to reinvigorate historical studies, then it has achieved its purpose in my case. From the first of these essays – published late in the 1960s – to the most current at the end of the 1980s – my imagination has always been fixed on the problem of historicism: which historicism, of what variety, how practised, in which rhetorics and tropes and genres? I am thus in no sense a convert: having begun historical – as the head notes detail – I remain historicist. All my doubt has rested on a more proper approach to a deep-layer historicism, especially for Enlightenment studies, than the ones we have at present. But the great challenge of theory during my adult lifetime has been its extraordinary possibilities for historicism. If I did not believe that, I would long ago have abandoned cultural history and returned to the old methods in which I had been trained. Theory, especially feminist theory and the theory that privileges sex, gender and class, has never appeared to me the gremlin it symbolises to some of my university colleagues and fellow scholars because of its inherent ability to re-energise history and challenge conventional wisdom. The challenge of a theorised academy, such as we now have, is a healthy and positive one because theory's ability to ask questions requiring a higher threshold of explanation than prevails in times when theory is not so widely dispersed and ingrained as a natural habit of mind.

Furthermore, during my adult life I have lived through a revolution in knowledge created in large part by the disciplines represented in these essays. In cultural anthropology after Mead and Lévi-Strauss, and the new history of science after Kuhn, Latour, and Bordieu, are found some of the sources of the *post*disciplinary transformations these essays imply. But not all. Much is also owing to Western society at the end of the twentieth century: its global shifts, unprecedented pluralism, run-away technology, and renewed quest for freedom and egalitarianism at any price. This is perhaps why disciplines such as science and medicine have been so important in our time. Without a serious critique of medicine we could not understand how previous men and women had resisted the temptation to cave in under the stresses and strains of the postindustrial age. Yet 'sex' has no academic disciplines, no institutionalised filiation. To be blunt, in which faculty or department would sex and its history be studied? This is the question Foucault often asked, but he supplied no satisfactory answer. Psychology, psychiatry, history, philosophy, sociology, literature? Surely all of these. That is why we cross borders in the first place, to understand evolving discourses like the one of sexuality. But then, why do we still retain disciplines at all?

Finally some readers may wonder why I have been so biographically explicit, and whether it would not have been preferable to write an autobiography or publish memoirs. It is a good question readily responded to. My purpose has not been to document my own development in regard to my *life* – that I will do elsewhere, in another genre altogether – but rather, to suggest the various ways in which that intellectual development was prescribed and determined somewhat beyond my control. Those who contend that I have tried to model myself (to return to the old trope used above) on the Renaissance man have perhaps missed the point, which has been this: do what I could, I seem to have been unable to narrow my concerns and practice in one discipline only; incapable of remaining within the traditional mould and tending to the local agenda. My condition, it seems to me, has been symptomatic of the age.

If this energy appears wildly promiscuous, so it must be. More specifically, if it represents the developing, broad contexts for which many themselves are striving for today, then it will have served to encourage those also on this or a similarly unconventional quest. From my vantage, which is admittedly myopic as well as oblique, it has always appeared that the crossings would eventually open up contexts that had previously remained too narrow. This is one reason the borders are so perilous. Anyway, time will tell.

WORKS CITED

S. Allen (ed.), *Possible Worlds in Humanities, Arts and Sciences: Proceedings of Nobel Symposium 65, 1986* (Stockholm, 1989), section 1: Philosophy: T. S. Kuhn: 'Possible Worlds in History of Science'. Session 3: Literature and Arts: Lubomir Dolezel: 'Possible worlds and literary fictions', with commentaries by Umberto Eco and others. Kuhn's chapter contains some of the ideas of the two worlds of science and language which he developed in his 1984 Thalheimer Lectures at the Johns Hopkins University.

Pierre Bourdieu, *Distinction: a Social Critique of the Judgement of Taste* (1984).

George Dickie, *Art and the Aesthetic in Institutional Analysis* (Ithaca and London, 1974).

Michel Foucault, *Les Mot et les choses: une archeologie des sciences humaines* (Paris, 1966).

Michel Foucault, *Discipline and Punish* (New York, 1977).

Michel Foucault, *The History of Sexuality*, 3 vols. (New York, 1978–86).

E. H. Gombrich, ' "They Were All Human Beings – So Much Is Plain": Reflections on Cultural Relativism in the Humanities,' *Critical Inquiry*, XIII (summer 1987), 686–99.

Penelope Gouk, 'The Union of Arts and Sciences in the Eighteenth Century: Lorenz Spengler (1720–1807), Artistic Turner and Natural Studies', *Annals of Science* XL (1983), 411–36.

Loren Graham, Wolf Lepenies, and Peter Weingart (eds.), *Functions and Uses of Disciplinary Histories* (Dordrecht, 1983).

Jürgen Habermas, 'Michel Foucault: the Critique of Reason as an Unmasking of the Human Sciences', in *The Philosophical Discourse of Modernity*, trans. Frederick Lawrence (Cambridge, 1987).

Russell Jacoby, *The Last Intellectuals: American Culture in the Age of Academe* (New York, 1987).

Thomas S. Kuhn, *The Structure of the Scientific Revolution* (Chicago, 1970).

Thomas S. Kuhn, 'Commensurability, Comparability, Communicability', in Peter D. Asquith (ed.), *Philosophy of Science Association, 1982*, 2 vols (East Lansing, 1983), II, 669–716.

Thomas S. Kuhn, 'Scientific Development and Lexical Change' (The Thalheimer Lectures, 1984), unpublished lectures.

Bruno Latour, *Science in Action: how to Follow Scientists and Engineers through Society* (Cambridge, 1987).

Jean-François Lyotard, *The Postmodern Condition: a Report on Knowledge*, Theory and History of Literature (Manchester and Minneapolis: 1984).

Joseph Margolis, 'Theory and Method in the Cultural Sciences', in Robert S. Cohen (ed.), *Boston Colloquium for the Philosophy of Science* (Boston, 1988–9).

M. J. Mulkay, *The Social Process of Innovation: a Study in the Sociology of Science* (1972).

M. J. Mulkay, *Science and the Sociology of Knowledge* (1979).

M. J. Mulkay, *The Word and the World: Explorations in the Form of Sociological Analysis* (1985).

M. J. Mulkay and Will Outhwaite (eds.), *Social Theory and Social Criticism: Essays for Tom Bottomore* (Oxford, 1987).

Alan Sinfield, 'New Historicism and the Primal Scene of US Humanism' (UCLA Department of English talk, spring 1989).

Reba Soffer, 'Why Do Disciplines Fail? The Strange Case of British Sociology', *British Journal of Sociology* XCVII (1982), 767–802.

E. P. Thompson, *Albion's Fatal Tree: Crime and Society in 18th-century England* (New York, 1975).

Weber, Samuel (ed.), *Demarcating the Disciplines: Philosophy, Literature, Art* (Minneapolis, 1986).

I

Towards a social anthropology of the imagination

This was the first of the long essays attempting to define an anthropology of imagination based on the science and medicine during the Enlightenment. I began composing it while at Harvard during the late 1960s, before entering what I have called the partial poststructuralist phase of the 1970s. I was immersed in materialist and ideological treatises of the period, as well as in its mechanism and vitalism, but I had not yet read Foucault, Adorno, Althusser, or some of the other thinkers who would influence my later essays in this section. I wrote it in considerable astonishment that science and medicine had been omitted so consistently from the discourses about the Enlightenment. All that has by now – of course – changed; and one is no longer saying anything new by writing, for example as I did in this essay in 1969, that 'there are more metaphors . . . of the mind and references to mental institutions in the literature of the eighteenth century that literary critics have noted – indeed the artist's personal struggle to define himself in relation to the world of sanity or insanity is so pervasive that it may be called a leitmotif'. Then, it seemed crucial to make precisely these points, not only as a corrective to the empirical facts of Enlightenment agendas but also to provide an escape valve for those of us who were becoming college and university teachers working under the powerful tyranny of a still malingering New Criticism. My other aim in what then seemed a solitary attempt was to bring the various critiques of the sixties closer together.

The essay was fundamentally an effort to demonstrate how imagination had been medicalised in the early Enlightenment and why this development in turn had such profound effect on the Enlightenment discourses of mind and body. By using this medicalisation as a beacon, I hoped to demonstrate that the history of science and the philosophy of science were essential disciplines for literary historians, of whom I considered myself one. What I really sought was a social anthropology of imagination that integrated the medicalised discourses within a larger cultural view; but I did not see how this could be done, coming from a perspective grounded in intellectual history. Moreover, during those years – the late 1960s – the notion of bringing these various discourses together seemed a rueful enterprise; fraught with difficulty and peril, not least to one's own career and advancement. My encouragement came largely from Marjorie Hope Nicolson, with whom I had recently co-authored 'This Long Disease, My Life': Alexander Pope and the Sciences *(Princeton University Press, 1968). But by the time this essay was published two years later, she was already seriously ill and I had to look elsewhere to find my way.*

Late in the seventeenth century man discovered his imagination[1] and, as Densher in Henry James's novel *The Wings of the Dove* says, 'we shall never again be the same'. When they tell the story of this discovery, historians of science will probably insist that it was part of a long, continuing process of discovering the body. Not until man discovered a considerable portion of his anatomy could he earnestly formulate a scientific model by which to account for the physiology of imagination. The discovery of the imagination does not imply that man suddenly realised he had one; for example, that he had now located the faculty which permitted him to dream at night and daydream,[2] or to envision objects and places not actually present before the retina. What he did discover – with the help of scientists and philosophers – was that the imagination was a real essence, as material in substance as any other part of the body, and that it therefore could be medically described. An important consequence of this development in physiology is that leading thinkers of the next century deified the new 'organ', endowing it alone with the means of salvaging the soul of man while on earth. Such deification was restricted to philosophers and artists, men like Kant and Coleridge, who felt compelled to reject the modes of explanation of the physiologist, not upon methodological grounds but because it thwarted the expectations it raised. Science and literature were perhaps never closer in their ultimate aims than in the century (1680–1780) that discovered imagination.

Such discovery cannot accurately be said to have occurred over a long period of time as in the case of the chemical composition of the blood. It occurred precisely in the second half of the seventeenth century in Western Europe, particularly in England and France, largely the result of certain medical and physiological experiments and at a time when the scientific spirit, to use the language of the day, was at its zenith – as is evidenced by the establishment in 1660 in London of a Royal Society for the Advancement of Natural Philosophy and the hitherto unprecedented number of experiments undertaken. It was discovered, moreover, at that moment in history when Aristotelian scholasticism could no longer hold water and when the new science, particularly the new corpuscular physiology of Harvey, Boyle, Willis, and Newton, created a revolution in scientific thought.[3] This revolution was not so much a methodological one as it was an awareness that psychology was of paramount importance in the realm of ethics; and that moral conduct was ultimately predicated upon the passions and not the innate ideas of men. The thinker to whom the *literati* in England owed more than to any other single man for their knowledge of psychology is the monumental genius John Locke. And it is reasonable to conjecture that without Locke's theory of association (primary sense impressions combining and commingling), the whole course of eighteenth- and nineteenth-century British literature would be different.

The Platonic notion of the imagination as a source of suspicion and distrust (according to the *Timaeus* located in the liver), as a pander to the passions and the appetites, was so soon superseded by the Aristotelian conception in European thought that it can be over-looked as inconsequential in its influence. In Aristotle's ontological world of real and less real essences, the mind and its sub-members (fancy, the imagination, the appetitive faculties, the passions) play a small role in the observer's perception of these essences.[4] Trees, rocks, and drops of water exist in an objective and absolute sense; they ought to appear the same to the baker, bricklayer, or candlestick maker. If they do not, that is the fault of the perceiver (not the perceived), who suffers from a privation of the correct perception of matter. Descartes, Hobbes, Malebranche, and, more significantly, Locke toppled an aged empire of thought when, in their various ways, they introduced for the first time in European thought the possibility of a real imagination: substantive, existential, working physiologically through the mechanical motions of the blood, nerves,[5] and animal spirits.[6] The revolutionary thought of these men is sometimes referred to as the greatest advance ever made in the history of the 'mind–body' problem, but it is more accurately described as the 'discovery of the imagination' since the former was as old as the pre-Socratic philosophers and could not radically redefine its terms until the imagination was physiologically created.

From the literary historian's vantage, the most significant aspect of this discovery was the decline of mimetic art, that aesthetic preference for imitative art that had governed and guided art from ancient times through the late seventeenth century.[7] If the imagination is physically non-existent, then trees must be represented as trees, rocks as rocks, and water as water; but as soon as the imagination is acknowledged as real substance containing matter, it may then transform the perceiver's sense of trees and rocks and permit him to represent these materially tangible objects in artistic shapes that are not immediately recognisable. A belief in the physical existence of the imagination implies a belief in psychology – the science of the psyche – and belief in psychology substantially alters the number of possibilities for imitation. If the imagination contains substance and is material, then, like trees, rocks, or drops of water, *it* may be imitated in art. An observer gazing at Correggio's *Leda and the Swan* or Poussin's '*Et in Arcadia Ego*' can instantaneously recognise true nature in the likeness of the painter's forms, but who has ever seen an 'imitation of the imagination' represented in a form of art that could be called realistic – true to nature?[8] Such non-realistic art (in painting, literature, music) would pose insurmountable difficulties of interpretation. For this reason there was much resistance by philosophers and artists in the eighteenth century to the theory of the physiological existence of the imagination; resistance, however, eventually gave way, and symbolic art (art that imitates, if anything, the life of the imagination) inherited the throne formerly occupied by mimesis.

It was not possible for symbolism to flourish until mimesis died, and the decline of mimesis occurred only when psychology was established as a science. In the late seventeenth and eighteenth centuries psychology was more neurological than it has been at any time until the last few decades (when it appears to have reverted to its original state). Medical theories of physicians like Sydenham, Willis, Charleton, Hooke, and Boyle must be invoked, for without their bold ideas the imagination must have lingered for a longer time in an inchoate state of universal darkness. Although John Locke is famous today as an empirical philosopher and the author of the ethical treatise *An Essay Concerning Human Understanding* (1690), his reputation in his own time was as a leading physician. Scientifically trained at the University of Leyden, which then contained the most advanced medical school in the world, he had studied medicine with Boerhaave, the eminent physician and Professor of Chemistry, and learned physiological theories that later were to enable him to base his ethics and epistemology upon current physiological principles.

The aspect of Locke's *Essay* most important for our purpose is that his deepest questions are ultimately physiological. To be sure, he investigated the science of the mind in order that he might advise men better regarding virtuous conduct. And it is true that he succeeded *most* in his ethics, *least* in his physiology, and not without abundant reason, for he never undertook the kind of scientific investigation and experimentation (as had Boyle and Newton) necessary to explore adequately the neurological aspects of his questions. And yet, his questions were physiological from the start.[9] The imagination, he argued, *must* exist; observation and induction teach that no two men behold and describe a tree similarly; they cannot and indeed are not capable of expressing it alike or suggesting an identical connotation; therefore, while the tree exists, it is not existential in the sense the imagination is; in fact, the tree can exist only in the eye and imaginative faculty of the beholder. So important is the formation of this 'mind', its impressions and ideas, Locke asserted, that it deserves more attention than the tree. In focussing his attention, Locke's problem was always 'how', rarely 'why'. He was not a moralist asking *why* men are as they are, nor why they perceive as they do; he knew they are creatures of passion and ruled by irrational desires; he was the physiologist asking 'how' they perceive. Locke was perennially interested in the formation of the imagination as a complicated network of secondary ideas in various associative patterns and in the organic relation of the imagination to the nerves, blood, and animal spirits.

Although it was not possible for Locke to answer the physiological questions he asked, his *Essay* influenced the path of science, not merely epistemology, for more than a century. George Berkeley the Irish philosopher, David Hartley the London physician and associationist philosopher, David Hume and Joseph Priestly, and many others followed in his footsteps, asking the same basic questions. If eighteenth-century medical-philosophical thought was unable to explain the physiology of imagination, that failure should be regarded, first of all, with humility (the most advanced brain theorists today know virtually nothing about the physiology of memory),[10] and secondly, in perspective. No mechanical model could satisfactorily explain the associations of the imagination until the controversies raging over the 'animal spirits' had subsided and ended in less troublesome waters. Precise chemical composition of the substance in the blood giving motion to life eluded definition. It was not until the early nineteenth century, when the reputation of the theory of animal spirits had diminished,[11] that scientists were inclined to believe the problem had always been definitional. And yet, the eighteenth-century physiologists and neurologists conducted their experiments on the nerves in an attempt to understand the secondary associations of the imagination.

The literary effects of the numerous physiological investigations of the century 1680–1780 were considerable, and scientific exploration as significant as this in one segment of the culture would not be expected to remain self-contained. There are more metaphors of the mind and references to mental institutions in the literature of this century than literary critics have noticed – indeed the artist's personal struggle to define himself in relation to the world of sanity or insanity is so pervasive that it may be called a leitmotif. The Restoration and eighteenth century battled out questions relating to the role and place of the imagination in works of art with an ardour that is rare in literary controversies, and the latter part of the century carried on the argument just as ardently. In so doing, thinkers looked to Locke's psychology again and again, and often quoted or commented upon his now celebrated distinction between 'wit' and 'judgement'.[12] In the first half of the eighteenth century, poets like Richard Blackmore in *The Creation* (1712) found a store-house of opulent poetic images in the physiological terminology of the scientific controversies over the definition of imagination; images taken directly from the language of 'the learned', who, in Blackmore's words, 'with anatomic art/Dissest the mind, and thinking substance part'. For the second half of the century, Dr Johnson's chapter 44 of *Rasselas*, 'On the Dangerous Prevalence of Imagination', with its insistence that 'all power of fancy over reason is a degree of insanity', is emblematic of the thinking of the day and of the mode in which physiological thought was creeping into non-scientific literature. Writers like Addison, Swift, Pope, James Thomson, and Dr Johnson were persuaded – however strongly they may have agreed or disagreed with Locke's system – that the role of imagination in literature was perhaps the most vexing aesthetic problem of their time. Without the stirrings of the new physiology these aesthetic questions would never have been asked in the first place.

If the 'imagination' exists, then it must be described by anatomists and its functions must be delineated by physicians and other theorists. Obviously this could not be done in the eighteenth century; nor could it be partially completed without a scientific, molecular model that includes neurons and protons. Yet, it was attempted again and again.[13] The clearest verbal descriptions of the physiological dynamics of the imagination took a mechanical form: the imagination does not work through and by itself although it alone causes the physical motions and chemical processes within the body that result in passions (pleasurable and odious) and second-ary, associated ideas. One of the many comprehensive summaries of the physiology of the imagination is found in the *Medicinal Dictionary* (1743–5) by Dr Robert James, inventor of the famed 'James's fever powders':

> The whole Bent of the Soul is to court and embrace it [the imagination], earnestly endeavouring to be united to it. She is, as it were, expanded in Pleasure; while the animal Spirits, in a kind of Ovation, being carried within the Brain, are constantly exciting the most pleasing Ideas; and, acting in a lively Manner upon the nervous System, causes the Eyes and Countenance to sparkle, while the Hands and every Member exult for Joy: Besides, the Influence of the Brain affecting the Praecordia, by means of the Nerves, they propel the Blood with more Rapidity, and pour it with Vigour on every Part of the Body . . . Such are the Effects of the Power of Imagination; Effects which are sometimes almost incredible, and which have been thought sufficient to restore and renovate, to ruin and destroy, the human Structure.[14]

Such definition immediately implies two kinds of imagination: healthy and sick, normal and diseased, and the distinction was increasingly discussed as the eighteenth century progressed. It is an ironic contrast that the supposed 'Age of Reason' should have produced so many cases of insanity among its writers, in England William Cowper, Christopher Smart, and others. That the so-called 'Enlightened Age' should have concentrated so much of its energy on such distinction should not, however, seem strange to us in a post-Freudian age in which the effects of both kinds of imagination are visible daily: the healthy imagination exhibited in creative art and science, and the diseased imagination of the hallucinating schizophrenic.

The distinctive mechanical operations of each type were of concern to eighteenth-century neurologists, although they had more to say about the latter. Disregarding for the moment the distinction, the imagination was explained by various models, most often as an image-producing aspect of the 'mind', sometimes as the lens of a camera, and sometimes as a multi-motion process of the frontal lobe which throws up images of things or places not present to the mind. Eighteenth-century English poetry, particularly scientific and didactic poetry, possesses a large vocabulary for images describing (analogically) the imagination: cameras, lenses, mirrors, lamps-of-alabaster and lamps-of-reflection, optical instruments then popular, and even the *camera obscura*. A long list of didactic poems explaining the physiology of imagination can be compiled for the period 1750–1820; a late example is L. F. Poulter's *Imagination, a Poem* (1820). There was a tenacious belief that memory was crucial in accounting for the associative modes and chronological order in which these images stream forth. In maintaining this belief, many physiologists were palpably 'modern', for it is still firmly adhered to by brain theorists.[15] Intensity of imagination was felt to depend upon the size of the vestigia, or tracks, through which the animal spirits flowed, and the animal spirits themselves to depend upon 'the lines or strokes of those images'.[16] The medical writings of Dr James and his contemporaries explain that displeasing objects are recalled from the memory without being present by a process of contraction and, then, by relaxing of the fibres.

Not until philosopher–physicians like Locke had addressed themselves to questions relating to the physiology of the imagination could the mechanics of ideas (whether innate or acquired) be explained. And yet, almost immediately after Locke formulated questions regarding the association of ideas – a form of 'madnesse' in itself, as he explains in the *Essay* – medical men were quick to distinguish the associative processes under normal and abnormal conditions. The neurological bases of *dementia* had come a long way from Malebranche's indefinite definition, 'L'imagination est la folle du logis'[17] – imagination is the madwoman of the house, less literally the mad creation of the brain. The fact that Enlightenment physiologists centred their attention on the diseased rather than healthy imagination is of tremendous consequence for the development of European poetry; for it was not until culture scientifically defined the very same madness it wished to condemn that poets turned to the writing of 'mad verse' for catharsis and relief. Stated otherwise, the imagination had to be scientifically authenticated before it could be declared ill by physicians, and in turn cured. One cannot cure an unknown disease. In this connection it is interesting to note that the confinement of lunatics to asylums was an institutional creation peculiar to the seventeenth century and unheard of before them; reformation and attempted cure of lunatics occurred only when physicians of the eighteenth century had shown that the disorders of madmen were physiologic, not religious. Madness was thereby torn from the imaginary freedom which permitted it to flourish in the Renaissance at that moment historically when scientists could demonstrate that body and mind worked hand in hand in a mechanistic and organic fashion.[18] Such demonstration – by seventeenth- and eighteenth-century physicians like Willis, Sydenham, Locke in England, Boerhaave in Holland, Stahl in Germany, La Mettrie in France – ripped religion out of madness and left it (madness) hovering in an orbit of mechanical cause and effect; as in the case of Newtonian gravity, whose forces everyone could calculate but which no one could explain away, madness was defined as a mechanical disorder of the animal spirits relative to their speed of flow and density, but in almost all cases without the slightest indication of an apparent external cause, i.e., a horrific object or alarming circumstance.[19]

Society, in discovering the 'diseased imagination' within the imagination at large, thereby created the notion of a physiological condition: a melange of similar symptoms constituting a 'condition', or as it is called today in medical parlance, a neurosis. By so doing, it also rendered the theoretical possibility of man's functioning well in certain areas and poorly in others. For the first time in the history of medicine it was possible for man's body to be sick and his psyche healthy. Never before the rise of psychology in the eighteenth century had this been true; if man was ill, that was because of some radical disorder in the arrangement of the 'humours' which had been caused, in the first place, by a ruptured relationship to God. The sacred causes of illness were once and forever made profane.

Michel Foucault, the French structuralist philosopher and opponent of Jean-Paul Sartre, who has written an award-winning book *Reason and Civilization: Madness in the Age of the Enlightenment*,[20] notes magisterially that hysteria is the true eighteenth-century disease, far more typical of the age than gout, dropsy, or ague, because it alone was explained by the new dualism that replaced Cartesian dualism, the mechanical operation of the *imagination* in relation to the *body*. '[Hysteria was] the most real and the most deceptive of diseases; real because it is based upon a movement of the animal spirits, illusory as well, because it generates symptoms that seem provoked by a disorder inherent in the organs, whereas they are *only the formation* [italics mine], at the level of these organs, of a central or rather general disorder; it is the derangement of internal mobility that assumes the appearance, on the body's surface, of a local symptom.'[21] The writings of eighteenth-century physicians – works like Mandeville's *Treatise of the Hypochondriack and Hysterick Passions* (1711) – support such a theory of hysteria or hypochondria as a condition, not a disease (a condition embraces many diseases), but not until powers of triggering every kind of physical illness had been delegated to the imagination, could the general malaise of the polite, refined age have been called a disorder of both the imagination and the animal spirits. This malaise was, of course, the well-known 'English Malady', a neurotic type of melancholic hysteria.

The etiology and taxonomy of the science of 'diseased imagination', a phrase that by 1720 was common in medical parlance,[22] was unable to rupture the 'holy alliance between science and religion', although it eventually did. 'It is evident', Dr Robert James wrote in the article on 'Mania' in his medical dictionary, 'that the Brain is the Seat . . . of *all* Disorders of this nature [i.e., madness]. It is there that the Creator has fixed, although in a manner which is inconceivable, the lodging of the soul, the mind, genius, imagination, memory, and all sensations.' And although madness was explained, by James and other physicians, by a mechanical model in which there is an irregular agitation of the spirits, it was now also the obstruction of the body and the imagination, not merely the obstruction of one or the other; an obstruction, moreover, which had grave consequences, as James noted, 'causing stagnation of the humours, immobilisation of the fibers in their rigidity, fixation of ideas and a kind of manic concentration on a theme or idea that gradually prevails over all others'. To be sure, some of this explanation was residual Cartesianism, but it was more than that and incorporated the new psychology of Locke and the new physiology of the doctors. Much of eighteenth-century medicine reads like a commentary on Locke's definition, 'Madnesse seems to be nothing but a disorder in the imagination, and *not* in the discursive faculty.'[23] Science never became so mechanistic as in her attempt to explain 'the obstruction' suggested by Locke and mentioned by James. From the theory of the diseased imagination arose a new conception of the madman. This in turn gave rise to a whole etiology of illnesses created by the 'diseased imagination', which in turn spurred a series of associationist and sensationist controversies[24] that were to leave indelible scars on literature. The astonishing thing is that Enlightenment medicine dismissed as uninteresting the healthy imagination and concentrated exclusively upon the diseased. It arrogated powers to the diseased imagination in its influence on the body that earlier had been reserved for the Deity himself; imagination, in obstructed and consequently diseased forms in the female or male, could destroy the seed of life, the foetus at any stage of conception or gestation. The last vestiges of Cartesian dualism (mind and matter) were now reduced to a form of tyrannical monism in which all bodily functions – especially those of the fibres and animal spirits – were enslaved to the will of the imagination. This imagination, still undefined, was recognised as an irrational 'super passion', as significant for the body as gravity was for the earth, and as the totality of an infinite number of sensations associated and combined in patterns as yet unexplained.

'To the Virtue of the Mother's Fancy [alternate words for the Imagination] have been ascribed the Lineaments of the Embryo or Foetus', Dr James wrote in his *Medicinal Dictionary* in the article on 'Imagination', 'with the Marks imprest upon its Body, both at and after any Time of Conception . . . Transplantation of Diseases, the Strange Alterations of Bodies by the Virtue, Reliques, and the Invocation of Saints, are all imputed to this Power of the Imagination.'

All nascent insanity was believed to result from the mother's diseased imagination, although some theorists thought the father could transmit it during copulation. Medical insistence on the validity of this belief gripped literary and artistic sensibility in a profound way, in a manner that transcended mere influence of science on literature in the form of allusion or demonstrable awareness. Mrs Pickle's perverse craving for 'pineapples of the finest sort' during Peregrine's gestation in Smollett's *Peregrine Pickle* (1751) raises the medically valid fear that Peregrine may be born deformed and – to carry the idea one step further – there is no shadow of doubt that Tristram Shandy's disordered sense of time is caused by his mother's ill-timed ejaculation, uttered at the very moment of sexual coition with Mr Shandy, 'Pray, my dear, have you not forgot to wind up the clock?'[25] Eighteenth-century literature is permeated with examples of women whose imaginations are 'diseased', thereby illustrating more than casual interest of the literary man in medical theories of the day. No science throughout the century was more influential on philosophical thought than medicine, and no science did more to unseat the *literati* from a lingering medievalism based on hierarchy and order, which was now finally obliterated. In the hundred years from 1727 to 1827 there were no Newtons in astronomy, or for that matter in any other science, and while vortices, rainbows, and gravity had enthralled an earlier generation of poets like Pope, John Hughes, and James Thomson, the organic sciences now prevailed and were causing the largest ripples in that ocean of science we have come to call 'the Enlightenment'. As early as 1726, one year before Newton's death, Pope wrote to Swift that the possibility of the 'Rabbit Breeder woman', Mary Tofts, giving birth to seventeen rabbits had stimulated his imagination more than anything since he indulged in 1713 in 'astronomical dialogues with William Whiston', whose explications of planets, orbits, and worlds–upon–worlds without end had sent Pope soaring to a fanciful cloud where he remained for some years.[26]

A survey of the vast medical writings of eighteenth-century England and on the Continent, in Russia and the East European countries, shows a preponderence of works concerned with madness and the malfunctioning imagination.[27] The history of the medical concept 'imagination' in this epoch is therefore also the history of madness. It is hardly surprising that the diseased imagination, rather than the healthy, should have claimed most theoretical attention: Once derangement was deprived of its former freedom, it was the task of physiologists and neurologists to place still stronger limitations upon it; limitations in the form of incessant redefinition. Madness became a subject of greatest interest to methodologists in science, who made it conform to technological constructs then emerging in the organic and inorganic sciences. Indeed, it is not much of an exaggeration to note that the most creative eighteenth-century medical theory appears to be one long record of reconsiderations of the concept madness. In almost every case an attempt was made to demonstrate the precise dynamics of the new dualism, interaction of the imagination and the nervous system. It is as if theoretical physicians were looking for Newtonian laws of motion of the disordered physiology. Their search was for a calculus, as their spokesman Dr Thomas Morgan made perfectly clear in his treatise on the *Philosophical Principles of Medicine* (1725), in which imagination (force) is the product of nerves (mass) and animal spirits (acceleration).[28] Why should it be thought extraordinary that recently discovered mathematical laws – the Newtonian calculus – would be applied to psychology at a time when other sciences (post-Newtonian astronomy and physics, French chemistry, Priestleian electromagnetism), as well as Leibniz's 'science of morality', were turning to them? Albrecht von Haller's experiments in the 1740s and 1750s on animal 'sensibility' and 'irritability'[29] stimulated further laboratory research on the nervous system: here was a physiologist of the highest calibre who appeared to be on the threshold of discovery of the sensory dynamics of the imagination. His experiments on the sensory perception of animals provided partial answers to Locke's associationist questions, and his separation of all sensations into categories of 'irritability' (impressions which do not reach the cortex) and 'sensibility' (those which do) added new fuel to the fire of theoretical physiologists. Whether mania or melancholy were in question, the cause of mental illness initiated by the 'diseased imagination' is always in the movement of the animal spirits. Haller's explorations into the nervous system confirmed the suspicions of empirical scientists like John Gay and David Hartley.[30] What had been put forth by these men as philosophical speculation was now given the stamp and seal of the medical world. Haller was not only the Professor of Medicine at Göttingen (the most esteemed German university of the day); he was also one of the most reverenced physiologists of the century. Associationism and madness were now wedded, and what had earlier passed for mere hypothesis was now proved scientific fact.

There had been much talk about derangement, of course, in medical circles at the turn of the eighteenth century. In fact, there was so much speculation that Jonathan Swift in 1704 alluded abundantly in *A Tale of a Tub* to one of the current theories, that of 'rising vapours', and fully expected his readers to grasp his allusions without spelling them out in detail.[31] But at that time, the etiology of madness was an unknown province. In clinical terms, at that time (*c.* 1700), the etiology was also the sign and the symptom, and the manifestations of the diseased imagination were thought to be the cause. By 1800 the picture altered considerably. Society at large had heard much about scientific theories of the sick imagination,[32] had observed social reform attempting to improve the lot of the madman, and had even grown somewhat weary by the inability of medicine to cure what it professed to understand. Some of the dissatisfaction was owing to a general suspicion of doctors – 'quacks, empirics, and mountebanks', to use Jane Austen's invective – but much was more particularised. There was little visible evidence that the new physiology was better than the old: lay people praise theoretical science only when it abets their daily life. We know today that the neurology of the late eighteenth century had advanced to a point far beyond that of the previous century's, but there is little evidence that laymen of the time knew it. To them, discussion by the 'doctors' regarding madness often appeared pedantic and petty, as one long never-ending controversy. There is, thus, as aspect of staleness and a tone of weariness in the creation of Mathew Bramble, Smollett's ailing hero in *Humphry Clinker* (1771), who suffers from 'a natural excess of mental sensibility' and 'whose every attendant disorder of the Body arises from one originally in the Mind'. So, too, is there in Goldsmith's kindly Dr Primrose in *The Vicar of Wakefield* (1766) whose path of vicissitude proceeds from 'an imagination in discord with its body'.

Greater literary artists than these men absorbed in a curious and sometimes profound manner the findings of contemporary medicine, and began to write in new empirical modes that implied a marriage between 'the diseased imagination' and the normatively accepted 'creative sense' – between sickness and health. The origins of Romantic and, later, symbolic poetry were probably as intrinsically involved with this marriage as they were the decay of the so-called 'rules' and 'genres'; or, again, with the decline of mimesis, a decline that had occurred in the first place as a result of psychology and the empirical view of human experience.

Of the various sciences studied in the eighteenth century, geology has been shown to have played a significant role in the development of romantic nature imagery, particularly in poems like Coleridge's 'Kubla Khan' and plays like Shelley's *Prometheus Unbound*.[33] It has been less clear that the organic sciences generally and medicine particularly played a greater role in the formation of the temperament in art we now call 'Romantic'. Without a century of controversy about the 'diseased imagination', Wordsworth could not have composed his *Prelude* as we know it, the 'Growth of a Poet's Mind'. He was not, to be sure, a scientific poet but if his reaction against physiological law is difficult to pin down, his epic-of-the-imagination – a poem that is now considered to be the greatest achievement of English Romantic poetry – is a direct answer to the inadequacies of associationist medicine and sensory physiology. His language was new, but there was nothing new about his subject, the imagination.

It is a paradigm that art does what science cannot. Whitehead has written that the great defect of eighteenth-century science was its failure to provide for the deeply felt experiences of man or to tolerate the sense that nature is organic. Enlightenment scientists, try though they did, were unable to explain adequately the interaction of the imagination and the animal spirits.[34] If they had tackled a less important matter, they might have been forgiven, but theirs was the single most important problem of physiology, and physiology was the only science of the eighteenth century in which serious research was conducted. Some aspects of their failure were overlooked because culture, particularly in England, was prepared to accept these failures. The inability of the neurologist, for example, to devise a calculus for this interaction was viewed less disappointedly because society at large had not as yet become quantified in the sense we have known technological quantification in this century.

Had it been apparent to the eighteenth century that the physiology of imagination was tearing God from his seat and creating a new kind of deity – a Godhead of the machine: impersonal, predictable, artificial, thrifty – resistance might have been greater. As it was, the resistance was feeble and inconsequential. There was considerable opposition from all segments of the Church, particularly to La Mettrie's theory of 'man as a machine',[35] but set in proper perspective and evaluated on balance, this resistance was not influential and gradually gave way. The greatest disappointments of eighteenth-century science were medical, and are most widely viewed in the natural philosophy and romantic poetry of the late eighteenth and early nineteenth centuries; in the poetry of Blake,

> O Divine Spirit, sustain me on Thy wings,
> That I may awake Albion from his long & cold repose;
> For Bacon & Newton, Sheath'd in dismal steel, their terrors hang
> Like iron scourges over Albion: Reasoning like vast Serpents
> Infold around my limbs, bruising my minute articulations.
> I turn my eyes to the Schools & Universities of Europe
> And there behold the Loom of Locke, whose Woof rages dire,
> Wash'd by the Water-wheels of Newton . . .[36]

or that of Coleridge, who was convinced that the materialist tradition of Boyle, Locke, and Harley had 'untenanted creation of its God'[37] and substituted

> a universe of death
> From that which moves with light and life informed,
> Actual, divine, and true.

For too long it has been thought that the 'revolt' of the Romantic poets was essentially a reaction to a decaying empiricism that could not satisfy the promises it made and the expectations it raised with regard to human progress, a reaction that begged for a new empiricism regarding human experience. Some part of the revolt was certainly due to unfulfilled promises. But much was also the inability of science to formulate laws of organic relationship between the imagination (healthy or diseased) and the animal spirits; that body of physical laws which, if they had been satisfactorily formulated, may have permitted man to be free once again – free in health and free in madness, free as the spirit had been in the Renaissance. The failure of Enlightenment physiology was a genuine, scientific disappointment. Judged by expert standards, it was more than the consequence of an immature science wallowing in a Sargasso Sea and hindered by an absence of genius.[38] It extended beyond the artist's desire that science fulfil in the same way as art; and it is most probably correct to speculate that if science had not taken the turn it did – towards an ever greater impersonality in the march towards technology – Romantic thinkers would not have rebelled as monolithically and strenuously as they did. Surely the point to be gathered is not *only* that eighteenth-century science actually forced the human spirit into a strait-jacket, but that the Romantics were convinced it had. There can be no doubt, additionally, that eighteenth-century science damaged the artist and impelled him almost against his will, as it were, to indulge his desire for a new variety of empirical experience based on moments of transcendental truth. Claims of impersonality, predictability, artificiality, and thriftiness – claims all made in the name of science and technology – were not enough to satisfy the ilk of a Blake, a Wordsworth, or a Coleridge.

There is, however, still another aspect of the 'revolt'. When science makes promises she must fulfil them however inchoately. In this sense, experimental science as a cultural force is radically different from that of the humanities. Once imagination was created by physiologists, it had to be nurtured, permitted to mature, to evolve into adulthood and ripen into old age. The abortive attempts of eighteenth-century physicians and theoretical physiologists were perfectly visible to all who could see; by late century the record of neurological research read like an antiquarian's journal: Of interest to historians only, these neurological works often repeated, sometimes undigested, the research of earlier physicians, particularly those at mid-century, men like Boerhaave, Whytt, and Hartley.[39] Only Pinel,[40] the French theoretician and physician at the Bicêtre and the Salpétrière, had genuinely new ideas about the pathology of the diseased imagination, and Englishmen were resistant to these for several decades.

With the promise of an organic marriage of the spiritual (imagination) and the material (animal spirits, fibres, nerves) thwarted, it remained the task of non-scientists to formulate a mythical set of laws uniting them. That poets and philosophers should somehow have felt this their 'task' is significant in itself. More consequential was its effect on literature. Such a 'task' may not have been auspicious for the history of physiology; it was for Romantic poetry and natural philosophy.

Madness was once again returned to sacred grounds, to camps of mysticism and to cults of pantheism which had no basis in scientific fact. Under the influence of powerful minds like Coleridge, Wordsworth, and the German naturalists, neurology regressed in the popular mind, particularly in England, and associationist psychology was declared an invalid. The way was paved for the new phenomenology. The diseased imagination was instead romanticised, endowed with an aura of glory it had never known; so much so that Wordsworth's famous lines may be read almost literally: 'We Poets in our youth begin in gladness,/But thereof come in the end despondency and madness.'[41] The long wars of truth over the supremacy of the body by the mind, or the mind by the body, were finally brought to an end, mind triumphant, as Wordsworth notes subtly, though plainly, at the conclusion of his lyrical ballad of *Goody Blake and Harry Gil* based on a story in Erasmus Darwin's *Zoonomia*.

What appeared in the 1740s and 1750s as the start of a genuine revolution in neurology turned out to be merely an incomplete mechanics, an abortive attempt so far as literature was concerned. Associationist psychologists could not explain the inseparability of matter and force, particularly in the association of secondary ideas. Theoretical physicians instead of keeping their promise to solve the greatest riddle in medicine fell back upon themselves and, in defence, returned to older subjects: redefinitions of madness and the vital substance within the animal spirits. The theory of sensationism lapsed into a kind of vitalistic archaeology. Romantic philosophers like Kant and poets like Coleridge were thus the heirs of an inchoate scientific breakthrough, of what seemed to be an inert materialism, their task of demolition carried out in the name of humanism, the preservation of man as an organic creature: whole, unfragmented, non-disintegrated.

Consequently, it is probably true that the etiology of European Romanticism is located as much in the medical researches of the eighteenth century as in the disturbance of the sacred and profane in an increasingly industrial society. Newton's discovery of mathematical laws of light waves contributed directly to concrete imagery in poetry and painting, as Professor Marjorie Nicolson has shown,[42] and his discovery of gravity, to belief in a living centre of every moving object, a centre forever attracting its parts.[43] But the implications of the neurological 'discovery of the imagination' – as I have been using this phrase – were of equally great consequence. The seat of all creative endeavour was established. Man was irredeemably bifurcated into (1) a physically existential imagination and (2) a complex of fibres, nerves, and animal spirits. Not until these distinctions – now more precise than Descartes's unwieldy pineal gland and a body proper composed of many organs – could be once again united would creative thinkers who valued mental freedom rest.

European Romanticism as we know it was therefore in part a final answer to Cartesian dualism and to the mind–body pathologists who followed Descartes. I know of no moment in the history of modern European culture in which science and literature were more intrinsically interrelated. It cannot be denied that the multifacets of this interrelationship have warded off students. It is easier, after all, to survey the interworking of the two in direct linear fashion, as for example, in the poetry of Donne who explicitly refers to Copernican cosmology, or in the prose satires of Swift who lambastes the ludicrous experiments of the Royal Society in London.[44] More difficult, by far, is it to correlate developments in science and society, such as Robert Merton's thesis – to my knowledge still unchallenged in a demonstrable way by those who maintain that latitudinarian men were equally engaged in scientific experimentation – that puritanism, protestantism, and science developed together, the latter a result of the former two. Still more elusive is the influence of science on modes of human thought and revolutions in aesthetic taste. Any conclusions regarding such influence must be viewed tentatively and skeptically until historians of science catch up with historians generally.

Professor Robert Merton has written, 'It has become manifest that in each age there is a system of science which rests upon a set of assumptions, usually implicit and seldom questioned by the scientists of the time.'[45] Would that historians applied such criteria to the Enlightenment, at least as a prolegomenon to understanding. It would then be apparent that one reason among several for the relative wasteland of great imaginative literature, especially in England, was caused by more urgent problems,[46] crucial problems which occupied and deflected men from writing great poetry in abundance and which caused them to turn to the study of 'natural philosophy' – the sciences. The Carlylean tendency to regard the history of human achievement as a succession of inexplicable geniuses arbitrarily bestowing knowledge upon mankind has finally been abandoned as simple-minded and mythical. And Matthew Arnold, in assessing the age of Pope, never understood the reasons that caused men to turn away from verse.[47] Actually, economic conditions in eighteenth-century England were such that a larger portion of the population than in any earlier time could have devoted itself to the writing of creative literature if it wished. To be sure, some portion did, but considered on a per capita and not an absolute basis – and it is an important distinction – the writing of poetry diminished in the eighteenth century. The largest number of educated men became scientists, doctors in particular.[48]

Throughout the eighteenth century, scientists conducted their experiments in the name of morality, or thought they did, and it is amazing to discover how religious most actually were. Scientific empiricism and inductive rationalism were accordingly canonized, beatified, and deified. And yet the fruits of their research seemed underdeveloped. The followers of Descartes in France, who took the physiological half of his dualism (including an early theory of associationism based on nervous traces in the brain) and ignored the rest, were to be answered and repudiated by the German metaphysicians and, slightly later, by English thinkers like Coleridge. Coleridge's theories of the sympathetic and esemplastic imagination are thereby best understood as another chapter in the medical history of the discovery of the imagination. His philosophical thought ultimately rests upon a complete rejection of Locke's associationism and Hartley's sensationism. His flirtation with Hartleyian mechanism is vividly documented, and he may certainly be described as one who sought to heal the Cartesian rift. He is, in a sense, an inquiring physiologist and a sceptical biologist attempting to explain the rift of mind and body in the previous age.[49] There is also a scientific side of Blake, particularly in his demands for an organic union of the senses and the imagination in the non-fragmented man. At no point in Blake's writings – notwithstanding the momentary vision at the end of *Jerusalem* of Locke, Newton, and the bard holding hands – is there hope for the progress of the materialist philosophy or Enlightenment physiology. Indeed, Blake claims to have abhorred Locke and Voltaire from his first reading of them. These and other poets were the posterity – not always consciously, but still the posterity – of Enlightenment science. They accepted associationism as a temporary paradise only to discover shortly thereafter that it was a permanent exile; accordingly, they rejected it and formulated their own theory of imagination. Their thinking had more in common with scientists than with poets of the previous century; their writings were alien to, yet not completely divorced from, the neurologists. John Stuart Mill has written that 'the Germano-Coleridgean doctrine expresses the revolt of the human mind against the philosophy of the eighteenth century'.[50] It was more specifically a revolt against its physiology. As late as 1923 Valéry created in his

Dialogues a Romantic physician, Eryximachus, who attempts to cure Socrates by combining his nerves and imagination into one, unfragmented,
whole framework.

The romantic temperament thrives by indulging in private visionary
experience based on moments of transcendental truth; it dwells in a mythical sphere of abundant revelation, however unreal to an outsider, which
is similar to the madman's. No earlier thought beatified madness as it did,
particularly in its apotheosis of the mad poet, the mad lover, the mad
hero, the mad sufferer. I believe it is inaccurate to conceive of the decline
of the baroque and the rise of the Romantic habit of mind without recourse
to physiology and medicine.[51] In their aspirations and ends, the theories
of Enlightened medicine and Romantic imagination were similar: Both
considered matter and force as inseparable, and both believed that if any
ratiocinative process separated them, the result would be disintegration of
the organic creature.

The longing to remain whole is not yet inert; it is as ancient as recorded
history and it antedates the beautiful and ridiculous myth of Aristophanes
in Plato's *Symposium*. It seems evident that in 1650–1800 the human conception of what it was to be human in the first place suffered an unprecedented trauma, one that fragmented conscious creatures and left them
materially divisible. Not until the collective spirit could repair the damage
of the physiologists would educated Europeans return to their former,
more unitary, selfhoods: one man, one woman, however sane or
demented, but at least one human being. The 'sciences of man', Peter
Gay's memorable recent phrase, were born out of this search to recast and
repair a treacherous view that anatomy was embodied destiny. Too much
had been extrapolated from this anatomy and physiology. It was time to
elevate human beings by elevating them from this place in nature. But
mind and its attendant psychology – its passions, capacities for pleasure
and pain, views of virtue and conduct – could not be reconstructed until
anatomy and medicine were viewed in a different light. It is my contention
that the origins of Romantic sensibility are incomplete until we survey
the cataclysmic shift in physiological thought that occurred in the Enlightenment, a shift that probably contributed more to change man's image of
himself that anything since the introduction of gunpower into Europe in
the fourteenth century. Robert Boyle, perhaps the greatest chemist of the
period but also a highly original mind, seems to have anticipated this shift
when he commented in *The Usefulnesse of Experimental Naturall Philosophy*
(1663) that 'those great transactions which make such a noise in the World,
and establish Monarchies or ruin Empires, reach not so many Persons
with their Influence as do the Theories of Physiology'.[52]

NOTES

This paper was originally read as the major address at a conference on Literature and Science, SUNY, Nassau Community College, Garden City, New York, 2 May 1969.

1 Throughout this paper I use 'imagination' in the strict physiological sense and not in its loose and now common usage, e.g., 'the literary imagination', 'the artistic imagination', or imagination as connoting a degree of sensitivity, intuition, or creativity. See Gerhardt von Bonin, *The Evolution of the Human Brain* (Chicago, 1963) and Harry J. Jerison 'Interpreting the Evolution of the Brain', *Human Biology*, XXXV (Sept. 1963), 263–91. Most brain theorists today define the imagination scientifically as the number of associations per unit time. The number of associations depends upon four physical and biochemical processes: (1) the number of neurons in the frontal lobe of the brain; (2) the speed of nervous conduction and synopsis of their neurons; (3) memories which hinder or abet the processes described in (2); and (4) hormones that may or may not affect the whole process. (1) and (2) are best understood, almost nothing is known about (3), and little has as yet been learned about (4). It is possible, and perhaps probable, that the interaction of all four processes may radically change present notions regarding an individual one. Dr Jerison conclusively shows that there has been no known change in the brain size of the *homo sapiens* since Cro-Magnon man. Brain theorists discuss the healthy and sick imagination in terms of the above four factors. Biochemists surmise, although it is not proved, that (3) and (4) account for most mental illness. It is important to note that the most advanced brain theory may be incorrect: the brain can imagine only that which it is capable of, and it is at least possible that functions (1)–(4) do not permit comprehension of the very process that limits it. E.g., the gorilla knows how to peel bananas, but the limited number of associations per unit time prevent it from formulating theoretical questions. By analogy, the same may be true of man. I am very much indebted to Dr Saul Zamenhof, Chief, Brain Research Institute, UCLA, for assistance in this note and for discussions in 1968–9 which permitted me to explore the scientific aspects of my subject.

In the strict sense, 'Enlightened England' is meaningless; I use it merely to designate the period 1660–1800. The most comprehensive scientific definitions for 1660–1800 are found in medical and other dictionaries of the period. See John Harris, *Lexicon Technicum* (1704); Ephraim Chambers, *Cyclopaedia: or, An Universal Dictionary of Arts and Sciences* (1728); Robert James, *A Medicinal Dictionary* (1743–5), *Encyclopaedia Britannica* (1768). The *OED* provides a guide to changing concepts of the word in non-scientific usage. In this period the 'brain' was thought to consist of 'inner' and 'outer' fibres and to correspond to different parts of the body: see William Drage, 'A Tractate of the Diseases of the Head', *A Physical Nosonomy* (1665); Thomas Willis, *Pathologiae Cerebri* (1667), *An Essay of the Pathology of the Brain*, trans. S. Pordage (1681) and *Two Discourses Concerning the Soul of Brutes* (1683). I have found no agreement regarding definition of the 'fibres' in the brain; most scientists of the time liken them to textile fibres and are ambivalent about their hollowness or solid state. Later on I discuss medical definitions of the imagination, 1660–1800.

2 The theories of Artemiodorus (the most important collector of ancient theories of the subject) were transmitted through the Renaissance to the seventeenth and eighteenth centuries, some of which are summarised in *Sir Thomas Browne's Works*, ed. Simon Wilkin (1835). See Philip Goodwin's *The Mystery of Dreams, Historically Discoursed* (1658).

3 Aspects of this revolution have been studied by Alfred North Whitehead, E. A. Burtt, A. O. Lovejoy, R. S. Crane, R. F. Jones, M. H. Nicolson, Herbert Butterfield, and R. K. Merton. The most conclusive evidence demonstrating that it was a genuine scientific revolution has been gathered by T. S. Kuhn in *The Structure of Scientific Revolutions*.

4 See Aristotle, *De Anima, passim* and *Poetics, passim*; also Plato, trans. Jowett (New

York, 1937), *Apology*, 22; *Republic*, 378; *Ion*, 534. An example of anti-Aristotelianism is Akenside's *Pleasures of Imagination* (1744), in which it is significant that Akenside abandoned the definite article of his original title, *Pleasures of the Imagination*.

5 Nerves were defined variously as (1) hollow tubes through which vital liquids flowed; (2) hollow tubes containing undefined but stationary substances; and after the 1740s as (3) solid tubes conducting electric impulses from cell to cell. There was little agreement about all three major explanations and there were several other minor ones. I know of no secondary study that has surveyed eighteenth-century theories of nerves or, as I state in n. 6, of animal spirits. Listed chronologically, some of the works involved are: *Philosophical Transactions* (1661–1780); Ephraim Chambers, 'Nerve', *Cyclopaedia: or, an Universal Dictionary of Arts and Sciences* (1728), II, unnumbered page; George Cheyne, *The English Malady: or, A Treatise of Nervous Diseases* (1733): H. Boerhaave, *Academical Lectures on the Theory of Physic*, 2nd ed. (1751–7), II, 284–5; Thomas Reid, *An Inquiry into the Human Mind* (Edinburgh, 1764). In a series of essays: G. S. Rousseau, 'Discourses of the Nerve', F. Amrine (ed.), *Literature and Science as Modes of Expression*, (Dordrecht, 1989) 29–60; G. S. Rousseau, 'Towards a Semiotics of the Nerve: the Social History of Language in a New Key', Peter Burke and Roy Porter (eds.), *The Social History of Language II*, (Oxford, 1991) 000–000; G. S. Rousseau, 'Cultural History in a New Key: Towards a Semiotics of the Nerve', Joan and Andrew Weir Pittock (eds.), *Cultural History*, (1991), 25–81.

6 Even more controversial were theories of the 'animal spirits'. Basically, the problem was one of defining the vital substance within the spirits themselves. This problem of definition was further complicated by contemporary theories of acids – in the air, body, and blood – which defied chemical identification. Most of the works cited in n. 5 also discuss animal spirits. Endless debates over the motion of animal spirits sometimes created humility in physiologists. Dr Robert Whytt, an important neurologist and physician to King George III, wrote of the difficulties of explaining the passions that arise from particular movements of the animal spirits: 'To ascend from small things to great, altho' Sir *Issac Newton* did not pretend to explain the cause of gravity, yet he made no small improvement in physical Astronomy, when, from this principle alone, he accounted for the various motions of the planets, and banished the imaginary *vortices of Descartes*, which had been contrived, but unsuccessfully, to explain the phenomena of the solar system' (*Observations on the Nature, Causes, and Cure of . . . Disorders* (Edinburgh, 1765). VII, preface). The animal spirits controversies have not been surveyed. Important works include: Thomas Willis, 'Treatise of Musculary Motion', *A Medical-Philosophical Discourse . . .* , trans. S. Pordage (1681) and *Two Discourses Concerning the Soul of Brutes Which Is That of the Vital and Sensitive Soul of Man*, trans. S. Pordage (1683): *Philosophical Transactions*, 1680–1750 (more than thirty articles on animal spirits); John Harris, 'Nervous Spirit', *Lexicon Technicum* (1704), II, un-numbered page; Nicholas Robinson, *A New Theory of Physick* (1725) and *A New System of the Spleen, Vapours and Hypochondriack Melancholy: wherein all the decays of the Nerves . . . are Mechanically Accounted for* (1729); Robert James, 'Animal Spirits', *Medicinal Dictionary* (1743–5); *Gentleman's Magazine*, 1740–65 (seventy-two entries on animal spirits); Malcolm Flemyng, *An Introduction to Physiology: Being a Course of Lectures on the Most Important Parts of the Animal Oeconomy* (1759) and *The Nature of the Nervous Fluid; or Animal Spirits Demonstrated* (1751); Laurence Heister, *A Compendium of the Practice of Physic*, trans. E. Barker (1757); 'Spirits', *A New Medicinal Dictionary*, ed. George Wallis and G. Motherby, 4th ed. (1795).

7 See J. D. Boyd, S.J., *The Function of Mimesis and Its Decline* (Cambridge, 1968).

8 For commentary on the imitation of the imagination in symbolic painting of the eighteenth century, see Erwin Panofsky, *Iconology* (Princeton, 1955) and Ralph Cohen, *The Art of Discrimination* (1964).

9 See John Yolton, *John Locke and the Way of Ideas* (Oxford, 1956); Kenneth Dewhurst, *John Locke, Physician and Philosopher: a Medical Biography* (1963); Maurice Mandelbaum, 'Locke's Realism', *Philosophy, Science and Perception* (Baltimore, 1964); *John Locke:*

Problems and Perspectives, ed. J. Yolton (Cambridge University Press, 1969). Richard Ashcraft has recently shown that Locke was known to his contemporaries as a physician as well as political rebel; see R. Ashcraft, *Revolutionary Politics and Locke's Two Treatises of Government* (Princeton, 1986); John Harrison and Peter Laslett have written *à propos* of the unusually large number of medical books in Locke's library: 'Whether Locke's ownership of works by Glauber, Gesner, Mayerne, Borelli, Gabelchover, Huyghens, Malpighi, Borrichius, Sachs, Rolfinck, Pisanelli, and the rest make of his catalogue a landmark in the literature of the scientific revolution is for historians of science in our own time to decide' *The Library of John Locke* (Oxford, 1965), 24–5.

10 Eighteenth-century physiologists stressed the role of memory in influencing the process of association; see Locke, 'Of Retention', *Essay Concerning Human Understanding* (1690), I, 193–201; 'Memory' in Locke's *Medical Journals 1675–1697*, quoted in Dewhurst, *op. cit.*, 100–2; David Hartley, *Observations on Man* (1749), I, 3, 374. Hartley's chapter, sect. iv, 'Of Memory', I 374–82 summarises the differences of opinion regarding memory held by the physiologists. Much controversy took place over the function of memory in moral ideas that are innate. It was believed by some physiologists that certain of these innate, moral ideas could not be learned by the usual neurological and associationist processes. See also Richard Burthogge, *An Essay upon Reason, and the Nature of Spirits* (1694); Burthogge had studied medicine at Leyden and was a practising physician.

11 By 1740 there had been so much controversy about the animal spirits that some scientists discredited them altogether, and literary men satirised and described them. See Henry Brooke's exposition in *Universal Beauty, a Poem* (1735), part iv, II, 243–52:

Quick, from the Mind's imperial Mansion shed
With *lively Tension* spins the *nervous Thread*
With Flux of animate Effuvia stor'd,
And Tubes of nicest Perforation bor'd,
Whose *branching Maze* thro' ev'ry Organ tends,
And Unity of conscious Action *lends*;
While Spirits thro' the *wandring Channels* wind,
And wing the Message of informing Mind;
Or Objects to th' ideal Seat convey;
Or dictate Motion with internal Sway.

See also Garth, *The Dispensary* (1699), I, 15–19, III, 82–86; Malcolm Flemyng, *Neuro-pathia; sive, De Morbis Hypochondriacis et Hystericis* (1740, a Lucretian epic in Latin hexameter), 3–4; Addison, *Spectator*, ed. Bond (Oxford, 1965), I, 367, 471; II, 8, 197, 383, 451, 460, 525, 563; James Thomson, 'Spring', *The Seasons* (1728), 865–76; Henry Fielding, *Tom Jones*, ed. W. E. Henley (1902), II, 9; V, 9.

12 Locke, *An Essay Concerning Human Understanding*, I, 203.

13 See Nicholas Robinson, *A New System of The Spleen* (1729); P. Frings, *A Treatise on Phrensy* (1746); Jerome Gaub, *De Regimine Mentis* (Leyden, 1747–63), printed with annotations in L. J. Rather, *Mind and Body in Eighteenth Century Medicine* (1965); David Hartley, 'Of the Pleasures and Pains of Imagination', *Observations on Man* (1749), I, 418–42; Richard Mead, *Medical Precepts and Cautions* (1751), 77–84; see also the index of the *Gentleman's Magazine 1731–1786*, which lists several dozen entries on imagination, many of which are letters to the editor concerning recent books dealing with the imagination. Among the most influential medical definitions of imagination were those of Descartes, who placed its activity entirely in the pineal gland; Thomas Willis, who believed its operations took place in the *corpus allosum* and those of common sense in the *corpora striata*; and La Mettrie (among the associationists), who carried Locke's theory of perception so far as to reduce the entire mind (i.e., judgment, reason, memory, the mechanical parts of the soul) to imagination. Many physicians considered the imagination as the chief cause of all bodily illness: see Thomas Knight, *Transmutation of the Blood* (1725), 45. Chambers, in the *Cyclopaedia*, believed the imagination works

by mechanical means although he distinguished its operation from that of sensation: 'Whenever there is any motion in that part, to change the order of its fibres, there also happens a new perception in the soul, and she finds something new, either by sensation of *imagination*; neither of which can be without an alteration of the fibres in that part of the brain.' In this note and others I attempt to provde sufficient definitions to imply a 'discrimination of imaginations'. In order that such a list of definitions be complete for 1660–1800 it would be necessary to survey literary analogies as well as scientific ones. Space does not permit that here.

14 Article on 'Imagination'. James's definition is as clear as one can find in medical dictionaries of the age. His *Dictionary* was considered by philosophers and physicians of the age to be the single best summary of contemporary medicine. See Diderot, Eidous, and Touissant, Preface to their translation of James's *Dictionnaire Universel* (Paris, 1746): 'Ce Dictionnaire est précédé d'un Discours historique sur l'origine & les progrés de la Medecine . . . Il montre enfin Harvey, jettant par sa découverte les fondemens d'une nouvelle theorie sûre & lumineuse & propre à nous faire appercevoir les ressorts cachés qui produisoient des effets dont la cause si long-tems cherchée, avoit jusqu' alors été inconnue.'

15 See n. 1. Chronological assocations (*a*) within a time span $(t^1 - t^2)$ are now thought to depend on the four variables listed in n. 1. Stated mathematically, although such an equation is meaningless since there is as yet no way of calculating (3) and (4): $a(t^1 - t^2) = f(1,2,3,4)$

16 Ephraim Chambers, *Cyclopaedia*, article on 'Imagination', unnumbered page.

17 'Entretiens sur la métaphysique et sur la religion', *Oeuvres Complètes*, ed. A Robinet (Paris, 1965), XII, 30.

18 See William Battie, *A Treatise on Madness* (1758) and John Monro, *Remarks on Dr. Battie's Treatise on Madness* (1758), who comment on this point, and in modern commentary, Michel Foucault, *Madness and Civilization: A history of Insanity in the Age of Reason* (New York, 1965), pp. 101–32. The idea of the freedom of the deranged in the fifteenth and sixteenth centuries is noted in a medical treatise by Jacques Ferrand, *De la maladie de l'amour, ou Mélancholie érotique* (Paris, 1632), translated into English by E. Chilmead in 1640 and issued in many editions by 1700.

19 This belief was repeated in most works discussing the 'diseased imagination' and in medical treatises by Nicholas Robinson, *A New System of the Spleen* (1729), 174–6; Edward Synge, *Sober Thoughts for the Cure of Melancholy* (1742); J. D. T. de Bienville, *La Nymphomanie, ou Traité de la fureur utérine* (Amsterdam, 1758), trans. into English by E. S. Wilmot (1775).

20 Originally published as *Histoire de la Folie* (Paris, 1961).

21 P. 124. See also G. S. Rousseau, introduction to Sir John Hill's *Hypochondriasis: a Practical Treatise* (1766; pub. for the Augustan Reprint Society, Los Angeles, 1969), in which this point is discussed at length.

22 See the controversies over the etiology of the 'diseased imagination' in the 1720s: James Blondel, *The Power of the Mother's Imagination . . . Examin'd* (1729); Daniel Turner, *De Morbis Cutaneis* (1726), *A Discourse Concerning Gleets . . . in respect to the Spots and Marks impressed upon the Skin of the Foetus* (1729), *The Force of the Mother's Imagination upon her Foetus in Utero* (1730). A full study of the medical controversies concerning the diseased imagination is found in G. S. Rousseau, 'Pineapples, Pregnancy, Pica and *Peregrine Pickle,' Tobias Smollett: Bicentennial Essays*, ed. G. S. Rousseau and P.-G. Boucé (New York 1971) (*Enlightenment Borders*, chap. 7).

23 John Locke, *Journals: 1675–1679*, ed. Dewhurst, p. 89.

24 They were, respectively, answers to Locke's *Essay* and Hartley's *Observations*. See John Yolton, *John Locke* (Oxford, 1956) and Robert Hoeldtke, 'The History of Associationism and British Medical Psychology', *Medical History*, XI (1967), 46–65.

25 Respectively *Peregrine Pickle* (1751), I, 21–36 and *Tristram Shandy*, ed. James A. Work (New York, 1940), 2.

26 See Marjorie Nicolson and G. S. Rousseau, *'This Long Disease, My Life': Alexander Pope and the Sciences* (Princeton, 1968), 131–238.

27 I have made a study of the number of such works and find the percentage very high. This may be due, in part, to the large quantities of medical satire written in the eighteenth century and to the many physicians (bona fide doctors, apothecaries, quacks, mountebanks, medical hacks) then writing. The point is emphasised by one writer of the period in an anonymous pamphlet in the Bodleian Library, *An Enquiry into Dr. Ward's Practice of Physick . . . With An Examination into the Origin, and Meaning of the Words Empiricism, Empirick, Quack-Doctor, and Quack. And, An Exact Account of the Present State of Physick* (1749).

28 The Newtonian equation $f = ma$ was actually applied to the animal spirits, although there was no means of calculating a (in Newton, $a = dv/dt$). See the anonymous, *Philosphical Conjectures Concerning the Animal Spirits* (1746), 6–7, in the Royal Society of Medicine, London. There was some opposition to Newtonian equations applied to body motion by anti-Newtonian groups like the Hutchinsonians. Some discussion of developments influencing the slow progress of physiology 1700–1800 is found in Joseph Needham, 'Limiting Factors in the Advancement of Science as Observed in the History of Embryology', *Yale Journal of Biology and Medicine*, VIII (1935), 1–18.

29 See Albrecht von Haller, *A Dissertion on the Sensible and Irritable Parts of Animals* (1755), trans. by Tissot, *Bulletin of the History of Medicine*, supp. iv (1936), 651–99, and for Haller's reception in England, *Phil. Trans.*, 1748–57, *Gentleman's Magazine*, XXII (1753), 592–3, and Stephen d'Irsay, *Albrecht von Haller: Eine Studie zur Geistesgeschichte der Aufklärung* (Leipzig, 1930).

30 See John Gay, *A Dissertation Concerning the Fundamental Principle . . . of Virtue* (1732), and David Hartley, 'Of the Doctrine of Vibrations and Assocations in General', *Observations on Man* (1749), I, 3–100; see also Hoeldtke, *Medical History*, XI, 48–51, and Joseph Priestley's comments in the introduction to his *Abridgement* (1755).

31 See Miriam Starkman, *Swift's Satire on Learning in 'A Tale of a Tub'* (Princeton, 1950), 3–48.

32 The best evidence of this is found in the correspondence columns of the *Gentleman's Magazine*, 1740–1800. Few subjects received more attention, if letters written by readers (to the editor) are an indication. Studies of mesmerism and hypnotism are also helpful in this connection. See Robert Darnton, *Mesmerism and the End of the Enlightenment in France* (Cambridge, 1968). The imagery of nerves, fibres, and animal spirits, in addition to that of the diseased imagination, is common in English and French novels 1740–1800. See some illustrative passages in Smollett's *Ferdinand Count Fathom*, 2 vols. (1753), II, 46, 156, 260.

33 See John Livingstone Lowes, *The Road to Xanadu* (Boston, 1927) and G. M. Matthews, 'A Volcano's Voice in Shelley', *English Literary History*, XXIV (1957), 191–228.

34 I mean in a manner satisfactory to educated men outside the world of experimental science. The response of other scientists alone would not be sufficiently broad to gauge opinion. An analogy in modern science may be current dissatisfaction with the techniques of psychotherapy. The point is studied in detail by E. H. Carr, 'History, Science, and Morality', *What Is History?* (Cambridge, 1961), 70–112.

35 See Aram Artanian, *La Mettrie's l'Homme Machine: a Study in the Origins of an Idea* (Princeton, 1960); F. A. lange, *History of Materialism* (1877).

36 'Jerusalem: Plate 15', in *The Poetry and Prose of William Blake*, ed. by D. Erdman and H. Bloom (New York, 1965), 157. See Jean Hagstrum, 'William Blake Rejects the Enlightenment', *Proceedings of the II Congress on the Enlightenment* (1964), II, 142–55.

37 'The Destiny of Nations', 35–97, in *The Complete Poetical Works of S. T. Coleridge*, ed. E. H. Hartley (Oxford, 1912, rev. ed. 1966), 132–3.

38 Such is the opinion of recent historians of physiology. See Sir Michael Foster, *Lectures on the History of Physiology* (Cambridge, 1901); J. R. Fulton, *Physiology of the Nervous System* (1938); numerous studies of Oswei Temkin's, including 'The Classical Roots of Glisson's Doctrine of Irritation', *Bulletin of the History of Medicine*, XXXVII (1964), 297–328, and June Goodfield, *The Growth of Scientific Physiology; Physiological Method and the Mechanist-Vitalist Controversy* (1960).

39 Other less important scientific writers include Drs William Hunter, John Gregory, William Finch, Hugh Farmer, James Vere, Thomas Arnold, William Cullen, James Makittrick Adair.

40 See Phillipe Pinel, *Recherches sur le traitement moral des aliénés* (Paris, 1800); *Traité médico-philosophique . . .* (Paris, 1801; Eng. trans. by D. D. Davis, 1806); *Nosographie Philosophique* (Paris, 1818). The introductory remarks to D. D. Davis's translation, *A Treatise on Insanity* (1806), are of considerable interest.

41 William Wordsworth, 'Resolution and Independence,' 48–9.

42 *Newton Demands the Muse* (Princeton, 1946).

43 It is curious that the considerable influence of Newton's *Principia* on English literature in the eighteenth and nineteenth centuries has not been surveyed.

44 'The First Anniversary', ll. 205–26 and *Gulliver's Travels*, part iii.

45 Robert K. Merton, 'Puritanism, Pietism, and Science', in *Social Theory and Social Structure* (rev. ed., New York, 1957), 586, originally in *Sociological Review* (1938). See also the same author's 'Science, Technology and Society in Seventeenth-Century England', *Osiri* (1938), IV, 360–632.

46 Here I am evaluating the poetry of England in the eighteenth century with respect to other centuries, and it must be admitted that periods like 1550–1620 or 1798–1850 seem richer in the quality of their poetry. This does not, of course, diminish the achievement of Dryden, Pope, or Johnson.

47 Matthew Arnold, 'Literature and Science' in *Discourses in America* (1885), 90–4.

48 T. McKeown and R. G. Brown, 'Medical Evidence Related to English Population Changes in the Eighteenth Century', *Population Studies*, IX (1955–6), 119–41.

49 See Joseph Needham, 'S. T. Coleridge as a Philsophical Biologist', *Science Progress*, XX (1926), 692–702; Gordon McKenzie, 'Organic Unity in Coleridge', *University of California Publications in English* (1939); Basil Willey, 'Coleridge on Imagination and Fancy', *Proceedings of the British Academy*, XXXII (1946), 174–87; Elisabeth Schneider, *Coleridge, Opium and Kubla Khan* (Chicago, 1953); James V. Baker, *The Sacred River: Coleridge's Theory of the Imagination* (Baton Rouge, 1957); Althea Hayter, *Opium and the Romantic Imagination* (Berkeley and Los Angeles 1968). Coleridge's medical thought as found in *Philosophical Lectures* has not as yet received scholarly study. Some of Coleridge's attack on the physiology of the eighteenth century is found in a lecture entitled 'Materialism, Ancient and Modern', 15 March 1819: the advertisement in *The London Times* read, 'Mr. Coleridge's Lecture for this Evening is on Dogmatical Materialism – in its relations to Physiology as well as to the religious, moral and common sense of Mankind'.

50 F. R. Leavis (ed.), *Mill on Bentham and Coleridge* (1950), 108.

51 See the last section of Walter Pagel, 'Religious Motives in the Medical Biology of the Seventeenth Century', *Bulletin of the Institute of the History of Medicine*, III (1935), 97–128, 213–31, 265–312. Pagel discusses the importance of vitalism in biology 1750–1820 and in the formation of the metaphysical doctrines of some of the Romantics. For discussion of this subject later in the nineteenth and twentieth centuries, see Jean-Paul Sartre, *The Psychology of Imagination* (1950), 141–218. Among the best scientific statements for and against vitalism are D. Dix, 'A Defence of Vitalism', *Journal of Theoretical Biology*, II (1963), 338–40 and several books attacking vitalism by F. Crick (the noted biologist),

particularly *Of Molecules and Men* (Seattle, 1966). See also Frank Barron, 'The Psychology of Imagination', *Scientific American*, CXCIX (Sept. 1958), 151–68.

52 Second Part, 3.

___

2

Le Cat and the physiology of Negroes

In 1971 Richard Popkin, the doyen of historians of scepticism, invited me to participate in a symposium on racism during the Enlightenment held under the auspices of the American Society for Eighteenth-Century Studies. Its results were published in Studies in Eighteenth-Century Culture *(Columbus, 1973). Soon after being invited I discovered that little had been written then about the racist views of Enlightenment scientists and doctors. Having already worked on the medicalisation of the imagination, and by now immersed in Foucault, I was interested in the way the discourses of anatomy and physiology marginalised certain groups within society.*

Nicolas Le Cat, a little-known physiologist, seemed a perfect test specimen. He was one of the few licensed physicians of the period who actually took a stand on race by addressing the etiology and epistemology of skin colour. Except for a few glances here and there by a handful of historians of science, no one, it seemed, had written about him. During my study, I became aware that Le Cat was a tremendously important figure for an anthropology of Enlightenment culture, and had I been undertaking to write one, I would have cast him among the protagonists. Even so, my approach, as I now see, was sorely limited, and I would cast the essay altogether differently now if I were working with the same materials.

'The origin of *Negroes*,' Ephraim Chambers wrote in the 1728 *Cyclopaedia*, 'and the cause of that remarkable difference in complexion from the rest of mankind, has much perplexed the naturalists; nor has anything satisfactory been yet offered on that hand.' A generation later, in the 1750s, this was still true, although Claude Nicolas Le Cat was to influence the picture considerably. It is hard to know if Chambers, no scientist or medical man, would have been at all impressed by Le Cat's theories. But if he had heard or read them, he might have modified somewhat his statement in the *Cyclopaedia*.

From the vantage of the history of science, Le Cat's entire career, quite unsurveyed, incidentally, is as exciting as that part of it represented by his contribution to the age-old debate about the colour of Negro skin, its origins and history, from the beginning of man to the eighteenth century. Born in 1700 and dead by 1768, Le Cat was the chief physician and surgeon of the Hôtel-Dieu, the leading hospital in Rouen, a member of many French and foreign scientific societies, and the author of over a dozen medical treatises. In 1762 he retired from his hospital post, and during his remaining seven years wrote most of the books that utilise his researches, observations, and reading of over fifty years.[1]

His scientific contribution to the race argument has either been neglected or thought so insignificant until now that one looks in vain for his name in most modern reference books in the history of science and medicine as well as in encyclopaedias and dictionaries of biography. And yet, careful scrutiny of his works reveals that he played a role in advancing biological understanding of skin colour. He himself was apparently aware of this role, and he accordingly devoted his greatest scientific energies to what we today must regard as his most significant medical work, *Traité de la couleur de la peau humaine en général & de celle des Nègres en particulier*, published in Amsterdam in 1765.[2]

Le Cat's treatise contradicts previous theories maintaining that bile is responsible for the colour of human skin; this argument had been advanced as indisputable scientific fact in the earliest writings of Egyptian medicine, later appeared in Homer, Strabo, Ovid, and Pliny, and was advanced throughout the Renaissance and for much of the eighteenth century. The *Teatro crítico* of Father Feijoo is typical of the impressionistic manner in which the bile argument was set forward: succinctly, without experimental support, and as an *ipse dixit* argument.[3] Other eighteenth-century naturalists, including Raymond de Vieussens, Buffon, La Mettrie, D'Holbach, and numerous travel writers, also repeated the argument as if it were gospel truer than truth.

In Italy, Albinus and Sanctorini supported a bile theory (although these men recanted and at several junctures even displayed scepticism about the belief), and in France, where it seems to have been extremely popular, it attracted numerous advocates, and none more vocal than Pierre Barrère, a Perpignanese physician and medical author who strenuously championed it in 1741 in a dissertation on the cause of skin colour, *Dissertation sur la cause physique de la couleur, des Nègres, de la qualité de leurs cheveux, & de la génération de l'un & de l'autre*. Germans, Scandinavians, and Englishmen also gave the belief their stamp and seal, and it is accurate to say that by 1750 the belief was prevalent – truly as popular as the 'monster-mongering' sport, to use the phrase of Professor Jordan in his edition of Samuel Stanhope Smith's *Essay on the Causes of Complexion*[4] – that blacks were another species of man, *sans* the ordinary human organs, tissues, and heart, and (of course) *sans* soul.[5] Le Cat's theory, in contrast, introduces a black substance, 'ethiops' (in other words, melanin and its cell the melanocyte), which, he maintained, is present to some extent in all creatures, white and dark, but to a greater degree in blacks; and it is this that distinguishes them. This theory had been Malpighi's,[6] and as I shall show in the paragraphs below, Le Cat, who had read and studied Malpighi's works, developed it. Establishment of the precise connection between the theories of the two men is important because one cannot understand the significance or implications of Le Cat's theory of ethiops without first understanding Malpighi's.

Both Malpighi and Le Cat believed that ethiops is contained in the nerve tips, where it permanently resides. But whereas this idea is merely suggested, without detailed development, in Malpighi's writings, Le Cat made it the central focus of his argument. Furthermore, he tried to show that ethiops is not governed by the liver, pancreas, or gall bladder, but is indigenous to the membrane surrounding the tips of nerve cells. Le Cat based this assumption on microscopic experiments he had done with frogs and other animals. In the frog, for example, 'ethiops' (i.e. melanin) *is* in fact present anatomically in nerve cells, but not in human beings. In our anatomy, pigment is exclusively located in epidermal tissue, which is apart from the nerve cells. Le Cat would not have known this; microscopes in the 1730s and 1740s were not powerful enough to distinguish sharply within human dermal tissue. Nerve tips, under weak miscroscopes of the type Le Cat is likely to have used, would appear to extend as far up as the epidermis, whereas, in fact, they do not; they are subdermal. It was not until the nineteenth century that microscopy enabled medical men to see that an epidermal-subdermal barrier (basement membrane) exists and that nerve cells do not penetrate this barrier.

Le Cat, who was logical and reasonable in his inference that human anatomy is almost identical with animal anatomy (frogs, chameleons), was so much convinced of the presence of ethiops in nerve cells that he directed his energies to other questions about the physiological nature of ethiops. For example, he asked how blacks originally acquire this ethiops – a question we might think would have interested Malpighi but which apparently never did. Le Cat tried to formulate an answer, but it was not as clear as we would hope: ethiops, he maintained, comes not from the sun, climate, or torrid zones alone, but from these climatic conditions in conjunction with the peculiar physiological traits Negroes developed over longs periods of time. Not a perfectly clear formulation, to be sure, but in 1765 there was no Darwinian evolutionary theory of selection. Yet Le Cat's staunch belief that ethiops is somehow indigenous to blacks reveals a colour argument scientifically more sophisticated than the theories of his contemporaries or near-contemporaries Malpighi, Feijoo, Sanctorini, and Barrère.

Like all scientific hypotheses, Le Cat's must be judged for its ultimate accuracy. In this regard it fails, as I shall show in detail below. But it ought also to be viewed in the context of his basic assumptions concerning physiology and the common assumptions of his age. In this regard, Le Cat's theory shows up rather well on several counts, not merely one. First, he believed that the nervous system controls the organism – not a revolutionary assumption in the 1760s, but one that was in constant need of focusing and that required application to the racist debates in medicine. In assuming this view, he was in line with the most progressive mainstream of current European medicine and physiology. It was a view demonstrating that he had read and understood Willis's brain theory and Haller's radical but nevertheless accurate thesis about nervous action in relation to muscular contraction. Second, he was right to assume that ethiops is somehow controlled in its action by the nervous system. We today know that the pituitary, an integral part of the nervous system, regulates many of the functions of melanin; Le Cat could not have known this, but was not very far from the truth in assuming that nerve tips extending into the epidermis regulate pigment cells.

If his conception of the nervous system is lacking in certain areas, we ought to be tolerant within reasonable limits. For example, Le Cat believed that the animal spirits, not subject to the laws of physics and chemistry, pervade the hollow tubes of the nerves. This is untrue, but most scientists – good scientists – of his epoch also believed it. Moreover, Le Cat held that a mucous sheath (*corps muqueux*) wraps the entire nerve cell.[7] Although this idea is not entirely true, it is closer to the truth than the notion of many of his contemporaries, and it is certainly a more advanced concept of the anatomy of this part of the nervous system than Malpighi's. Controversies about the precise physiological structure of the 'outsides' of nerve cells had vigorously been carried on throughout the eighteenth century in England, where the question was debated in the Royal College of Physicians and in the Royal Society, as it was too on the Continent by Boerhaave, Hoffman, and lesser-known figures. It is true that Le Cat could not add substantially to these debates or radically change the theories of these men. But he did spend more time than they examining ganglions, the ends of nerves, under the microscope, and eventually he developed a fairly sophisticated conception of nerve tufts (*papilles nerveuses*) which he likened to the nipple-like structures of the tongue. Furthermore, he demonstrated that they expand and contract mechanistically, especially when regenerating themselves.

Considering the assumptions of physiologists in his age, therefore, Le Cat did not fare badly. In fact, he did exceptionally well, erring only in the points described above and, importantly, in his mistaken idea that the nervous system of humans is exactly, or almost exactly, the same as in frogs. To summarise his anatomical reasoning, he built his theory on some of the best physiology of his day and buttressed his assumptions with microscopic observations of several decades.

But even so, he was unsatisfied about the precise nature, histologically, of ethiops. And as a result of his dissatisfaction he reconsidered the matter, he says in his *Traité*, many times before satisfying himself. The most puzzling question, he believed, related to the *origin* of ethiops. He had seen this substance expand and contract under the microscope, so there could be no question of its physical nature: it could not be non-material, as were animal spirits. He was also certain, although it is hard for us to know why, of its presence at birth in blacks, and that there was no possibility of its being acquired after maturation. It was transmitted from generation to generation by the sun's rays, he thought, but these rays alone could not *produce* the substance. Heat could expand it, he believed, in the same way that heat causes other types of physical expansion.

Since Le Cat's experiments with various animals played an important role in his theory in the *Traité*, something, however brief, must be said about these, as well as about the significance of these experiments for modern medicine. Le Cat was convinced of the necessity of microscopic investigation, unlike many of his contemporaries, rationalists at heart who placed little faith in the microscope. He had seen ethiops in many animals and fish, but especially in the cuttlefish or squid (*sèche*). For two decades (1740–60) he observed their large black cells under various kinds of microscopes and deduced that human skin tissue must be similar. What he actually saw under the lens were melanocytes, microscopically quite prominent and very large in squid; but he was ultimately incorrect to assume that melanocytes in black men were structured similarly to those he observed in cuttlefish. Such reasoning by analogy was far from outlandish (scientists today, for example, experiment on mice and then extrapolate all their findings to humans); nor was his thoroughly logical assumption that Negroes have some sort of greater melanocyte production than do whites. Time has proved him correct, although his reasons were different from ours. But he had no conception of the melanocyte cell itself, its nature, anatomical structure, boundaries within the basal layer, accumulation at the base of the epidermis, chemical composition, and evolution throughout the life of a normal human being.[8]

If Le Cat's theory is 'translated' into modern medical terminology (and extreme caution must be employed in such a translation), these approximate statements obtain. Melanocytes are scattered throughout the epidermis but do not appear, whether in whites or blacks, in the basement membrane or dermis. These two layers, dermis and epidermis, are separated by a boundary (the basement membrane) through which nerve tissue does not penetrate. Therefore, it is quite impossible, by the standards of modern anatomy, to imagine melanocytes in the dermis, or, conversely, nerve cells in the epidermis. Moreover, these melanocytes do not differ significantly, if at all, in chemical composition in whites and blacks, although their number does. Blacks are known to have many more melanocytes per epidermal area than whites, but present-day knowledge of the hormonal activity of melanocytes is not sufficient to indicate if this disparity influences bodily functions. But it does influence skin pigmentation, thereby accounting in part for the difference between fair and dark peoples. There are of course other factors, mostly genetic, that influence this coloration, but they need not be explained in detail here.

To turn now to Le Cat within this brief 'translation': as I have already indicated, Le Cat was wrong on several counts, especially in his notion that nerve cells penetrate through the basement membrane. But he must be given credit for his intuitive leap in suspecting that bile cannot influence pigment, and thus for changing the whole course of physiological theory about skin. He must, it seems to me, also be given credit for his suspicion that the nerves play a more extensive role in the body than was thought at this time. Haller, Whytt, and other neurologists demonstrated in his own age that the brain required further examination, but it was Le Cat who suggested, however primitively, that the blood channel and nervous system were connected more intimately than most medical men thought.[9] Le Cat, viewed in this light, clearly emerges as a more important physiologist than Malpighi, especially if his contribution to the racist debates is the yardstick of measurement.

Malpighi, who died in 1694 (only six years before Le Cat was born), believed in an altogether different theory, one much less scientific and sophisticated: that all men were originally white, but that sinners among them had degenerated into black. In putting forward this remote divine cause of black skin, Malpighi impeded rather than advanced arguments regarding race among scientific men. It is true that he later abandoned his divine cause and substituted a proximate physiological cause: namely, a mucous sheath separating the dermis from the epidermis, recognition of which solved the physiological riddle puzzling anatomists for centuries. But he was wrong here, as wrong as Le Cat, although in a different way: the basement membrane, Malpighi's mucous sheath, does not contain melanin. Malpighi also theorised about a 'mucous liquor' determining skin colour, but he never stated where this liquor is located or how it operates, and Le Cat sensed this gap early in his researches. He dedicated his experiments, in part, to a refinement of this theory, but never could convince himself that ethiops was confined to a single sheath within the dermis. In other words, Le Cat argued for more area within skin tissue, for the whole basal cell and its surroundings as a zone wherein ethiops was contained. Malpighi, on the other hand, was persuaded that a localised substance must necessarily be the cause of differences in skin colour.[10] Having established to his own satisfaction that the cutis as well as cuticle of blacks is white, he reasoned that blacks differ anatomically only in this mucous liquor. In this regard he was certainly more advanced than all his seventeenth-century colleagues, but not so advanced as Le Cat, who consciously tried to *show* the connections between the 'mucous liquor' and the nervous system – a connection that we are now just beginning to learn does exist.[11] Le Cat, in his own way, was saying that the nervous system (brain, nerves, etc.) has some control of pigment activity (we know that the pituitary controls the hormonal activity of melanocytes). No one would wish to argue that this discovery in anatomy should bear Le Cat's name, but he was closer to the truth than his colleagues in France, and certainly those in England. And it is precisely in the bold imaginative leap of this connection, however primitively made, that Le Cat demonstrated his sound scientific intuition.

His contemporaries failed to understand him. Most never deemed his ideas worthy of the labour of serious comprehension: they continued the racial debate, usually asserting once again all the inadequate previous theories – but no one veered from the age-old lure of the bile theory. Riolan, Littre, and Morgagni, for example, were perplexed by the origin of black skin, and hypothesised that since most Negro skin had white patches, black men must originally have been white: a curious argument possessing little anatomic veracity. Later on, the sun turned their bile black (so the argument continued) and also their skin. For these scientists the relation of sun and bile was cause and effect: too much sun caused bile to blacken, and bile determined skin colour. QED. Albinus, an eighteenth-century Italian scientist (whose name, incidentally, has no connection to 'albino') proved to his own satisfaction that Negro bile, both hepatic and cystic, was black.[12] Sanctorini concurred with Albinus in considering bile the *only* substance in the body capable of influencing skin colour.[13] These men, oppressed by the tyranny of the ancient theory of bile, with centuries of weight behind it, had either not read Malpighi or did not comprehend him. (It is naturally possible that they read and rejected him, but this seems unlikely in view of the zeal with which Sanctorini and Albinus approached the theories of others; one wonders, moreover, why they would not have refuted him in print if they had renounced his theories.) Elsewhere than in Italy, the situation was not different. Winslow in Denmark was undecided,[14] and Grossard, a Le Cat student who later became a professor at the medical school in Montpellier and who also happened to have undertaken important research into the lymph system, impressionistically speculated that *lymph* was more important than bile in determining colour; but he was surprised to discover in autopsies that Negro lymph is every bit as white as the white man's.[15]

Then in 1741, a momentous episode in the eighteenth-century history of this medical debate occurred. Barrère, in France, published experiments asserting that Negro bile is black, and that it alone causes the black pigment in Negro skin.[16] Not the theory but the experiments won him attention. The bile theory was centuries old; but Barrère now endowed it with an authority it had never had. His book stated that his conclusions were based entirely on laboratory studies, thus creating the impression that black bile and its effects, long suspected but never seen, were as verifiable as the second law of motion. But the careful reader would have found that Barrère gave himself away. Blacks acquired the black bile, he postulated, by dwelling in hot jungles. He himself had not, of course, seen black bile in Negroes, nor could he account for the fact that generations of white men living in Africa never turned black. He somehow took black bile on 'faith', having viewed something abnormal resembling it, perhaps, in a few diseased bodies.

It is therefore greatly to Le Cat's credit that, only twenty years after Barrère's theory won universal acclaim, especially in France, he intuited and then demonstrated that it was specious. Historians of science may in the future show that certain French and English medical men anticipated Le Cat in this regard, but even so, some credit, however little, must go to him; at least, he must be rescued from the total oblivion in which he has until now remained. This is all the truer when it is remembered that towns like Rouen were somewhat isolated. If Le Cat had done his experiments in Paris, with the aid of many exceptional colleagues, we might feel more wary of granting him much honour; but he swam against the tide alone, in a small northern French city that had never been a medical centre. An idea of his courage in rejecting the dominant belief in bile as the single and sole determinant of skin colour is glimpsed by examining reviews of Barrère's theory in comparison to those of Le Cat. If Barrère was recognised and praised, Le Cat was disparaged as a shallow rationalist, even by English scientists who ought to have known better. Monsieur Eloy, author of the four-volume *Dictionnaire historique de la médecine*, published in 1778, commented favourably upon Barrère's bile theory but criticised Le Cat's nerve–ethiops theory as a wild hypothesis: 'Il explique ensuite le sentiment qu'il a adopté, mais comme il n'est fondé, ni sur l'observation, ni sur l'expérience, on est en droit de le renvoyer dans la classe des hypotheses qui sont plus ingénieuses que concluantes.'[17]

Two years after Le Cat's systematic demolition of the bile theory in the *Traité*, the Abbé Demanet published a *Dissertation physique et historique sur l'origine des Négres et la cause de leur couleur* (1767),[18] wherein he repeated the old bile arguments without mentioning Le Cat. Such an omission in itself is insignificant, but it reveals the typical neglect of Le Cat before the beginning of the nineteenth century. While it is true that his research on skin was occasionally mentioned during the last quarter of the eighteenth century – for example, in Jean Paul Marat's *Philosophical Essay on Man* (London, 1773) – his theory, however inchoate, of the interactions of ethiops and the nerve system was either too advanced or physiologically too radical, or appeared too clouded by physiological details, to admit of acceptance or recognition in his own time. Or it may have been left unregarded altogether, though this possibility is hard to understand in view of Le Cat's reputation. This was the man, after all, who had won the esteemed Berlin prize in physiology and about whom the editors of the *Gentleman's Magazine* said in 1753 he 'ought to be universally read'.

Throughout the last quarter of the eighteenth century, the scientific-medical community debated questions regarding the origin of Negroes and their black skin. As revolution approached and man's thoughts were deflected, it abated; but until then the question consumed them, though it seemed to arrive nowhere. Although some writers pointed out the loopholes inherent in the hot sun-black bile argument, none gave quite such specific reasons as Le Cat. Samuel Stanhope Smith professed to have read much literature before turning up any tangible conclusions in his *Essay on the Causes of Complexion . . .* , and ultimately admitted that not much new could be said on the subject. Essentially a synthesiser, he was satisfied to relegate Le Cat to a single mention in a voluminous footnote in which the Rouen surgeon is, of course, lost.[19] Whether Smith actually read Le Cat is doubtful, but his estimate cannot be misconstrued under any circumstances. (He had at least heard of Le Cat and his theories, which is more than can be said for other writers; most authors simply disregarded Le Cat altogether, and I have already suggested that this is not likely to have been prompted by his obscurity.) In 1768, three years after Le Cat's *Traité* was published, the first edition of the *Encyclopaedia Britannica* appeared. In the article entitled 'Negroes', the anonymous author commented: 'Dr Barrère alleges that the gall of Negroes is black, and being mixed with their blood is deposited between their skin and scarf-skin.' But no mention appears of Le Cat, or of his magistral, though cautious, challenge to the theory of bile as the cause of colour. Though this anonymous author took notice of 'Dr. Mitchell of Virginia' (John Mitchell, author of 'an Essay upon the Causes of the Different Colours of People in Different Climates'), he apparently had never heard of Le Cat, or if he had, could not see the difference between the sophistication of Le Cat's theory and the primitiveness (as well as repetitiveness) of Barrère's.[20] Like Barrère, he confused himself in this article by citing bizarre cases of colour change; yet he never paused to ask what the physiological basis of skin colour was.

Le Cat himself took time out to study such fantastic cases of blacks turning white, or whites turning black, but in each instance he attributed the change to severe illness, body change during pregnancy, or wild growth of the 'ethiops'. That is, he perceived these were exceptional cases, and drew no paradigms from them. His balance of induction and deduction was intelligently managed, and one observes few cases in the *Traité* of his going out on a limb or forcing a conclusion from an isolated example. But when it was time to generalise, he surrendered prejudice and tradition to his empirical findings. He ruled out climate as a primary cause: a Norwegian clan migrating to the Sudan could never become black, at least not in the course of a few centuries. He thereby discarded adaptive conditions and concentrated on physiological processes. If he could have known the approximate age of the world, he might have been able to anticipate Charles Darwin in *The Descent of Man and Selection in Relation to Sex*, and might also have reasoned that there must have been selection for lightly pigmented individuals in higher latitudes since they could better utilise sunshine. But the chronology of the world in 1765 was still in doubt, and so it remained until the nineteenth century; the age of man, indeed, is still to be determined. And Le Cat, who really cannot be criticised for this lack of knowledge, demonstrated his abilities as a model-maker by refuting the bile theory and turning to the nervous system's interaction with other systems.[21]

The significance of this essay for a symposium on racism in the eighteenth century is not easily grasped. For the men it treats, Le Cat, Malpighi, and to a lesser extent Albinus, Sanctorini, and Grossard, were never involved in the debates about race. Philosophers like Voltaire and Diderot held their personal opinions about the real status of black men, and especially about their physiological similarity or dissimilarity to white men. But Voltaire and Diderot never engaged, to my knowledge, in medical experiments, as did Le Cat; besides, they allowed other concerns – nationalistic, economic, religious, philosophic – to influence their final decision about the species to which black men belonged.[22]

Le Cat, so far as I know, had no such complicated concerns. He was not a 'philosophical' scientist in the way his English colleague Dr Robert Whytt was; he was content to experiment and report his observations. This is not to imply that his scientific assumptions were simple or lacking in any way, but Le Cat, unlike the French *philosophes* discussed elsewhere in this volume, had less ambitious plans for himself. He desired, understandably, to rise as high as possible in medical research, and for this aspiration he was respected in his own age. Yet he remained content to leave it to others to comment on the social implications of his discoveries.

Perhaps, then, the significance of Le Cat's work is that there is no significance. I am personally persuaded that thinkers who debate a topic like racism without understanding something about the physiological bases of skin colour cannot be sophisticated thinkers. They may have a great deal that is important to say about other topics, e.g. the nature of man, God, the life process, the human condition, and so forth. But this is a different matter from making a significant statement, one worthy of recording in the annals of history, about racism. Too many examples of my point abound in this volume for me to provide detail; and no one is going to think less of a Montesquieu or a Voltaire because either thought blacks were a different species of man, without taking the trouble to read contemporary scientists like Le Cat. But we may be certain that if more people in the eighteenth century had read scientists like Le Cat, the nature of the debates discussed today would be different. Laymen cannot be expected in any age to comprehend the technical writings of medical men, but the ideas of a Le Cat, for example, were explained in popular magazines like the *Gentleman's*, and were epitomised in everyday language for the common man.

If I may conclude on a modern note, it seems to me that the situation today is not altogether different from that in Le Cat's age. Thinkers from the common man to professional philosophers have their personal views about the black man, his capabilities, limitations, potential.[23] Yet not very many of these thinkers have taken the trouble to read the recent radical theories of Dr Jensen and his team.[24] The content of these theories is not in question: they may be right, they may be wildly wrong. But they have been put forward by scientists of very high calibre, with credentials beyond question, who hopefully have scientific truth as their first concern. Who knows if historians of science two centuries in the future will prove Jensen and company correct? Who knows what changes in the social structure of American life will be effected by Jensen's theories, if they are accurate? Or has a monumental change occurred, and do we now live in an age when certain theories are simply too dangerous to be put forward regardless of veracity? These are big questions, but must be left for another occasion.

NOTES

1 There is no biography. Information, and precious little exists, is scattered: see N. F. Eloy, *Dictionnaire historique de la médecine ancienne et moderne* 4 vols. (Paris, 1778), I, 565–71, for the only brief sketch. Nothing at all is said about Le Cat in the standard histories of medicine by Arturo Castiglione, Fielding H. Garrison, Sir William Osler, Theodor Puschmann, Henry F. Sigerist, Charles J. Singer, René Taton, and E. A. Underwood. René Taton's *Enseignement et diffusion des sciences en France au xviiie siècle* (Paris, 1964), briefly discusses Le Cat's anatomy courses at the Hôtel-Dieu in Rouen. Robert Darnton, *Mesmerism and the Enlightenment* (Cambridge, 1967), mentions Le Cat in relation to hypnotism. Le Cat's private papers survive and are available in the Archives of the City, Rouen, France. On 31 January 1739, Le Cat was elected a foreign member of the Royal Society, London (Thomas Thomson, *The History of the Royal Society* (London, 1912), appendix xli). After this time his anatomical works were regularly translated into English and reviewed in English journals. His interactions

with Dr James Parsons, F.R.S., are described by John Nichols, *Literary Anecdotes of the Eighteenth Century*, 6 vols. (1812), v, 475–6. By 1753 Le Cat, many of whose communications were now published in the *Philosophical Transactions of the Royal Society of London*, was sufficiently well known to be referred to by a columnist in the *Gentleman's Magazine*, XXIII (1753), 403 as 'the ingenious writer . . . who ought to be universally read'. In 1765 Le Cat won the prize of the Berlin Academy by answering their set of physiological questions on the structure of nerves. Offered by the Academy since 1753 but without a candidate, the prize answers were published as Le Cat's *Dissertation sur l'existence & la nature du fluide des nerfs & son action* (Berlin, 1765). The actual questions and an account of Le Cat's achievement in answering them are found in A. von Harnack, *Geschichte der Königlich Preussischen Akademie der Wissenschaften zu Berlin* (Berlin, 1901), I 400. Le Cat was congratulated by the acclaimed scientist Haller for his attainment.

2 Extending to almost two hundred pages, it was not translated into English or reviewed in English periodicals as almost all Le Cat's other works had been. The reasons are not clear: perhaps the subject matter was too controversial for the more sedate reviews and too conservative for others.

3 Benito Feijoo, *Teatro Critico Universal* (Madrid, 1736), VII, third discourse, 69–94.

4 Published in the John Harvard Library Series (Cambridge, 1965), viii.

5 A long list of comments and works could be compiled for the period 1700–80. Without making a search, I have found no fewer than two dozen comments in travel books alone. See, for example, Edward Long, 'Negroes', in *The History of Jamaica* (1774), chap. i, the third book. Some of these works appear in Winthrop Jordan's 'Guide to Smith's References', in Smith, *Essay*, pp. 253–68.

6 See *Opera Omnia* (1686), II, 221.

7 *Traité de la couleur*, 30 ff.

8 This concept arose in the mid nineteenth century and required at least Schwann's theory of the cell. See Bobbie Williams, 'Human Pigmentation', *General Anthropology* (1973), 487–523, the best scientific treatment of skin colour I have seen. I am grateful to Professor Williams, Department of Anthropology, University of California, Los Angeles, for making this unpublished material available to me.

9 This is a chapter of the history of science not yet surveyed.

10 *Opera Omnia* II, 215–38. This notion was transmitted to the eighteenth century as is made clear by dictionaries and encyclopedias. See, for example, Abraham Rees's article 'Complexion' in *The Cyclopaedia; or, Universal Dictionary* (Philadelphia, 1810–24), IX, no pages.

11 I.e., the pituitary regulating functions of melanocytes. Precisely why this is the case is unknown as yet, as most histology textbooks explain. In general, little is known about the influence of the nervous system on hormonal activity. As an example of another area in which the influence of the nervous system is not well understood there is the glyal cell, separating the blood system and the brain. Before the 1920s it was not known that medicines could pass through this barrier, i.e., penetrate from the blood into the brain, and consequently affect the nervous system.

12 See Bernardus Albinus, *De Sede et Causa Coloris Aethiopum* (Leiden, 1737), 267–78.

13 *De Statica Medicina* (The Hague, 1664), 221. Sanctorius, an influential writer of aphorisms, never developed his theory.

14 Jacob Winslow, *An Anatomical Exposition of the Structure of the Human Body*, trans. G. Douglas, 2 vols (1733), and *A Description of the Integuments of the Vessels* (1784).

15 Grossard never published books, but his ideas and writings were circulated in France among interested doctors. He consulted frequently with Le Cat in Rouen and at scholarly meetings.

16 *Dissertation sur la cause physique de la couleur des Nègres, de la qualité de leurs cheveaux, &*

de la génération de l'un & de l'autre (Paris, 1741). A brief survey of Barrère's life appears
in Elroy's *Dictionnaire historique de la médecine*, 1, 265. Although Barrère's books never
attained the same important in England as Le Cat's, his name and theory (i.e., as
champion of the bile theory) carried great weight there. Nothing in France contributed
more to the prestige of Barrère's theory than the extensive review and serious treatment
he received in the *Journal des Sçavants* (February 1742), 97–107. See, for example,
Edward Long's discussion of the scientific origins of Negro skin in his important
treatise *A History of Jamaica*, 3 vols. (1774), II, 351–2, which reckons with Barrère but
has never heard of Le Cat: 'Anatomists say, that this *reticular membrane*, which is found
between the *Epidermis* and the skin, being soaked in water for a long time, does not
change its colour. Monsieure Barrère, who appears to have examined this circumstance
with particular attention, as well as Mr. Winslow, says, that the *Epidermis* itself is
black, and that if it has appeared white to some that have examined it, it is owing to
its extreme fineness and transparency; but that it is really as dark as a piece of blackhorn,
reduced to the same gracility [*sic*]. That this color of the *Epidermis*, and of the skin, is
caused by the bile, which in Negroes is not yellow, but always as black as ink. The
bile in white men tinges their yellow skin; and if their bile was black, it would doubtless
communicate the same black tint. Mr. Barrère affirms, that the Negroe bile naturally
secrets itself upon the *Epidermis* in a quantity sufficient to impregnate it with the dark
colour for which it is so remarkable. These observations naturally lead to the further
question, "why the bile in Negroes is black?" ' The tone and weight of Long's prose
in this passage makes it clear that Barrère's authority is beyond question and that he
represents the most valid school of thought. Only Buffon receives an equal amount
of esteem in Long's chapter.

17 I, 571. An earlier version of the dictionary appeared in 1755.

18 Published in Paris. I have found no biographical information about Demanet of any
note.

19 *Essay*, 53.

20 The author throughout refers to Barrère as an authority. The truly amazing thing,
from my vantage at least, is the attention Barrère's treatise received and the almost
complete neglect of Le Cat's.

21 A study in depth of Le Cat's scientific writings would, of course, have to explain why
Le Cat was able to posit connection. His books on the physiology of the nervous
system made him eminently qualified. See, especially, his prize-winning volume,
Dissertation sur l'existence & la nature de fluide des nerfs (Berlin, 1765), in many ways one
of the genuinely radical theories of the age. Also of help were his medical treatises on
the anatomy of the passions, such as *Traité des sensations & des passions en général* (Paris,
1767).

22 Much 'history' can of course be accumulated documenting virtually every aspect of
the racism debates of the eighteenth century. But every age adheres, whether it knows
it or not, to primitive assumptions about what constitutes 'scientific belief'; and we
cannot penetrate to the core of racism in the Enlightenment unless we know precisely
what it believed about the scientific bases of the skin question.

23 This is an important point. What a vast sense of the monumental changes of belief
and emphasis, as well as theories of cause and effect, one derives by approaching the
problem vertically rather than horizontally, starting, let us say, with Robert Boyle's
analysis in Peter Shaw (ed.), *The Works of the Hon. Robert Boyle* (1772; ed., 1699), I,
714–19, 'Of Colours: Experiment xi'. A brief reading list after 1780 might include: E.
G. Bosé, *De Mutato per morbum colore corporis humani* (Leipzig, 1785); Robert Know
(ethnologist), *The Races of Man* (1850–62) and *Man: His Structure and Physiology* (1857);
Franz Pruner-Bey, 'Notions preliminaires sur la coloration de la peau chez l'homme',
Bulletins de la Société d'Anthropologie, v (1864), 65–135; C. H. G. Pouchet, *Des colorations
de l'épiderme* (Paris, 1864); L. Dunbar, *Ueber Pigmenterungen der Haut* (Berlin, 1884);
Ashley Montagu, *Man's Most Dangerous Myth: the Fallacy of Race* (New York, 1952,

3rd ed. rev.); Richard Bernheimer, *Wild Men in the Middle Ages* (Cambridge, 1952); J. S. Slotkin, 'Eighteenth Century Social Anthropology', in *Readings in Early Anthropology* (1965), 244–356; John S. Haller, *Outcasts from Evolution: Scientific Attitudes of Racial Inferiority, 1859–1900* (Urbana, 1971).

24 Arthur R. Jensen has argued that genetic rather than environmental factors account for differences in IQ for the most part. He further claims that those environmental factors that do operate are likely to be nutritional, dating to the prenatal period: 'How Much Can We Boost IQ and Scholastic Achievement?', *Harvard Educational Review*, xxxix (winter 1969), 1–123. Those who replied to Jensen in the next issue of the journal seem more bent on airing their own views than in considering his: 'Discussion', *HER*, xxxix (spring 1969), 273–356.

3

Foucault and Enlightenment

During 1970–1, when I was writing this essay, Foucault's works remained for the most part untranslated and as a consequence largely unknown to North American scholars who tilled the field of Enlightenment Studies. At that time only Madness and Civilization *and* The Order of Things *had appeared in English.* The Archaeology of Knowledge *and* The Birth of the Clinic *were being translated but had not yet been released in America.* Discipline and Punish *would be published much later in the 1970s, as would the first volume of* The History of Sexuality. *The various collections of essays and interviews in English that proved so influential – such compilations as Donald Bouchard's* Michel Foucault: Language, Counter-Memory, Practice *– had not yet appeared, nor such important bio-critical works as Alan Sheridan's* Michel Foucault: the Will to Truth. *Even Baudrillard's* Oublier Foucault, *first published in 1977, remained unavailable in English translation for another decade, until 1987.*

Around 1970, there had as yet been no critical response to Foucault in either Britain or America. R. D. Laing and Maurice Cranston had each written short appreciative, popular, essays, but Hayden White had not yet 'decoded Foucault' from 'the underground', and Lawrence Stone, the distinguished social historian, had not penned his scathing attack in The New York Review of Books, *claiming that Foucault was an intellectual bandit (using language such as the Nazis, Stone would later charge that Foucault had committed unforgivable crimes against humanity). Nevertheless, it was then clear to me that it was only a matter of time before Foucault would become a household word. I therefore sought to interpret some of his work for my colleagues in seventeenth- and eighteenth-century studies.*

While dazzled by Foucault's brilliant insights, I also recognised the perils of his method, especially his (typically French) refusal to read criticism and scholarship written in English. No one since Cassirer at the latest had displayed even a fraction of his uncanny ability to transform current perceptions of the great European Enlightenment. This very original approach, it seemed to me, would globally alter the way I and every other scholar in the field worked; on the other hand, it seemed crucial to call attention to those aspects of his cultural anthropology and historiography that would never stand the test of time.

*So it was with a great deal of trepidation that I wrote this essay. At the same time some of my friends were warning me that I would come to regret this rash act. I could not know that J. G. Merquior, the Brazilian theoretical scholar then at the London School of Economics, would later commend my effort in his own book on Foucault (*Foucault, *University of California Press, 1985), nor that in his much later 'unmasking of Foucault'*

Jürgen Habermas would make some of the same points in his Philosophical Discourse of Modernity *(Cambridge, MIT Press, 1987).*

Michel Foucault writes like a prose-poet, yet wants to be treated as a philosopher, and added to this anomaly is the fact that most of his critics have been evaluating him (as I will) on the uncompromising basis of scientific proof and concrete demonstrability. He also denies that he can or ought to be judged scientifically; moreover, his critics don't seem terribly excited about him as a poet writing in prose. If his message were insignificant such misunderstanding would not matter at all. But the message, at least in the book I shall discuss here,[1] is nothing less than monumental and has not been put forward with such vigour since the nineteenth century: that 'man' was born in the Classical Age,[2] subsequently 'died', and that today he is entering a new era in which he merely plays a Lilliputian role. Strange as it may seem, this proposition conveys to Foucault a profundity that has taken him four hundred pages to fathom. It is as meaningful to him as Dionysian and Apollonian energies were to Nietzsche or the past, present, and future of history to Hegel.

But the 'message' is not the problem. I shall conclusively, and on scientific grounds, demonstrate it is not much more than one man's hypothesis without proof of any hard, scientific validity. The problem, as I have already hinted, is the medium (hard as I have tried to avoid this McLuhanesque antinomy, it has not been possible). And precisely because Foucault's medium is so apparent, it coerces some of his critics into believing that a didactic poet writing in prose ought not to be judged mathematically, as if he were writing a treatise on calculus. But Foucault *au fond* is a poet: writing in prose, to be sure, philosophically erudite and sometimes prodigiously learned, possibly more polymathic than any French intellectual living today, obsessed by arcane knowledge and obscure out-of-the-way books – but still at heart a philosophical poet.

Imagining him otherwise will not do.[3] Readers of this journal may well question this prolegomenon: why not plunge directly into the theory itself? Because Foucault's poetic philosophy, no less than Lucretius', Dante's, Kierkegaard's, or Sartre's, requires an *a priori* context and introduction before his thought can be estimated.[4] Moreover, wishing him otherwise will not dissipate the difficulties inherent in his philosophical system. Cavilling because Foucault is not as prudent in his research and austere with data as, for example, Lawrence Stone (history), George Sherburn (English literature), Joseph Schumpeter (economics),[5] or any number of other pioneering scholars of this century, is an exercise in futility inasmuch as a thoroughbred ought not to be expected to race against a

ploughhorse even though each may perform his assigned tasks effi-
caciously.

One either takes the man and his writings at their face value (i.e., as
dramatic philosophy written in a highly poetic and personal style) or
leaves him alone altogether. Those who are partial toward the former will
become enriched by a kind of literary experience; or as D. W. Harding
nicely put it, 'If you get excited by the experience of having thoughts,
especially wordily inflated thoughts, then the book as it stands will give
you all you can ask.'[6] The others ought not to read Foucault unless they
wish to inflict upon themselves a masochistic torture. My stance is more
literal. I consider it the task of this essay to evaluate logically and scientifically the philosophy of *The Order of Things*, forgetting for the moment
that I have just contradicted all my earlier strictures and also relegating
Foucault's literary style to other critics.[7] Here it will suffice merely to
explicate his theory, or at least the parts of it that are sufficiently comprehensible to be explicated, and to demonstrate its inconclusiveness.[8]

THE THEORY

Foucault suggests that all modern thought is built on unspoken assumptions rarely, if ever, articulated. While this notion is hardly new (see, for
example, its role in the important writings of Robert K. Merton),[9] it has
received little attention. It takes daring to free oneself from all preconceptions, let alone to plot the history of the hardening of the preconceptions themselves. But Foucault, taking his inspiration from a text of
Borges communicating an imaginary Chinese classification system, braves
it and considers himself an 'archaeologist of modern thought'; i.e., digging
up, or out, the remnants of other systems of thought in which the preconceptions were different. The nexus, or meeting point, of radically different
preconceptions he calls 'mutations' – in other words, a mutation occurs
when one body of preconceptions gives way to another. I will have more
to say in a moment about Foucault's metaphor, since mutation implies,
indeed requires, a radical change; at present, however, it is more important
to chart his archaeological tableau.

Cataclysmic mutations occurred, according to Foucault, in the seventeenth and eighteenth centuries;[10] at the very end of the eighteenth and
the beginning of the nineteenth century; and a third mutation is happening
right now. For our purposes, the first two are most important.

Foucault believes that before the seventeenth century, words and
things (thus his title) were not separated but rather enjoyed a 'sympathy
of similitudes'.[11] The sympathy was somehow good, wholesome, utilitarian, and nonfragmented. It bound men to their cosmos, especially to
the naturalistic universe, and kept them in touch with sensuous nature,

rocks, trees, rivers, oceans; it was 'profound kinship.' Whole sets of 'signatures' existed to relate things and words, as in Foucault's example of the affinity between the plant called aconite and diseases of the eye: 'This unexpected affinity would remain in obscurity if there were not some signature on the plant, some mark, some word, as it were, telling us that it is good for diseases of the eye. This sign is easily legible in its seeds: they are tiny dark globes set in white skinline coverings whose appearance is much like that of eyelids covering an eye.' Here the 'sign' is not a word but a resemblance, and Foucault is talking about the Renaissance doctrine of signatures, especially as it was apparent in magic, demonology, and astrology. In all the examples he gives, he tries to show that knowledge consisted 'in relating one form of language to another form of language; in restoring the great, unbroken plain of words and things, in making everything speak' (40). That this language of signatures existed is true beyond any shadow of doubt; but it never encompassed '*all* knowledge', not even at that moment in the late Renaissance when writers wrote most about it.[12] This, however, is a minor quibble about degree and extensiveness and must not bog us down.

Then a *sudden* break in adherence occurred and the first 'mutation' took place. Words and things *suddenly* (Foucault inflates his language to evoke a melodramatic atmosphere of earth-shaking cataclysmic change) stopped relating by sympathy and signs: '. . . from the seventeenth century, one began to ask how a sign could be linked to what it signified. A question to which the Classical period was to reply by the analysis of representation; and to which modern thought was to reply by the analysis of meaning and signification. . . . The profound kinship of language with the world was thus dissolved. . . . Things and words were to be separated from one another.'

If I understand Foucault correctly, he means that all doctrines of signature (not merely those involving words and things) *suddenly* dissolved and were replaced by science. In other words, men no longer passively accepted the affinity between aconite and diseases of the eye, or walnuts and diseases of the brain; now they asked *how* aconite or walnuts could cure ('how a sign could be linked to what it signified'). If nothing else, this implies that they had not asked the question about cure before the seventeenth century. And yet every history of medicine with which I am familiar reveals dozens of Renaissance physicians actively asking how a plant such as aconite or an herb such as satyrion (used to calm insatiable sexual appetites) effected their cures.[13] It is naive of Foucault seriously to believe that the history of medical science began in the seventeenth century. Stated otherwise, namely that medical science was developing in the Renaissance concomitantly with the doctrine of signatures, there remains nothing to comment upon. Walter Pagel has shown the impact of signatures on the lay mind,[14] and several other important historians of medicine have clearly shown the strides made by Renaissance medicine, without which, incidentally, Harvey probably would not have been able to discover in 1618–28 the circulation of the blood. But, again, we must not get bogged down.

Now that people were preoccupied with questions relating signs (aconite) to their significations (diseases of the eye), the way was paved for the next mutation.[15] Words and things grew more disparate than ever before as various sciences arose. Since the old signs were now inadequate, a new set had to be invented, hastily and arbitrarily. Foucault, rationalist though he is, never entertains the possibility of utilitarian agents here. If people at the beginning of the seventeenth century were no longer satisfied to apply aconite leaves for eye trouble, and if they now asked *how* aconite cured, can their shift not have been prompted by dissatisfaction with this herbal remedy? Foucault, who seems uninterested in this question, would retort by asking, why had they been satisfied with it for centuries? And most medical historians would inform him that the incessant, almost unrelenting, plagues during the period 1580–1640, as well as the expectations raised by the new science after 1660, were largely responsible for the great acceleration in popular dissatisfaction.[16] Throughout the sixteenth century there had been few serious plagues, but toward its close plague after plague took its toll of human misery.

Yet Foucault insists that the new signs were arbitrary and that they

> introduced into knowledge probability, analysis, and combination, and the justified *arbitrariness* of the system. It was the sign system that gave rise *simultaneously* to the search for origins and to calculability; to the constitution of tables that would fix the possible compositions, and to the restitution of a genesis on the basis of the simplest elements; it was the sign system that linked *all* knowledge to a language, and sought to replace *all* languages with a system of *artificial* symbols and operations of a logical nature. At the level of the history of opinions, all this would appear, no doubt, as a tangled network of influences in which the individual parts played by Hobbes, Berkeley, Leibniz, Condillac, and the 'Idéologues' would be revealed. But if we question Classical thought at the level of what, archaeologically, made it possible, we perceive that the dissociation of the sign and resemblance in the early seventeenth century caused these new forms – probability, analysis, combination, and universal language system – to *emerge*, not as successive themes engendering one another or driving one another out, but as a single network of *necessities*. And it was this network that made possible the individuals we term Hobbes, Berkeley, Hume, or Condillac. (63)[17]

These and other similar thinkers, according to Foucault, toiled away for almost two centuries (1600–1800) until they recognised that their individual endeavours were directed at one object, man.[18] Thus, a Linnaeus

developing natural taxonomies, an Adam Smith discovering the flow of
trade among men, or a Lancelot sensing the transformational levels of
grammar – all somehow, whether individually or collectively, recognised
that their inquiries were about a single object, *man*, and that they were
consequently contributing to his 'birth':

> Before the end of the eighteenth century, *man* did not exist – any more than
> the potency of life, the fecundity of labour, or the historical density of
> language. He is a quite recent creature, which the demiurge of knowledge
> fabricated with its own hands less than two hundred years ago: but he has
> grown old so quickly that it has been only too easy to imagine that he had
> been waiting for thousands of years in the darkness for that moment of
> illumination in which he would finally be known. (308)

Now that man was 'born' and could be studied scientifically, he, like
other organisms, evolved:

> There is no doubt that the natural sciences dealt with man as with a species
> or a genus: the controversy about the problem of races in the eighteenth
> century testifies to that. Again, general grammar and economics made use
> of such notions as need and desire, or memory and imagination. But there
> was no epistemological consciousness of man as such. The Classical *episteme*
> is articulated along lines that do not isolate, in any way, a specific domain
> proper to man. And if that is not sufficient, if it is still objected that, even
> so, no period has accorded more attention to human nature, has given it a
> more stable, more definitive status, or one more directly presented to dis-
> course – one can reply by saying that the very concept of human nature,
> and the way in which it functioned, excluded any possibility of a Classical
> science of man. (308–9)

There is much attractiveness here, especially in the mythic appeal of
the birth of human nature and the prognostication of another 'mutation'.[19]
But from our vantage – as students of the eighteenth century – it is more
important to notice the three specific realms in which words and things
(or signs and their significations) were growing apart:

> There took place therefore, towards the last years of the eighteenth century,
> in *general grammar*, in *natural history*, and in the *analysis of wealth*, an event
> that is of the same type in all these spheres . . . What came into being with
> Adam Smith, with the first philologists, with Jussieu, Vicq d'Azyr, or
> Lamarck, is a minuscule but absolutely essential displacement, which top-
> pled the whole of Western thought: representation has lost the power to
> provide a foundation – with its own being, its own deployment and its
> power of doubling over on itself – for the links that can join its various
> elements together. No compositions, no decomposition, no analysis into
> identities and differences can now justify the connection of representations
> one to another. . . . (236–9)

This is (of course) the Romantic point of view about fragmentation, and there isn't much more intellectual content here than is present in Blake's verses, 'Mock on, Mock on, Voltaire, Rousseau'. Pared and stripped of its inflated rhetoric, this passage, like much of his book, comments on faulty empiricisms. But Foucault's notion that 'an event towards the [end] of the eighteenth century' in linguistics, biology, and economics dealt a final death blow to whatever little profound kinship remained between words and things, requires serious refutation, if for no other reason than his contention that such dislocation and alienation of representations took place during 1650–1800. While it may appear flattering to some scholars with a vested interest in restoring the eighteenth century to prominence and in endowing these years with majestic powers of dismemberment, Foucault's hypothesis is actually more specific: (1) that the 'event' took place at the end of the eighteenth century, and (2) that all the ensuing dislocation (i.e., mutation) resided in the development, or evolution, of *three* (no more, no less) sciences – in his words, 'in *general grammar*, in *natural history*, and in the *analysis of wealth*'.

LINGUISTICS

Until about a decade ago, any competent historian of linguistics would have considered it safe to assert that the two most significant developments during the period 1650–1800 in his science were (1) the Port Royal grammar and (2) the genetic theory.[20] Stated roughly, the first introduced transformational grammar[21] and the second demonstrated that all Indo-European languages originated from a common source and were therefore related. The transformational grammar of Lancelot and Arnauld is usually considered responsible for the first, and a statement made in 1787 by Sir William Jones for the second.[22] By 1820 philologists such as Bopp and Grimm began to study comparative grammars, and the genetic theory of language was on its way to acceptance.

But the significance of the discovery of transformational grammar by Port Royalists is another matter altogether. For one thing, their transformational grammar is of another parity than the genetic theory of language: i.e., it does more than collect data and classify facts. The difference between them may be compared to Coleridge's new literary criticism, on the one hand, and to the encyclopaedic efforts of the *philosophes* on the other. For another, the two developments were separated in time by almost a century and a half. Lancelot's two important grammars appeared in 1644 and 1653; the *Grammaire générale et raisonée*, compiled by Lancelot and Arnauld, appeared in 1660. The genetic theory, on the other hand, was not introduced until *c.* 1800. Thus, while Foucault considers *both* developments crucial to his argument, no linguistic scientists with whose writings I am familiar would agree with him, for the genetic theory of language cannot have had any power of separating signs and their significations. Transformational grammar, on the other hand, most certainly can.

Then came Noam Chomsky, announcing in 1966 that transformational grammar was owing to the influence of Cartesian philosophy and psychology, and that it is first apparent in the Port Royal grammars of the 1660s.[23] How, then, can Foucault possibly argue that his 'event' (see p. 236) 'took place towards the last years of the eighteenth century'? Granting that Foucault published *The Order of Things* before Chomsky's *Cartesian Linguistics*, ought he not to be capable of keeping simple chronology straight?

Such oversight is only the beginning. Chomsky's critics quickly demonstrated that transformational grammar was not original with the Port Royalists at all.[24] The most devastating blow came from Robin Lakoff of the Language Research Center in Cambridge, Massachusetts, herself a student of Chomsky:

> We have mentioned the claims made by Chomsky that Descartes was a seminal influence on the Port Royal grammarians. If this were so, we might expect him to be mentioned in the preface to the *Nouvelle méthode pour facilement et en peu temps comprendre la language* or the *Grammaire générale et raisonnée*, and Lancelot's and Arnauld's debt to him noted. Yet, curiously, in neither book is there any mention of Descartes or Cartesian philosophy. . . . It seems as though, by Lancelot's own testimony, the most important influence on his (and Arnauld's) theory of language was not Descartes, but rather Sanctius. If we wish to find the origins of this early transformationalist theory, we should look at Sanctius.[25]

Several independent scholars did,[26] and confirmed Lakoff's contention: Chomsky seems to have overlooked entirely this important Spanish grammarian (1523–1601), whose actual name was Francisco Sanchez de las Brozas. And yet, Sanctius's most important book, *Minerva, seu de causis linguae latinae* was published in 1585, *at the very same time* that the doctrine of signatures was most popular. Regardless of a linguist's estimate of the book's degree of transformation, the fact is that it contains within its thousand pages many, if not most, of the revolutionary linguistic ideas found in the writings of the later Port Royalists. How, then, in the name of anything, can Foucault's thesis hold water? What 'event of the late eighteenth century . . . in *general grammar*' took place? Signatures (or correspondences) and Sanctius were contemporary bedfellows. Every deep insight in *Minerva* demonstrates that Sanctius was a protolinguistic scientist engaged in querying how surface structures could be related to deeper structures. In fact, there is good reason to believe that his syntactic theories are scientifically more sophisticated than those of the Port Royalists of the 1660s.[27] Not until Du Marsais and Beauzée, writing in the 1760s,[28] is there such clear evidence of transformational grammar.

Foucault's cataclysmic 'event' in linguistics is therefore a Renaissance phenomenon, published in 1585, but one whose origins and inspiration were the influence of earlier teachers of the 1550s and 1560s, and of writers from Quintillian to the Modistae in the fourteenth century.

BIOLOGY

Foucault is harsh on those who write, or even conceive of writing, histories of biology in the eighteenth century; who

> . . . do not realize that biology did not exist then, and that the pattern of knowledge that has been familiar to us for a hundred and fifty years is not valid for a previous period. And that, if biology was unknown, there was a very simple reason for it: that life itself did not exist. All that existed was living beings, which were viewed through a grid of knowledge constituted by *natural history*. (127–8)

Once again, it is questionable whether there is anything serious here to examine. After stripping this prose of its rhetorical flowers (e.g., the overly dramatic use of 'exist') and accepting the enslavement of its metaphors ('a grid of knowledge'), little intellectual content remains. Foucault wants to say that (1) biology cannot 'exist' until man 'exists' and that (2) man – that is, man as the object of scientific enquiry – could not 'exist' until the great 'mutation' at the end of the eighteenth century, at which time simultaneous developments in three sciences created an unprecedented contrast between successive strata of thought systems. Stated less elaborately and theoretically, this says that one can study genes or cells and not necessarily be studying biology. The necessary condition for studying biology, as we today know it, is an *a priori* concept of man as an objective entity.[29] Thus Harvey and Vesalius, according to Foucault, were not biologists in the same sense that Schleiden and Schwann were; their degree of empiricism counts for nothing, nor does imagination and native ability.[30] Only a sense of life (i.e., of an organism and its whole history throughout time) can turn a naturalist (Linnaeus) into a biologist (Schleiden); and Foucault uses the example of Linnaeus to disqualify the Swede from the ranks of biologists: 'As Linnaeus says, the naturalist – whom he calls *Historiens naturalis* – "distinguishes the parts of natural bodies with his eyes, describes them appropriately according to their number, form, position, and proportion, and he names them." The naturalist is the man concerned with the structure of the visible world and its denomination according to characters. Not with life.'

Where then does life archaeologically begin? According to Foucault, with Cuvier (*c.* 1800) and the discovery of the organic structure of living things:

> From Cuvier onward, it is life in its non-perceptible, purely functional aspect that provides the basis for the exterior possibility of a classification. The classification of living beings is no longer to be found in the great expanse of order; the possibility of classification now arises from the depths of life, from those elements most hidden from view. Before, the living-being was a locality of natural classification; now, the fact of being classifiable is a property of the living being. So the project of a general *taxonomia* disappears . . . 'Nature,' too, disappears. (268)

Linnaeus's particular system of bisexual taxonomy, its foundations and relation to other taxonomical systems before 1750, is not in question here, nor is that of any of his predecessors or contemporaries. Foucault's suggestion is rather that 'life begins' when a non–visible, internal principle for ordering, not merely for classifying, nature arises; and by 'arises' he means that it alone is the basic foundation for all hierarchical order. Such a principle he finds in the idea of organic structure: 'It subordinates characters to one another; it links them to functions; it arranges them in accordance with an architecture that is internal as well as external, and no less invisible than visible; it distributes them throughout a space that is other than that of names, discourse, and language.'

Granted, this is done (although in scientific practice less poetically than here), but *only in a sense*, metaphorically speaking. That is, internal taxonomy based on organic forms may be metaphorically more attractive to theoretical speculators than external taxonomy such as that found in Linnaeus and Bichat.[31] But I am unaware that any evidence exists to prove that it is scientifically more accurate, or even to prove that either description makes one bit of difference to everyday experimentation. Only among metaphysicians, such as Coleridge or the German Romantic philosophers, does it play an important role, and recently the importance of this role seems to be diminishing. Even if it did make a difference, the notion Foucault entertains about its being the source of 'archaeological life' is dubious because historians of science long ago demonstrated that organic structure as a dominant metaphysical assumption was nothing new with Cuvier.[32] And if Foucault can't prove that Cuvier, or his contemporaries (*c.* 1800), were responsible for its rise, then his case for a new 'mutation' based on it must be discredited, no less than his case in linguistics must be discredited purely on factual grounds.

No point exists in dispelling the wild notion that organic form begins about 1800. It is an ancient idea conceived long before Plato but pursued by him, and it had a long history from Aristotle to Albertus Magnus, da

Vinci, and Vesalius.[33] Leibniz's philosophy in the next century has been construed as a search for a universal formal system of reasoning,[34] and Newton's *Principia* (1687), written long before Cuvier was born, discusses it as a basic principle: '. . . it is not to be conceived that mere mechanical causes could give birth to so many regular motions.'[35] Shaftesbury developed the idea of inward form in the *Characteristics*, an inner psychological process by which form is realised, and Vico's *Scienza Nuova* emphasises a morphological approach to the study of cultures and human history.[36] The line to Cuvier is continuous, with Kant's view of time and space as *a priori* subjective forms and Goethe's explorations in botany filling its gaps. Cuvier, Foucault argues, was the first to apply an external principle to classify *every single living form*, thereby introducing a continuity nonexistent before. But all the seeds of this application in comparative anatomy are evident earlier.[37] Scientific progress, as Bacon knew and stressed, requires a continuum of achievements, and even the accomplishments of individual geniuses must be estimated within their context.[38]

Yet Foucault continues to idolise Cuvier because organic structure alone seems to possess an ability to heal the rift between words and things: 'At the beginning of the nineteenth century, [words] rediscovered their ancient, enigmatic density; though not in order to restore the curve of the world which had harboured them during the Renaissance, nor in order to mingle with things in a circular system of signs. Once detached from representation, language has existed, right up to our own day. . . .' The connections of thought are sufficiently obvious: Cuvier, organic structure, words now returning to things, a 'profound kinship' is restored. It is, again, a romantic theory, based on a dialectic of opposites attracting and repelling each other, but also founded on a most defective logic and the faultiest of historicisms; and is, furthermore, Eliotan and 'modern', as it were, to the extent that it disparages literature between Milton and the Romantic poets.[39] Neat also is the seeming resuscitation of great imaginative literature (Sade, Blake, Goethe) precisely at the time (1800) of Cuvier and organic form.

But on scientific and rigorous grounds it is no more than a hypothesis: beautiful, symmetrical, labyrinthine in its cerebrational intricacy, but also ridiculous. Ridiculous to the extent that it is predicated on any impossibly weak philosophy of history that neither marshals facts correctly nor attempts to grapple with the monumental problems of *cause* and *change*.[40] And no history of biology, or for that matter of *natural history* (to take Foucault on his own terms), can hope to achieve acceptance without adequately taking *cause* and *change* into account.

ECONOMICS

Foucault masters his last domain more successfully than the previous two. Here his interest is 'that moment' when 'the analysis of wealth becomes economics', especially as exemplified in thinkers from Copernicus and Bodin to Adam Smith, Ricardo, and the physiocrats: 'This domain, the ground and object of "economy" in the Classical age, is that of *wealth*. It is useless to apply to it questions deriving from a different type of economics – one organized around production or work, for example; useless also to analyze its various concepts . . . without taking into account the system from which they draw their positivity.'

This 'system' is, according to Foucault, the creation of economic values, and he firmly believes the physiocrats to have been responsible for its establishment. For they, not Adam Smith, conceived of *value* as an organic master plan encompassing trade, deifying production, and idolising utilitarian ends:

> Let us imagine the most rudimentary of all exchange situations: a man who has nothing but corn or wheat confronted with another who has nothing but wine or wood. As yet, there is no fixed price, no equivalence, no common measure. Yet if these men have gone to the trouble to collect the wood, to sow and harvest the corn or the wheat, it is because they have passed a certain judgement on these things; without having to compare it with anything else, they judged that this wheat or that wood was able to satisfy one of their needs – that it would be *useful* to them. (196)

Here Foucault suggests that the physiocrats, especially Condillac and Turgot, always exercised judgement in the name of utility. Utilitarian values, he continues, were thereby created in the middle and late eighteenth century, giving rise in turn to a new concept of 'political economy' based on the relation of value and prices. Some of this argument is conventional, but Foucault's sense of the arbitrariness of 'certain judgements' is not. While many human needs are arbitrarily fulfilled (both at the literal and 'archaeological' level), economic ones rarely are; one need not strictly adhere to doctrines of economic determinism to subscribe to the view that when men 'judged that this wheat or that wood was able to satisfy one of their needs', they were not acting so randomly as Foucault suggests. The rapidly accelerating pace of economic expansion in England during the period 1720–60, the political pessimism in France created by a losing battle with England throughout the eighteenth century, and the unprecedented rate of economic development throughout Europe at the very end of the century – all combined to create an intellectual climate in which mercantilist doctrines could be finally toppled and paved the way for Turgot, the econometricians, and the new economics.[41]

Yet, even such arbitrariness is largely ancillary to Foucault's key point, that in the transition from the *analysis of wealth* (A. Smith) to the study of *economics* as we know it today (Ricardo), there exists something mysterious and inexplicable.[42] Ricardo is chosen because he (like Cuvier) symbolises the hero at the moment of mutation, in this case because he clearly anticipates Karl Marx. And the abundantly documented fact that Ricardo's innovations in labour-quantity theory have a history of anticipatory economic notions and functioned in a continuum whose beginning it is impossible to know, could not matter less to Foucault.[43] What counts is Ricardo's presence at the crucial moment (1775–1800) and Foucault's firm belief that it is impossible to explain adequately the gap between his (Ricardo's) theories and those of Smith. Here Foucault supposes the reason may be owing to the difference between economics, on the one hand, and linguistics and biology on the other, but the reasons given are feeble and cannot convince:

> It is true that the analysis of wealth is not constituted according to the same curves or in obedience to the same rhythm as general grammar or natural history. This is because reflection upon money, trade, and exchange is linked to a practice and to institutions. And although practice and pure speculation may be placed in opposition to one another, they nevertheless rest upon one and the same fundamental ground of knowledge. (168)

Such speculation does not (of course) begin to solve the problem – it merely emphasises that Foucault is at a loss to explain pure economic theory from 1750 to 1800. Then follows, at the conclusion of the above quoted paragraph, a rare statement, unusually crisp and clear, which contains the pith of all these issues. Here he is especially worth quoting:

> In any given culture and at any given moment, there is always only *one* *episteme* that defines the conditions of possibility of all knowledge, whether expressed in a theory or silently invested in a practice. The monetary reform prescribed by the States General of 1575, mercantilist measures, or Law's experiment and its liquidation, all have the same archaeological basis as the theories of Davanzatti, Bouteroue, Petty, or Cantillon. And it is these fundamental necessities of knowledge that we must give voice to. (168)

Ricardo's role is therefore as arbitrary as the equally arbitrary economic values Foucault promises to delineate; Condillac, Turgot, Malthus, or Marx could have fulfilled this role equally well. It is rather the 'one and only *episteme*' that has guided Foucault all along. This superlative and often latent principle governing the knowledge of knowledge, hence knowledge's deepest substratum, is the pillar upon which everything else – mutations, their causes, man's destiny – is predicated, and not linguistics, biology, or economics.[44]

RESOLUTION

Ultimately Foucault leaves his reader with a metaphysical dilemma that he (Foucault) can't prove or disprove. Nor can anyone else.[45] For if knowledge at any moment depends exclusively upon 'one and only one' *episteme*, it logically follows that we cannot fathom the archaeological principle of our own time. To do that requires removing ourselves from present time in order to gain the perspective and necessary distance to view today's *episteme*. And since mutations occur *only* when a given *episteme* radically alters, then removal in time and space is a necessary, not merely sufficient, condition. But since every *episteme*, according to Foucault, evolves organically through cycles of life (birth, maturation, death), and since it is necessary to view the total death, not merely the gradual decaying, of one *episteme* as well as the birth of another before obtaining the prerequisite empirical materials for observation, an impossible condition is introduced. Stated less cumbersomely, one can have knowledge only of a dead, not a moribund, *episteme*. At least this is Foucault's supposition.

How, then, can he possibly know about this moment in 1972?

> . . . the entire modern *episteme* – that which was formed towards the end of the eighteenth century and still serves as the positive ground of our knowledge, that which constituted man's particular mode of being and the possibility of knowing him empirically – that entire *episteme* was bound up with the disappearance of Discourse and its featureless reign, with the shift of language towards objectivity, and with its reappearance in multiple form. . . . Ought we not to admit that, since language is here once more, man will return to that serene non-existence in which he was formerly maintained by the imperious unity of Discourse? (385–6)

Foucault later admits to a certain scepticism about his own prognosis: 'Of course, these are not affirmations; they are at most questions to which it is not possible to reply; they must be left in suspense, where they pose themselves, only with the knowledge that the possibility of posing them may well open the way to a future thought' (386).

Such doubt pleases the sceptics among us, but its positive counterpart, the last thought Foucault expresses, revives our fears, not only on logical and epistemological grounds but because of the gloom it forebodes:

> One thing in any case is certain: man is neither the oldest nor the most constant problem that has been posed for human knowledge. Taking a relatively short chronological sample within a restricted geographical area – European culture since the sixteenth century – one can be certain that man is a recent invention within it. . . . In fact, among all the mutations that have affected the knowledge of things and their order . . . only one, that

which began a century and a half ago [1800] . . . has made it possible for
the figure of man to appear. (386)

The particular combination of the ways of knowing *in the eighteenth century*
is the *cause* ('has made it possible'), however much Foucault may deny
this cause; and his book must therefore be construed as inimical to the
efforts of the man of that century.[46] But the death knell of all men is
then trumpeted so blaringly that Foucault's methodological vagaries are
temporarily forgotten: 'If those arrangements were to disappear as they
appeared, if some event of which we can at the moment do no more than
sense the possibility . . . were to cause them to crumble, as the ground
of Classical thought did, at the end of the eighteenth century, then one
can certainly wager that man would be erased, like a face drawn in sand
at the edge of the sea.'

Men of flesh and blood will naturally remain, will still enjoy the
fruits of their labours and shed tears over their woes, but archaeologically
speaking – and this is the quintessence of Foucault's hypothesis – man will
no longer count an iota, will no longer be the subject of unified scientific
enquiry.[47] Peter Caws has called this prophecy 'one of the most powerful
structuralist blows against traditional humanism'.[48] Actually it is much
less than that, having been constructed on the shakiest of historical foundations and unrelenting in its almost personal vendetta against randomness
and the possibility of wholly new patterns, never seen or heard of before.
Foucault, the absolute rationalist whose entire metaphysics is predicated
on airtight historical patterns cyclically repeating themselves, cannot conceive of combinations hitherto unknown.[49] He cannot imagine that man
may, in an archaeological sense, discover a new 'way of knowing' in order
to save himself from oblivion, any more than he (Foucault) can conceive
of Sophocles' celebrated ode to man in the *Antigone*[50] as abundant proof
that man 'existed' before the end of the eighteenth century, or perceive
the extent to which he (Foucault) has been tyrannised in this book by
enticing but dangerous metaphors entrapping him at every turn.

Poet, Romantic, Blakean heretic, romantic pessimist, imaginative
rationalist thriving on the lure of the Platonic 'One and Many', universalist
terrified of the possibility of an empty nominalistic universe, child of
Hegel and brother of Nietzsche – Foucault is all of these.[51] But even at
his best moments (and there are many), he cannot persuade by crystalline
thoughts and rigorous demonstrations. Those who know little more than
he about the culture of Europe in the centuries he professes to study may
be convinced, and those who respond to poetic talent diffused over a vast
panoramic verbal spate will regard this book as gospel truth heralding a
'breakthrough'; they will consider him the new seer in a long line of high
priests extending from Blake and Nietzsche to Camus and Sartre. But the

others who appeal for less verbiage and greater proof, who prefer to look for truth to Harvey and Newton, Russell and Wittgenstein, Namier and Gödel, Quine and the logicians, will be sorely disappointed at this necromantic performance.

NOTES

1 *The Order of Things: an Archaeology of the Human Sciences* (New York, 1970); originally appeared as *Les Mots et les choses* (Paris, 1966). Although the English translation is generally faithful to the original, Pantheon has committed a hideous blunder in leaving the translator unnamed. Can Foucault himself have wished to suppress this translator? It is unlikely since he has been named in earlier translations.

2 Roughly the seventeenth and eighteenth centuries in Europe generally. Foucault is unconcerned with labels to a degree of utter neglect: when it seems profitable for his purposes he moves the 'Classical Age' back to 1575 and forward to 1825. But he is at least consistent in using the same label throughout this book, even if he has no sense of periodisation. Chronological labels actually play no part in Foucault's hypothesis, and it is therefore a waste of time to examine them seriously. In his earlier book, *Histoire de la folie à l'âge classique* (Paris, 1961), Foucault used the same vague term to describe the sixteenth, seventeenth, and eighteenth centuries.

3 Because he has evolved a long way from the Foucault of the *Histoire de la folie*, in which he was tied to solid facts and still concerned with historical accuracy, and because he has violently abjured structuralism and repeatedly denied having anything in common with the French structuralists, most notably Lévi-Strauss.

4 I.e., to try to understand the thinker on his own terms. Here it is essential to point out that Foucault was trained in philosophy (he was recently appointed to the plush Chair of Philosophy at the Collège de France) but has been most influenced by linguistics and its role in human knowledge. Moreover, he has been concerned with aspects of the history of medicine (especially its social history) ever since he began writing and as the titles of his books themselves demonstrate: e.g., *Histoire de la folie*; *Naissance de la clinique: une archéologie du regard médical*. But he has continually blasted all his critics who cannot fail to notice this matrix: philosophy, linguistics, medicine. He insists that he is not a medical historian, and disparages the structural linguists. This leaves Foucault where he wants to be left, as a philosopher.

5 Respectively for their classic works: *The Crisis of the Aristocracy, 1558–1641* (Oxford, 1965); *The Restoration and Eighteenth Century: 1660–1789* (Oxford, 1948); *History of Economic Analysis* (New York, 1954).

6 *The New York Review of Books*, XVII, 12 Aug. 1971, 22. All reviews I have thus far seen have been dispraising, especially that of George Steiner, *New York Times Book Review*, 28 Feb. 1971, 8, 28–31. To this attack Foucault replied in his most visceral tone yet in 'Monstrosities in Criticism', *Diacritics*, 1 (fall 1971), 57–60. Jean-Marc Pelorson has so adequately savaged Foucault for his explication of *Don Quijote* (*The Order of Things*, 46–57) that I neglect this aspect altogether; see 'Michel Foucault et l'Espagne', *La Pensée*, No. 152 (Aug. 1970), 88–99.

7 Presumably critics of the future; at this moment, readers want to know *what* Foucault is saying. Briefly and inadequately: his prose consists of impossibly long sentences, inflated rhetoric ('there is not and cannot even be the suspicion of'), and the dramatic use of verbs ('emerged', 'arose', 'awakened') and adverbs ('suddenly', 'at this and no other moment'). His technique also includes sustained personification of centuries ('the eighteenth century awakened to its . . .') and subjects ('biology did not exist then'). Repetition abounds to such a great degree that some readers will be coerced into believing the truth of propositions by virtue of the number of times they have heard it repeated. See n. 17 below.

8 Without arguing *ad hominem*. One could write another kind of review, for example psychoanalytic, showing why Foucault-the-man distrusts so profoundly Freud-the-thinker. My interest here is merely to show the factual lapses in Foucault's thought and the areas where his thinking transcends empirical testing.

9 See his 'Puritanism, Pietism, and Science', rep. in B. Barber and W. Hirsch, eds, *The Sociology of Science* (New York, 1962), 41: 'It has become manifest that in each age there is a system of science which rests upon a set of assumptions, usually implicit and seldom questioned by the scientists of the time.' The same notion is also found in the writings of Whitehead and E. A. Burtt.

10 More specifically, in the last quarter, 1775–1800. For the term *mutation*, Foucault is especially indebted (although he does not say so) to the theories of the Dutch botanist Hugo de Vries (1848–1935) and François Jacob (1920–), Nobel Laureate in physiology in 1965 and Foucault's colleague at the college de France, who introduced the concept of *epismes* into the genetics of mutation.

11 All quotations unless otherwise stated are Foucault's; to conserve space only indented citations are given page numbers.

12 From 1550 to 1620, especially under the influence of Paracelsus and evident in writers like Croll. Even Frances Yates, the most studious student of Renaissance *arcana* in this century, would have to assent to this as she does in the preface to *Giordano Bruno and the Hermetic Tradition* (London, 1964).

13 The number of able sixteenth-century scientists opposed to all doctrines of signatures is considerable: Vesalius, Leonicenus, Linacre, Fracastorius, Benivieni, Giovanni Battista della Porta, Cesalpino. Such surgeons as Paré, Gersdorff, Franco, Würtz, Tagliacozzi, Bartisch, Clowes, and others, while not always opposed to curing by homeopathy, devoted time to studying the ways in which surgical procedures succeeded or failed. See Fielding Garrison, *History of Medicine* (New York, 4th ed., 1929), 225–31. The sophistication of these scientists is open to question, but their firm opposition to the theory of signatures is not. No one, not even a Foucault, can make out of a Vesalius or Fracastorius a Paracelsus.

14 *Paracelsus: an Introduction to Philosophical Medicine in the Era of the Renaissance* (Basel, 1958).

15 Precisely how and when this 'mutation' occurred is never stated, nor is Foucault fazed by the question; he narrates its account as if composing a modern Platonic myth for the twentieth century, one replete with allegorical figures who engage in geological ('cataclysmic change') and genetic ('the next mutation') activities.

16 There were also other contributing influences: e.g. (1) the role of science in a Protestant world view; (2) political distrust of magic, demonology, and witchcraft; (3) after 1660 in England the activities of the Royal Society; (4) pro-scientific propaganda by men of every variety.

17 Italics mine – to illustrate Foucault's melodramatic use of language. Later on in this section his dominant metaphor changes from the sudden birth of an organism to that of 'a grid of knowledge', the 'grid' is sustained throughout the rest of the book.

18 Foucault gives no evidence for this recognition, nor is it to be found explicitly stated in the writings of the principal heroes of his drama. Yet it is crucial to his argument.

19 The only other contemporary author I have also read who presents this nebulous area of the history of human imagination so attractively is Mircea Eliade; see his *Cosmos and History: the Myth of the Eternal Return* (1954); *Birth and Rebirth* (1958); *Images and Symbols* (1961).

20 See the works of G. Sahlin, O. Jesperson, L. Bloomfield, C. Hockett, and W. Howell. Howell's *Eighteenth-Century British Logic and Rhetoric* (Princeton, 1971) is especially useful for providing the historical background of these developments.

21 In Chomsky's sense: there exists in all language a surface structure and a deep-base structure whose governing principle is syntactic rather than logical.

22 In a letter dated 27 Sept. 1787, quoted in *Memoirs of Sir William Jones* (1807) II, 128.

23 Noam Chomsky, *Cartesian Linguistics* (New York, 1966); see also his *Language and Mind* (New York, 1968).

24 For example, Hans Aarsleff, 'The History of Linguistics and Professor Chomsky,' *Language* XLVI (1970), 570–85. See also his important book *The Study of Language in England, 1780–1860* (Princeton, 1967).

25 Robin Lakoff in *Language*, XLV (1969), 343–64. Her explanation of Chomsky's omission of Sanctius and his inclusion of Descartes appears on p. 359: 'Sanctius, Chomsky would say, was an applied linguist, not a theorist. But since the *Minerva* is inaccessible to anyone who does not read Latin, Chomsky has been forced to rely on the judgments of [other] writers . . .'

26 Most significant is the doctoral dissertation of Richard Ogle of the Language Centre, University of Essex, England, which deals with Sanctius and transformational grammar. I am greatly indebted to Dr Ogle for reading and commenting on this section of my essay.

27 According to both Robin Lakoff and Richard Ogle in the works cited above. The matter must, however, remain unsettled until conclusive proof one way or the other is given.

28 Respectively, *Logique et principes de grammaire* (1769) and *Grammaire générale* (1772).

29 But the reasoning is circular: (1) scientific experimentation and classification must recognise that all their labours are directed at an independent object called 'man' before either qualifies as a science; (2) yet it is virtually impossible to test whether any experimenter or classifier (or group of these) has such a notion. And even if a scientist or group of scientists enjoyed such a metaphysical notion, it might have no bearing whatsoever on their scientific experimentation and classification. Foucault dismisses the possibility of individual genius altogether: knowledge is the result of archaeological mutations and never one of man's brain. Ultimately the matter concerns nominalism and realism, and Foucault is the realist *par excellence*, endowing every major development in the history of science with an elaborate rational cause.

30 Most historians of science will not agree, however, with this estimate. Much of the problem in *The Order of Things* is that Foucault reads the wrong historians of science; he reads *only* French scholars, although he possesses the linguistic ability to read many languages well; for the history of biology he reads Henri Daudin, who wrote six decades ago, rather than Lovejoy, Temkin, William Coleman, E. Mendelsohn, and Jacques Roger.

31 And yet who can say that the contribution of either scientist is in any qualitative way less significant than later ones? Linnaeus's taxonomy had a profound impact, especially methodologically, on all the organic sciences; and Bichat's tissue theory affected biological research for decades.

32 A list of authors here would be long. The best of these is Philip C. Ritterbush, *Overtures to Biology: the Speculations of the Eighteenth Century Naturalists* (1964).

33 See D'Arcy Wentworth Thompson, *On Growth and Form* (Cambridge, 1943); E. W. Sinnott, *The Problem of Organic Form* (New York, 1963); Lancelot L. Whyte (ed.), *Aspects of Form* (1951); G. S. Rousseau (ed.), *Organic Form: the Life of an Idea* (1972).

34 By his critics in the eighteenth and nineteenth centuries, and most recently by Gerd Buchdahl, 'Leibniz' in *Metaphysics and the Philosophy of Science: the Classical Origins Descartes to Kant* (Oxford, 1969), 388–469.

35 *Principia*, trans. Andrew Motte, rev. F. Cajori (1962), II, 544.

36 Many other examples of thinkers before 1800 could be given. Surely the question is not whether these writers possessed a notion of organic structure or whether they articulated it fully in their writings, but rather to what extent it functioned in forming the basic tissue of their thought.

37 This also raises the question of Foucault's strange treatment of Lamarck: in beatifying Cuvier he seems, if I understand him correctly, to be limiting considerably the role of Lamarck in the development of modern biology. And yet most historians of science I have read consider his contribution important, especially in genetics.

38 The argument for context and continuum, as well as for individual genius in scientific innovation, has been set forth eloquently by Sir Peter Medawar: see 'Hypothesis and Imagination' in *The Art of the Soluble* (1967), 147–73 and *Induction and Intuition in Scientific Thought* (Philadelphia, 1969).

39 Sade, as could have been predicted, is the literary hero of Foucault's drama, primarily for his attempt to use language for 'naming': 'Sade attains the end of Classical discourse and thought. He holds sway precisely upon their frontier. After him, violence, life and death, desire, and sexuality will extend, below the level of representation, an immense expanse of shade which we are now attempting to recover, as far as we can, in our discourse, in our freedom , in our thought' (p. 211). If Foucault here extols Sade beyond his merits, he also gratifies his French readers who at this time seem to be engulfed in a turbulent ocean whose god is Sade (see *Tel Quel* (winter 1967), 'La Pensée de Sade', especially the essay by Roland Barthes). Once the revaluation of Sade now underway comes full circle, literary critics will be able to give 'archaeological' reasons for his eminence, for their 'Sadisme'. Perhaps this will be known to future students of the eighteenth century as 'le Foucaultisme' and Foucault will be metamorphosed into a kind of Kant. In any case Foucault should be happy at his reception; he has received far more attention in this decade of intellectual life (1962–72) than did his paragon, Nietzsche, who wasted away throughout his lifetime in painful obscurity, scarcely read or translated anywhere (see D. S. Thatcher, *Nietzsche in England 1890–1914: the Growth of a Reputation* (Toronto, 1970), 3–51).

40 Even though Foucault anticipates in the preface to the English translation of *Les Mots et les choses* that he will continue to be dispraised for his weakness here. His writing in this preface is marvellously evasive and suave, as if created under a dark slippery veil; but he finally fails to answer his critics regarding the laws of *cause* and *change* in the realm of the archaeology of knowledge. And the deep questions raised by recent students of these problems, such as Patrick Gardiner, Louis Mink, and David Hackett Fischer, never enter his thinking. If only some Humean scepticism had been shown in all this incredible maze!

41 All these ideas have been studied at length by Joseph Schumpeter in his monumental *History of Economic Analysis* (1954), although Foucault's account of Turgot is different in its emphases from his. But whereas Foucault's imagination is quick in its brilliant leaps to see connections of every sort, Schumpeter is usually cautious and circumspect. For example, in his chapter on 'The Econometricians and Turgot' he wonders if the whole idea of 'the flow of trade' as found in Cantillon and Quesnay could have been owing to a scientific discovery: 'It is tempting to assume that this idea came independently to Quesnay, the physician, through analogy with the circulation of the blood in the human body. William Harvey's (1578–1657) discovery of the latter was then a century old but had lost nothing of its freshness' (240). Under Foucault's imprint there would have been less scepticism and much more brilliant imagination. The question, as I have tried again and again to emphasise throughout, is not the indisputable fecundity of Foucault's imagination but the possibility of seriously testing his theories.

42 See, for example, *The Order of Things*, 101. Foucault approaches moments of 'mutation' with religious awe, as if they were the only sacred events in an otherwise profane succession of times. The period 1775–1800 captivates him because of its political events

and his own Marxist leanings; in the *Histoire de la folie* he showed the same reverence for the sixteenth century (another moment of mutation).

43 Here, again, the problem is not that Foucault values Ricardo more or less than Turgot, or that his emphases are unconventional and will not gain acceptance by historians of economic theory, but that he nowhere considers the possibility of, or explores the archaeology or topology of, continuums; and this is remarkable for a thinker who has spent so much time studying the contexts of continuity and discontinuity.

44 Foucault's *episteme* at first glance seems to resemble Kuhn's *paradigm*, but close scrutiny shows fundamental differences and I cannot imagine that he is indebted in any way to Kuhn. Space does not permit me to delineate the differences here; yet an important question about Foucault's *episteme* must be raised – its modality. Unlike other conceivable *epistemes* this one is mutually exclusive in relation to all others, always predetermined, rationally (or cerebrally) comprehensible, and deductively capable of demonstration. Since none of these four attributes is capable of conclusive empirical authentication, ought not Foucault to have considered the possibility of other modalities?

45 Eventually leading to the nominalist-realist question and to one's belief about God and the creation of the world.

46 In the same manner that Matthew Arnold and his nineteenth-century contemporaries were, although more insidiously.

47 In his everyday life man does not care about 'archaeologically speaking' and he will not moan if he is metaphorically 'dead'. Or to turn to another realm: the Russians today have the poorist economic thinkers yet they are rich; the British enjoy the best economic advisers in the world yet they are poor.

48 Peter Caws, 'What is Structuralism?', *Partisan Review*, XXXV (winter 1968), 86.

49 Foucault's already brilliant imagination would have further soared here if he had read the Princeton mathematicians on the theory of games rather than French semiologists or German students of hermeneutics.

50 Many the wonders but nothing walks stranger than man.
This thing crosses the sea in the winter's storm,
making his path through the roaring waves . . .
Language, and thought like the wind
and the feelings that make the town,
he has taught himself, and shelter against the cold,
refuge from rain. He can always help himself.
He faces no future helpless. There's only death
that he cannot find an escape from.
(D. Grene and R. Lattimore, (eds.), *Complete Greek Tragedies*, (Chicago, 1966–8) I, 192–3, ll. 332–4, 355–60).

51 And according to Jean Piaget he is also important for our understanding of French structuralism, although Piaget despises the nature of Foucault's contribution. In chap. XXI ('Structuralism without Structures') of his book *Structuralism* (Paris, 1968; trans. 1971), 128–35, Piaget laments that Foucault 'keeps only the negative aspects of contemporary structuralism', and later on: 'To call Foucault's structuralism a structuralism without structures is, accordingly, no exaggeration. All the negative aspects of static structuralism are retained – the devaluation of history and genesis, the contempt for functional consideration . . .' (134–5). Whether Foucault's structuralism will prove important for higher literary criticism today, much of which is already blurry and fuzzy, time alone will tell. My greatest concern, however, throughout this essay focuses on the concrete aspects of Foucault's theory, not intuitive aspects appealing to the imagination or emotions. For every Piaget there will be dozens of readers of this journal and elsewhere who will be deeply impressed by Foucault's seemingly rigorous system of thought and who will be lured into its network of ideas. If Foucault (like Theodore Roszak, author of *The Making of a Counter Culture*) had merely written about

present times, then any sensible student of his writing ought to grant him leeway. But Foucault essentially concerns himself with the past, with a major chunk of European intellectual history extending from 1500 to 1900, and enough time since then has elapsed to permit his students to judge the validity of his theories. If Foucault wishes to be taken seriously ever again, he ought to abandon the past altogether and concentrate exclusively on the present. Then his audience will agree or disagree but never label him a scholarly naïf.

4

The discourses of psyche

During 1979–80 I was in Cambridge, England, as a Visiting Fellow at Clare Hall, reading Foucault, Lévi-Strauss, and Althusser, and working on eighteenth-century primary texts in many disciplines. By then, the academy had been theorised on both sides of the Atlantic, as both Quentin Skinner and Frederick Crews noted later. 'Theory' was less evident around the Cambridge colleges than I would have expected, present only among a few prominent outsiders such as Raymond Williams and George Steiner. (Cambridge, incidentally had not yet been rocked by the explosion set off by Colin MacCabe, Christopher Ricks, and Frank Kermode.)

I also met Roy Porter, the British social historian, who was then still at Churchill College. We had already entered into a correspondence in which we had agreed to collaborate on a large-scale revaluation of the historiography of eighteenth-century science. We completed it during my visiting year there at Cambridge (1979–80); it was published late in 1980 by the Cambridge University Press as The Ferment of Knowledge: Studies in the Historiography of Eighteenth-Century Science. *Each of the chapters was designed to cover a specific modern 'science', and my contribution was entitled 'psychology'; the term which seemed best to describe the river of discourses and practices – anatomical, physiological, philosophical, medical, psychiatric, theological in so far as the soul is involved – feeding into the nineteenth-century ocean we now call psychology.*

I now see that I had set myself an impossible task. On the one hand, I hoped to produce a reliable account of the development of the discourse of psychology from about 1650 to 1800 – the 'long eighteenth century' – without worrying properly about such immense barriers as subject-object relations and dialectical and dialogical considerations, to say nothing of the differences between discursive practices and their rhetorics in these developing fields. On the other, despite these obstacles I was groping for a way to understand the great underbelly of Enlightenment psychology, especially its mystical, irrational, and darker sides, and its politics and ideological visions. This goal, I now see, could not be reached, given my historicist position and particular angle of vision then: wanting to see everything and see it at once – so to speak, see it diachronically and synchronically. As a result I now realise that although the essay did break ground by providing all sorts of new information (including an approach to Foucault that had not yet been articulated), it is defective in several ways.

Yet many historians of science and medicine found it useful for its privileging of anatomical and physiological categories over the more common-sense versions, but I doubt that any of us then saw precisely how ideological its concept of materialism was: i.e., the anatomy capable of producing the complex physiological and psychological processes under discussion. My conclusion now is that I was then too close to the material – saw it exclusively from an eighteenth-century vantage, and that I would actually have profited by further distinction. Still, I had broken out of the conventional mould used in earlier accounts of the rise of psychology, which are described in the early sections of the essay.

Only connect . . . (E. M. Forster, *Howards End*)

In the history of Western medicine, from the school of Salerno to that of Freud, the content and structure of its four principal ingredients – its conception of the nature of man, its technical capacity to do medical research and to give treatment, its sense of religion, and the social structure of medical aid – have changed continually; but the exclusive concern of pathology with the physical side of man's being has not disappeared or changed. (Pedro L. Entralgo, *Mind and Body: Psychosomatic Pathology* (1955)

If one poses, for a science such as theoretical physics or organic chemistry, the problem of its relations with the political and economic structure of society, doesn't one pose a problem which is too complicated? Isn't the threshold of possible explanation placed too high? If, on the other hand, one takes a knowledge [*savoir*] such as psychiatry, won't the question be much easier to resolve, since psychiatry has a low epistemological profile, and since psychiatric practice is tied to a whole series of institutions, immediate economic exigencies and urgent political pressures for social regulation? Cannot the interrelation of effects of knowledge and power be more securely grasped in the case of a science as 'doubtful' as psychiatry? It is this same question that I wanted to pose, in *The Birth of the Clinic* apropos of medicine: it certainly has a much stronger scientific structure than psychiatry, but it is also very deeply involved in the social structures. What 'threw me off' a bit at the time was the fact that the question which I posed did not at all interest those to whom I posed it. They considered it a problem without political importance and without epistemological nobility. (Michel Foucault in an interview in 1967 with Alessandro Fontano and Pasquale Pasquino, published in Meaghan Morris and Paul Patton (eds.), *Michel Foucault: Power, Truth, Strategy* (Sydney, 1979), 29–30)

THE 'PHYSICK OF THE SOUL'

I am a literary, not a scientific, historian, as a consequence of which I tend to see the entire world in terms of 'languages' – printed texts, verbal discourses, symbolic gestures – rather than 'systems of classification'. On the other hand I do not perceive the so-called 'revolution' in the history of science that has occurred in the last generation in precisely the same terms that others do: I view it as neither pronounced to the same degree nor significant to the same extent, although I unequivocally view it as a 'revolution'. Furthermore, and more locally within the so-called 'science'

I want to discuss here – psychology – I do not believe we know enough as yet about the history of medicine to differentiate meaningfully between psychology and psychiatry in the eighteenth century: it is easier to contrast the 'philosophy' and 'psychiatry' of the period. But the psychiatry and psychology of the age overlap again and again, sometimes in unpredictable ways, as I attempt to demonstrate below, rendering it almost impossible to chart three distinct areas: psychiatry, psychology, philosophy.

All these obliquities and vantages would seem to leave me in unfortunate and uncomfortable circumstances. There are, however, many common grounds I share, among these terrains a sense of 'what actually happened' during the eighteenth century so far as its ideas and practices related to psychology are concerned: to mention just a few, the roots of understanding about the psyche; concepts of soul, spirit and spirits; endless debates about free will versus determinism; further endless debates about nature and man's ability 'to nurture', about the presence of innate ideas and sensations, about natural genius and education, and about the dynamism of active versus passive minds.

The flow of these and other developments then – especially their unfolding and overlapping – is not the subject of this essay, and readers who expect it to be will be disappointed. Many historians named and discussed below have described the life of these ideas and practices. I consider my task here to be an exploration of the ways they have described these developments, not a detailed and comprehensive treatment of the development themselves.

Why is my essay not titled psychiatry, or, perhaps more comprehensively, psychology *and* psychiatry? First of all, there was no sustained distinction between them at that time, and I see little advantage, except for purely pedagogic reasons, to impose one now. After all, there cannot be a historiography of something that never existed. Moreover, what is today called psychiatry (i.e. study of the administration of a wide repertoire of therapies ranging from chemical injections to psychotherapy and psychoanalysis) enjoyed little, if any, direct correlative then; and an essay that merely tried to compare or contrast the psychiatry (or the psychology) then with ours now would stray very far indeed from our intention: to survey changing aspects of the scholarship of certain sciences in the eighteenth century.

Instead, it seemed more sensible to admit my own limitations and to take a more catholic view: to call the essay 'psychology', without too great a fear that I would be accused of slighting the period's psychiatry, and then, having made this decision to survey scholarship in several of the areas, not merely psychiatry, which constitute the matrix or nexus of ideas and human practices we today would call psychology *and* psychiatry. Such a procedure seemed plausible and practical for one who had witnessed, even in his relatively short 'history of science' life, a radical alteration in the type of scholarship being written about these areas of human activity; one that in fewer than three decades seems to have moved from mere biographical accounting to detailed analysis, often in depth, of the play of complex ideas, cultural assumptions and practical applications of medical techniques.

Yet there is a caveat, as will soon become apparent. I cannot disguise my bias: the belief that the consequence of all this radical alteration is ultimately linguistic. That is, the sense that one language has been substituted for another, in this case the language of the social sciences for that of biography and the natural sciences. The notion that this great alteration in scholarship has occurred is, of course, unassailable. But, one must inquire, precisely what fields has it opened up and how has it opened them? Those who have expanded the fields of psychological history remain scholars concerned to relate certain developments *in terms of* other developments. They are, in a sense, similar to the early Boyle Lecturers in England who related Newtonian science to audiences who could comprehend it 'in other terms', in this case in religious terms. Such 'translation' or 'relation', whenever or wherever it occurs, necessitates linguistic analysis at a rather deep base-level.

This is why I begin my account with some consideration of the word psychology. There is disagreement about the first use of the term in English. Nevertheless it is clear that it begins to appear at the close of the seventeenth century, perhaps having first been used in 1693 in the English translation of the second edition of Blanchard's *Physical Dictionary*, although it is also found in Nathan Bailey's (the London lexicographer) popular English dictionary: 'Psychologist, one who makes a study of, or is skilled in psychology; a student or teacher of the science of mental phenomena'.[1] The Latin term 'psychologia' was naturally much older – according to the *Oxford English Dictionary* it is a term used in scholarly treatises by the sixteenth century, as in the German-produced *Psychologia anthropologica* (1590–7) – and if one searched ardently enough one could probably find a dozen references to the Greek version. The point here is neither to trace the history of the concept, which has already been done,[2] or to speculate about the conditions under which it originated, but rather to suggest that as an area of human knowledge *psychology* possesses a *historiography*, not only a history, in our period, the eighteenth century, precisely because – and the cause is the important aspect – four or five trends were converging *c.* 1700. These 'convergences' are very much the subject of this essay.

Yet convergences of historical trends – incremental secularism, economic conditions, political developments, scientific societies and schools – are not enough for the student of historiography, though they may be sufficient for the more straightforward historian. The historiographer of psychology – for all periods, not merely for the eighteenth century – must be alive to other considerations as well, especially to written and unwritten assumptions guiding his or her own age. And then, he or she must be capable of leaping from the history to the historiography and back again without too great a sense of shock. Not only, for example, was psychology a rapidly developing speculative field throughout the period 1700–1800 (something that cannot be asserted for the previous hundred years – at least I am unaware of any scholar who has tried to make such a case), but also the unprecedented secularisation of European culture during the period made tremendous claims on the average person's sense of his own 'ego' and 'selfhood'.

The matter is, of course, even more complicated than this, depending primarily on whether the student holds a dialectical view of the relationship. Not to hold one is to omit its dynamic relationship; to maintain one, on the other hand, can render the relation unwieldy because no 'hard history' of psychology 1700–1800 exists, as I attempted to say at the outset. Even attending to the one (the history of psychology 1700) at the risk of excluding the other (modern historiography construed in a pluralistic age by students racked by radically new versions of intellectual scepticism), and neglecting their dialectical relation (the precise processes used in leaping back and forth), poses severe problems. The reason, simply stated, is that history is not historiography. In the one – the former – the subject of the discourse is the period or era itself; in the other – historiography – discourse replaces history as subject and history recedes to an ancillary position among the various subjects intrinsic to the discourse. In the history versus the historiography of psychology there are other intruding factors as well. Even for the so-called 'hard history' of psychology a question arises regarding 'point of view': politics, economics, science, literature, etc. In the now-popular phrase of the late Sir Herbert Butterfield,[3] there is a 'Whig' as well as a 'Tory' history of psychology. There are also others that remain to be written, from the vantage of, for example, the various economic classes (e.g. the poor man's view of psychology in the period of the Georges) or, in contrast, the budding behaviourist putting forward radical new theories. The reader will be able to supply others as well.

This large problem – history versus historiography – cannot be solved here. Nothing short of a vast research project of scholars or by modern computer methods to compile lexicons of psychological terms would satisfy scholars about the hard facts (what I have been calling 'hard history') of European psychology 1700–1800; and I doubt if even this would satisfy them. Moreover, an equally vast team would be needed to probe ancient and medieval writings to discover the origins of the concept 'psychology' and its cognates. Finally, since many contemporary historians, self-conscious of their methods, now believe there are no 'facts' whatsoever in history and that one reads even the best historian for his style or for his myths and fictions, perhaps we should turn our attentions elsewhere, to areas less hazardous than these.[4] One may lament in this connection that there exists, as yet, no history of the attitude of the masses, but the *Annales* school project of *l'histoire des mentalités* (Mandrou, Febvre and Butke) will some day fill the gap. Given this preliminary caveat, especially the reason why this is the place to scrutinise neither the 'hard history' nor the 'dialectical dynamic', we may cautiously explore the scholarship written about psychology in the eighteenth century.

THE 'QUADRUPLE ALLIANCE': THE FOUR TYPES OF HISTORIES

Essentially four types of histories have been written for our period: (1) chronological histories proceeding by year or period; (2) thinker-oriented histories; (3) thematic histories – which necessarily include the works of polemicists who use theme as pretext; and (4) teleological histories that are usually concerned to diminish the novelty of Freud's theories (although some expand it) by demonstrating on how much previous knowledge Freud built his own edifice. Each must be viewed individually since all current accounts of psychology in the eighteenth century, and hence a survey of its historiography, derive from these four types.[5]

Chronological histories. These are a province in themselves. Less interesting for their arrangement of materials and logical structure than for the historian's approach to the psychology of the period, they often appear to have been written by emptying index cards on to foolscap sheets. Concern with methodology and scepticism about validity in interpretation are almost universally absent in this genre. Thus a chronological history such as Gregory Zilboorg's *History of Medical Psychology* (New York, 1941), which reports a great deal of information about our period, is arranged diachronically and would seem to command little interest in its approach. After all, Zilboorg was an eminent practising analyst who wrote at a time when the field had been uncharted. More important than an 'approach' is the author's (not merely Zilboorg's) 'reading', as it were, of the psychology of a given epoch, whether ancient, medieval, or Renaissance. Generally speaking, the genre attracts genuine chroniclers far more capable of amassing materials than of theorising profoundly about them. These histories have generally not been accumulated by powerful analytical minds (Zilboorg was an exception) who have written histories of psychology as a pretext for announcing their own philosophies of history. In point of fact I have not discovered a single chronological historian of psychology who seems to care about problems of periodisation (to name one area of concern to theorists), although many historians since 1950 have grown so sceptical of the dangers of generalisation based on *a priori* 'period notions' that they have actually neglected their own work and probed that area.[6] Some of those who write in the journal *History and Theory* serve as a good example of the deflection: Louis Mink, Hayden White, John Passmore, W. H. Walsh, Leonard Krieger, Arnaldo Momigliano.

Chronological historians conceived of as a group have had little to say about eighteenth-century psychology, and the explanations for this silence may not be so simple as they appear. Since World War II they have written a vast literature about the psychology of the ancient Greeks[7] and have endowed it, it seems, with every type of label from the 'age of discovery' to the 'age of the birth of the mind';[8] but these same historians have been less excited, for reasons not altogether clear, about psychology in the Enlightenment. The labels they give to our period are an indication of lack of hard analytical thought: Zilboorg and Henry have called it an 'age of reconstruction', while other chronological historians have used similar catch-alls to denote respite and observation rather than to postulate radical activity or radical theory in the period. Such a procedure tallies with that of most contemporary historians of science, who continue to emphasise the seventeenth century as the age of systems and theoretical discovery and who view the eighteenth century merely in terms of collecting and classifying, or, or some of 'politicking' and 'ossifying'. Considering that most recent historians of psychology/psychiatry have been medical historians of one variety or another, it is not surprising to find this state of affairs. It appears that historians of science tend not to be quite as self-conscious of their methodology as others because they are so preoccupied with composing the 'hard history' of their as-yet unwritten history of science. This generalisation is, of course, a matter of great debate. But, the accuracy of the generalisation notwithstanding, the relatively conservative attitudes the historians of science embody are surpassed by those of another group: the historians of medicine. These are practitioners of an art – history – for which many are ill qualified, and, at bottom, a group that barely knows what historiography signifies.

Thinker-oriented histories. These histories of psychology are less easily typified; but here again their authors rarely possess an adequate concept of the period that is in touch with diverse types of the best scholarship. Rather than acquire a new view of the era they rely on a traditional concept and inherit as well as sense of the concept's inherent value. As in the case of chronological history, these authors generally invoke metaphors of evolution (*A* flowed from *B*, evolved from *C*, issued from *D*) and rely on acquired and often dangerous views of cause and effect (*A* resulted in *B*, caused *C*, was the reason for *D*). This genre is a favourite of historians of philosophy as well. It has been popular at least since the early Renaissance, when there arose a tradition of biographical sketches in conduct books and history books (e.g. *A Mirror for Magistrates*).

By the 1850s works such as George Henry Lewes's *The Biographical History of Philosophy from its Origin in Greece down to the Present Day* (1853) – a work containing much we today would call the 'history of psychology' – were being written and continued to be written for another century. More recently the following thinker–oriented histories have appeared: R. I. Watson's *The Great Psychologists: from Aristotle to Freud* (1963) and *Eminent Contributors to Psychology* (1974), organised according to thinker and containing almost no historical discussion; Denis Leigh's *The Development of British Psychiatry*, II, *The Eighteenth and Nineteenth Century* (1961), organised as the separate biographies of three thinkers and written in a type of historical vacuum, the scenario of three lives *sans* a context; and Richard Hunter's and the late Ida Macalpine's *Three Hundred Years of Psychiatry 1535–1860* (1963), a work that reprints dozens of selections and knits them together with brief introductions and prefaces, such 'lace work', lending an impression of historical cohesion – from great thinker to great thinker, or just from selection to selection – and often producing the illusion in the reader of having digested a type of history. But rigorous self-examination reveals that one has substituted 'facts' for 'analyses'. Furthermore, thinkier-oriented histories commonly focus on several major figures – usually the empiricists, Locke, Hume, David Hartley, Adam Smith, the Scottish 'common-sense' school, as well as Tuke and Pinel – in their sweeping panoramic views. In traversing large territories there is little chance of presenting a penetrating analysis and none is usually found; instead, the author conceives of his task as the amassing of large amounts of derivative material. He will read the philosophers: Locke, Berkeley, Hume, and some of the Scottish moralists. But he does not burrow in manuscript archives and does not reread primary material. In crude terms, what he produces is a rehash, and a list of works is not needed to prove that the genre is still alive and healthy.

Thematically arranged histories. These are more significant than the two former types and their yield for intellectual history is greater. They often isolate a theme – for example the 'theory of insanity' or the 'rise of madhouses' – and develop it. The old adage about 'wisdom within selection' is certainly evident here: compelled to abandon chronological organisation and a history centred on main figures, these authors inevitably produce social history or a type of 'history of ideas'. Thus R. G. Hill, the Victorian surgeon and follower of the non-restraint system for treating lunatics (he followed the lead of William Tuke, as well as the Quaker moralists) wrote a history of insanity entitled *Lunacy, its Past and its Present* (1870), a book containing little primary research but one using 'thematic history' to argue that non-restraint is the most successful way to treat the insane.

In practice, thematically arranged histories of psychology are often, as Hill's book illustrates, polemics in disguise. Sometimes the polemical base is not even concealed, as in James M. Baldwin's *History of Psychology: a Sketch and an Interpretation* (1913), which attempts to demonstrate that the eighteenth century was a dull era but does so under the guise of a 'thematic history' of eighteenth-century psychology. Histories of 'emotion' or 'feeling' also fall into this category, although they possess a more interesting aspect: depending upon whether they are written by historians of psychology or by research physiologists, they emphasise, to a lesser or greater degree respectively, the role of the nervous system.[9] Histories of the unconscious in particular fall prey to this polemical tendency, in part because a history of the unconscious can readily form itself into a history of anything, and in part because such vast topics attract historians or scientists with broad cultural interests. As a result, books about the history of the unconscious have fared both worse and better than books on other topics: worse as a consequence of the amorphousness of the subject, better because the author will not confine himself to narrow terrains possibly lacking in significance for a large audience of readers.[10] The books by Whyte and Margetts cited in note 10 are examples: in addition to the willingness of each to survey large terrains, each is brave enough to chart an area where most other historians would fear to tread. Whyte crosses national boundaries, looking at all of Europe, even central Europe and the Slavic countries; Margetts reads primary authors ranging from the Scottish common-sense philosophers to the early German Romanticists before positing her conclusion: 'There was no clear-cut division between consciousness and unconsciousness [in the eighteenth century]. The principle of continuity was followed; the one shaded into the other – unconscious perception (*petites perceptions*, vague and obscure, ideas, subconscious activities) gradually merged with the unconscious apperception.'[11]

Another strength of thematic historians is evident in Georges Canguilhem's *La Formation du concept de réflex au xviie siècle* (Paris, 1955), a book often referred to by both general historians and specialist historians. Dedicated to Gaston Bachelard (Canguilhem's teacher and by now the much-discussed structuralist thinker), *La Formation* proceeds diachronically from roughly 1550 to 1850, as do the chronological histories. Its strength, though, lies not in its diachronic arrangement but in its narration of the 'life of an idea' (an idea woefully neglected until the 1950s), just as more recently scholars have been surveying the life of another idea, 'organic form'.[12] Canguilhem also resuscitated the work of Thomas Willis amidst a milieu of historians of science who had paid no attention to Willis, and made 'connections' in *La Formation* between areas (philosophic, biological, physiological) others would have left underdeveloped. His two earlier books, *Essai sur quelques problèmes concernant le normal et le patholo-gique* (1943) and *La Connaissance de la vie* (1952), which were historico-philosophical studies that also explored large terrains, should have pro-vided a clue to his method. Although Canguilhem was for a time a practising physician, he wrote as a cultural historian and *La Formation* still has great value today. It is probably valid to assert that Canguilhem is among the best thematic historians to have written on psychology since 1950.

Teleological histories. These are my last category, and I call them 'teleological' because they 'inexorably lead to' something. They set out to seek sources for Freud's discoveries, not in order to depreciate his work nor to show that he was right or wrong but to demonstrate on what a long tradition his own thought was constructed. Such histories are usually restricted to a single country, though they occasionally cross boundaries and frontiers. Moreover, teleological histories have a sub-set, i.e. those aiming to show that Pinel was the 'founder of modern psychiatry' – always a dangerous label – and demonstrating his (Pinel's) antecedents: the task originally assigned to Freud's work is thereby transferred to Pinel's, and in this genre Pinel becomes a minor-league Freud. These histories thrive on metaphors such as 'evolution',[13] 'revolution', 'change', 'flow', and other terms designating continuity and discontinuity, although it is perfectly clear that their authors are far more enamoured of the genuine *telos* (Pinel, Freud, Jung) of the history than of any aspect of the historical process. Lancelot Whyte's *The Unconscious before Freud*, already mentioned, is an example of teleological history because it purports to show that the whole history of psychiatry from the ancient Greeks onward results in Freud's theory of the unconscious.[14] This pronouncement is made not to reduce Whyte to simple-mindedness but rather to isolate the assumptions a practising analyst who also writes history of psychology may hold.

Whyte's method and his conclusions reveal how teleological history usually proceeds. He divides the eighteenth century in half – a pre-1730 and post-1730 segment – and postulates that Lord Kames was the first Western thinker (he does not discuss Eastern traditions) to employ the terms 'conscious' and 'unconscious' in a form resembling modern psycho-logical usage. Intellectual historians will be interested in the dates of the segments. 1730 is given because it divides thinkers who stressed the cogni-tive aspects of the unconscious from those (post-1730) whose main interest was the unconscious mind as the seat of the passions: 'It will be noted that in the eighteenth century the unconscious mind had already been linked with a primary organising activity or formative principle, with organs of generation and the *élan* of desire, and with illness. The nineteenth century developed these early speculations in various directions, but added little that was new to the general conception.'[15] Aside from one's attitude to the barrier date or to Whyte's lexicographical research, the conclusion is noteworthy here because it lays great weight on the eighteenth century.

But does it say enough? Presumably even Whyte would concede that the difference between sophisticated and unsophisticated psychological theories rests, perhaps exclusively, on a sense of an unconscious psychic mechanism (the eighteenth century called it 'ruling passion', 'monitor', 'censor', 'demon') guiding the individual's decisions and determining his behaviour; and the eighteenth century is the first to develop it. One can argue, as Boyle did in the Restoration, that physiology is the key to human behaviour and to most 'systems' rationalising it;[16] but a concept of the unconscious does not ultimately depend on a sophisticated notion of human anatomy or physiology – in this instance a developed science of the brain and nervous system – for either its genesis or amplification. Again, the eighteenth century is the crucial period here. Lord Kames and other Scottish philosophers were important in the rise of psychology because they popularised a concept, however metaphysical at first, of 'the other self', the 'self' that is the shadow of the outer self but nevertheless the 'truer self': in the words of the most lyrical poet of his day, Thomas Gray, the self who is 'the stranger within thee'.[17] No similar concept exists in didactic thought before the eighteenth century, and although in earlier times the philosopher Juan Luis Vives, author of the important psychological study *De Anima et Vita* (1538), and certain other authors, especially Cervantes and Shakespeare, have more than an inkling of 'the stranger self', they do not hypothesise about it. But one ought not to turn to Gray and other eighteenth-century sentimentalists – Henry Mackenzie's *The Man of Feeling* – for respectable theories of psychology. These doctrines about the self are reflected in more highly regarded literary forms in Swift, Pope and Johnson. The last author is a reliable, even scientific, commentator on the unconscious, and is quoted by several eighteenth-century physicians in their treatises on insanity.[18] Swift reflects some of these notions, however parodically, in his 'Digression on Madness' in *A Tale of a Tub*, as does Pope in his discussion of the 'Ruling Passion' in *An Essay on Man*, epistle II. After 1740, however, one begins to discover abundant speculation about 'the stranger within', the unconscious, and it may even be (to be historically rather than historiographically discursive) that the poets rather than the scientists generated this and allied concepts, as they did so many others assumed by historians of science to have no literary bearings.

Teleological histories whose *telos* is Pinel are fewer but necessitate commentary in a discussion of the historiography of Enlightenment psychology. Pinel's contribution to psychology and psychiatry is too well known to be discussed here: it is sufficient to note that he was one of the first physicians – Sydenham, Boerhaave, Johann Christian Reil, Cullen, and Benjamin Rush were others – to maintain that lunatics could be cured, and one of the first to erect the social and medical conditions, many taken from his original theoretical writings, necessary for recovery. Pinel is mentioned with good justification in every serious history of psychiatry in France; in social histories, as well as histories of the French Revolution, the poor movement and the humanitarian movement.[19] He has been the subject of numerous biographies, and most phases of his life and works have been annotated. It is perhaps not going too far to maintain that he has been to eighteenth-century psychiatry what Newton was to its natural philosophy and Linnaeus to its taxonomy. What has been lacking in the 'Pinelian field of research' is integration of these aspects with broader developments in France: its politics, economics, and intellectual life. There has been no attempt to relate Pinel's accomplishments to 'mob psychology' in the century – to George Rudé's theory of the 'Paris mob', for example. Nor has Pinel been viewed within the context of Andrés Piquér's psychiatric treatises, which antedate Pinel's. Some historians of psychiatry have argued that Spain, not France or Britain, preserved Roman notions (transmitted by the Moors) of humanity to lunatics;[20] and it may be profitable to determine how many of Pinel's concepts are found in Piquér's treatises. In another context – the philosophic – Pinel has found few students, and this may reveal more about the nature of medical history today than about Pinel's studies. Studies of the philosophical origins of Pinel's psychiatric thought are needed, that include discussion of eighteenth-century conceptions of sex, the family, and the cycle of life,[21] as well as the sociology of French society before and during the Revolution.

There is no point in lamenting these lacunae; an all-important reason why these problems have not been studied involves the realisation that there are few scholars anywhere who possess the necessary learning. Only the French structuralists and Marxists today seem capable of making the required connections: leaps from point to point within a framework, or grid, able to contain such a vast edifice; but they have recently turned their attention elsewhere than to these subjects. Even in *Surveiller et punir* (Paris, 1975), and *Histoire de la sexualité* i: *La Volonté de savoir* (Paris, 1976), Foucault is concerned with very different matters; but we must not forget that his very first book, *Maladie mentale et psychologie* (Paris, 1954), though barely read today, is a teleological history in the sense I have been describing.

Teleological histories dealing with Pinel as their fountainhead cannot be abandoned so facilely as this, for Pinel and Tuke are the protagonists in the recent historiography delineated here. As such, they are the 'subjects' of vast amounts of recent scholarship, much of it still undigested. But

how are we to conceive of them – whether individually or taken together
– as 'subjects'? And how did they, in contrast to other figures, become
constitutive subjects in the first place? Perhaps the answer, as usual, lies
in the reconstruction of a whole field of study – psychiatry or psychology
– through its historiography. This is why the details of Pinel's contribution
are so crucial, and why they can never be adumbrated often enough.
These so-called Pinelian facts have, of course, been laid out by recent
scholars in a literature barely summarised here; and while they have not
been delineated at a length sufficient to satisfy all readers, the basic stones
have been set. But the stones are solitary and unorganised, as it were,
without a surrounding edifice and landscape. The cultural contexts of
Pinel's thought – not merely in the sense of causation but of concomitancy
with other developments – remain to be explored and laid out by someone
able to take account of parallel developments in medicine and who is at
the same time informed enough to write sophisticated history. William
Bynum has written elsewhere the most penetrating essay on this subject,[22]
but does not have space to take the argument far enough. He demonstrates
two distinct lines of thought that have developed in England since the
Renaissance: first the notion that every mental state depends on functions
of the brain (i.e. insanity is a physiological/anatomical aberration in every
case) and, second, the notion that the aggregative secularisation and gradual acceptance of certain mental states such as depression and anxiety has
shaped our sense of mental illness. Bynum views Pinel within this context,
showing how his humanitarian treatment of the insane related to each
development. Such an approach renders Pinel important in the evolution
of what we would call 'mechanistic medicine' (not to be confused with
'psychosomatic medicine') and also endows him with cultural significance.
Moreover, Pinel sedulously argued that what was 'psychologically caused'
was most effectively 'psychologically treated', an approach that challenged
the physician's authority and categorised Pinel as a member of the tribe
of the unorthodox, even the revolutionary.

For these proximate reasons Bynum and others consider Samuel
Tuke important: not merely for his proselytisation and popularisation of
Pinel's ideas, especially in translating them from French into English, but
also for Tuke's book describing the 'York Retreat' asylum for the insane
run by laymen rather than medically trained personnel.[23] 'The success of
moral therapy', Bynum argues, 'thus threatened to change the rather
newly established place of the medical man in the treatment of insanity.'[24]
This approach does not depart altogether from Michel Foucault's in the
Histoire de la folie (Paris, 1961), in that it takes a hard look at the politico-
moral dimensions of insanity. But, as Bynum notices, this was also the
period (the late eighteenth century) in which 'moral therapy' was practised,
and its application was a mixed blessing to 'healthy' and 'sick': the treat-

ment of George III's bouts of madness typifies the mixture.[25] By the Regency, though, medical practitioners such as John Haslam, the prolific psychiatric author, were insistent that the cure of lunatics should be the exclusive right of medically certified men. He argued that 'mental derangement is *always* accompanied by physical derangement of some sort', a valid enough position in light of the two developments surveyed by Bynum; but the more probable reason for Haslam's stand is that medical practice had now become a profession and, consequently, the notion of entrusting lunatics to paramedics constituted a genuine threat.[26]

Haslam's position hinges, as Bynum shows, on the ties between mental and physical states. Without this concept the exclusive claim that 'lunatic spaces' (the hospital, its landscape, the patient, the mythology connecting them) fell within the sole province of the physician was impossible. Every psychic state had to be correlated with a mechanistic explanation in the body. But whereas this accounts for the development of a segment of the medical profession, it says little about the English scene at the time it received Pinel; and it does not account for the origins of Pinel's thought nor for psychiatry in France from 1740 to 1790, i.e. the half century before he innovated. One can reply that no account is necessary; that Pinel was a humanitarian – as simple as that; that before the 1790s attitudes toward madness in France were morally rather than medically determined, and, more importantly, that these same attitudes coloured medical belief: thus, the logical chain becomes a vicious circle of reasoning. One can also postulate that the psychological relativism evident at the end of the century – the notion that mental health is not an absolute state but a relative one depending upon socio-economic norms – is the singlehanded work of Pinel. But I doubt that the matter is so simple, or that attitudes were as monolithically conservative as the 'teleological historians' extolling the work of Pinel would have us believe. Just as Freud had his predecessors in the nineteenth century, so did Pinel in his century, and the major figures should not be given all the credit when some is owing to the minor: in France to the labours of du Petit, Lorry and Saucerotte, in Germany to Stahl, in Italy to Vignoli, and in England to men such as Tyson, Battie, and the Monros (who are an ambiguous case since much of their practice was traditional). To return to France, medical history of the period before the Revolution is still in such a sorry state – as two recent works abundantly testify[27] – that it is no wonder teleological history exists. For example, Singer's widely consulted *Short History of Medicine*, revised by E. A. Underwood and published in 1961, leaps from the sixteenth century to Revolutionary France in the 1790s, proceeding as if nothing whatsoever happened in between. The lament that there is no medical history of Enlightenment France available in English is a theme of this essay.

THE PROBLEMS OF COPING

The above four types of historical treatment are influenced by, perhaps even determined by, factors demonstrating the difficulty one faces in coping with the abundance of primary material. Chronological histories taken as a class appear to have been written in a tunnel that omits all the light of cultural history. In this genre one proceeds from event to event, from development to development, without any attention paid to the rest of the picture. It is as if the author has painted the bare features, even the dark silhouettes of the characters represented on his canvas, without filling in their shapes, colours, textures. Thinker-oriented histories proceed in almost identical fashion so far as 'coping' is concerned; but their biographical reductionism is so patent (i.e. the mere rehearsal of facts of a life without interpretation: the *ad hominem* approach) and their cultural sophistication so limited that one wonders if Carlyle's theory of history as the mere imprint of the minds of a few geniuses has ever really been laid to rest.[28] It is important (of course) to learn what Kames or Pinel contributed to the history of psychiatry. But when each is considered as if he had been merely the representation of 'some one thing' (Kames his use of a term and Pinel his humanity), and this 'one thing' is isolated as a moment without a background or a future – without an enriched context – then the result is unsatisfactory.

The two categories of 'thematic history' and 'teleological history' fare better because their authors have broader interests and greater intellectual curiosity, yet the way they 'cope' is at best merely different. Thematic histories normally proceed by isolating ideas (e.g. the brain or soul as the seat of madness; social conditions in a given region or country; religious forces in relation to secular ones), but often they reduce competing ideas (antitheses, alternative hypotheses, ideas emerging from radical methodologies) so much that logical falsification as well as historical invalidity obtains. There is another difference too: the 'thematic historians' of psychiatry are interested in change and, at their very best, process; 'static' matters (an event, a moment, a life) claim little of their attention. It is not inappropriate here to consider as an analogy the relation between anatomy (the static study of organs) and physiology (their functioning). 'Chronological' and 'thinker-oriented' historians resemble the anatomists: they have little notion of the life of ideas. 'Thematic' and 'teleological' historians resemble the physiologists: they describe the flow of ideas, the fluidity of medical terminology and the movement of terrains adjacent to their main one in psychology. The difference, as noted, is elusive, and some may pause before they concur that one exists.

Subject areas in the Enlightenment in which thematic histories would be successful (because they lend themselves to this type of treatment and because such studies have not been undertaken) are: (1) study of the madhouses of a locale or region; (2) intensive study of the 'condition' known as hypochondria in men and hysteria in women (especially a study of actual cases, not merely of theory, as in Sydenham's *Epistolary Dissertation to Dr Cole*); (3) delineation of the decline of the larger condition, melancholy, as a peculiarly 'English illness', with analysis of its sociological dimensions and comparison of it in England and other Western European countries.[29] In each case the culture in which the medical condition evolved should not be viewed narrowly.

How authors cope with teleological history is less capable of brief synthesis because, of the four types, it alone addresses itself to philosophic issues in a major sense. Teleological histories inquire into causative questions (in the lowest sense as *cause* and *effect*) by pleading eclecticism. That is, they do not pretend to gaze at every aspect of their province, even fleetingly, but select this or that for the most specific of reasons. Concomitantly, they indulge in constant value judgements: Pinel's reform was more important than *A*'s, Tuke's than *B*'s. More often than not the 'teleological historian' possesses a philosophy of history – perhaps because he is constantly asking questions about change and process, how *E* led to *F* – and coerces himself to view history merely as moving forward in linear time.[30]

The writings of Michel Foucault, the Olympian master of the opaque style within the impersonal mode, defy precise classification, but if one had to choose from our four categories one would probably place him here, amidst the 'teleological historians', although he himself would be the first to deny, and rightly so, that he is an historian of any variety. Nevertheless Foucault synthesises large terrains, by depicting the changes in language used to describe psychiatric developments: in his *Histoire de la folie* he even glances at the history of these metaphors and at iconographical representations of madness for evidence. Foucault has been faulted, especially by the Americans, for many aspects of his methodology. But objection in itself cannot detract from the worth of the undertaking: to trace the prose language of psychology and psychiatry in France, particularly at the end of the eighteenth century.

THE IMPACT OF PHILOSOPHY

Anatomy and physiology would seem to have been the two shaping forces in the history of psychology. All Western theories of the mind, no matter how primitive, ultimately own their origin and subsequent development to these two domains, although there are moments when political circumstances (e.g. France 1789–98) are as influential. The history of European psychology can be viewed, to echo Whitehead on Plato, as a footnote on the history of this relation between anatomy and physiology, not merely of the one considered in isolation from the other. While religious and secular concepts also shape psychology, they have not done so to a degree that can compare with the role of anatomy and physiology.[31]

True as this precept may be, it overlooks philosophy which, if not as influential in shaping the ideas of Western psychology, certainly has a more problematic role than either anatomy or physiology. The difficulty of philosophy in relation to psychology is one of definition: it is almost impossible to fix the boundaries of each, to say where the one begins and the other ends. So many types of overlap are found in the writings – medical practice is not in question here – of the two groups in the eighteenth century that one wonders if they should be treated in isolation from one another at all, or as distinct from psychiatry. The difference between psychology and psychiatry does not become pronounced until the nineteenth century; therefore, concern about the precise boundaries of these areas can be minimised for the eighteenth century. But the differences between and overlaps of psychology and philosophy in the seventeenth century are crucial. They cannot be dismissed or made light of.

In a sense, the problem of definition and overlap is practical rather than theoretical. Philosophers do not usually treat lunatics, nor did they even in the eighteenth century; but eighteenth-century 'psychiatrists' – Drs Battie, Monro, Cheyne, Whytt – though certified medical men, often wrote as if they were also certified philosophers, defining provinces of knowledge and fixing the boundaries of each. If, by the term 'philosopher' is designated a thinker with a logically rigorous system, then many eighteenth-century physicians qualify for the title, as Lester King has recently shown in *The Philosophy of Medicine: the Early Eighteenth Century*.[32] If the criterion is the resolution of an important logical or epistemological problem that previous philosophers could not solve, then most of these physicians, perhaps all, are eliminated; but most eighteenth-century philosophers would be also eliminated on these grounds. Besides, the last criterion seems to distinguish degrees of importance among philosophers, not whether they are 'philosophic' in the first place.

Thus, the definitional and semantic issue about the meaning of 'philosopher' and 'philosophic' reduces to a practical matter of classification. When Robert Whytt, M.D., often called 'the philosophic doctor', published in 1764 *Observations on the Nature, Cause, and Cure of those Disorders commonly called Nervous, Hypochondriac, or Hysteric*, he thought he was writing an informative treatment of a baffling – perhaps the most puzzling – medical condition.[33] Surely he did not ask himself, at any stage, whether the book ought to be classified as 'medicine' or 'philosophy'; and even while granting that his classification, if he had made one, would not be the definitive one, it is significant that these categories did not seem of consequence to him. The issue was hysteria, its elusive aspects, and he did not care whether readers or future historians classified his *Observations* as medicine or philosophy so long as he got his medical point across. Nor would he have considered that 'nervous diseases' were more properly classified as 'medicine' than 'philosophy': what counted was the disease, and the possibility that he could develop a system of thought about nervous diseases that would permit new treatment and cure. Of course Whytt knew that as a practising physician and professor of medicine (in the Chair at Edinburgh) his books would be viewed as 'medical books' in essence; yet this fact did not impede him from intruding philosophical content into his books or from commenting on the non-medical aspects of the diseases he studied: the nature of man in general, his human condition, the role of his reason and passion, and so forth.

The crucial issue, then, appears to be not whether the doctor writing about this or that medical condition is also a 'philosopher', but to what degree he is 'philosophic'. Resolution of the point does not reside in the counting of asides and references: the fact that a medical author of the eighteenth century refers to hard philosophy or digresses from his subject into metaphysical disquisitions does not render him a 'philosopher'. His logic and epistemology must be sufficiently sophisticated to permit him to develop a system, as Dr King has shown in *The Philosophy of Medicine*, and the system needs to be airtight even when judged by the most rigorous demands of cause and effect, necessary and sufficient condition, *a priori* and *a posteriori* reason, and the like.

Even these discriminations are insufficient, though, because when considering the overlaps of philosophy and psychology in this period, the one (psychology) blends into and seems to emerge from the other (philosophy), philosophy being the much older subject. This admittedly sweeping generalisation is only valid so long as the dictates of anatomy and physiology are borne in mind: a philosopher can invent systems by the use of reason and imagination, but that same reason and imagination is determined in the strictest sense by another anatomic system, the brain and its nerves. It is therefore probably accurate to claim, though it is impossible to prove, that psychology in large part 'emerged' (even the verb is problematic) from philosophy; but in doing so anatomy and physiology must not be relegated to a distant background. Such a heavy-handed law would seem to be less valid in times of anatomic stagnation – such as the late Middle Ages – or when physiology is out of fashion or vogue and when, as a consequence, its tenets are given no credence; but when physiology's advocates are active, as in the period of Vesalius or Boyle, or when it is reverently viewed, as it was in the eighteenth century, it must play a rather significant role in shaping even the best philosophy of the day.

To maintain all this is naturally to rehearse the rise of philosophic empiricism, the movement associated with Locke, Berkeley and Hume. But lest one gets bogged down in the quagmire of British empiricism and by so doing avoids the real issue at hand – the boundaries between philosophy and psychology in the eighteenth century – further inquiry must be made into the influence of anatomy and physiology on philosophy. Afterwards, a return to philosophy and psychology can be made. Much of the reason for such procedure is owing to the curious volution of madness: not as an 'idea' tied down to a particular 'field' or 'subject' – say medicine or philosophy – but as a coherent cultural notion transmitted from century to century. Madness, insanity, lunacy, mental derangement – call it by whatever name one wishes – it is the *sine qua non* of psychiatry.

The Renaissance in Europe inherited a theory of madness almost exclusively dependent – to the extent that it was a 'theory' divested of religious and other secondary causes – on Aristotelian concepts of the soul.[34] Long before the sixteenth century, however, there had been speculation about the brain,[35] but little discussion about psychological health in relation to the brain. By the middle of the sixteenth century Vesalius had made a set of discoveries which were later applied by several physicians (especially Harvey and Willis) to a subject we would call brain theory. Descartes's dualism, especially the dichotomy of soul and brain, significantly influenced this picture. This is not the appropriate place to rehearse Descartes's contributions to the development of psychology,[36] but it is necessary to glance briefly at Cartesian historiography as it bears on the eighteenth century.

Crudely speaking, historians of psychology have tended to make too little rather than too much of Descartes's contribution, not because it is essentially metaphysical but because it requires importation from another area, philosophy, and until the 1960s even serious students of the eighteenth century were unable to integrate medicine and philosophy. Some practising contemporary psychologists and psychiatrists are shocked to learn that philosophy now plays or has played any significant role in their 'clinical practice'; this may be a sad situation but is nevertheless true. Most consider themselves the practitioners of a 'science' (although they are cautious in their use of the term) whose roots were recently discovered by Freud. Nothing, however, could be farther from the truth. Philosophy, construed not loosely as unwritten assumptions but as informed printed texts guided by rules of logic and language, remains an intrinsic concern to the best practising psychologists; those who deny it are usually the least knowledgeable clinicians and display their ignorance by the assertion. No thinker in modern European cultural history proves the paradigm better than Descartes. The issue then is not Freud or, more germanely, Pinel, but knowledge of the mind–body problem by historians of psychology.

artes and physicians contemporary with him acknowledged the proximity of medicine and philosophy – this indeed is one of the themes of
this book, as its title and chapters reiterate – but modern historians have
been loath to do so, and one reason may be that ours is an age so much
less philosophical than the Enlightenment.

Other matters impinge on the philosophic as well as the anatomic
bases of eighteenth-century psychology, especially their boundaries and
overlaps. During the seventeenth century, anatomy made such rapid
advances that almost any scientific hypothesis was soon invalidated.
Research on nerves and their interaction with the brain threatened to
change everyone's conception of the cause of insanity; now, for the first
time in modern culture, it seemed impossible to refute a physiological
basis of madness. Thomas Willis, the great English physiologist, was
among the first to accept the validity of this concept, viz. of the mechanistic and physiological bases of insanity. He turned away from other
pressing work because he believed he could not proceed until he had
solved certain riddles about the brain's anatomy.[37] Yet recent historians of
psychology have paid little attention to these developments. An example is
their analysis of psychosomatic medicine. The first thing to notice is its
neglect. No history, however Procrustean, of psychosomatic concepts
now exists for psychotherapy,[38] neither for the seventeenth or eighteenth
centuries, although no one questions that such concepts were then significant. This is odd as so many practitioners today consider these concepts
of crucial importance.[39] Most American postgraduates studying the history
of medicine would be hard put to answer questions about the origins
of modern psychosomatic medicine, its essential texts and ideas, or its
development from the seventeenth century to the beginning of the nineteenth.[40]

The anatomic bases of Enlightenment psychology are plagued by
other problems as well, as it is not enough merely to note gaps. These
must be filled, and directions for the future given. One thing is clear:
given that the role of the senses is imperfectly understood in Englightenment thought, most of all their capability of influencing thought processes,
it is probably hoping for too much to expect a clear picture of the age's
psychosomatic medicine. This may be why the imaginative (i.e. non-
scientific) literature of the age is, as I have already indicated, ultimately
our most reliable gauge of the degree to which psychosomatic ideas then
permeated French and English culture. This may not be a fashionable
position to take in a discussion of the historiography of eighteenth-century
science, but it is the accurate one. Historians of Enlightenment literature
know that all the literary forms – poetry, prose, drama – then invoked
are replete with characters whose mental life reflects their physical: in the
'humour' characters in the drama, in Swift's *Mechanical Operation of the*

Spirit, in Goldsmith's *Vicar of Wakefield*, everywhere in *Tristram Shandy*. The reciprocity is too blatant to be missed, but it barely exists in previous literature.[41] There are dozens of examples, of which Smollett's irascible hero, Matt Bramble, in *Humphry Clinker* (1771) is a perfect although simple one: when Bramble, whose name reveals his 'ruling passion' (to use psychological jargon of the day), writing to the physician in whose care he has placed himself, complains that he is 'equally distressed in mind and body', we know there is no simpler expression of the paradigm. His nephew, Melford, repeats the assertion over a dozen times in the novel's opening pages lest any reader miss the point. 'Mind and body' were believed to affect each other 'equally'; but the equation in reciprocal inter-action was nothing invented by a novelist. It rather derived from anatomic research of the previous century, the seventeenth, that had only just reached the masses – the popular sensibility.

Literature demonstrates how science infiltrates culture; this is why literature, or the relations of science and literature, is so vital in any discussion of psychology or psychiatry, not yet a 'science' but striving to be predictive. When the imprisoned Caleb Williams, Godwin's protagonist in his novel by the name (1794), recovers from a violent bout of sickness at the precise moment when his illness is at its worst, Godwin suggests at the triumph of mind over body: it is a form of Priestleyanism transposed to the terrain of literary character. For Caleb has just learned that things are looking brighter for him outside jail; and he brings about this amelior-ation by following a psychosomatic medical tradition almost a century old. Godwin turns the plot at this point so subtly that contemporary readers unaware of popular culture then may miss the detail; but eighteenth-century readers probably did not. They assumed a reciprocity we doubt; and while not all of them were *au courant* with medical theories of psychosomatosis, they believed in mind–body reciprocity in a way we never would. It is undeniable that today no thorough or even partial history of this theoretical relation between mind and body exists, and certainly none that charts its progress down through the eighteenth cen-tury.

The reciprocity of science and literature, and the reflection of each in the other, illuminates the semantic issues raised earlier about philosophy and psychology as separate and overlapping domains, but does not resolve their boundary disputes. If an adequate definition of philosophy could be superimposed on the discussion, the problem might be resolved, but no such superimposition is anywhere to be found, and even eighteenth-century philosophers disagree on the nature of the philosophic enterprise, as their disputes over the merits of leading philosophic systems indicate. Furthermore, it is not altogether patent, nor will it soon be, precisely what aspects of philosophy psychological theory absorbs. Eighteenth-century psychology clearly plundered the logical and epistemological areas, but it did so in the name of being 'empirical', of collecting data and not speculating further until its speculations could be verified by repetitive observations. Moreover, the 'rationalism' of both philosophy and psychology is problematic to assess: often it is not what it seems to be. Locke and Berkeley considered themselves 'rationalists' of a type; so too did Battie and Monro, as the prefaces to their treatises on madness indicate. All this dangerous labelling raises the further problematic matter of philosophic texts versus psychological, or psychiatric texts, a distinction almost impossible to substantiate when the contents of both varieties are scrutinised.

These impediments accounted for, one can begin to assess the impact of philosophy on psychology without the charge of lack of definitional rigour. This is exactly the task Lester King recently performed in *The Philosophy of Medicine*,[42] except that King does not discuss psychology. His book is nevertheless germane to this topic because it demonstrates how far afield the scholar must range if his subject depicts the interaction of medicine (whatever its branch) and philosophy. In psychological realms King discusses 'mind and body', the 'imagination', and theories of reciprocal influence in psychosomatic medicine. He prudently observes that all three topics are more or less 'philosophical', especially to the degree that each is based on logical explanations of cause and effect, and he ably argues that no picture of the general medicine of the period is complete without shading in its philosophical dimensions. Presumably King does not believe this to be true of other periods or he would not have confined himself to the 'Enlightenment'.[43] The question for us then is the following: if King's contention about philosophy and medicine obtains for the general medical theory of the age, does it not necessarily obtain for its psychological thought?

The question grows unwieldy unless there is a clear sense of its existence in the Enlightenment. Historians of ideas are right to maintain that in matters regarding the history of concepts over the sweep of time, the inspection of change is a clue. Almost all historians of psychiatry (whether 'chronological', 'thinker-oriented', or of any other type) agree that theories of the emotions were undergoing the most radical and rapid alteration in the Enlightenment: from 'innate ideas' combined at birth according to environmental factors to 'mechanistic chains' of nerves and fibres,[44] the combination of which made for the 'ruling passion' or, the late-nineteenth-century term, 'the personality'. There was as yet little sense of the relation of domestic environment (from birth onward) to eventual adult personality, but early-eighteenth-century theorists (in England Francis Fuller, Nicholas Robinson, Richard Blackmore, George Cheyne, John Midriff, John Purcell, William Stukeley, John Woodward and others) were beginning to classify human types by their 'nervous' dispositions. Even medically uneducated poets such as Pope had heard a great deal about these notions, as is perfectly evident in the second epistle of *An Essay on Man* (1733), which deals in large part with concepts of the 'ruling passion'.

Now while there is nothing new in the classification of character according to 'character type' or 'humoural type', categorisation according to the 'ruling passion' is innovative and points to the type of classification Battie and the Monros make later in the century when they write that, for example, *A* is principally lecherous or religiously inspired. What signals the 'ruling passion' as an advance is its dependence on the nervous system to an extent that the 'humoural type' never was. The latter, to be sure, was directly tied to the body – to its humours, digestive tract, saline state, the release of recrements – but the nervous system, especially the 'tone of the nerves, fibres and solids' did not loom large. Over the course of the eighteenth century this nervous state was to assume ever greater importance in determining psychological disposition and outlook. The genealogy of psychological advance, then, is this: from 'humoural' theory to 'nervous' analysis to discussions of 'anxiety' and 'insensibility' (Dr Battie's term especially) as the basis of derangement; or, in terms of thinkers, from Burton's legacy to Cheyne to Battie and Cullen. Cheyne, a Newtonian of a curious sort, portends what is to come in eighteenth-century psychological theory when he pronounces at the beginning of *The English Malady* that nearly all infirmities ultimately can be traced to fibres that are too lax or too rigid:

> That there is a certain *Tone, Consistence*, and Firmness, and a determin'd Degree of *Elasticity* and *Tension* of the Nerves or Fibres, how small soever that be . . . necessary to the perfect Performance of the *Animal Functions*, is, I think, without all Question, from an Excess over or Defect under which, in some eminent Degree, Diseases of one Kind or another certainly arise.[45]

And Battie validates the concept by the weight of his authority and its endorsement in his *Treatise on Madness*, when he contends that 'anxiety' and 'insensibility' are the preconditions of mental illness, and that both result from the 'ill conditioned state of the nerve itself'.[46]

Such decoding of the lineage of psychological theory forces one back, again and again, to the old problem of the separation of philosophy and psychology in the eighteenth century. For if mental health and illness depend upon the state of the nerves, as Cheyne and Battie had contended, then the relation of the nerves to one's perception of external objects becomes a matter of paramount importance. Yet these topics are no sooner tapped than one is driven back to empirical philosophy, as it was emerging

c. 1680–1720. There is no escaping the elenchus in a discussion of the rise
of psychology, as there is no refuge from the perpetual question of what
it meant to be a 'rationalist' then.

Locke had changed the course of some English and European thinking about perception, as Morris Mandelbaum has shown;[47] and Hartley,
the influential philosopher–physician, would probably not have generated
his mechanistic theory of the association of ideas ('vibrations') had he been
unable to build upon earlier models of memory.[48] These and others were
often philosophers as well as physicians; Locke was a trained and certified
physician who occasionally practised. They were also 'rationalists' (i.e.
speculators who build systems of thought) with deep empirical proclivit-
ies, but they themselves saw less contradiction than we do today in being
both rational and empirical; nor did they seem to worry whether they
were being styled 'philosophers' or 'physicians'. In the case of some other
contemporary rationalists, the act of 'integration' of the disparate realms
caused concern. Shaftesbury and Hutcheson (Adam Smith's teacher), primarily rationalistic rather than empirical, continued to care about the
'ruling passion' in relation to human physiology, but did not face the
matter squarely in their writing, nor could they accept Cheyne's argument
about the supremacy of the nerves.[49] In contrast Adam Smith, Lord
Kames, and some members of the Scottish common-sense school extended
the 'integration' by combining theories about the private and public self
into one system about man in society. Here, of course, are the origins of
nineteenth-century sociology; but more pertinent to our discussion is the
historical fact that these rationalists – whether primarily empirical, antiempirical, logical, optimistic, or the purveyors of common-sense – were
generating the very ideas from which the most important practising 'psychiatrists' of the day (the Cheynes, Batties, Pinels, Chiarugis, Tukes, and
others) built up their hospitals and eventually unchained the insane.

The conclusion should not be drawn that these psychiatrists were
optimists or sentimentalists. They read Hobbes as well as Shaftesbury,
and knew all too well that man is not an 'innately good creature', as
Shaftesbury would have him in the *Characteristics*, 'engaging in innately
good actions'. These doctors of the mind have not usually left behind
catalogues of the books they owned or commentaries on the philosophers
they read, but their writings make it perfectly clear that they were educated
thinkers who had read the pessimistic as well as the optimistic philosophical record. A doctor whose medicine is 'the physick of the soul' will be
alive to the anxiety of the 'unconscious'; and the more probing of these
physicians went to the works of Mandeville, Swift, and Johnson to read
about those tensions of the unconscious. In the case of Dr Cheyne, whose
long correspondence with the novelist Samuel Richardson survives, the

evidence is straightforward: one gleans from his letters exactly what he is reading and sees how literature permeates his medico-psychological ideas.

The ideas articulated in the previous paragraph were, therefore, concepts found in the writings of 'rationalists' of different backgrounds. Who knows if Dr Battie, for instance, did not consider Swift or Johnson as 'influential' a psychologist as Locke or Shaftesbury; even if he did not rank them so highly, he had to be highly knowledgeable about the philosophic legacy from Hobbes onward or his psychiatric writings would not be as they are. For even an early psychiatrist does not conjure ideas merely from other similar thinkers: he learns from such men, but learns as much, if not more, from disparate terrains.

Still another aspect of the 'philosophical' should not go unnoticed. If philosophical impact includes the religious, then the influence of philosophy on psychology must be construed even more widely than we have suggested. In the Restoration and early eighteenth century in England clergymen such as the Cambridge Platonists and latitudinarian divines wrote treatises containing seminal chapters on the memory, senses, imagination, soul; and it was from these books that the 'psychiatrists' of the eighteenth century formulated some of their theoretical ideals and shaped their practice. The degree to which *episteme* was put into *praxis* depended on the doctor's courage and ingenuity; nevertheless there is no question about these writings as a major tributary of psychological knowledge. Thus Locke's critics – especially John Norris and John Sergeant, authors respectively of *A Philosophical Discourse Concerning the Natural Immortality of the Soul* (1708) and *The Method of Science* (1696) – promoted a theory about 'ideas' in relation to 'memory' that was eventually absorbed into medical writings (Robinson, Cheyne, Hartley); and Samuel Clarke, the parsonical and learned Bishop Warburton, and Andrew Baxter, the prolific mid-eighteenth-century Aberdeen tutor,[50] all generated theories about dreams which are repeatedly referred to by early psychiatrists such as Battie and Cullen.

Granted, these and other doctors had little of Freud's sense that the analysis of dreams is a pivotal means by which to cure the patient. Nevertheless, they possessed a sense, however impressionistic, that dreams ought to be discussed when patients were examined. Even James Carkesse, a layman–lunatic confined to Bedlam for much of his life, realised that dreams were important and included many in his valuable 'anatomy of a madman's mind'.[51] Anyone who surveys the literature on dreams from *c.* 1680 onwards will note the radical change that occurs in the following hundred years. Such a work as Philip Goodwin's *The Mystery of Dreams, Historically Discoursed* (1658) is altogether different from Andrew Baxter's chapter on dreams in his *Enquiry into the Nature of the Human Soul* (1733; 2nd ed. 1750), and these two differ again from mechanistic treatments in which it is held in/that dreams are the result of chemical actions conveyed by the body to the brain (or, as William Godwin affirms in his novel *Caleb Williams* (1794), that bad dreams, which pave the way to anxiety and thereby to insanity, are mechanistically based on 'sensations linked together').[52]

The philosophic assumptions of the age are additionally germane because so much of the 'polite physician's' attention was then devoted to theory, so little to practice. The doctor was still a gentleman, and 'theory' – cast in whatever literary mould – issuing from his pen was the best proof of gentility. He rarely saw patients but often read a great deal. Pope's physician, William Cheselden, was not atypical of the physicians of the time: he assisted Pope in editing Shakespeare and Pope came to rely on him as a serious scholar.[53] Richard Blackmore wrote epic poems – *King Arthur, The Nature of Man, Creation: a Philosophical Poem in Seven Books* – in his carriage on the way to house calls. Other 'gentleman physicians' were interested in discovering the nature of emotion, feeling, intuition, of dissecting the most interesting of the passions: fear, lust, anger, love. In part this is why treatises such as Adam Smith's *Theory of Moral Sentiments* (1759) were so popular and were reissued so often (five editions and four translations of Smith appeared by the end of the century) and why these works are found in the libraries of medical men, especially physicians, of the period.[54] As we shall see later, the best application – best in that it could actually touch on real lives – of these theories was made by medical men. Doctors like Battie and Cullen, already referred to, spent much of their energy transforming insanity into a constitutive subject and also persuading their less enlightened medical colleagues that insanity *ought* to be cured; they had to engage in this activity before they could be in a position to effect cures themselves. They were philosophers and propagandists, as it were, before they were physicians, and this progress has not been noted by the historians as clearly as it ought.

It is probably inaccurate to contend that the period from 1680 to 1780 saw any revolution in the *practice* of psychiatry, although the management of madhouses seems to have been improving after *c.* 1770. 'Practical revolution' came much later, in the 1790s, when Pinel unlocked the chains of the insane in France, and when others followed his precedent in other countries. But to view practice alone is to have a narrow view of the history of medicine, or of any practical science. The earlier period, up to *c.* 1780, created a revolution in knowledge about psychology – if not a revolution then certainly a ferment – that was drawn upon at the end of the century when Pinel and others enacted monumental reform. Any deep study of this revolution or ferment will lead the student to the rationalists we have been discussing here, primarily 'philosophers', although by no means philosophers only.[55] Since 1950 there has been considerable interest in these thinkers, not only from philosophers of science and general historians, but from practising medical men such as Lester King.[56] Yet the medical-rationalists – Robinson, Mandeville, Cheyne, to mention but three among dozens – are always left out. Furthermore, while there is usually a good deal of discussion about abstract ideas such as progress, freedom, happiness, love, and education, the equally abstract but quasi-psychiatric ideas about memory, imagination, the soul, perception, the senses, intuition, and the emotions are rarely discussed in any depth except in obscure history of medicine journals. Those who have written, such as those cited in notes 35, 43, and 48, have scrutinised the rational literature of the age with a fine microscopic eye; but no one has systematically examined this same literature to understand how practising physicians were assimilating this knowledge and putting it to use in medical contexts and physician–patient situations, especially in cases involving the cure of disease. We are so far behind in this area that it would even be helpful at this point to isolate and study the prefaces and conclusions of medical works (of which there is no dearth from 1680 to 1780). Here, again, the minor works should be consulted as well as the major, for they may display the processes of assimilation discussed above far more clearly than the books which everyone read[57] and which are, perhaps, more subtle in this category.

PSYCHOLOGY AND SOCIAL HISTORY: METAPSYCHOLOGY

This relation is so vast that one can best grasp its perplexities by looking at specific texts. Garrison, author of the much-consulted *History of Medicine*, devotes a grand total of two and a half pages to the mentally ill in his very long chapter on 'The eighteenth century'.[58] Written in typical Garrisonian fashion it is a passage permeated by concrete detail and assumed to be fact, but the more intriguing aspect of it, and the reason why I have selected it to present the essential problem of 'psychology and social history', is that it comes to an abrupt stop – as if Garrison had feared he was suddenly in dangerous waters. The passage so clearly reveals the kind of writing that has been done since the 1930s in this vein (i.e. charting the social contexts of psychiatry) that it is worth quoting almost in entirety, even at the risk of fatiguing the reader with a very long passage:

> Bad as was the management of hospitals, the treatment of the insane was even worse. They were either chained or caged when housed, or, if harmless, were allowed to run at large, the Tom o'Bedlams of England or the wizards and warlocks of Scotland (Lochiel in Campbell's poem). The earliest insane asylums in the northern countries were Bedlam (1547), the Juliusspital at Wurtzburg (1567), St Luke's in London (1757), the Quaker or County

Asylum at York (1792), and the *Narrenthurm*, or 'Lunatics Tower' (1784), one of the showplaces of old Vienna, where, as in ancient Bedlam, the public were allowed to view the insane, like animals in a menagerie, on payment of a small fee. The latter institution was described by Richard Bright in 1815 as a fanciful, four-story edifice having the external appearance of a large round tower, but consisting on the inside of a hollow circle, in the center of which a quadrangular building arose, joined to the circle by each of its corners. The enclosed structure afforded residence for the keepers and surgeons. The circular part contained 300 patients, 'whose condition,' says Bright, 'is far from being as comfortable as in many of the establishments for the insane which I have visited.'[59] It was not closed until 1853. Until well into the nineteenth century, insanity was regarded as not only incurable, but as a disgrace rather than a misfortune. Heinroth (1818) even regarded it as a divine punishment for personal guilt of some kind . . . In such later asylums as those erected at Munich (1801), Sonnenstein (1811), Siegberg (1815) and Sachsenburg (1830), the sad lot of the insane was that of Hogarth's engraving and Kaulbach's celebrated drawing.[60] Monkemoller's researches on German psychiatry in the eighteenth century, based on the records of Hanoverian asylums at Celle and elsewhere,[61] confirm what Reil wrote of German asylums in his 'Rhapsodies' of 1803, and go to show that the theoretic part of the science in this period was nebulous philosophic speculation. Insanity was still attributed to yellow and black bile or to heat in the dog days, and symptoms, such as exaggerated self-esteem, jealousy, envy, sloth, self-abuse, etc., were regarded as causes. Kant, in his *Anthropologie* (1798), actually improvised a semeiology of insanity and maintained that, in criminal cases, it was the province, not of the medical, but of the philosophical faculty.

The point about Kant is significant enough, especially the matter of 'medical' and 'philosophical' faculties in criminal consultations. The actual passage from Garrison quoted above has gone unnoticed by almost all historians of psychiatry including Hunter and Macalpine; but the rest of the paragraph reveals how Garrison 'rounded out' his picture of insanity in the Enlightenment with details culled from his German education (though he himself was an American) at the University of Berlin. Conditions and cures are of unusual interest to him:

> The cases treated were all of the dangerous, unmanageable, or suicidal type, and no hope of recovery was held out. There was an extensive exhibition of drugs and unconditional belief in their efficacy. A case that did not react to drugs was regarded as hopeless. Melancholia was treated by opium pills, excited states by camphor, pruritus by diaphoresis, and a mysterious power was ascribed to belladonna: if it failed, everything failed. Other remedies were a mixture of honey and vinegar, a decoction of *Quadenwurzel*, large doses of lukewarm water, or, if this failed, 'that panacea of tartarisatus.'[62] The costly aqua benedicat Rolandi, with three stout ruffians to administer it, a mustard plaster on the head, venesection at the forehead and both

thumbs, clysters, and plasters of Spanish fly, were other resources. Barbarities were kept in the background, but the harsh methods of medieval times were none the less prevalent. A melancholic woman was treated with a volley of oaths and a douche of cold water as she lay in bed. If purgatives and emetics failed with violent patients, they came in for many hard knocks, with a regime of bolts and chains to inspire fear. A sensitive, self-conscious patient was confined in a cold, damp, gloomy, mephitic cell, fed on perpetual hard bread, and otherwise treated as a criminal. The diet – soup, warm beer, a few vegetables and salads – was of the cheapest. There were some attempts at open-door treatment, such as putting the patients to mind geese, sending them to the mineral baths at Doberan, Toplitz, Pyrmont, Vichy, Bath or Tunbridge Wells, or sending them as harvest hands to Holland (*Hollandgeherei*). Marriage was also recommended as a cure.

With these last few remarkable words Garrison concludes his single paragraph on madness in his chapter on the eighteenth century. His 'conditions and cures', enumerated in the last section, tally with the most detailed description of 'conditions and cures' in the period, at least the most detailed in any English work, the one found in Smollett's *Life and Adventures of Sir Launcelot Greaves* (1760–2). This is the story of an ill-fated couple, Sir Launcelot Greaves and Aurelia Darnel, who, though they are 'fated' to marry from the start, are 'doomed' to stray apart and be 'consigned' to a madhouse before they can unite.[63] Garrison's repertory of panaceas is not dissimilar from theirs. Both range from the most common purgatives to the most obscure, such as the 'Roland water' he mentions.

Looking elsewhere, Garrison's last sentence relates that marriage was often considered a cure. He does not say on what authority; the researcher must substantiate or disprove it for himself. There are numerous major and minor female characters in eighteenth-century fiction who are sent off to be married in order to be cured. Arabella in Charlotte Lennox's *The Female Quixote* (1752) may be the parent of the type, but there are dozens of others. Three generations earlier, Sydenham combated medical authorities who recommended that hysterical women marry; he was controversial in maintaining that the condition would be passed on to the daughters. Sydenham, however sound his intuition in this matter, lost out, and physicians continued to prescribe marriage at least until Richardson's time, and probably afterwards. Gideon Harvey, one of Sydenham's opponents, is an example of the dominant medical attitude. In *Morbus Anglicus . . . To which is added, some Brief Discourses on Melancholy, Madness, and Distraction, occasioned by Love*, published in the year of the 'Great Plague', Dr Harvey demonstrated that Sydenham was wrong. Five months after the South Sea Bubble burst, John Midriff, another physician, argued that economic reversal could be as influential as lost-love in causing insanity. The subtitle of his major medical work reveals the drift of his anti-Sydenham position: 'Containing Remarkable Cases of Persons of both Sexes, and all Ranks, from the aspiring Directors to the Humble Bubbler, who have been miserably afflicted with these Melancholy Disorders since the Fall of South-sea, and other public Stocks'. Young women, it is true, were not carted from the asylums to the marriage bed, but many who suffered the 'vapours' – the Lydia Languishes, Pamelas, cast-off mistresses – and who were portrayed as deranged, required a man in the end if they hoped to get well.[64]

Now all this is wrong Garrison volunteers; even in the last sentence of the long passage quoted above he relates psychological history in descriptive rather than analytical terms. He enjoys no inclination to scrutinise conditions, to probe motives and explore reasons; nor does he have a clue why these deplorable social conditions went unchallenged or take a stand against the progenitors of such intense human misery. If Garrison's mode is compared to Foucault's in *The Birth of the Clinic*,[65] a book dealing with the same subject, the difference between each mode is apparent. Foucault's language substitutes metaphor and metonymy for concrete detail; the narrator hides himself, as it were, behind a veil, and the direction of his paragraphs, written in an opaque style, is so unpredictable that any clear statement of their 'subjects' or 'themes' may suffer from *reductio ad absurdum*. Nevertheless, Foucault states at the start of his book that

> I should like to attempt here the analysis of a type of discourse – that of medical experience – at a period when, before the great discoveries of the nineteenth century, it had changed its materials more than systematic form. The clinic is both a new 'carving up' of things and the principle of their verbalization in a form which we have been accustomed to recognizing as the language of a 'positive science'.[66]

Foucault's rhetorical inventory of themes and concepts is essentially this: the history of medicine construed as a branch of knowledge and the history of ideas; *excursus* on time and space that glance at the Marxist and structuralist writings of Gaston Bachelard, Gilles Deleuze, and Roland Barthes; orations to persuade the reader that 'contextuality' is everything and that the crucial period in the development of the asylum in France and England occurs between 1750 and 1800;[67] further arguments contending that the period before 1750, after 1800, or even after 1850, is not nearly so essential; persuasion through the use of arcane materials (names, places, events) – so arcane that the reader grows distracted from the main subject that there is a language of 'medical spaces' in the Enlightenment; discourses on discoursing in the impersonal self-reflexive mode, in which the effective subject disappears; a political ideology that is explicitly anti-authoritarian; the 'clinic', 'asylum', or 'hospital' as essential imagery invoked in discourse aimed at demonstrating that no subject in history or philosophy is so crucial (i.e. superlatively) as the announced 'principle of verbalisation'.

These 'inventories' do not answer the question of whether or not Foucault is concerned with the so-called 'straight' history of medicine: that is, history of medicine conceived in traditional terms and traditional rhetorical moulds, and without preoccupation with the historian's metaphors, degree of self-reflectiveness, or other 'principle of verbalisation'. This is why the inclusion in the book of a passage such as the following, that appears on the fourth page of Foucault's preface, is so ambiguous:

> In 1764, J. F. Meckel set out to study the alterations brought about in the brain by certain disorders (apoplexy, mania, phthisi); he used the rational method of weighing equal volumes and comparing them to determine which parts of the brain had been dehydrated, which parts had been swollen, and by which diseases. Modern medicine has made hardly any use of this research. Brain pathology achieved its 'positive' form when Bichat, and above all Récamier and Lallemand, used the celebrated 'hammer, with a bread thin end' . . .[68]

It may have been true in the early 1960s, when Foucault was presumably writing these passages, that 'modern medicine [had] made hardly any use of this research', and it may have been equally true that brain pathology achieved the 'positive forms' Foucault affirms it did after 1800 under the conditions he describes (i.e. Bichat, who died in 1802 and performed most of his important work at the end of his very short life of thirty-one years). But all this substance notwithstanding, it is Foucault's empirical accuracy, or lack of, that constitutes the *least* reliable and interesting aspect of his method; the aspect, also, that has least attracted students to his books. The matter seems simple but should not be casually dismissed, for analysis of historical accuracy reveals the truest clue to decoding the recent historiography of scholarship in our field of inquiry.

In the passage just cited, for instance, Foucault derives his date of 1764 from a journalistic account of Meckel's experiment published in a popular Paris weekly.[69] Foucault may or may not know the difference between the significant and insignificant work of the elder Johann Friedrich Meckel, or at least the less significant work of his son of the same name. But *The Birth of the Clinic* offers no evidence that Foucault has actually read any of the elder Meckel's works – a charge that speaks for itself. Moreover, the sentence about 'modern medicine', translated literally from the same two French words, is ambiguous. Does Foucalt mean 'the practitioners of modern medicine', or recent scholarship in the history of medicine, or something else? Surely the basis of his claim here depends upon clarification of his ambiguity. After all, why should modern medicine rehabilitate Meckel's medicine?[70] The point about the 'celebrated hammer' is less controversial; every American, and probably European, medical student learns about it. Historians of medicine concur about its significance and usually there is little to discuss. But why are Rêcamier and Lallemand given more credit ('above all') than Bichat? Does Foucault know something medical historians do not? Is he withholding some information? The real issue in deciphering this prose lies in 'moving from sentence to sentence'; after sufficient decoding it becomes clear that any ostensible subject of the discourse is ancillary to Foucault's verbal pyrotechnics. But Foucault must be trusted when he discloses in the preface, already quoted, that he is most concerned 'with the analysis of a type of discourse'.[71] Such qualification ('a type') would seem to absolve him.

Further study of *Naissance de la clinique* and similar Foucaultian books would demonstrate the reason for their success. These texts do not isolate the 'psychiatric history' or 'medical history' as a constitutive subject. Rather, they transform the old 'text' into new 'discourse' and the old 'medical history' into new 'contextuality'. Therefore they represent, as the Swiss scholar Jean Starobinski has noticed, 'an experiment in a new way of writing the history of science, a testing ground'.[72] I would add that the 'experiment' is rhetorically loaded: it contains just the right amount of obnubulation, to use T. S. Eliot's term,[73] to mystify and confuse the unsuspecting reader, and to cause the suspicious reader to pause from his own writing and investigate the new mode. But, further to account for the success of these historico-medical texts, Foucault also possesses what Garrison did not: a sufficiently brilliant imagination to connect the most disparate terrains. By so doing Foucault successfully constructs a rhetorical illusion of having broken ground – i.e. discovered a new epistemology – for the history of medicine. Furthermore, it is crucial to compare Foucault's passage quoted above with what Garrison wrote about the elder Meckel in his internalist and quasi-prosopographical study of the history of medicine:

> Johann Friedrich Meckel (1724–74), of Wetzlar, graduate at Göttingen in 1748, with a noteworthy inaugural dissertation on the fifth nerve (Meckel's ganglion), became professor of anatomy, botany, and obstetrics at Berlin in 1751, and was the first teacher of midwifery at the Charité. He was the first to describe the submaxillary ganglion (1748), and made important investigations of the nerve-supply of the face (1751) and the terminal visceral filaments of the veins and lymphatics (1772).[74]

Foucault, by way of contrast, does not provide as much verifiable information but inflates Meckel's position by rhetorical hyperbole ('Modern medicine has hardly made any use of this research', etc.) and cajoles the reader into believing that a new area of late eighteenth-century psychology has been tapped – even into thinking that the whole history of psychology and psychiatry can be rewritten in this new mode. It may be that it can and that it will be, for to study Foucault's mode is to probe the insufficiencies of the internalist school, i.e. Garrison.

Historiographically speaking, several points are to be gathered. First and foremost is the fact that Garrison and his admirers or followers provide almost no analytic content whatsoever, while Foucault and his Franco-American epigoni probably include too much.[75] Yet an author such as Foucault is revered (he is already a cult figure everywhere except in America) because medicine, especially psychology, has enjoyed no analytical history for the period studied in this volume. The books by Garrison and others discussed above are contextual orphans and analytical surrogates; likewise, one could compose a bibliography of essays and articles that shed some light on facets of the subject. But no single book exists wherein one can learn about the evolution of psychology 1700–1800 from a trained, authoritative cultural historian who also writes clearly and perceptively. Richard Hunter and Ida Macalpine's book (see note 5 above) is the only attempt at a checklist, and it is an anthology, not a descriptive or analytic work in any sense of the term. Thus, when a shrewd and gifted stylist such as Foucault enters the vacant arena, he can ransack the primary sources in any manner he desires and still lend the impression that he is doing precisely what traditional medical and social historians should have done decades ago.

A second crucial observation needs to be made about historiography, this one in connection with the work of the late George Rosen, perhaps best known for his book *Madness in Society: Chapters in the Historical Sociology of Mental Illness*,[76] the middle sections of which deal with our period. Economic conditions and rational ideas form the two cornerstones of Rosen's explorations into mass mental illness, the first to correlate psychological movements with social status, the second, the ideational, to relate societal attitudes at a given time to philosophical movements and currents then apparent. The result is a work of lasting worth; but the diachronic period surveyed is so vast (from the ancient Greeks to the present day) that superficiality necessarily arises. Moreover, Rosen has not usually discriminated between the varieties of historical scholarship; trained as a physician, his sense of solid grounding in history was the compilation of an exhaustive number of index cards.[77] The result is fragmented discourse, to import Foucault's term, of the telephone-directory variety, 'discourse' that reads well only for those wishing to know what the terrain is, not for those searching to understand it.

Other materials available for the social history of psychology in our period require brief commentary: scattered in journals are many useful observations about the hospital movement, its conditions for patients and doctors, its facilities and conditions.[78] Much less accessible is information on the economics of this development, especially the fees paid to hospital physicians, their surgeons and apothecaries, and the costs to the public of all these services. After 1758 treatment was obtainable in England, usually without hope of total cure, but little is known about its precise nature, especially that in outlying areas, and we have failed to unearth even a few manuscripts that would significantly alter the picture of our knowledge. It may be that all this 'history of psychology' is of little importance in comparison with the type of analysis that has existed now for almost fifty years – that evident in the gulf that lies between a Garrison and a Foucault – but it is hard to pronounce on this matter too definitively. What is certain is that one can pick one's favourite historian, for example Perry Miller, author of *The New England Mind*, ponder his discussions about psychology in that book,[79] and then comprehend his discourse by measuring its proximity to or distance from the Garrison–Foucault poles, the extremes of internalism and externalism. Garrison never speculates about any cultural or social development; even his value judgements – what is good or bad for medicine – are suppressed. Foucault proceeds by an opposite method, never recording fact *qua* fact but collapsing traditional subjects and their objects (e.g. a specific author, a given text, an episode or moment) into discourse about newly constituted subjects (e.g. the 'history of medicine', 'systems of medical classification'), and then setting this discourse into the broadest possible context. As a result, Foucault is the externalist *ne plus ultra*. He is, in fact, the externalist's externalist. That a thinker of his idiosyncratic brilliance and with his particular political matrix (i.e. Marxist *manqué*, anti-establishmentarian, sexual anti-hero, spokesman for all those who are sexually and mentally chained), should dwell repeatedly on the history of medicine as a primary category is endlessly fascinating in itself. That he began his career writing about discontinuities in the history of psychiatry must never be forgotten by readers interested in the historiography – especially the Enlightenment historiography – of psychology. But what perhaps ought to engage us more than the moment of Foucault or his perpetual medical interests is the formula for his literary blend. I dare to say 'ought to' because it is not easy to persuade internalist historians and internalist scientists that language, in any sense, is the crux of the matter.

THE SOCIAL HISTORY OF PSYCHOLOGY

Measured against this rhetoric of history should be the stark facts of the social history of the period's mental life – otherwise no interpretation of whatever variety, no progress in scholarship, whether internalist or externalist, linear or dialectical, can be made. The chart that follows is admittedly reductionistic and pertains to one country only, Britain, but nevertheless epitomises the germane developments as they evolved in the country most alive to humanitarian needs in the eighteenth century:

1674– James Newton opens 'a Mad-house' in Wood's Close in the parish of St James's, Clerkenwell, which flourishes until the end of the seventeenth century.[80]

1695– John Miles opens a madhouse at Hoxton in Islington, in a road just north of the present Old Street tube station.[81]

c. 1700– Lack of regulation permits relatives to incarcerate persons who are not deranged, and English law renders it almost impossible for the imprisoned to escape.

1713–14 A parliamentary effort to combine the numerous Poor Laws results in the passage of an act to shelter homeless lunatics (13 Anne, c. 26, Vagrancy). This is part of a continuing attempt to regularise and simplify laws related to vagrancy in Britain.

1715–43 Throughout the Walpole administration regulation continues; no attempt under Walpole to effect reform.[82]

1742 Parliament sets up a 'committee' to investigate solutions to problems that arise from the attempts to administer the existing vagrancy laws, including those sections concerning the nuisance of lunatics.[83]

1744 The committee makes recommendations leading to a Consolidation Act of 1713 (17 George II, c. 5), but these merely 'consolidate' the various laws enacted in 1713–14, and do not add new laws, and especially do not regulate private madhouses.

1751 St Luke's Hospital for Lunatics opens, with Dr William Battie, member of the College of Physicians, as its first physician.[84] This is the second public hospital for lunatics in England.

1751–2 Dr Battie opens a private facility for lunatic patients in the Islington Road.[85]

1753 Battie begins to admit medical students to St Luke's to permit them to observe the mentally ill firsthand.

1754 Battie assumes proprietorship of Newton's private madhouse in Wood's Close.[86]

1761 The case of Rex v. Turlington rocks England. In this case one John D'Vebre committed his allegedly insane wife to Turlington's Chelsea madhouse to rid himself of her. But her physician and relatives obtained a court order securing her release.[87]

1760–2 Tobias Smollett writes a popular novel, *Life and Adventures of Sir Launcelot Greaves*, the first to be serialised in a British magazine, satirising the conditions in private madhouses. The heroine is Aurelia Darnel, a sane woman unlawfully confined. The conditions of Aurelia's imprisonment are nowhere mentioned; Sir Launcelot Greaves, however, is confined in the same madhouse as Aurelia and treated as badly.

1763 A new 'select committee' is appointed by parliament to investigate the regulation of private madhouses but does not investigate thoroughly. It produces an insubstantial report on which parliament fails to act.[88]

1766 The Manchester Hospital for Lunatics is opened.

1774   Parliament passes an 'Act for Regulating Private Madhouses' (14
George III, c. 9) which has greater legal than administrative significance.
Kathleen Jones has admirably summed up its importance: 'Even if the
visitation envisaged by the Act had been carried out systematically and
conscientiously, the proprietors of private madhouses would have
remained almost as free from the fear of legal penalties as before. The
Act said nothing on the subject of the medical supervision of patients,
diet, overcrowding, mechanical restraint, or deliberate brutality of treatment. Its primary purpose was to provide safeguards against illegal deten-
tion, but it failed even in this simple object, since there was no means of
forcing the proprietor to comply with the orders of the Commissioners.'[89]

1777   The York Hospital for Lunatics is opened.

1788   The King's second bout of illness opens legal questions about regency
and, once again, about madness.[90]

1790   The Liverpool Hospital for Lunatics is opened.

After 1790 the pace of change, at least in England, was so accelerated
that one wonders if it should be considered in this survey. It may be that
its nature, inspired in part by certain reforms occurring in France and
reported in England almost daily, belongs to the activities of the next half
century. Be this as it may, the above reduction may demonstrate that
while things were getting better, they were nevertheless improving at a
slow pace; even one predisposed to anti-Whiggish judgements would have
to be blind not to concede that, in view of the number of years involved,
progress was slow.

In contrast, however, to this basically optimistic picture is the
country's dark side – dark so far as madness and sanity are concerned.
This aspect of the Enlightenment embraces everything other than so-called
light and reason, and has only recently grasped the attention of some of
the best students of the period: E. P. Thompson writing on crime in
Albion's Fatal Tree (1976), Lawrence Stone on problematical sexuality in
The Family, Sex and Marriage in England 1500–1800 (1796), and Foucault
on repressed sexuality in *Discipline and Punish: the Birth of the Prison*
(1977). The improvements discussed above must be balanced against this
very different state of affairs if one hopes to formulate an accurate picture
of the times.

MYSTICISM AND WITCHCRAFT: THE DARK UNDERBELLY OF
THE EIGHTEENTH CENTURY

Every epoch enjoys or suffers – depending on one's point of view – secret
cults and psychic epidemics, ranging from the Orphic rites of the ancient
Greeks to the massacre in 1979 in Guyana. Oddly enough, the eighteenth
century also witnessed a mass suicide in Guyana. This fact is not recorded
to reawaken interest in Guyana or claim modernity for the eighteenth

century, but rather to suggest that in some essential ways, for those that cut through the superficies of historical events, centuries resemble each other. George Rosen says this about the activities of our period:

> The eighteenth century, like most other periods of history, is difficult if not impossible to characterize with a few limited phrases. It was not all enlightenment, rationalism, urbanity, and good sense. At the very time when religious enthusiasm was considered with suspicion and reproach, there appeared in several parts of Europe and America religious groups and movements which found a characteristic expression not only in their doctrines but equally in strange bodily agitations and extravagant behaviour.[91]

Rosen's point is valid, especially the quip about 'all enlightenment, rationalism . . .'. But his analysis of the behaviour and appearance of these 'doctrines' and 'agitations' must engage us more:

> These include the Camisard prophets of the Cévennes in Southern France; the Jansenist convulsionaries at the cemetery of St Médard in Paris; the sect called Shakers; the Great Awakening initiated by Jonathan Edwards in New England; the early methodist movement; the mystical, enthusiastic Russian sects, particularly the group known as Chlysti; and the Jewish sects, specifically the Frankist group and the Hasidism of the Baal-Shem Tov, that developed in the wake of the messianic movement of Sabbatai Zevi. To discuss these developments in detail would exceed the bounds of this presentation, and I shall limit myself to the essential features of some of them.

Rosen's 'essential features' are those noticed by every historian: the mass rituals, occult ceremonies, secret divinations practised in dens of sorcerers and conducted in gothic surroundings; but one wonders why no one has followed his lead and fathomed the whole story of these movements of 'great awakening' in England and France.

As early as 1677 John Webster, the radical reformer of the English universities and a practising physician, connected witchcraft with mental illness and magic with derangement. In *The Displaying of Witchcraft* Webster affirmed 'that there are many sorts of deceivers and imposters' who are 'but divers persons under a passive delusion of melancholy and fancy'.[92] But the medical doctors did not take up the cudgels for Webster: only preachers and other clerical types did, pouring forth a literature *contra* enthusiasm on grounds that it was but insanity in disguise. These ephemera, as Christopher Hill has shown in various of his books,[93] were directed primarily against 'radical madness', the insanity of a carefree nation overrun by political rebels. William Erbery's *The Mad Mans[sic] Plea* (1653) is an example of the genre in the century before the one of interest here. After 1688 and the Revolution, political circumstances change 'the island of Great Bedlam': there is less enthusiasm and, conse-

quently, less radical madness. From roughly 1700 onward this variety
of insanity is replaced by the derangement that results from wretched
environment, ill-starred love, and, of course, in Dr Battie's words, the
'ill-conditioned state of the nerve'.

One brief interlude, however, rocked the island at the beginning of
the century, the history of which remains to be told. This is the episode
of the French Camisard prophets. They had revolted in 1704 and virtually
disappeared into England after that time.[94] Some Camisards committed
suicide and others migrated into the hinterlands of central Europe; but
those who fled to Britain gained quite a few followers, not the least
vocal among whom were Sir Richard Bulkeley, the Irish baronet who
established a 'cult' at Dunlavan in county Wicklow,[95] and John Lacy, the
fanatical Englishman who was known to many of the wits including
Addison, Steele, Defoe, Swift, Whiston, and D'Urfey.

Both Bulkeley and Lacy spoke 'in tongues', prophesied hard days
for England, and gained many hundreds of English converts to the 'French
religion of the Camisards'.[96] For ten or twelve years their influence was
considerable: witness, for example, the sheer size of the British satirical
literature directed against them in the years 1707–9.[97] But after the death
of Queen Anne they seem to have become extinct, never to be reinvigorated in a similar shape or form, not even in the fanatical excesses of George
Whitefield. This is not the place to speculate about the reasons for their
temporary success in Britain, yet Rosen is surely correct to notice that the
French prophets 'did not allow the tradition of ecstatic trance and violent
transport to die out' and that these are the psychic phenomena that
interested the British. But it is impossible, without the performed research,
to know precisely what region of the mind of the average person in
England and France they occupied. Historians of the Quaker movement
in eighteenth-century England, for example, continue to suggest that the
country 'practised' far more agitation and ecstasy than we usually think
and that much of this supernatural experience has literally been obliterated
by prolific 'Whig historians' such as George Saintsbury and George Trev-
elyan who have a vested interest in propagating myths about the peaceful
eighteenth century as an Age of Reason; but it is impossible to generalise
adequately, let alone authoritatively, about this aspect without a thorough
revaluation of the religion of the century.[98]

In France the darkness regarding madness and sanity was somewhat
less intense. Eighteenth-century France was more centrally organised than
England in the regulation of its asylums. Its national programme built
public hospitals for the mentally deranged and administered them more
adequately than the English did theirs. France did not have 'private madhouses' *per se*, and there are no equivalents in France of the English
legislation of 1713–14, 1744 and 1774; what private asylums there were

existed at the discretion of the landlord or manager of the property. These distinctions, however, may not do justice to the differences between the two countries. The clue is the legal action, described above, of 1774: regulation of the insane, especially the type of treatment they ought to receive, was frequently discussed in England before this date, but until 1774 lunatics were merely considered as a subgroup of vagrants.[99] Not until then did the British government do anything genuine to help lunatics *qua* lunatics. All these differences may combine to explain why the activities of the Jansenist convulsionaries at the Parisian cemetery of St Médard, mentioned *en passant* by Rosen, are to be expected, and why one can readily conceive that the common people of France were far more capable than the English of embracing such religious enthusiasm. Robert Favre, the contemporary French social historian, has recently demonstrated that French conceptions of death in the period had deep-rooted medical implications, especially in the area of 'God-willed illness'.[100] Here, again, is an aspect in which the two countries differed significantly: the secularising effects of English medicine had occurred before 1700 and influenced, in turn, popular conceptions of disease, dying, and the life after death. Such differences between French and English medicine and religion, and the differing governmental policies towards each, cause one to wonder whether a 'national approach' to the historiography of psychology in the eighteenth century is not sensible after all.

Considering England again, far more knowledge about the undercurrents of popular psychology can be gained by microscopic examination of the 'enthusiastic' aspects of methodism, a field barely tapped, and the rites of secret societies such as the Medmenham Monks and the Beef-Eaters, than by cross-cultural comparisons of England and France, France and Holland, Holland and Spain, and so forth. It is true that the clubs were not religious cults as such; but they reached out to the contemporary religions, especially radical dissenting ones, to propagate their private rites and ceremonies – for example in the religious ecstasies and erotic activities of the 'Monks'. The methodological difficulty here is that so much of the evidence needed to reconstruct these so-called 'cults' has disappeared, or was never written in the first place.[101] Furthermore, sociological factors involving class structure, political position, and psychological environment (i.e. urban planning, architecture, available space) also influence the reasons why these various clubs existed in the first place. Then there is the zone of the erotic imagination, especially the fantasy life, of the period, a territory illuminated in erotica, in controversial tracts on *Onania*, and, of course, in the imaginative literature of the day. The imaginative literature in England is illustrated by the fictions of Defoe, Richardson, Cleland, and Sterne, but even more lucidly by the works of those female novelists who gazed into the world of 'male sexual fantasy': Mary Manley's *The*

Adventures of Rivella (1714); Mary Davys's *The Accomplish'd Rake* (1727); Charlotte Charke's *The History of Henry Dumont esq* (1755); and, most notably, Eliza Heywood's *Love in Excess* (1719), *The Secret History of the Present Intrigues of the Court at Caramania* (1727) and *Life's Progress through the Passions* (1748).

Methodism, on the other hand, is a less difficult phenomenon to get hold of: from the differences between a Wesley and Whitefield one can gauge, even at this removal of time, what factors must have influenced the people, and in what ways they were being affected by social progress. But all this, perhaps surprisingly, has not been done, and remains an open territory for the historian of culture, especially the historian with a broad gaze who can integrate various areas of human concern.

Nevertheless, it is one thing to study the 'radical fringes' of a culture and another to determine norms and middle grounds for that culture at large – for its degree of superstition and its submission to a popular mythology. One can summarise, as George Rosen did, the mystical traditions of the century, which ranged in scope from the activities of those just discussed to the various Masonic orders, Rosicrucian sects, and other heterodox cults. But bibliographical summary, as all will agree, is one thing and exploration with a view to microscopic analysis another; and unless these in-depth studies are correlated with the conservative and middle zones of eighteenth-century psychological behaviour they will lack significance and expose themselves to charges of triviality. This, *au fond*, is the inadequacy of books such as Knox's *Enthusiasm*. It is excellent in what it attempts – the charting of the evolution of religious enthusiasm throughout English culture – but it hardly synthesizes its terrain, synthesis being the only attribute that would give it a context meaningful enough for one to know how to interpret it. And then the late author, a prominent member of the Catholic Church, was so confident about his own point of view of 'the true God' that his bias is soon evident. It is true that Peter Gay, the German-born Yale historian, has performed this act of synthesis for the 'century of illumination',[102] but he has, alas, so very little to say about psychic epidemics, extravagant behaviour and strange bodily agitations; and, furthermore, he has such a simplistic teleology of improvement, that one cannot imagine him seriously perplexed, as was Rosen, with the dark underbelly or radical fringe of his period. At the very least, these topics remain desiderata.

SAINTS AND HAGIOGRAPHERS: THE 'GREAT SCHOLARS'

The number of pioneering scholars in the field of psychology is few. If the criterion is seminal books, then this assertion gathers strength. There have been two kinds of metaphorical saints: those who have discovered significant new information, and those who have surveyed the whole field. The former group, as I shall try to demonstrate, sometimes interprets as well and sometimes does not; the latter spends all its time assimilating and interpreting.

Precisely how our 'saints' interpret is another matter: what values, assumptions, even political predispositions do they bring to the act of interpretation? With the exception of one case (i.e. Hunter and Macalpine), which I have already discussed (see p. 68 above), the group that has discovered significant new information has strangely not been accorded greater scholarly kudos than the broad surveyors. Indeed there is every reason to believe that many students of the subject cannot tell the difference between the two groups. So little attention is given to historiography in the history of medicine that most practitioners do not even know what it is, or how it differs from history.[103] Scholars since 1950 who properly ought to be considered in the first group – those who 'discover' – include, as already mentioned, Richard Hunter and Ida Macalpine, a team which has compiled the single most important anthology of primary documents with critical commentary.[104] Also to be included are Kathleen Grange, who studied British psychological theory in the 'age of Johnson',[105] C. A. Moore, the American literary historian, who first pointed out the significance of the condition melancholy in imaginative literature from the time of Dryden to that of Sterne,[106] and George Rosen, whose important work has already been discussed. All five followed on the heels of Gregory Zilboorg, M.D., discussed above, who also engaged in primary research. But most of Zilboorg's work was completed by 1950, the agreed-upon point of departure for this appraisal of the historiography of psychology, and whereas it is admittedly an arbitrary date, it nevertheless compels omission of one scholar, one saint, without whose work the landscape of this field would look altogether different.[107] This is not because Zilboorg discovered a multitude of facts unknown before, but rather because he established the categories and the framework in which Enlightenment psychology has been viewed ever since: rational and irrational, normative and aberrant, accepted and unaccepted, prevalent and scarce, in fact all the categories and assumptions underlying the essay the reader now reads, with the exception of those dealing with the politics of knowledge (my concluding section) and the territory of historiography.

The second group – those who survey – has had somewhat less impact on the subject and includes those who have written histories such as those discussed above. With the possible exception of George Mora's *oeuvre* and Franz Alexander's, which are eclectic and refine their points by assessing a variety of contributing factors, most similar 'histories' are derivative.[108] For example, if one were to isolate a theme such as the condition of madhouses or the theory of the mentally ill, and were to examine books where these subjects are treated, it would soon become evident that each 'history' had consulted its predecessors – in most cases plundered its ideas from those works. It may even be true that some recent structuralist obsessions with 'origins' (although it would be nonsense to imply that all the structuralists have been interested in this question) are applicable here:[109] namely, that unless one goes back to the earliest 'histories' of insanity, such as those written in the 1790s, one cannot comprehend why the categories of our post-1950 surveys exist.

Among the various 'saints' Foucault is the exception, an anomaly in both classes, perhaps because he is a philosopher of sorts rather than an historian. He has performed in both groups: presented new information, especially in the resuscitation of obscure eighteenth-century French medical theory, and he has written many 'histories', such as the *Histoire de la folie*[110] and the multi-volume series dealing with the history of sexuality.[111] He stands alone in our hagiography because his point of view is oblique. His politics shapes his 'histories' to such a degree, and his language is so rhetorically charged, that his contribution to each category – both the new information offered and the resulting survey – must be viewed sceptically. Politics and rhetoric do not render him a lesser 'saint', indeed there is reason to believe that he will be read when others discussed in this essay have been long forgotten, but he will be read as 'literature' rather than 'scientific history'. Moreover, I believe that Foucault's works, especially his 'histories' (I use this term cautiously) of madness and sexuality, will be more appreciated when he is dead and his biography made known – when all the parts of his life, as it were, can be viewed organically. Only then will it be clear what emphasis Foucault has given to the period of the Enlightenment in all his medico-historical works. Fortunately, Foucault's style is growing less rather than more obscure. But even in his most recent volumes the language is dense and opaque, and his blend of considered elements consistently elusive. All this notwithstanding, he is the one writer, if one had to choose, who seems to know how to revolutionise the field: first by selecting it and elevating it to new significance;[112] then by discovering arcane primary materials and integrating them (whether he reads them or not) with his political and linguistic beliefs; and finally by constructing a matrix of thought in such compelling prose language that others hypnotically forget their own work under the compulsion to read and assimilate his. For no one else writing about the life sciences in the Enlightenment can the same be said. One must grant that an exception is found in the work of Gilles Deleuze. His massive project on schizophrenia and society is as important as Foucault's various histories. One volume, written in collaboration with Félix Guattari, has already appeared: *L'Anti-Oedipe* (Paris, 1972), and a second entitled *Schizo-analyse* is in preparation. But Deleuze is not read very much outside France, and that is why I have omitted discussion of his works here.

The *raison d'être* for treating of supposed 'saints' in the first place is to weigh their comparative merits. It is the single moment in a topical survey such as this one when one can stand away and compare, place substance beside substance and imagine its worth in eternity. In this connection it may not be unprofitable to compare the work of Foucault with that of George Rosen.[113] One is French; the other American. Foucault's training was humanistic, largely philosophical; Rosen's was medical – he came rather late to medical history. Foucault reads mostly French, the language of 95 per cent of his citations; Rosen read and cited in all languages, even Polish, Russian, Czech, Japanese. Foucault uses the footnote sparingly; Rosen used it profusely. Foucault's language is dense, grammatically paratactic, highly metaphoric; Rosen's prose antithetical to Foucault's. Foucault's academic posts have been in the 'history of systems of thought' – although the American universities have recently offered him visiting professorships in literature; Rosen, at least for the last ten years of his life, was professor of medical history and epidemiology at Yale. Foucault has no professional medical training; Rosen was both M.D. and Master of Public Health. Foucault and Rosen dwell on the same crucial period: the end of the eighteenth century. Each covers the very same chronological years in some of his books, but no one reading *Histoire de la folie* and *Madness in Society* side by side could possibly contend that the two books have anything in common except their historical period.

This is not the place to extend the survey. Suffice it to say that while Rosen thought and wrote as an empiricist – finding his material, finding out what others had said about it, and then reporting it without an axe to grind – Foucault never worked or works in this way. The last thinker to have empirical tendencies, he is a thoroughgoing rationalist, a system-builder no less than Descartes, Hegel or Kant. An original thinker with an original mind, his medico-historical terrain is merely a touchstone from which to spring to his own hypotheses. Whether these hypotheses are capable of verification; whether two independent researchers would confirm any of his findings; whether his notion of the evolution of 'Enlightenment madness' is 'scientifically' valid is far less important to Foucault than the fact – the blatant fact – that they are *his* hypotheses. Among recent 'saints' he is our thinker, Rosen our historian. A study in historiography such as this one makes the distinction palpable, hopefully even concrete.

THE POLITICS OF KNOWLEDGE: FUTURE FERMENTS

I have already suggested that many projects in the history of Enlightenment psychology are crying out for students, and I have named the main areas. It remains for me to suggest that many of these are politically determined, by which I mean that both the project (e.g. a reconsideration of the types of therapy offered lunatics in England 1750–1800) and the finished artefact (i.e. a book on this subject) will have political colouring. This is not a notion readily grasped by English-speaking scholars, who have tended, especially in America, to view all scholarship *qua* scholarship and as distinct from political considerations; but even a cursory glance at the history of European scholarship, particularly on the continent, makes it evident that the matter is not so simple. For our period, the politics of Newtonian science is today undergoing radical revision,[114] and I am going to suggest, albeit briefly, that the same is true of 'psychological science'. I would even go as far as to contend that this aspect – the politics of knowledge – has been the least understood, the least researched, and commanded the least amount of attention in all the secondary literature I have surveyed. It ought to be the theme of my essay, and is the one territory I would explore if I were writing a history rather than an historiography of psychology.

If we consider, for example, the regulation of private madhouses in eighteenth-century England, a vexing issue about which many Britons had something to say from the start to the very end of the century, it is evident that the matter is anything but straightforward. Scholars have demonstrated that it was not in the best interests of the various 'appointed committees' (who 'appointed' them is all-important) to search too hard for irregularities,[115] but no one has bothered to determine why. Those 'select committees' should be reconstructed, as Namier reconstructed parliamentary committees. For we need to know the background of the members: their moneyed interests, party affiliations, private ideologies. One wonders whether it can have been economically advantageous or politically shrewd for the committee member to overlook the irregularity of the asylums. And one asks whether there is any evidence to show that eighteenth-century 'lunatic physicians' also had vested interests; if they were in collusion with asylum owners who gave them rake-offs for incarcerated but healthy patients about whom the physician had lied. The Batties and Pinels, men of standards and character surely, are exceptions – humanitarians in an age often barbarically insensitive to the needs of the mentally ill – but one learns almost nothing about the others in recent literature.

Explanations of the melancholy and hysteria endemic to women and certain segments of the upper classes in the eighteenth century have also suffered somewhat from a low threshold of explanation. It is true that much has been written in the last twenty years about 'the English malady'.[116] Yet, curiously, no one has gazed at the politics of melancholy: at the *social* fibre of the organism, at its economic, sociological, political dimensions, especially the political allegiances of patient and physician in a relationship that was clearly understood by both. It is now widely accepted that melancholy was then the most fashionable of diseases; that it afflicted the rich far more than the poor (although the literature boasts some bizarre cases where it touched the poor);[117] that it especially attacked high-class women; and that the flood of remedies, not merely pills and potions, that were administered to cure it often made millionaires out of those dispensing them.[118]

But the politics, especially the economics, of the matter has not been explored. The hypothesis, for instance, that those patenting 'melancholic medicines' paid a commission to ministers who praised them and news-papers that advertised them has not been investigated – although it may be the only reason medicines were advertised so regularly in the main London newspapers. This is a case in which economic historians have not ventured into medical fields and vice versa. Nor has the notion that hypochondria is a socially explicable phenomenon been studied in any detail by historians. Surely it was fashionable to be melancholic; the imaginative literature of the period, both in England and France, assures us of this. It was a trademark of upper-class gentility. Thus all types of socially mobile women, such as Moll Flanders in Defoe's novel, Miss Harlowe in Richardson's *Clarissa Harlowe*, and Elizabeth Bennett in Austen's *Pride and Prejudice*, to mention the three best-known heroines among dozens of similar types, may have developed their melancholy for purely social reasons, as 'signs' in the semiotic sense of a certain class conscious-ness, unaware that they were 'contracting' the awful condition. But the dynamics of contraction are not so facile as this: money-seeking doctors and apothecaries are involved; so-called 'patients' are involved; theorists spinning out large tomes are involved, as are their all-too-obscure pub-lishers; resorts and spas, such as Bath and Tunbridge Wells, are involved; newspapers and magazines – the media – are involved; a host of appurten-ances including 'melancholic gowns' and alleged 'pharmaceutical panaceas' are involved; and all these exist in the realm of the concrete. Nothing as yet has been said about these in the 'realms of gold', the imagination: literature, art, even music, where a myth begins to develop about the melancholic composer. To relate the whole story dynamically would further understanding of our period;[119] but it requires extensive research as yet not undertaken. What it reveals may change our whole sense of the politics of madness.

Another direction research ought to take is toward the relationship of psychology to other arts. This is, admittedly, a more nebulous field than most medical historians like to elect but nevertheless one whose history is very much needed at the present time. The Enlightenment is replete with 'mad' poets, 'mad' painters, 'mad' musicians; yet their alleged madness has generally been construed in narrow terms, viewed as a black-and-white issue. The existing biographies of some of these figures make this evident,[120] yet the advances of social history today render the approach defective and incomplete. Continuing in this suggestive vein is the representation of dementia and other mental states in the arts: insanity portrayed in painting and etching, especially in the self-analyses of such possessed lunatics as Christoph Haizmann (the Austrian painter) and in the caricature art enjoyed so much in the Enlightenment. We direly need an iconography of mental illness and mental states; nothing at present even remotely approximates this.[121]

Further along lines of social history, it would be surprising if political factors did not influence artists in the representation of mental conditions and mental states, but one ought not to pronounce before sufficient research has been undertaken. Likewise for the so-called 'sensibility movement' and for the 'melancholic conditions' discussed: its victims, if they may be called such, and symptoms are patent, as is the jargon of melancholy, by now an almost foreign tongue including a vernacular of words about black and white bile and neologisms barely known today. 'When I first dabbled in this art', Nicholas Robinson, the popular London 'hyp doctor', writes in a rare confessional mood just after George II had been crowned, 'the old distemper call'd *Melancholy* was exchang'd for *Vapours*, and afterwards for the *Hypp*, and at last took up the now current [1728] appellation of the *Spleen*, which it still retains, tho' a learned doctor of the west, in a little tract he hath written, divides the *Spleen* and the *Vapours*, not only into the *Hypp*, the *Hyppos*, and the *Hyppocons*; but subdivides these divisions into the *Markambles*, the *Moonpalls*, the *Strong-Fiacs*, and the *Hockogrokles*.'[122] None of these words is found in medical dictionaries, of the present or of the eighteenth century. Yet it is important to determine the extent and diversity of this jargon, particularly as a clue to the political, economic and social aspects of the condition. Even when that is accomplished more remains to be explained: namely the ways in which a medical or pseudo-medical condition, validated by the entire medical profession, was enlarged into a national myth, at least in Britain. Such mythology, as it deserves to be called, has still not been interpreted, neither its sociology nor its politics. Yet many of those who were afflicted continued successful, in clinical terms enjoying the secondary gain of the illness. Some of the 'gain' reflected the fact that, although suffering, they were succeeding professionally; some the old belief – as old as Burton's *Anatomy* – that melancholy of whatever type of Burton's eighty-eight varieties, had beneficial as well as negative aspects.

It is, therefore, not remarkable that James Adair, the astute Scottish physician, would write:

After the death of Anne and the demise of the 'Wits' there arose a fashionable disease the likes of which had never been seen in England. Some call'd it melancholy, others by names too various to be enlisted here; but one thing about its development was clear: it enjoyed a 'progress' as distinct as that of any medical condition, and it is known that it became a fashionable disease only at that time, and that persons of all manner wanting to advance themselves suddenly developed it.[123]

This is a fine passage, revelatory for the historian, but it probably will not suffice for decoding the complex phenomenon that C. A. Moore has called 'an age of melancholy'.[124] For that, its politics, the ways persons 'advanced themselves' professionally, must first be decoded, then its semiology interpreted.[125] This is why the politics of knowledge is so crucial to any study of the historiography of psychiatry and psychology in every age, not merely in the Enlightenment.

There are other urgent areas too. No one has asked why there is no adequate history of 'sensibility', a concept without understanding of which the psychology of the age dissolves. No one, it seems, has wondered how idiosyncratic was Dr Johnson's notorious fear of 'diseased imagination' – i.e. madness – and whether it had cultural determinants without which he would not have dreaded it so direly.[126] Recently there have been several studies of lunatics in literature, but drawn without enough sense of the cultural landscape to provide an interpretation that explains anything.[127] No one has related this social background to Smollett's penultimate novel, *Life and Adventures of Launcelot Greaves*, the work of imaginative fiction 'in the manner of Cervantes' already mentioned, whose main theme is madness.[128] This prose treatise of over 100,000 words needs to be analysed for its references to madness, as well as dissected for the 'mythology' of madness it provides. And if one inquiries why, the answer will be found in Freud's essay on 'Mourning and melancholia': 'The description of the human mind is indeed the domain which is not his [the creative writer's] own; he has from time immemorial been the precursor of science, and so too of scientific psychology.'[129] No scholars have concerned themselves, moreover, with the interpretations that arise when sheer 'teleological history' is written, or when national boundaries are not crossed.[130] Nor has anyone conjectured about the relation of sexual repression in the Enlightenment to consequential madness, a correlation that physicians in the twentieth century believe to be practically infallible.[131]

These and other questions are large, and they ask for much – perhaps too much for a young field, medical history, still thought by some to be in infancy.[132] Nevertheless, there is a common denominator among these desiderata that includes first the need to explore the social history of the period and then the necessity of interpreting it more imaginatively and daringly than has been done. The question, of course, is whether it ought to be interpreted as inventively and idiosyncratically as Foucault (and now Deleuze) has done: that is to say, to a degree that places 'the threshold of possible explanation', as Foucault has commented in the epigraph at the beginning of this essay, 'too high'.

In conclusion, this threshold may be too complicated. Certainly it is too high for the internalists who still view such a modest and cautious externalist as George Rosen – let alone the likes of a Foucault or Deleuze – with suspicion. These French thinkers stand apart from a Rosen and any number of other externalists by maintaining that at the moment when one decides to write about a state of affairs in human history one assumes the burden of coping with 'discourse' as opposed to the mere confrontation with 'texts', the latter construed simply as the word on the page. This is not the place to enter into discussion about the complicated differences between texts and discourses, and the implications of these differences for the history of science, but it is ultimately the reason why Foucault and Deleuze place their thresholds of explanation so high.

What remains to be charted by future students, then, is the course of externalism: not the simple history of its survival but the nature of its future life. Now, 'at the beginning of a new decade', there is every reason to believe that the internalist camp is beginning to lose ground. One sees the loss in fields other than the history of science and medicine, even in the so-called pure sciences. Certainly the internalists have lost some of the brightest young minds of the 1960s and 1970s to the externalists. Furthermore, the massive surveys included in this volume provide abundant signs of trends to come. Finally, if Foucault is indeed correct about psychiatry now enjoying such 'a low epistemological profile', then psychiatry – among the various sciences – must continue to stand in the foreground of externalist treatments; it must necessarily occupy the labours of scholars in the future who are as concerned with the social, political and economic institutions of past eras as they are with the history of psychiatry, psychology or any other science. The key issues, then, are those social institutions: their precise regulations, exigencies, manipulations, deceptions – every aspect of their nature. Only the externalist approach can begin to cope with a synthesis of the sciences of man in relation to these institutions. And it is hard to imagine in decades to come a return to internalism after the externalists have just delivered so much and promised even more.

ACKNOWLEDGEMENTS

I am grateful to Drs Gloria Gross, William Bynum, Norland Berk, Roger Hambridge and Roy Porter for commenting, sometimes harshly, on various drafts of this essay and for suggesting means by which I could focus better on the vary large terrains I attempt to cover. I am also indebted to Stephen Morris of Selwyn College and Simon Schaffer of St John's College, for discussions in Cambridge during the Michelmas term 1979 about the internalist–externalist debates. Without the unrelenting questions of the former and the enlightened provocation of the latter, I would not have known as well as I now do why I had constructed the essay as I did, and why I had to include discussion of 'the politics of knowledge'.

NOTES

1 See Nathan Bailey's *An Orthographical Dictionary* (1727), the second volume of his popular *Universäl Etymological Dictionary*, 1st ed. (1721). The first use of the term 'psychiatry', according to the *New Oxford English Dictionary*, does not occur until the early nineteenth century, but the concept is doubtless known before then. See, for example, the poet Pope's own annotation to *The Dunciad* III (A), 81–2: 'The *Caliph, Omar I*, having conquer'd Aegypt, caus'd his General to Burn the Ptolomaean library, on the gates of which was this inscription, *Medicina Animae, The Physick of the Soul*'.

2 See F. H. Lapointe, 'Who originated the term psychology?', *Journal of the History of the Behavioural Sciences*, VIII (1972), 328–35, who contends that Wolff, the German philosopher and populariser of Leibniz, was the first to use the term. For a broad survey of the term, see Lapointe's 'Origin and Evolution of the Term "Psychology" ', *American Psychologist*, XXV (1970), 640–5. Launcelot Law Whyte writes in *The Unconscious before Freud* (New York, 1960), 101–2, that Wolff 'may have been the first influential German writer to give the word *Bewusstsein* its present meaning of awareness, and that his [Wolff's] analysis of unconscious factors is clearer than that of any predecessor'.

3 See *The Whig Interpretation of History* (1931), and an important application of this theory to literary history during the Enlightenment: H. K. Miller, 'The "Whig interpretation" of Literary History', *Eighteenth-Century Studies*, VI (1972), 21–47.

4 For some of the problems involved in this distinction, see Hayden White, *Metahistory* (Baltimore, 1973), and S. Ratner, 'The Historian's Approach to Psychology', *Journal of the History of Ideas*, II (1941), 95–109.

5 I intentionally do not cite copious examples of the four types, because the ensuing notes are adequate proof in themselves. The point made in this paragraph is further assisted by these essential tools: George Mora, 'The History of Psychiatry: a Cultural and Bibliographical Survey', *International Journal of Psychiatry*, II (1966), 335–56; R. M. Young, 'Scholarship and the History of the Behavioural Sciences', *History of Science*, V (1966), 1–51; L. Zusne, *Names in the History of Psychology: a Biographical Sourcebook* (New York, 1975); O. Diethelm, *Medical Dissertations of Psychiatric Interest Printed before 1750* (Basel, 1971); and E. Clarke, *Modern Methods in the History of Medicine* (1973), discussed in the last section. Of great value also is Richard Hunter and Ida Macalpine, *Three Hundred Years of Psychiatry 1535–1860* (1963).

6 In American scholarship see E. Heischkel-Artelt, 'The Concept of Baroque Medicine in the Development of Medical Historiography', *Actes du Deuxième Congrès International d'Histoire des sciences* (Ithaca, 1962), IX, part 2, 913–6. In French scholarship see M. Gourevitch, 'La Psychiatrie française à l'époque romantiqué, *Perspectives psychiatriques*, XVI (1978), 5–99.

7 A few sources in this vast literature worthy of consultation include: G. Aigrisse, *Psychoanalyse de la Grèce antique* (Paris, 1960); Bennett Simon, M.D., *Mind and Madness in Ancient Greece* (Ithaca, 1977); E. L. Harrison, 'Notes on Homeric Psychology', *Phoenix*, XIV (1960), 63–80. A rich resource for the medieval period is E. Ruth Harvey's *The Inward Wits: Psychological Theory in the Middle Ages and Renaissance*, Warburg Institute Survey No. 6 (1975).

E

8 See Bruno Snell, *The Discovery of the Mind: the Greek Origins of European Thought*, trans. T. G. Rosenmeyer (Cambridge, 1953) and two important works by Erich Neumann, both in the Bollingen Series: *The Origins and History of Consciousness* (1970) and *Amor and Psyche* (1971).

9 See H. M. Gardiner and R. C. Metcalf *et al.*, *Feeling and Emotion: a History of Theories* (New York, 1937). Some useful remarks on this matter are also found in D. A. Schon, 'Psychiatry and the History of Ideas', *International Journal of Psychiatry*, v (1968), 320–7.

10 For an example of better and worse in one book, see L. L. Whyte, *The Unconcious before Freud* (New York, 1960), and E. L. Margetts, 'The Concept of the Unconscious in the History of Medical Psychology', *Psychiatric Quarterly*, xxviii (1953), 115–38.

11 See Margetts, *art. cit.*, 122.

12 See G. S. Rousseau (ed.), *Organic Form: the Life of an Idea* (1972), and F. Burwick (ed)., *Approaches to Organic Form* (Dordrecht, 1987).

13 An example is Richard Lowry's *The Evolution of Psychological Theory 1650 to the Present* (Chicago, 1971).

14 Other teleological histories include Walther Riese, 'The pre-Freudian Origins of Psychoanalysis', in J. H. Masserman (ed.), *Science and Psychoanalysis* (New York, 1958), 29–72; Colin Martindale, 'A Note on an 18th-century Anticipation of Freud's Theory of Dreams', *Journal of the History of the Behavioural Sciences*, vi (1970), 362–4; Richard Lowry, *The Evolution of Psychological Theory 1650 to the Present* (Chicago, 1971); Iago Galdston (ed.) *Historic Derivations of Modern Psychiatry* (New York, 1967); Hadley Cantril, *The Psychology of Social Movements* (New York, 1941); Mark D. Altschule, *Roots of Modern Psychiatry* (New York, 1965). Excellent specimens in French scholarship are René Semelaigne, *Les Grands Alienistes français* (Paris, 1894); H. Baruk, *La Psychiatrie française de Pinel à nos jours* (Paris, 1967), Bruno Cassinelli, *Histoire de la folie* (Paris, 1939). For thirty years at the turn of this century, René Semelaigne wrote 'teleological history' of psychiatry. His classic work is *Les Pionniers de la psychiatrie française avant et après Pinel*, 2 vols. (Paris, 1930–2). For the years 1950–75, a bibliography of more than fifty articles exists.

15 Whyte, *The Unconscious Before Freud* (see n. 2), 104.

16 The most eloquent of Boyle's many comments on this subject appears in *The Usefulness of Experimental Naturall Philosophy* (1663), pt 2, 3, 'Those great transactions which make such a noise in the World, and establish Monarchies or ruin Empires, reach not so many Persons with their Influence as do the Theories of Physiology.'

17 *Conjectures on Original Composition* (1759; facsimile repr. Leeds 1966), 52–3. The subject has recently been studied by S. D. Cox in ' "The stranger within thee", the Self in British Literature of the Later Eighteenth Century' (Ph.D. thesis, University of California, 1978).

18 See Kathleen Grange, 'Dr. Johnson's Account of the Schizophrenic Illness in *Rasselas* (1759)', *MH* vi (1962), 162–8, and R. B. Hovey, 'Doctor Samuel Johnson, Psychiatrist' *Modern Language Quarterly*, xv (1954), 321–35.

19 The typical remark is brief and states that Pinel reformed treatment of the mentally ill. One can readily compile a bibliography of several dozen articles written since 1950 with this as their main theme. Also a humanitarian, Vincenzo Chiarugi is the 'hero' for Italian Enlightenment psychiatry. See, as one example, A Balli (ed.) *Onoranze a Vincenzo Chiarugi nel secondo centenario* (Empoli, 1961); there are many others. The Americans did not have an equivalent; for a valuable survey of available care, see D. M. Blackman, 'The Care of the Mentally Ill in America, 1604–1812, in the Thirteen Original Colonies, *Nursing Research Conference*, ii (1968), 65–113. Recently, Milos Bondy has argued in xvi (1972), 293–6, that Johann Ernst Greding (1718–75), the German physician interested in the classification of mental diseases, has been overlooked. Kathleen Grange has epitomised this trend in her article, 'Pinel or Chiarugi?' *Medical History*, vii (1963), 371–80.

20 See P. Bassoe, 'Spain as the Cradle of Psychiatry', *American Journal of Psychiatry*, CI (1945), 731–8. Bassoe notes (p. 731) that Pinel himself had written in the *Traité médico-philosophique*, 2nd ed. (Paris, 1809), 238, that 'we must look to a neighbour for an example [of humanitarian reform of lunatics]; not to England or Germany, but to Spain'. This point seems not to have been mentioned again in the secondary literature until E. Ullersperger endorsed the Pinelian attitude toward Spanish reform in *Die Geschichte der Psychologie und der Psychiatrie in Spanien* (Wurzburg, 1871). But the matter turns out to be 'nationalistic' in the ways I described above. For Pinel did not personally view the Spanish asylums until 1808, long after he had written the first version of the *Traité* (Paris, 1801), in which this passage does not appear; and even in the first edition of 1801 he advocates massive reform of existing French hospitals. Outside Spain there is no study of Piquér's medical works. Of particular interest for this theory of insanity is his 'Discurso sobre la enfermedad del Rey Ferdinando', in *Colleciones de documentos inéditos para la historia de España*, XVIII (118 vols., Madrid, 1842–95), 156–226. This work was not published until 1851 and was unknown to Pinel; the original manuscript is still in the personal library of the Duke of Osuña.

21 Two exceptions are notable: see Lawrence Stone, *The Family, Sex and Marriage in England 1500–1800* (1976), and Randolph Trumbach, *Rise of the Egalitarian Family* (New York, 1978).

22 See W. F. Bynum, 'Rationales for Therapy in British Psychiatry: 1780–1835, *Medical History* XVIII (1974), 317–34. Also important as background to Pinel is Kathleen M. Grange, 'Pinel and Eighteenth-century Psychiatry', *Bulletin for the History of Medicines*, XXXV (1961), 442–53; E. A. Woods and E. T. Carlson, The Psychiatry of Philippe Pinel', *Bulletin for the History of Medicines*, XXXV (1961), 14–25; W. Riese, *The Legacy of Pinel: an Inquiry into Thought on Mental Alienation* (New York, 1969); B. Mackler, *Pinel: Unchainer of the Insane* (New York, 1968).

23 Samuel Tuke, *Description of the Retreat, an Institution near York, for Insane Persons* (York, 1813).

24 Bynum, 'Rationales' (see n.22), 324).

25 The fullest account of the king's 'madness' is found in Ida Macalpine and Richard Hunter, *George III and the Mad-Business* (1969). Sect. 4, 'Georgian psychiatry', 269–347, deals with the subject.

26 There is a difference of opinion about the moment when medicine became a true 'profession' in Britain. See Susan F. Cannon, *Science in Culture* (New York, 1978), 'Professionalization', esp. 137–41.

27 See George Rosen, *Madness in Society* (Chicago, 1968). Rosen's survey broke new ground but made no pretence of having covered *social* attitudes. Stone's book (see n.21), the more useful, is a goldmine of primary information; but madness is, unfortu-antely, not among the topics related to the author's constellation of 'marriage and the family'.

28 Actually the Carlylean tendency to view the history of human achievement as a succession of inexplicable geniuses arbitrarily bestowing knowledge upon mankind has never been abandoned. Certain origins of the nineteenth-century concept are found in my 1976 Clark Lecture in the University of California. See G. S. Rousseau, 'Sir John Hill, Universal Genius *Manqué*', in D. J. Greene (ed.) *The Renaissance Man in the Eighteenth Century* (Los Angeles, 1978).

29 Some comment on the historiography of each of these three fields is necessary. (1) In this case the information is difficult to locate and those who attempt to treat it usually say little about the period before 1790 (see, for example, W. Parry-Jones, *The Trade in Lunacy* (1972)). A. D. Morris's *The Hoxton Madhouses* (1958, privately printed), is an exception but it is practically unavailable. (2) The two best-known studies are Ilza Veith, *Hysteria: the History of a Disease* (Chicago, 1965), and C. A. Moore, 'The Age of Melancholy', in *Backgrounds of English Literature* (Minneapolis, 1953), but each is incomplete or defective, Veith because she neglects the eighteenth century, a period

that ought to have been her most important, and Moore because he is a literary scholar – and although he valued research and engaged in plenty of it, he was ultimately unaware of the history of medicine. More useful than either of these is John F. Sena's unpublished study, 'The English Malady: the Idea of Melancholy from 1700 to 1760' (Princeton University dissertation, 1967) and his *Bibliography of Melancholy 1660–1800* (1970). (3) Melancholy has of course been studied by many, but everyone overlooks its most significant side: the sociology of melancholy in an epoch that made it the most fashionable of diseases (see p. 000 below).

30 The historian of this variety may also be entrapped unawares by metaphors of flow and culmination. An example is found in the entrapment of Y. Pelicier in *Histoire de la psychiatrie* (Paris, 1976).

31 I am unaware of any history of medicine, except that of Karl Figlio in *HS*, which studies this particular matrix: the relation of the development of anatomy and physiology to religious and secular patterns. This is what is called for, and what one ought to keep calling for.

32 Cambridge, 1978. King does not address himself specifically to psychology but the kinship is implicit in the medicine he studies, and especially discussed in his chapter on 'Imagination'.

33 I.e. melancholy and hysterical diseases arising from the structure and sympathy of the nerves. The most authoritative account of Whytt's philosophical medicine – 'philosophical' because the soul plays such an important role and because the tradition of Descartes's dualism looms so large – is R. K. French's *Robert Whytt, the Soul, and Medicine* (1969). About the methodology invoked in Whytt's *Observations*, French comments (31): 'Apart from the prefatory chapter on the structure and sympathy of the nerves, Whytt writes primarily as a practising doctor; his interest is in the treatment of the diseases, and his efforts to understand the causes are directed toward that end.' French is right to reduce to two categories all nervous diseases in Whytt's classification: 'Sufferers from nervous diseases . . . on the whole fall into two categories, those in otherwise good health whose "uncommon delicacy" of the nervous system renders them liable to disturbance from any unusual internal or external circumstance, and those with a constant weakness in one or more of the seats of hupochondria or hysteria' (39).

34 Herschel Baker, 'The body–soul relationship', in *The Image of Man* (Cambridge, 1947), 275–92, is an eloquent statement of the Renaissance view. See also R. L. Anderson, *Elizabethan Psychology and Shakespeare's Plays* (1927).

35 This can best be grasped in papers delivered at the symposium on *The History of the Brain and its Functions*, ed. F. N. L. Poynter (1958). Also see L. G. Ballester, 'Diseases of the Soul (*Nosemata tes psyches*) in Galen: the Imposition of a Galenic Psychotherapy', *Clio Medica*, IX (1974), 35–43; Edwin Clarke, 'Aristotelian Concepts of the Form and Function of the Brain', *Bulletin for the History of Medicine*, XXXVII (1963), 1–14; A. C. Crombie, 'Early Concepts of the Senses and the Mind', *Scientific American*, CCX (1964), 108–16.

36 The literature is too vast even to be epitomised, but one will find discussion in any serious work treating of seventeenth-century dualism.

37 I have adopted some of T. S. Khun's language here from *Structure of Scientific Revolutions* (Chicago, various eds.). Willis is often viewed either in the narrow biographical sense – as a scientist without a life or milieu – or as one of several anatomists who contributed to brain theory. I have yet to see an integrated study of his contribution that combines the fields discussed here. It would be useful if Willis were placed in a wider context than he has been in the past. Some clues are afforded by consulting W. J. Dodds, the minor Scottish physiologist, 'On the Localization of the Functions of the Brain: Being an Historical and Critical Analysis of the Brain', *Journal of Anatomy and Physiology*, XII (1878), 340–63, 454–94, 636–60, valuable for demonstrating how a history of 'brain theory' was envisioned, and Karl Figlio's study of 'Theories of Perception and the

Physiology of the Mind in the Late Eighteenth Century', *History of Science*, XIII (1975), 177–212. The type of approach I am arguing against here constricts the contribution of Willis and unnecessarily limits it; see Horace W. Magoun, 'Early Development of Ideas Relating the Mind with the Brain,' in G. E. W. Wolstenholme *et al* (eds.) *Ciba Foundation Symposium on the Neurological Basis of Behaviour* (1958), 4–22, and A. Meyer and Raymond Hierons, 'A Note on Willis' Views on the *corpus striatum* and the External Capsule', *Journal of Neurological Science*, 1 (1964), 547–54.

38 Walter Bromberg's *The Mind of Man: a History of Psychotherapy and Psychoanalysis* (New York, 1959) is no exception: it cursorily dismisses our period and the little it says about it is what every university student already knows.

39 Most contemporary neurologists are persuaded that 'break-throughs' in brain theory will be discovered in the fields of anatomy and physiology. Such predisposition may change; at the present time there seems to be no doubt that contemporary research has laid its faith there. For a forceful statement of contemporary views, see Stephen Rose, *The Conscious Brain in Modern Research* (New York, 1973).

40 We have no history of psychosomatic medicine, let alone one that emphasised the Enlightenment. Valuable information is found in L. J. Rather's *Mind and Body in Eighteenth-Century Medicine: a Study based on Jerome Gaub's 'De Regimine Mentis'* (1965), but not even the author would contend that this specialised study could pass muster as a history of psychosomatic theory in the eighteenth century.

41 I have surveyed aspects of the reciprocity in 'Nerves, Spirits and Fibres: Towards Defining the Origins of Sensibility – with a Postscript 1976,' in A. Giannitrepanni (ed.), *The Blue Guitar* (Rome, 1976), II 125–53. This essay originally appeared without any postscript in R. F. Brissenden and C. Eade (eds.), *Studies in the Eighteenth Century*, III, *Proceedings of the David Nichol Smith Conference* (Canberra, 1975), 137–57, (also chap. 5 below).

42 See note 32 above.

43 Further evidence of this assertion is found in King's papers on the relation of philosophy and medicine. Especially see 'Stahl and Hoffman: a Study in Eighteenth-century Animism', *Journal of the History of Medicine*, XIX (1964), 118–30; 'Basic Concepts of Eighteenth-century Animism', *American Journal of Psychology*, CCXIV (1967), 797–807; and *The Road to Medical Enlightenment 1650–1695* (New York, 1970).

44 Those not wishing to use technical language speak of 'the passions' and develop a quasi-scientific theory of the passions and their role in psychological behaviour; others, more physiologically inclined, discuss the ventricles of the brain, often arguing that the front ventricle seats the imagination, the middle ventricle reason, and the rear ventricle memory. The clergy upholding an Augustinian world-view still considers 'psyche-ology' to be the moral *logos* of the soul and its significant choices. Yet an author such as P. Récamier, discusses none of these historical developments in *Le Psychanalyste sans divan* (Paris, 1970), purportedly a history of psychiatric institutions. For some significant discussion of these matters, see B. C. Ross, *Psychological Thought within the Context of the Scientific Revolution 1665–1700* (Durham, 1970), who has discovered that '19% (367) of the papers published in the *Philosophical Transactions* from 1665 to 1700 were relevant to psychological thought'.

45 George Cheyne, *The English Malady: or, a Treatise of Nervous Diseases of All Kinds* (1733), 66.

46 William Battie, *A Treatise on Madness* (1758), 34. Battie's explanation of madness is almost entirely, if not entirely, anatomic. The 'ill conditioned state of the nerve' derives from a defect in the fibres enveloping the nerves. Poorly constituted fibres simply will not shield the nerves from trauma and excitement. As a consequence, 'sensation of the nervous or medullary fibres, tho' they continue the same, will be in a reverse proportion to the cohesion of those minute particles which constitute the solid and elastic fibres. And in fact we find that Anxiety is almost always the consequence of morbid laxity' (p. 35). It is therefore not surprising that Battie should conclude the following relation

between madness and physiology: 'No wonder is it then that the straining or loosening the solid parts of human bodies should frequently render those bodies liable to be violently affected by such objects as are scarce felt or attended to by other men, who enjoy a natural or artificial strength and compactness of fibres' (p. 36).

47 See 'Locke's Realism', in *Philosophy, Science, and Perception* (Baltimore, 1964), and J. Yolton (ed.), *John Locke: Problems and Perspectives* (Cambridge, 1969). Also, see David B. Klein, *A History of Scientific Psychology, its Origins and Philosophical Backgrounds* (New York, 1970). So far as I am aware no scholarly study exists of the reception of Locke's theories in France 1690–1780 and their influence on psychological theory there in pre-Pinelian days.

48 There is no adequate study of theories of memory in the period, but for Hartley and psychology see R. Hoeldtke, 'The History of Associationism and British Medical Psychology', *Medical History*, xi (1967), 46–65, and B. Rand, 'The Early Development of Hartley's Doctrine of Association', *Psychological Review*, xxx (1923), 306–20.

49 I have attempted to isolate some of the problems in the rationalist–empirical trends of the philosophy and medicine of the period in ' "Sowing the Wind and Reaping the Whirlwind": aspects of change in the eighteenth-century medicine', in P. J. Korshin (ed.), *Studies in Change and Revolution* (1972), 129–59. An example of the treatment received by these empiricists in this century is found in 'Frances Hutcheson and the Theory of Motives', *American Journal of Psychology*, LXXIV (1961), 625–9, and Thomas Verhave, 'Contributions to the History of Psychology', *Psychiatric Reprints*, xx (1967), 111–16.

50 On the extant letter and manuscript remains of these authors one views the true assumptions of the age better than in dictionary definitions of dreams such as E. Chambers's *An Universal Cyclopedia* (1728) or Robert James's *Medicinal Dictionary* (1745).

51 See James Carkesse, *Lucida Intervalla . . . written at Finsbury and Bethlem . . .* (1679). Dreams also have an important religious component, although this topic cannot be probed here. In the period in question many of the sermons, religious treatises, even the Book of Common Prayer, offer valuable light on the interpretation of dreams and are in themselves, as a consequence, valuable psychological manifestos. In Catholic France, the power of confession was overwhelmingly important. Throughout Europe, the guilt-laden, patriarchal, orthodox Christian framework – Enlightenment or no Enlightenment – was an extraordinary factor in personal psychological development. Nowhere is this development better documented than in the theological literature of the times.

52 See Godwin, *Caleb Williams* (New York, Mod. Lib. ed., 1950), 354. The Abbé Richard Jerome's *Théorie des songes* (Paris, 1766) is also worthwhile in this connection.

53 The interplay of philosophy, psychology and physiology is nowhere clearer than in the case at hand. It was the same surgeon, William Cheselden, whose medical works stimulated the 'philosopher' Edmund Burke, though writing as a 'psychologist,' to conceptualise his particular new theory of vision in the *Philosophical Enquiry into the . . . Sublime* (1757). See, especially, pp. 144–5 in the 1958 edition, with notes by J. T. Boulton.

54 The valid question naturally arises of whether these physicians read the books in their libraries. It is difficult to generalise except in individual cases in which a particular library and author is involved and where evidence is discovered about a particular book. Nevertheless, it is reasonable to surmise that some of the philosophical material in the libraries of medical men was being absorbed into their medical thinking, and that some part of it dealt with dreams and the passions. From no other recent source could doctors plunder it. One must also consider the libraries of physicians as status symbols, but that cannot be done here.

55 Jacob Kantor's unusual theory about Newton should be considered in this context. See his 'Newton's Influence on the Development of Psychology', *Psychological Record*,

XX (1970), 83–92, which contends that 'Newton's misleading influence upon psychology is not generally accepted' (83). Kantor's argument is that Newton's theory of perception is 'false', that it misled his contemporaries who looked to it as gospel, and that it has unfortunately been accepted 'by such eminent modern physicists as Bohr, Heisenberg, Schrödinger and Bridgman'. All this may be valid, but the scientists mentioned have held little sway over modern post-Freudian psychiatrists who now generate theory used to treat patients. However, the case was different in our period, when theories of perception were plundered by medical men, usually second hand, without questioning any of their philosophical bases. Doctors such as Robert Whytt and William Cullen were exceptions to the rule.

56 See n. 32 above. To cite two non-medical examples, see Peter Gay, *The Enlightenment, an Interpretation*, 2 vols. (New York, 1966–9) and Laurens Lauden, *Progress and its Problems* (Oxford, 1975). Gay's fourth chapter, 'The Science of Man', II 167–215, considers psychological theory solely in terms of rational speculation which, while not inaccurate, is certainly only a part of the total picture.

57 An example is the preface of William Hillary's *A Rational and Mechanical Essay on the Small Pox* (1735), in which he insists that 'medical systems must be founded on a just mechanical way of reasoning'.

58 *History of Medicine* (New York, 1929; rev. ed.), 400–2.

59 See Richard Bright, *Travels from Vienna through Lower Hungary* (Edinburgh, 1818), 87–8. Bright, consultant physician to Guy's Hospital, discovered the class of nephritic diseases that still goes by his name, and travelled extensively in central Europe.

60 Referring to Wilhelm von Kaulbach's 'Das Narrenhaus', in his series of black and white satires, and Hogarth's eighth plate in *A Rake's Progress*. See n. 115 below.

61 Garrison's note reads '[see] Monkemoller: Zur Geschichte der Psychiatrie in Hannover, Halle, 1903', and lists the journals in which portions of Monkemoller's monograph had appeared.

62 Garrison does not provide a source for the quotation; it may have been taken from one of the popular eighteenth-century pharmacopoeias such as John Quincy, *Pharmacopoeia officinalis* (1726), entry under 'tartar tartarisatus', 349–50.

63 Smollett's sources in psychology have not been studied, nor is there an authoritative edition of his work. Suggestions about these sources have been made by R. Hunter and I. Macalpine, 'Smollett's Reading in Psychiatry', *Modern Language Review*, II (1956), 409–11, who note that Smollett read Battie's *Treatise on Madness* (1758), and by P. Miles in 'Bibliography and insanity: Smollett and the mad-business', *The Library*, XXXI (1976), 205–22. See also G. S. Rousseau, 'Beef and bouillon: a voice for Tobias Smollett, with comments on his life, works and modern critics', *British Studies Monitor*, VII (winter 1977), 33–51, who comments on some of these sources.

64 The conclusion is drawn on the basis of a bibliographical search and is confirmed, in part, by Stone, *The Family, Sex and Marriage in England* (see n. 21), and by Patricia Meyer Spacks, who has studied female characters in novels written by women; see *The Female Imagination: a Literary and Psychological Investigation of Women's Writing* (1976). Some of the implications of 'female melancholy' for literary tragedy were brilliantly analysed by Walter Benjamin during the years 1924–7 in an essay entitled *Ursprung des deutschen Trauerspiels*; see George Steiner (ed.), *Walter Benjamin: the Origin of German Tragic Drama* (1977), 145–63. In *The Concepts of Illness, Disease and Morbus* (Cambridge, 1979), 88, F. Kräupl Taylor suggests that 'female hysteria' was a nosological concept whose significance so thoroughly disappeared that total reconstruction is necessary to understand the 'morbus' (his term).

65 Originally published as *Naissance de la clinique* (Paris, 1963) and then under the above title in 1973, trans. A. M. Sheridan Smith. This approach to the 'clinic' or 'hospital' as a special kind of space needs to be compared to that of J. D. Thompson and Grace Goldin in *The Hospital: a Social and Architectural History* (New Haven, 1975).

66 *Birth of the Clinic* (see n. 65), xvii–xviii.

67 The 'national histories' discussed above consider the chronological distinction important, but Foucault does not, nor does he comment on the matter.

68 *Birth of the Clinic* (see n. 65), xii.

69 *ibid.*, 20, n. 18, for the account in the *Gazette salutaire*, XXI, 2 Aug. 1764.

70 Most histories of medicine written since 1950 do not mention Meckel, nor do histories
   of psychology. The only work about him appears in German medical journals; for an
   example see H. Schierhorn, 'J. F. Meckel', *Anatomische Anzeiger*, CXXXVII (1975),
   221–56.

71 *Birth of the Clinic* (see n. 65), xvii. I have attempted to interpret Foucault's method in
   R. Allen (ed.), *The Eighteenth-Century Bibliography for 1974* (Iowa City, 1975), 790–4,
   and in 'Foucault on Madness and Civilisation', *Eighteenth-Century Studies*, IV (1970),
   90–4. Hayden White has written admirably on similar matters in 'Foucault decoded:
   notes from under-ground', *History and Theory*, XII (1971), 52–7, but he focuses on
   Foucault's method of 'deconstruction' whereas I try to demonstrate that the rhetoric
   employed permits the categories found. Other secondary studies are listed in Meaghan
   Morris and Paul Patton (eds.), *Michel Foucault: Power, Truth, Strategy* (Sydney, 1979),
   92–100. But further analysis is necessary, for Foucault's prose style has altered considerably since the 1960s, especially in one crucial aspect: before this time his implied reader
   was anonymous – everyone, every man. Afterwards, Foucault began to write with
   specific reader–scholars in mind, not merely in his short essays but in books as well.
   Thus, 'Theatrum Philosophicum', originally published in *Critique*, CCLXXXII (1970),
   885–908, and now translated into English and printed in D. Bouchard (ed.), *Language,
   Counter-memory, Practice* (Oxford, 1977), 165–96, specifically addresses Deleuze and
   Pierre Klossowski. Whole sections of this important essay are written with a specific
   reader in mind. How else can one interpret pp. 190–1 of the English version and
   Deleuze's incredible footnote on p. 191?

72 See *New York Review of Books*, XXII, 22 Jan. 1976, 18–22. It is not widely known that
   although Starobinski writes abundant literary criticism, he is a trained physician who
   holds a chair in the history of medicine at the University of Geneva. His career sheds
   light on the boundaries of knowledge – philosophy, psychology, physiology – studied
   in this chapter. The same Starobinski who writes impressionistically about Rousseau
   and Baudelaire writes such essays as 'The Word Reaction: from Physics to Psychiatry',
   Psychological Medicine, VII (1977), 373–86.

73 In *The Function of Criticism at the Present Time* (1923), *Selected Essays of T. S. Eliot* (New
   York, 1960, new ed.), 12–22, the pages where Eliot develops the concept. Eliot's
   analysis of Rémy de Gourmont, the turn-of-the-century literary author who wrote on
   scientific topics, bears parallels with mine of Foucault: both are, in Eliot's phrase,
   'master illusionists of fact' (21).

74 Garrison, *History of Medicine* (see n. 58), 334.

75 In America, where Foucault's writing is taken mush less seriously than it is in Europe,
   Foucault's 'epigoni' are not historians of medicine or science, but literary critics and
   general philosophers and historians. American institutes of higher criticism rarely
   engage in analysis of Foucault's books, whereas there are no professional historians of
   medicine to my knowledge who take Foucault seriously. His work has parallels in this
   sense with that of T. S. Kuhn, who merely diverted many historians of science when
   he published his anatomy of scientific revolutions but who has few followers today
   and virtually no students who would actually call themselves Kuhnians. Perhaps
   Theodore Brown, author of a study on the iatromechanical movement in England is
   an exception. Time alone will tell, both about Kuhn and Foucault, and the 'internalist-
   externalist' debates in the history of modern thought.

76 Chicago, 1968. See also Rosen's 'Social Attitudes to Irrationality and Madness in 17th
   and 18th century Europe', *Journal of the History of Medicine*, XVIII (1963), 220–40.

77 Rosen obtained his medical degree from Berlin University in 1935, never having obtained any degree in history. See pp. 000–00 below.

78 See, for example, Richard Hunter and Ida Macalpine, who have written about the origins of the private madhouse system in England in *British Medical Journal*, II (1972), 513–15. Eighteenth-century madhouses have been surveyed by: A. D. Morris, *The Hoxton Madhouses* (1968, privately printed); David J. Rothman, *The Discovery of the Asylum* (New York, 1971); W. Parry-Jones, *The Trade in Lunacy: a Study of Private Madhouses in England in the 18th and 19th Centuries* (1972; various biographies of William Cowper the poet which treat of Dr Nathaniel Cotton's 'Collegium Insanorum', a lunatic asylum in St Albans where Cowper was incarcerated.

79 Disseminated through chap. 9, 'The Nature of Man', in I: *The Seventeenth Century* (New York, 1939).

80 Little biographical information is known about Newton, who was intimate with the Earls of Northampton and occupied their town house, the 'Manor House' at Clerkenwell. The private papers of the house are not extant, so far as is known, but a group of handbill advertisements remain in the British Library. See Add. MSS. C. 112, fol. 9. The 'madhouse' appears on the 1720 map of John Strype in book 4 of Stow's *Survey of the Cities of London and Westminster* (1747).

81 See Morris, *The Hoxton Madhouses* (see n. 78), who has studied Miles's house from the Restoration onwards. In 'The First Psychiatric Hospital of the Western World', *American Journal of Psychiatry*, CXXVIII (1972), 1305–9, R. D. Rumbant describes a lunatic asylum in colonial America during these same years.

82 British social historians have not delved into the matter. See M. Dorothy George, *London Life in the xviiith Century* (New York, 1925), who is as silent on the subject as Kathleen Jones, *Lunacy, Law and Conscience 1744–1845: the Social History of the Care of the Insane* (1955) and Parry-Jones, *The Trade in Lunacy* (see note 78).

83 Jones, *Lunacy, Law and Conscience* (see n. 82), sums up the committee as follows: 'In 1742, the Pretender and his son were still active on the continent, and the Hanoverian succession not yet fully established; yet the committee included both the King's friends and those who were potential enemies. Thus there is nothing to suggest that this was more than a routine investigation to find ways of mitigating a common nuisance.' The diversity of the large committee may support this generality but it would take more research than Miss Jones has performed, as well as more understanding of the politics of medicine (see pp. 000–00 below), to substantiate it.

84 No adequate biography of Battie exists, but some biographical material will be found in John Monro's, M.D., *Remarks on Dr Battie's Treatise on Madness* (1758; facsimile repr., ed. R. Hunter and I. Macalpine, 1964).

85 The evidence is found in Hunter and Macalpine, *Three Hundred Years of Psychiatry* (see n. 5), 402.

86 Newton's son (see n. 80 above), who had owned and managed the premises until his death in October or November 1750 (see *Gentleman's Magazine*, XX (1750), 525). It is not known who owned the house from 1750 to 1754, but Battie purchased it in 1754 (see *Gentleman's Magazine*, XXV (1754), 496). After Battie's death in 1776 the house was continued by John Monro, M.D., who bequeathed it to his son Thomas, who relinquished it in 1803. During this entire period preachers of whatever denomination were prevented from entering the premises: 'We [preachers] are forbid to go to Newton [i.e. the madhouse now owned by Battie] for fear of making them wicked; and to Bedlam, for fear of driving them mad.' See N. Curnock (ed.), *The Journal of the Reverend John Wesley* (1938; bicentenary ed., 8 vols.), III, 455.

87 Jones, *Lunacy, Law and Conscience* (see n. 82), discusses the case known as 'Rex v. Turlington' in the legal literature (see *The English Reports*, 176 vols. (Edinburgh, 1900–30), XCVII, 741).

88 Some consideration of the petition of Sir Cordell Firebrace of Melford Hall in Suffolk

to the College of Physicians attempting to regulate private madhouses may illuminate the social history of insanity in England during the 1760s. The College flatly turned it down. Sir George Clark's analysis of the rejection in *A History of the Royal College of Physicians* (Oxford, 1966), II, 582–4, is authoritarian and politically coloured. Jones's estimate in *Lunacy, Law and Conscience* (see n. 82), is shrewder: 'The impression left on the reader is that, although the Committee was bound to investigate, it did not *want* to investigate too deeply' (italics mine).

89 Jones, *Law, Lunacy and Conscience* (see n. 82), 39. Of chronological interest here is George Mora, 'The 1774 Ordinance for the Hospitalization of the Mentally Ill in Tuscany: a Reassessment', *Journal of the History of the Behavioural Sciences*, XI (1975), 246–56.

90 All the bouts have been studied by Hunter and Macalpine in *George III and the Mad-Business* (see n. 25), a controversial book that stirred up further controversy.

91 *Madness in Society*, 209. The following passage is also found on this page. I intentionally avoid discussion of Mesmer and 'Mesmerism' in this section, as it has little to do *au fond* with my subject.

92 The passage quoted is from the subtitle of Webster's tract. Information about Webster and witchcraft in the Restoration is found in Christopher Hill, 'Mechanic Preachers and the Mechanical Philosophy', in *The World Turned Upside Down: Radical Ideas during the English Revolution* (1972), 287–305.

93 *Ibid.*, 277–86 especially, in the chapter entitled 'The Island of Great Bedlam'.

94 See Charles Almeras, *La Révolte des camisards* (Paris, 1959), 41–50, for the Camisards in England after 1704, and Ronald Knox, *Enthusiasm: a Chapter in the History of Religion with Special Reference to the Seventeenth and Eighteenth Centuries* (Oxford, 1950), 356–71. See M. C. Jacob, 'Newton and the French Prophets', *History of Science*, XVI (1978), 134–42.

95 Illness seems to have been the cause of Bulkeley's conversion, especially his wish that the Camisards could cure his ailments: by 1707 he began to hold occult meetings in Ewell in Surrey, where he ministered over a church; in 1708 he wrote *An Impartial Account of the Prophets of the Cévennes in a Letter to a Friend*, one of several such treatises.

96 Lacy was converted shortly after the arrival of the prophets in 1705. In 1707 he translated Maximilian Mission's *Théâtre sacre des Cevennes* as *A Cry from the Desert, or Testimonials of the Miraculous Things lately come to pass in the Cevennes verified upon Oath and by other Proofs*. Danies Defoe, William Whiston, Richard Steele – all well-known persons – tried to reason him out of his belief but to no avail.

97 Written by many of the most popular wits of the period. The silence of Swift is a mystery: he spent the winter of 1707–8 in London, just at the time of the prophets' notoriety, and he was wholly opposed to their brand of enthusiasm, as he had made clear in *A Tale of a Tub*.

98 This has not been undertaken, and the little scholarship that exists is fragmented. Basically the situation in the country relative to the town is that of a gap beginning to appear between the administration of folk remedies used to cure mental derangements – or at least assuage them – and the remedial practices of physicians, a widening gap abundantly documented for England by Parson Woodforde's diaries; see N. C. Hultin, 'Medicine and Magic in the Eighteenth Century: the Diaries of John Woodforde', *Journal of the History of Medicine*, XXX (1975), 349–66. But even this is merely a facet of the entire picture: as English and French society grew increasingly secular, the question of what it meant to stand apart from so-called 'normal' and conventional men and women became more difficult than ever to answer and, furthermore, as the process of secularisation marched forward, and as technology changed the social fabric of daily life, some of the young especially found their religious needs unfulfilled. Some folk turned to religion with a zeal unknown to their parents and grandparents, and were consequently labelled 'mad' – lumped often together with incurables and those whose

grief had clearly deranged their wits. Some background to this development is found in T. J. Schoeneman, 'The Role of Mental Illness in the European Witch Hunts of the 16th and 17th Centuries: an Assessment', *Journal of the History of the Behavioural Sciences*, XIII (1977), 337–51, and R. E. Hemphill, 'Historical Witchcraft and Psychiatric Illness in Western Europe', *Proceedings of the Royal Society of Medicine*, LIX (1966), 891–902, but no one except George Rosen has extended the study beyond 1700. Then there is the matter of the behaviour of enthusiastic devotees of dissenting religions. Some eighteenth-century physicians believed these groups to be mentally ill, suffering from physiological 'mania' or demonically inspired 'deformity of the mind' (a phrase that needs scrutiny), but the manner in which religious belief coloured the opinion of 'mad doctors', as they were then called, has not, to my knowledge, been studied.

99 See the chart beginning on p. 000. No study such as Jones's *Lunacy, Law and Conscience* (see n. 82) exists for France. Instead, one discovers short pieces dealing with mental hospitals or medical treatment in a region. See, for example, E. H. Ackerknecht, 'Political Prisoners in French Mental Institutions During the Revolution, and under Napoleon I', *Medical History*, XIX (1975), 250–5, and J. Alliez and J. P. Huber, 'L'Assistance aux malades mentaux au xviiie siècle à Marseille', *Histoire de sciences médicales*, x (1976), 60–71.

100 R. Favre, *La Mort au siècle des lumières* (Lyon, 1978): 'La Médecine: du rêve à l'espoir', 221–43; 'Vers un politique de la santé publique', 244–72. See also Philippe Ariès, *Western Attitudes toward Death from the Middle Ages to the Present* (Baltimore, 1974), who notes that 'in the second half of the eighteenth century, things [I.e. attitudes to death] changed'. Such changes of attitude reflected a new concept not only of society but of personal psychology within that society.

101 This may be why there has not been an adequate description of their activities from the eighteenth century onwards. Existing works include L. C. Jones, *The Clubs of the Georgian Rakes* (New York, 1942), and Iwan Bloch's *Sexual Life in England* (1938).

102 In *The Enlightenment: an Interpretation* 2 vols. (New York, 1966–9), II, 'The Science of Man'.

103 This point is implicit in the essays collected by E. Clarke and is discussed further in an essay of mine entitled 'Ephebi, epigoni, and fornacalia,' *Theory and Interpretation: the Eighteenth Century*, xx (autumn 1979), 203–26. (*Enlightenment Borders*, chap. 3).

104 See n. 5 above. I have not found similar anthologies for French, German or Italian psychiatry.

105 See 'Dr Johnson and the Passions' (Ph.D. thesis, University of California, 1960), a pioneering but still unpublished work written before Hunter and Macalpine compiled the bibliographies now used.

106 C. A. Moore, 'The English malady', the longest section of *Backgrounds of English Literature 1700–1760* (Minneapolis, 1950). The defective aspect of Moore's work is his simplistic notion of the concept of 'disease'; he demonstrates little of the analytic ability valued in historians of ideas. The work of Ilza Veith on this subject is, in my estimate, less important.

107 See *A History of Medical Psychology* (New York, 1941); *Mind, Medicine and Man* (New York, 1943).

108 Such histories of psychology and psychiatry are many, and too lengthy to be listed here. Another exception may be S. Selesnick's *The History of Psychiatry* (New York, 1966), which appears to be much less derivative than most others.

109 See Edward Said, *Beginnings* (New York, 1975); G. Canguilhem, *La Connaisance de la vie* (Paris, 1952); G. Bachelard, *La Formation de l'esprit scientifique: contribution à une psychanalyse de la connaissance objective* (Paris, 1938); idem, 'La Double Illusion du continuisme', in M. Fichant and M. Pêcheux (eds.), *Sur l'histoire des sciences* (Paris, 1974), 155; M. Foucault, *Les Mots et les choses* (Paris, 1966); idem, *L'Ordre du discours* (Paris,

1971); Dominique Lecourt, *Marxism and Epistemology: Bachelard, Canguilhem, Foucault* (1975).

110 See n. 65 above.

111 One volume has appeared to date: *La Volonté de savoir* (Paris, 1976).

112 Gilles Deleuze, alone among recent scholars, seems to have understood this.

113 Whether their work *and life* should be compared is another matter, depending very much on one's notion of the relationship. I am reasonably certain that our sense of Foucault will shift rather noticeably when his biography is written and it is fully realised that all along he has been a member of the political–radical fringe. I would be surprised if anyone writes a biography of the late George Rosen, as fine a scholar as he was.

114 Others have discussed the work of M. Jacob and J. Jacob, who reinterpret the reasons for Newton's instantaneous success in England.

115 See Jones, *Lunacy, Law and Conscience* (see n. 82).

116 See Thomas Chaplin, *Medicine in England during the Reign of George III* (1919); R. H. Gillespie, *Hypochondria* (1928); William K. Richmond, *The English Disease* (1958); Charles Trench, *The Royal Malady* (New York, 1964); Ilza Veith, *Hysteria: The History of a Disease* (Chicago, 1965); G. S. Rousseau, *Introduction to Sir John Hill 'Hypochondriasis: a Practical Treatise'* (Los Angeles, 1969); T. H. Jobe, 'Medical Theories of Melancholia in the Seventeenth and Early Eighteenth Centuries', *Clio Medica*, XI (1976), 217–31. W. Lepenies, *Melancholie und Gesellschaft* (Frankfurt, 1969).

117 The class character of melancholy is described in many eighteenth-century texts – scientific, medical, social, literary. See, for example, *The Letters of Doctor George Cheyne to Samuel Richardson (1733–1743)*, ed. C. F. Mullett (Columbia, 1943); Dr John Gregory, the Edinburgh medical ethicalist, *A Father's Legacy to his Daughters* (1774), 126; James Makittrick Adair, *Essays on Fashionable Diseases* (1790), chap. on 'Fashionable Maladies'. For France see Anne Charles Lorry, the physician of the fashionable and author of *De Melancholia et Morbis Melancholicis*, 2 vols. (Paris, 1762), which recognises two classes of melancholics, one nervous the other humoural, both of which have class origins. Modern students (see n. 116 above) have often noticed this class distinction, but have not explained its dynamic.

118 The list is too long to be discussed here but it would include 'therapy sessions' for rich ladies, pills and potions such as Dover's drop, James's powders, Berkeley's tar-water and Hill's Hungary water – manufactured remedies that made these men rich.

119 A 'dynamic' explanation includes the socio–economic factors as well as psychological assumptions of the age. It does not consider an explanation adequate unless it deals with the interaction of these assumptions as a bare minimum, nor does it view with approbation surface-deep descriptive accounts that attempt to pass for genuine explanation. Therefore, it would not suffice to explain the history of melancholy in our period merely as a 'history of science'. To do that would tell only a fragment of the story.

120 Cowper, Smart, Collins, Samuel Johnson, and other British writers of the period are the exceptions because they have generally enjoyed adequate biographies, as have their physicians. E.g. see the essay on Smart's physician, Nathaniel Cotton, by B. Hill, 'My Little Physician at St Albans' *Practitioner*, CLXXXXIX (1967), 363–7. This fact notwithstanding, few modern students differentiate between eighteenth- and twentieth-century self-reflectiveness about insanity; i.e. it is one thing for something to happen to one, and quite another to explain away that occurrence. In this connection, Lady Mary, the noted female-traveller, is instructive. In a long letter about Richardson's novels written to her daughter-in-law, Lady Bute, she comments on the sexual attractiveness of demented women: 'He [Richardson] is not a Man Midwife, for he would be better skill'd in Physic than to think Fits and Madness any Ornament to the Characters of his Heroines, tho his Sir Charles [Grandison] had no thoughts of marry-

ing Clementina till she had lost her Wits, and the Divine Clarissa never acted prudently till she was in the same Condition, and then very wisely desir'd to be carry'd to Bedlam, which is realy all that is to be done in that Case. Madness is as much a corporal Distemper as the Gout or Asthma, *never occasion'd by affliction*, or to be cur'd by the Enjoyment of their Extravagant wishes. Passion may indeed bring on a Fit, but the Disease is lodg'd in the Blood, and it is not more ridiculous to attempt to relieve [*sic*] the Gout by an embroider'd Slipper than to restore Reason by the Gratification of wild Desires' (italics mine). See R. Halsband (ed.), *The Letters of Lady Mary Wortley Montagu*, 3 vols. (Oxford, 1967), III, 96. This position should be compared with other popular notions such as that found in the French traveller Pierre Jean Grosley's *A Tour to London; or, New Observations on England* (1772), I, 243: 'all the people here [in Bedlam] were here because it was occasioned either by love or religious enthusiasm'.

121 See notes 60 and 65 above. Historians of architecture have dissected the plans for mental asylums and prisons, but there is no iconography of its paintings and caricatures along the lines studied by Grace Goldin, the historian of architecture, in 'A Painting in Gheel', *Journal of the History of Medicine*, XXI (1971), 12–23. We need one that extends from Cuyp's turn-of-the-century caricatures of 'Bedlam' to J. C. Lavater's engravings of 'an idiot' in his 1789 *Essays on Physiognomy*. R. Herrlinger's *History of Medical Illustration* (1969) does not include psychiatry.

122 See Nicholas Robinson, M.D., *A New System of the Spleen, Vapours, and Hypochondriack Melancholy* (1729), 34–5.

123 See Adair, *Philosophic and Medical Sketch* (1787), 234.

124 See nn. 29 and 106 above.

125 Medical historians have been so inattentive to the history of hysteria as the malady of the century, even in the latest clinical research on hysteria (see Mardi Horwitz, *The Hysterical Personality* (New York, 1977), that it may not be unreasonable to demand a 'semiotics of melancholy' that isolates the chief signs.

126 See W. J. Bate, *Samuel Johnson* (New York, 1977), chap. 21, 'Approaching breakdown: religious struggles; fear of insanity', and E. Verbeek, M.D., *The Measure and the Choice: a Pathographic Essay on Samuel Johnson* (Ghent, 1971). Various scholars and physicians have argued that Johnson depicts a 'classic schizophrenic' in *Rasselas* (1759).

127 See Max Byrd, *Visits to Bedlam: Madness and Literature in the Eighteenth Century* (Columbia, 1974), and M. V. DePorte, *Nightmares and Hobbyhorses: Swift, Sterne, and Augustan Ideas of Madness* (San Marino, 1974). Both studies survey the literary aspects but their medico-scientific and socio-economic backgrounds are thin.

128 See P.-G. Boucé, *Les Romans de Smollett: étude critique* (Paris, 1971), 230–42.

129 See James Strachey and Alan Tyson (eds.), *The Standard Edition of the Complete Psychological Works of Sigmund Freud* 24 vols (1953–), XIV, 239–40.

130 In this connection see Toby Gelfand, *The Training of Surgeons in Eighteenth-Century Paris . . .* (Baltimore, 1973).

131 Stone, *The Family, Sex and Marriage in England* (see n. 21), 385ff., speculates about the matter, but not in relation to developmental insanity.

132 Edwin Clarke's collection, *Modern Methods in the History of Medicine* (see n. 5), lends the impression that there is an historiography of medicine; see especially p. ix, n. 12, and O. Temkin's essay, 'The Historiography of Ideas in Medicine'.

5

Nerves, spirits, and fibres: towards an anthropology of sensibility

In 1973 I travelled to Canberra, Australia, as an invited member of the David Nichol Smith Memorial Seminar, an international workshop devoted to discussion of Englightenment topics. My hosts requested that I address the scientific side of Enlightenment sensibility, a topic then eminently in need of discussion as so little had been written about it. The situation today has altered: there are probably over a dozen good books dealing with the concept of sensibility from the Renaissance to modern times, some of which urge us to take a broad view of the subject in view of T. S. Eliot's caveat about the 'dissociation of sensibility'. But at that time, the scholars were almost completely silent about its chronological development. Louis Bredvold, a specialist in the field, had written a slender volume called The Natural History of Sensibility *(1962),which was read only by people in English literature. Northrop Frye, whose positions were then much more influential than most of us now remember, had already pronounced English literature of the later Enlightenment to be 'the literature of an age of sensibility', prophetically claiming that sensibility equalled 'process', but without explaining how it arose at the precise moment that it did and why it triumphed over competing discourses and competing cultural practices. Professor Stephen D. Cox, my former student, had not yet published* 'The Stranger Within Thee': Concepts of the Self in Late Eighteenth-Century Literature, *which dealt so sensitively with sensibility in its purely literary contexts. So there was abundant reason to turn the tide of the discussion.*

In the essay I tried to contextualise sensibility more broadly and explain under what cultural conditions it could arise. It would not be my last attempt. The need was for discussion of its specific historical conditions, precise research agendas and cultural practices, and civic, ideological, and epistemological circumstances. I had already been immersed in the science and medicine of the period, had assimilated my reading of Foucault (i.e., having read everything he had published up to 1973), and, as I explain in the postscript, had begun to read Derrida. While composing the essay I was also deeply engaged in the debates of the historians of science over internalism/externalism and over Thomas Kuhn's conception of 'normal science' described in The Structure of Scientific Revolutions. *My 'postscript of 1975' was added in the second version of the essay at the request of Professor Angela Giannitrapani, then of the Universities of Rome and Messina, and is found in* The Blue Guitar, *published in English in Italy (December 1976).*

We have all heard a great deal in the last decade about Kuhn's 'paradigms'.

His definition in *The Structure of Scientific Revolutions* has itself become something of a classic:

> Aristotle's *Physica*, Ptolemy's *Almagest*, Newton's *Principia* and *Opticks*, Franklin's *Electricity*, Lavoisier's *Chemistry*, and Lyell's *Geology* – these and many other works served for a time implicitly to define the legitimate problems and methods of a research field for succeeding generations of practitioners. They were able to do so because they shared two essential characteristics. Their achievement was sufficiently unprecedented to attract an enduring group of adherents away from competing modes of scientific activity. Simultaneously, it was sufficiently open-ended to leave all sorts of problems for the redefined group of practitioners to resolve.
>
> Achievements that share these two characteristics I shall henceforth refer to as 'paradigms', a term that relates closely to 'normal science'.[1]

During the last decade we have also read and heard that large segments of the scientific community are not happy with Kuhn's definition. They argue that the deflection of human energy by unprecedented, open-ended theories is inadequate to describe the origin of scientific revolutions.[2] Nevertheless, Kuhn's paradigms have considerable worth; if nothing else, Kuhn's definition typifies and describes his own achievement. No other single concept in the last ten years has deflected serious thinkers so much from their own pursuits, nor is any other in the recent history and philosophy of science so open-ended as to have caused students of every background to scrutinise it and even to imitate it, as does Michel Foucault's theory of the *episteme* in *Les Mots et les choses*, first published in 1966.[3] Even today, in this post-Popperian age, and at the risk of labouring a now well-known theory, it is worth repeating that Kuhn's 'paradigm' refers to books, and that his concept of paradigms was formulated by examining the way that science textbooks charted the route to 'normal science'.[4]

What does such a theory do for us, students of the eighteenth century? We might extend Kuhn's list by adding many works, for example Locke's *Essay Concerning Human Understanding*, clearly an 'open-ended' work that deflected many through its use as a scientific textbook. But would we add Hume's *Treatise of Human Nature* or Adam Smith's *Theory of Moral Sentiments*? It all depends on the level at which we decode, and on our understanding of Kuhn's original definition. Application of the theory, as we can see, has already presented a slight problem; but in fairness to Kuhn we ought to remember that he reserved the term 'paradigm' for unprecedented works demonstrating open-ended theories and deflection in the highest possible degree. Thus, while it probably can be shown (and I say probably because it has not yet been shown) that Locke's *Essay* deflected all sorts of men in addition to ethical philosophers and soon established itself as a scientific textbook leading to understanding of the 'new science', the science of man – the same (and here I want to be somewhat the loose Humean) perhaps cannot be said of the treatises by Hume and Smith. If nothing else, we can probably prove beyond a shadow of doubt that these later works were far less tentative than Locke's; and furthermore, that in the case of Hume the point made was too precise to leave ensuing practitioners in open-ended doubt; and that in Smith's case the contents summarised the theories of others and made them available to everyone in a new form rather than put forward a radically new and open-ended theory itself. A similar case can be made for certain works by Diderot, Rousseau and other *philosophes*, for La Mettrie, Le Cat, Marat. In paradigmatic terms then, and if I may take the liberty of expanding on Kuhn's original term, the Rousseauistic doctrine *je sens, donc je suis*, is the end rather than the beginning of a revolution in knowledge.

We are therefore left with John Locke, a condition that will surprise or horrify some and that others will call reductionist or even patently foolish. But if we accept Kuhn's theory (and despite its difficulties it is still the best available) and follow it to its logical conclusion, Locke's *Essay* alone among textbooks about the 'new science' of man satisfies Kuhn's two extraordinary conditions. Is this in itself not extraordinary? Not at all extraordinary in the fact that Locke's is a seventeenth-century work (published in 1690), nor in the further fact that no scientific works other than Newton's, Franklin's, and Lavoisier's are mentioned by Kuhn for the eighteenth century, but rather in the fact that Locke's *Essay* is the first to deal with a science that had not as yet developed: the *science* of man. Here Kuhn's theory about Franklin and electricity is equally instructive. 'Only through the work of Franklin and his immediate successors did a theory [of electricity] arise that could account with something like equal facility for very nearly all these effects and that therefore could and did provide a subsequent generation of "electricians" with a common paradigm for its research.' Likewise, by the time Locke published his *Essay* in 1690, a *theory* of the new science of man had evolved that was sufficiently unprecedented and open-ended to deflect at least three subsequent generations of moral scientists: Mandeville, Shaftesbury, Hume, Adam Smith, La Mettrie, the *philosophes*, and dozens of others. Call this science what you will: social science, the science of morals, or, as Peter Gay has called it, the 'Science of Man',[5] and give it any label you fancy – a crisis, an ethical dilemma, a revolution, an epoch of transition. One thing, however, is clear: without Locke and his immediate successors, the theory could not have developed.

What then precisely was it about Locke's *Essay* that allowed for, indeed insisted on, this paradigmatic treatment? Surely it was his application of crucial aspects of the physical sciences to a realm – ethics and politics – that was not previously imagined to yield to scientific types of explanation. Locke's integration of ethics and physiology has little, if anything, to do with the fact that he himself was a physician. For every physician in 1690 who was integrating seemingly non-allied terrains, there were dozens, perhaps hundreds, who saw no connection at all. And even among the integrationists only one thinker's genius inclined him, for whatever mysterious reason now lost to time, to grasp at the one realm – ethics – most requiring an unprecedented theory to be arrived at by radical integration of disparate areas of study. Physico-theologists like the Boyle lecturers, like Ray and Derham, annually were integrating the physical sciences into the study of religion. The difference between their endeavours, which certainly led to no revolution in knowledge, and Newton's is evident: if there is one thing the *Principia* and *Opticks* are not it is physio-theologies. Newton, the man whose open-ended theories deflected men for over a century by replacing the old textbooks with his new ones, also kept science and religion apart when it came to writing books. We all know his protestation that he could not tell anyone 'why is gravity, only what is gravity'.[6] Paradigmatic achievement, therefore, does not depend upon integration as an efficient cause. In Locke's case it happens to function as such, but this is partly owing to the rapid acceleration of scientific research immediately after the Restoration, and partly to Locke's own monumental genius in recognising that integration working below the surface statement of these disparate realms – ethics and physiology – would result in the open-ended effect about which Kuhn speaks. Locke intuitively realised, as Descartes had not, that the whole argument about knowledge pivots upon the concept and definition of 'sensation'.

Now our isolation of Locke's *Essay* as paradigmatic is in itself of no great interest except that we have tended to think of 'sensation', and hence of the ensuing cults of 'sensibility' and 'sentiment', as mid eighteenth-century phenomena. We speak of a 'sensibility movement' commencing with Richardson in the 1740s, transforming itself until the 1790s, and persisting until something called 'Romanticism' eclipsed it. Here I wish to make clear my temporary suspension of belief in nominalism; for the moment, I am not interested in semantic labels and tags; it is paradigms and paradigmatic works, that is books, related to sensibility, that I wish to consider. Everyone knows that Northrop Frye has called English literature between Richardson and Wordsworth the product of an 'Age of Sensibility',[7] and those still hovering in doubt will be convinced by R. F. Brissenden's book, *Virtue in Distress: Studies in the Novel of Sentiment from Richardson to Sade*. And yet the half-century between 1690 and 1740, between the appearance of Locke's *Essay* and Richardson's *Pamela*, an epoch separating men two generations apart, has continued to elude us. If we follow Kuhn's argument and my subsequent reasoning to its apodic-tic end, should Frye's 'Age of Sensibility' not have occurred fifty years earlier? Have we been dangerously promoting an historical fallacy by alleging that its appearance was a mid, even a late, eighteenth-century phenomenon?

Not really. For such reasoning dangerously and erroneously assumes that imaginative literature – and by this I mean poetry, fiction, the drama – is influenced by science at once, and we know this is not true of the eighteenth century merely by noticing that it took Newtonian science at least one generation to 'demand the muse'. It is no less dangerous at this point and no less consequential for the future of eighteenth-century studies, for us to confuse *imaginative literature* and *speculative science*.

What I am therefore suggesting is that the eighteenth-century revolution in intellectual thinking regarding the 'science of man' owes its superlative debt to John Locke. Secondly – and this is the more important of the two points – that sensibility, not merely sentimentalism,[8] is at the very heart of this revolution (precisely for the two reasons given in Kuhn's definition of paradigms) and of subsequent revolutions. But sensibility was not a mid eighteenth-century phenomenon, certainly not in philosophy or the natural sciences. It was a late seventeenth-century development, owing its superlative paradigmatic debt to books – and here, again, I adopt Kuhn's emphasis – books like Thomas Willis's *Pathology of the Brain*,[9] and also to one unprecedented, integrative work, Locke's *Essay*. The mid-eighteenth-century neurological treatises of Haller and Whytt and the many others who entered the arenas of debate were not paradigmatic works that led to a revolution in the scientific approach to the study of man, or to the sensibility movement in literature. They were the deflections, not the deflectors. These were not the works that paved the way for *Clarissa, A Sentimental Journey*, and *Justine*: nor were the earlier treatises of Dr George Cheyne, with whom Richardson for example corresponded so prolifically. At the deepest level of decoding, the level at which I believe Kuhn has decoded, the revolution in sentiment occurred in the last quarter of the seventeenth century. It took imaginative writers like Richardson and Sterne a half century to 'catch up', as it were; and more importantly, it also took most scientific thinkers like Cheyne, Haller and Whytt almost as long to understand what had transpired in the interim.

This observation should not surprise us. Almost fifty years ago, R. S. Crane warned that if we wish to understand the origins of sensibility 'we must look to a period considerably earlier than that in which Shaftesbury wrote'.[10] And I am suggesting now that it is equally dangerous to think that the revolution in sensibility was a mid or late-eighteenth-century phenomenon. To trace its origin to Shaftesbury, or even solely to Locke, is to indulge in sheer mysticism and to have no philosophy of the influence of history on literature. I realise that I have been partly responsible for some of the confusion in my essay on science and the imagination in eighteenth-century England, but I am not so culpable as Mr Frye, who was satisfied to repeat what every Victorian and Edwardian schoolteacher knew, and to garnish his main point with consolation to the effect that English literature between Gray and the Romantics is not altogether dull.[11]

I must now demonstrate that at least in scientific thought the revolution in sensibility was *not* an eighteenth-century phenomenon; in other words show that unless one decodes at Kuhn's level one does not possess a meaningful, let alone cogent, model of literary change so far as contents are concerned, and moreover that decoding at the level Kuhn's paradigms imply is essential for students of the eighteenth century today. If this is done and accepted, one significant consequence is that propositions of the form 'the social sciences were born in the eighteenth century' must be thrown out of court on grounds of false aetiology. They may have matured and flowered then; they were not born then. The social sciences of man, about which mid eighteenth-century Frenchmen had much to say, may not have had an influence on the manifold aspects of routine daily life until the mid eighteenth century, but it is absurd to suggest 'birth' at that time if we decode at the level of Kuhn, Michel Foucault, Lévi-Strauss, some of the literary phenomenologists and other recent powerful analytical minds.

What then were the 'paradigms' of sensibility, and was a revolution in knowledge about man created by them? Crudely speaking they were sets of physiological texts published shortly after the Restoration that were sufficiently 'open-ended' (like Willis's *Anatomy of the Brain* and *Pathology of the Brain*) to deflect all types of scientists, not merely other anatomists and physiologists. (This is not to suggest that the physiological dimension of these texts is the crucial aspect. It is not: physiology text books were being written certainly by the second century A.D., when Galen published his paradigmatic physiological work, *On the Natural Faculties*.)[12] After 1660 their numbers increased owing to regental and internal university support of scientific research. It is essential to note that these books (however cognisant or not their authors) were ultimately attempts to answer Cartesian science. That is – and here again I follow certain of Kuhn's philosophical theories, especially his notion that the precise nature of scientific works is never accidental – the history of science is best conceived of as a continuum in which paradigmatic works periodically deflect 'groups of practitioners'.[13] Until we discover which are the paradigms and which the deflected responses, we cannot understand revolutions in intellectual thought: the rise of sensibility is a good case in point, especially as regards the continuum in which it takes place.

Before the Restoration, Descartes's *Discourses* and his *Passions of the Soul* were paradigmatic works, especially for anatomy, and deflected all types of natural scientists, directing them almost compulsively to the study of physiology. But for various political reasons, the Interregnum among them, their influence in England was temporarily abortive. The next such paradigmatic works in the biological and medical sciences were Thomas Willis's texts on the brain published in the 1660s and 1670s and translated in the early 1680s. Although there were other paradigmatic texts before the nineteenth century (e.g. Whytt, Haller, Cullen), these were not of the same class as Willis's. His special genius, like Descartes's before him, lay not in the scientific veracity of his theory but in his ability to deflect men. The theory itself was of course unprecedented: he was the first scientist clearly and loudly to posit that the seat of the soul is strictly limited to the brain, nowhere else. Shadows and anticipations of this revolutionary theory can be found before 1660, but nothing loud and plain.[14] In the sense of cause and effect, it was this theory that inspired a revolution in intellectual thought concerning the nature of man and that greatly enhanced the doctrines of anti-Stoic and anti-Puritan divines of the Latitudinarian school about which R. S. Crane has written so brilliantly.[15] Every competent physiologist of the late seventeenth century knew that nerves, morphologically speaking, carry out the tasks set by the brain. But not every physiologist or anatomist suspected – (or if he did know Willis's work, would have agreed), that the soul is located in the brain. Without this knowledge, an imaginative leap of the first order, it is impossible to account for the intense interest after the Restoration (but not before) in nerve research, and consequently for the emergence of diverse cults of sensibility.

Here it is delightful and amusing, but no more, to recount that Willis was Locke's teacher at Oxford, that Locke is known to have voluntarily copied into notebooks everything he (Locke) thought he might later use in his own work. It is no exaggeration to say that Willis's brain theories had a profound influence on Locke in some of his most formative years. It would be nothing less than teacherous, however, to argue that it was Willis's theory of the brain that 'deflected' Locke into writing the *Essay*. In rehearsing the influence of Willis on Locke my intention is not to minimise other factors (especially religious and political) in the development of Locke's imagination, but to question whether the deepest substratum of the *Essay*, especially its unspoken assumptions, is not more intelligible when viewed in the light of Locke's education at Oxford.

If we continue this line of inquiry regarding the revolution in physiology, it becomes evident why nerves, and their subsidiaries, fibres and animal spirits, could not be accounted the basis of knowledge, and consequently of human behaviour, until the seat of the soul was limited (not merely moved) to the brain. For this organ alone depends upon the nerves for all its functions. Once the soul was limited to the brain, scientists could debate precisely how the nerves carry out its voluntary and involuntary intentions, and what the relation between nerves and other systems, especially blood and lymph, is. The history of science reveals that they did this: no topic in physiology between the Restoration and the turn of the nineteenth century was more important than the precise workings of the nerves, their intricate morphology and histological arrangement, their anatomic function. It is true, this collective scientific endeavour could not have been undertaken without Harvey's discovery in the 1620s of the circulation of the blood, expounded in another paradigmatic work, *De Motu Cordis*. Nor would it have been possible without Willis's revolutionary theory of the brain.

These admittedly sweeping abstractions about a chapter in the history of science have now been minutely documented by Edwin Clarke, our most distinguished historian of physiology. In an important article entitled 'The Doctrine of the Hollow Nerve in the Seventeenth and Eighteenth Centuries', he concludes: despite the welter of speculation and observation concerning the supposed hollow or porous nerve which had accumulated in the seventeenth and eighteenth centuries, little advance beyond Galen's original suppositions had in fact been made'.[16] Why did this 'welter' exist in the first place, and what difference does it make to a history of sensibility? If indeed the soul is limited to the brain, as Willis and his followers in the 1670s contended, then nerves alone can be held responsible for sensory impressions, and consequently for knowledge; it also follows that the nerves must necessarily be hollow tubes rather than solid fibres, so that the brain's unique secretion, animal spirits, can freely flow through them to the body's vital organs. It was essential to the deepest and probably most unconscious assumption of these physiologists that the old model of nerves as hollow tubes be sustained. But the rapid and marked acceleration of the 'welter of speculation' after Willis's paradigmatic books on the brain is equally notable. Once Willis's paradigms are understood by us, a context for physiology manifests itself, and we can begin to perceive how the war between mechanists and vitalists, a war about which we have heard so much, developed at the end of the seventeenth century.

The mechanists, like their vitalist or animal opponents, were dualists. Followers of Descartes, they accepted his mechanistic explanation of all bodily functions except that of the soul, which, again like Descartes, they located everywhere in the body but whose activities, they asserted, do not act in any known mechanistic fashion. When asked by vitalists how the soul does act, mechanists from the time of Descartes to that of La Mettrie and Haller more than a century later, answered that in essence it does not matter how, because the soul has little power in and of itself – virtually everything depends on the clockwork movements of the body, a perfectly constructed machine whose basic motions would be enacted whether or not the soul willed them voluntarily. After Willis brilliantly limited the soul to the immediate area of the cerebrum and cerebellum and its surrounding network of nerves, the mechanists avidly set about to prove, although they did not succeed, that all nerves were in fact hollow tubes through which the quasi-magical fluid secreted by the brain flowed. Unless they could prove that nerves were porous, cavity-like structures, they would need to surrender their most fundamental assumption about the dualism of body and soul (or mind).

But precisely this fierce attempt to prove that nerves are porous cavities gave animists like Stahl and his many followers in the eighteenth century their biggest impetus. Monists of varying degree, the Stahlians – Stahl, Whytt, Cullen, to mention just the most celebrated – had never accepted Descartes's dualism of body and soul, although they had been deflected by his theories from the very start. Instead they preferred to adhere to an animate, functioning soul whose mechanical operations throughout the body were maximised to the greatest possible degree. In other words, every part of the body was chemically and physically governed by this soul, which did not function predictably, rationally, or mechanistically, but was influenced by non-mechanical, unconscious phenomena. It is hard not to notice how the whole dispute between Cartesian mechanists and Stahlian animists was radically displaced (altered would falsify the facts) by Willis's limitation of the soul to the brain. After 1680 mechanists and animists alike, dualists as well as monists, had no choice but to refute Willis's unprecedented contention by demonstrating unequivocally that nerves are in fact solid, or to agree with him. For if the nerves were solid fibres rather than porous hollow tubes, no avenue existed by which to explain the brain's control over the rest of the body – not, at least, before the discovery of electricity in the mid eighteenth century. That is, no means existed otherwise by which to account for knowledge gained by experience, for non-innate knowledge. But no one in the eighteenth century could prove the solidity of the nerves; i.e. no one could disprove Willis's theory by adducing concrete microscopic evidence.[17] The only remaining alternative was to work away at proving the one condition that would in turn prove Willis's theory, the hollowness of the nerves.

If we stop at this point, surely we scatter to the wind the most essential thread and consequences of the argument: the manner in which the idea that nerves control human consciousness gradually took hold. We also lose sight of the fundamental concept of 'sensation' upon which the entire debate had centered.

If Willis had not appeared on the scientific scene with his striking theory about the autonomous brain, the question of nerves could never have held the dominant sway it did. For by the 1660s the study of anatomy was sufficiently well developed, especially with regard to circulatory and respiratory systems in the body, for scientists to insist that the nerves are the slaves of the brain and, conversely, that the brain is thoroughly enslaved to the nerves and unable to function without them. This had been unequivocally demonstrated by Vesalius, Van Helmont, and their contemporaries. Without Willis, physiologists and other scientists would have continued to debate the problem of how to prove the hollowness of nerves, the precise morphology of their fibres (which no one had seen microscopically), and the chemical composition of animal spirits. But other organs than the brain, such as the heart, stomach, bowels, would then have commanded superior positions as subjects for investigation by philosophers as well as anatomists.

Willis's paradigmatic leap, if we continue in this line of decoding, was to locate the brain in the soul in a series of experiments and books possessing just the right balance between observed fact and unprecedented hypothesis to deflect bewildered scientists for over a century, to the time of Haller, Whytt and Cullen – that is to say to the very end of the eighteenth century.[18] Unless the consequences of this imaginative leap are fully understood we can never comprehend the origins of those ideas resulting in the diverse cults of sensibility so clearly visible by the middle of the eighteenth century. A new assumption about the fundamental anatomy of man arose through Willis's deflection of several generations of scientists, including mechanists, vitalists and animists of every variety and persuasion. The unspoken assumption was hardly a 'paradigm' in Kuhn's sense; but a radically new assumption arose about man's essentially nervous nature. From pure anatomy, it was one step to an integrated physiology of man and just another to a theory of sensory perception, learning, and the further association of ideas. Locke, in the course of time Willis's best student, took these steps perhaps not visibly in the written *Essay* but in the stages that may be construed as the preformation of the *Essay*; and the schools of moral thinkers he in turn deflected – Shaftesbury, Hutcheson, Hume, Adam Smith, and many others – carried his brilliant act of integration to its fullest possible conclusion.[19] Collectively they developed a scientific approach to every aspect of the study of man by means of a theory of sensory perception and a theory of knowledge that directly followed from their understanding of the physiology of perception. Today, we are still the heirs of the revolution. Witness our specialised scientific approaches to the study of man: psychology, sociology, anthropology, psycho-history, psycho-linguistics, and so forth. If we understand the revolution set in motion by Willis and Locke, and the theories of the former without the latter would not have have had an impact as quickly as they did, then we can at last begin to come to terms with sensibility. We still require narration of the whole story of this development; for I have outlined the crudest sketch and essential features only. Even so, the outline demonstrates some salient facts about European intellectual history in the seventeenth and eighteenth centuries: first that no adequate theory of perception arose, or could arise, until physiological questions pertaining to anatomy were at least partially solved, not by actually *answering* the deepest questions – we know they were not answered – but by endowing the answers with enough authority to permit men seriously to study them, i.e. to permit the serious study of physiology. Second, that a scientific approach to the study of man, such as the one we see flourishing in the eighteenth-century schools of Scottish morality, English empirical philosophy, and even French ethical thought (persuasively presented by Lester Crocker in his books on the subject), required as a prerequisite a developed science of physiology. Call this science anatomy or morphology of the nervous system if you will; in either case it was new. Speculation about it had existed for centuries as a marginal aspect of more general science, but at the end of the seventeenth century it came into its own and permitted, as it were, the new science of man to begin to practise. To decode further at this level, the 'revolution' in anatomical thinking was not an eighteenth-century phenomenon but a late seventeenth. Mechanism, animism and vitalism were responses to previous radical ideas and not radical new ideas themselves. All three depended for their life-blood on the institutionalisation of physiology as a serious endeavour in itself, and there is good reason that all three philosophical positions were not hotly debated before the end of the seventeenth century. While Willis and his contemporaries can hardly be credited with making the study of physiology respectable by their own teaching, studying and restudying it, texts like his *Anatomy* and *Pathology of the Brain* and those of his student John Locke directly contributed to the 'revolution' we now call the scientific study of man. Whether these men also made it possible in the first place depends almost exclusively on one's theory of cause and effect.

We can now begin to understand all sorts of connections not evident earlier. By comprehending precisely how 'sensation' was at the heart of the revolution in physiology, we can observe how it was also the parent of a child called the science of man. We can, furthermore, see why theological systems, even dissenting theological systems, based on a theory of the soul that was more or less anatomically grounded, were ultimately asked to account for the phenomenon of sensation. But we can do much more. We can now understand realms that hitherto have seemed disparate: the cults of melancholy, hypochondria, as a national institution, the 'English Malady', as Cheyne called it, Richardson's novel of sentiment, later on the well-formed and mature 'man of feeling', Sterne's bizarre variations and subtle alterations on this theme, the eighteenth century's eventual attack on all forms of sentiment as fake; throughout the century the insistence, indeed obsession, with the relation of mind (soul) to body, and, still later, Romanticism with a capital R. We can begin to understand why Mrs Donnellan, no scientist or learned lady, could directly link (in the sense of outright cause and effect) Richardson's wretched health with his far more than usual sensibility as a writer:

> Misfortune is, those who are fit to write delicately, must think so; those who can form a distress must be able to feel it; and as the mind and body are so united as to influence one another, the delicacy is communicated, and one too often finds softness and tenderness of mind in a body equally remarkable for those qualities. Tom Jones could get drunk, and do all sorts of bad things, in the height of his joy for his uncle's recovery. I dare say Fielding is a robust, strong man.[20]

That is, unlike Richardson! This is no 'attempt to console Richardson for his perpetual ill-health', as Ian Watt has suggested;[21] rather than consolation this is the clearest possible indication, at the deepest and most unconscious level, of a revolution in thinking that had been set in motion in the late seventeenth century. All Mrs Donnellan's unstated premises had been scientifically worked out for her by Willis, Locke, and many others. Crudely stated in the form of a syllogism: (1) the soul is limited to the brain; (2) the brain performs the entirety of its work through the nerves; (3) the more 'exquisite' and 'delicate' one's nerves are, morphologically speaking, the greater the ensuing degree of sensibility and imagination; (4) refined people and other persons of fashion are usually born with more 'exquisite' anatomies, the tone and texture of their nervous systems more 'delicate' than those of the lower classes; (5) the greater one's nervous sensibility, the more one is capable of delicate writing. The ordering of the unspoken assumptions here could not be clearer if it tried. They – the assumptions – may conceal a mythology only partly grounded in physiological research; this notwithstanding, they doubtless thrive on an innate and steadfast distinction between persons of different social origins and economic backgrounds. But these assumptions nevertheless formed part of the substratum of thought of an epoch extending over several generations until the early nineteenth century and are not easy to reconstruct at this removal of time. Richardson represented to contemporaries like Mrs Donnellan the man *par excellence* of exquisite and truly delicate sensibility, and other women as well knew why he was able to write so delicately, even if we do not today.

We can now begin to understand that the novel of sentiment in all its multitudinous forms, especially as it developed in the 1740s under Richardson's influence, ultimately owed nothing to the notorious neurological debates between Haller and Whytt, or even to Richardson's earlier debt to Dr George Cheyne with whom he was on intimate terms and from whom he learned so much about his perverse bodily constitution. Nor did it owe much to Hutcheson's *Passions and Affections* published in 1728, or to his *Ideas of Beauty and Virtue* published in 1725, or to Shaftesbury's *Characteristics* published in 1711. The debate between Haller and Whytt did not erupt until 1751,[22] four years after *Clarissa Harlowe* was published. Even if it had broken earlier, even if it had erupted before Richardson composed *Clarissa*, and even if it could be proved beyond a shadow of all doubt that Richardson absorbed every detail of the Haller-Whytt controversay; even if Richardson himself had revealed to us in the preface to *Clarissa* or elsewhere that his knowledge about sensibility and science, sentiment and the heart, derived from his intensive reading about the controversy – that would prove nothing more than token influence.

For we, like Kuhn early in the 1960s, have not been decoding at a level of mere surface and linear relation or of necessarily one-to-one and direct influence. And it is consequently of no more concern to us whether Richardson read Haller and Whytt, or Haller *or* Whytt, for example, than whether he read Dr Cheyne or Hutcheson or Shaftesbury before them. His reading is of immense concern to Richardsonians only as Sterne's is to Sterneans. What counts to those among us who would understand the deepest levels, the most original ideas, which made the many cults of sensibility possible in the first place – whether in the novel or elsewhere in imaginative literature – is the simple fact (and it is so simple that we have never bothered to notice it) that no novel of sensibility could appear until a revolution in knowledge concerning the brain, and consequently its slaves, the nerves, had occurred. If Sterne or Smollett, or even Jane Austen with *Sense and Sensibility*, had chronologically preempted Richardson by writing for the first time about the delights of moral sentiments or charitable sensibility, it would make no substantive or even impressionable difference to the historian of ideas. For Mrs Donnellan has already told us *why* Richardson could perform so well in this species of writing, and presumably she would have found similar explanations for an ailing Sterne or Smollett or Austen, or for that matter a suitable Hogarth, Reynolds, or Gainsborough, a Handel or Boyce. Her explanation for exquisite refinement in painting or music would not have substantially differed from the one she gives for the physiologically sensible Richardson; and her testimony is valid because, like dozens of other similar passages in eighteenth-century letters, it was uttered without any degree of forethought or premeditation and in a moment of total sincerity. She is obliged to give *no* elaborate reasoning, because her unstated assumptions are precisely those of the age. Nor does it matter in the least whether she was right in any absolute sense: each age is entitled to believe what it wishes, to create the revolutions in knowledge it desires; and even if we profoundly wish it otherwise, generations of men in the future will continue to fabricate their own mythologies despite subsequent protestations.

It is our task – and I hope I will be forgiven for such heavy-handed moralising – neither to falsify the unspoken and unwritten ideas of previous ages, nor to give emphasis or credit where it is not due. But an even greater task for contemporary intellectual historians is a steadfast refusal to reduce highly complex contents to embarrassingly simple structures that neither do justice to reality nor ask or answer the 'big' questions. The simple fact of literary history, for example, that it took almost thirty or forty years for English writers to grasp the full extent of the brain-nerve revolution, is of no greater interest, except to literary specialists, than what Richardson actually read. Recent imaginative writers in this century have taken that long, if not longer, to understand at the level of unspoken assumption paradigmatic works by Darwin, Einstein, Freud, Heisenberg, and others – and some still have not. The exact chronological distance in years between writers of sensibility (such as Richardson, Sterne, Mackenzie, Sade) and the intellectual revolutionaries themselves – in this case Willis and his pioneering Oxford and London colleagues – must remain an academic sport to engage the attention of highly specialised scholars of the interrelations of science and literature. So, also, must the precise manner in which the brain-nerve revolution influenced the totality of medical research from 1680 onwards. That must concern a small group of medical historians primarily.

Our task is to chart the blurry interconnections of seemingly non-related realms. In doing so for sensibility, we can also understand why it is virtually unnecessary for us to demonstrate the influence of particular thinkers on these writers of sensibility when we decode at this substratum of uttered thought. It would indeed almost be improper. For given that a physiological theory of perception was a necessary condition to explain feelings of every sort (whether genuine or otherwise) and especially the diversity of simple and complex passions, it is of little concern to us, and certainly no cause for celebration, if we discover an identical passage or perfectly clear analogue in a scientific work known to have influenced the writer in question. We must consider as arbitrary which scientific author wrote the following: 'Feeling is nothing but the Impulse, Motion or Action of Bodies, gently or violently impressing the Extremities or Sides of the Nerves, of the Skin, or other parts of the Body, which . . . convey Motion to the Sentient Principle in the Brain'.[23] It is immaterial to us, who would understand the truest origins of sensibility, if the author of this passage is Haller, Whytt, Hartley, La Mettrie, Hume, Cheyne, William Hunter, Nicholas Robinson, Ephraim Chambers, Hermann Boerhaave, Hutcheson, Shaftesbury, or any one of a dozen other scientific thinkers. It happens to be Dr Cheyne, Richardson's confidante, but any of these men could have written it. Only if it appeared in a work written before the paradigmatic books of Willis, Locke and their colleagues would we be concerned.[24] My contention all along is that it could not have appeared earlier; that is was impossible before the revolution in brain theory to expect the totality of human feeling to be nothing but motion in the nerves. Considered in the broadest sense, this implies that every response to a moral crisis is physiologically grounded, fated, and determined in the *a priori* sense.

Even more important, we can now begin to understand why all diseases, not merely those considered hysterical and hypochondriacal, were eventually classified as 'nervous' and after a reasonable amount of time were internalised by persons of fashion as visible emblems of refinement and delicacy – thereby functioning as tangible proof of distinct upper-crust difference from the lower and middle classes. Slowly but surely, it becomes painfully clear that Richardson, Sterne, Diderot, Rousseau, Mackenzie, and even the Marquis de Sade were the posterity of two generations of thinkers who had increasingly 'internalised' – and that is the important word – the new science of man, directing thought about man from his visible eyes and expressive face to his unseen nerves and controlling brain, from what he looks like to what he feels, and from what he feels to what he knows. Internalisation as a process means that man is no longer satisfied to understand himself as a doer of deeds and a thinker of thoughts. He – man – wants to know precisely how his feelings have shaped his knowledge; and for the first time in European history he is unable to keep them separate, unable not to relate his emotions to his percipience. Richardson penetrates his own fictive creation Clarissa, as Sade does his Justine, by turning inwards and internalising the relation between Clarissa's anatomy, feelings, actions, and finally knowledge. Clarissa must die, as many heroines before her must die, but in her case for the first time, we know precisely why: we have watched her quest for respect proceed from the smallest animal spirit and nerve through all her exquisite delicacy and sensibility to a full knowledge of herself. As Clarissa and her maker further know, internalisation is impossible without an analogue, whether stated or implied, of body and mind. But we would falsify matters if we continued to believe that such an analogue owed its birth to the mid eighteenth century; in fact it was already fairly mature in Shaftesbury's formative years in the first decade of the eighteenth century.[25] Smollett's analysis of his last and greatest hero, Matt Bramble, couched in words well-meditated at the level of unconscious assumption only, could be the epigraph of all writers from Richardson to the Marquis de Sade: 'I think his peevishness', says his nephew Jery Melford, 'arises partly from bodily pain, and partly from a natural excess of mental sensibility.'[26] And Goldsmith's account of Sir William Thornhill (Mr Burchell in disguise) in *The Vicar of Wakefield*, the man who saved the Vicar and his family from destruction, and who is perhaps Goldsmith's most genuinely benevolent character, loses no opportunity to ground itself in a body–mind analogy that was old by 1766: 'Physicians tell us of a disorder', says Goldsmith, 'in which the whole body is so exquisitely sensible, that the slightest touch gives pain: what some have thus suffered in their persons, this gentleman felt in his mind. The slightest distress, whether real or fictitious, touched him to the quick, and his soul laboured under a sickly sensibility of the miseries of others'.[27] Body–mind analogies could not have become conventional in sentimental literature without an antecedent theory of nervous diseases widely disseminated throughout the culture, and this theory ultimately owes little to Burton, Bacon, Thomas Browne, and other seventeenth-century anatomists of melancholy. It is as if the infintely expanding universe, upon which Addison and Pope had dwelt at such length, had to close up again, this time involuting itself on man's inner universe, before the process of internalisation could come full circle at the end of the eighteenth century.

But we can also begin to understand why that most puzzling of modern enigmas, Romanticism, was in turn the heir to a heritage of the cults of sensibility, thereby going beyond the best all-encompassing definition we thus far have, that of Harold Bloom. For if one accepts his enticing idea that it is proper to speak of Romanticism in literature only at the moment when conventional motifs of 'the quest' are internalised,[28] then we can start to see why the intricate process of internalisation itself required a specific neurological legacy. It is not true that Romanticism, understood in this way, could have occurred at any time. First a revolution in knowledge about man, set in motion by certain paradigmatic works, had to occur; and then the diverse cults of sensibility, religious, social, moral, literary, even fashionable, had to play themselves out. While they did, theories about man became increasingly internalised and it was no longer important to pretend, as Swift had, that man could or even ought to be merely a cerebrating creature. Imaginative writers could now return to 'the quest', then centuries upon centuries old, and internalise it – that is, accommodate their feelings to a new set of ideas about it – as readily, as naturally, as scientific thinkers of every persuasion had been internalising philosophical theories about the nature of man throughout the eighteenth century.

NOTES

1 Thomas S. Kuhn, *The Structure of Scientific Revolutions* (Chicago, 1962), 10.

2 The literature of Kuhnian criticism is enormous and cannot be reduced to a few bibliographical references. Perhaps the single best criticism is one not directly attacking

Kuhn but substituting for his 'paradigm' a different but not unrelated theory of the 'episteme'; see Michel Foucault, *Les Mots et les choses* (Paris, 1966); English version, *The Order of Things: an Archaeology of the Human Sciences* (New Yor, 1970). Although I vigorously disagree with Foucault about the simple facts of European scientific history 1600–1800, I have been enormously influenced by his way of doing intellectual history, i.e. decoding beneath visible surfaces, as I have by Robert K. Merton's theory 'that in each age there is a system of science which rests upon a set of assumptions, usually implicit and seldom questioned by the scientists of the time'; in Bernard Barber and Walker Hirsch (eds.) *The Sociology of Science* (New York, 1962), 41. Kuhn's own revaluation of his concept of the 'paradigm' is of considerable interest; see his 'Postscript – 1969', in *The Structure*, 2nd ed., enlarged (Chicago, 1970), 174–210.

3 I have attempted to show some of the differences between Kuhn and Foucault in 'Whose Enlightenment? Not Man's: the Case of Michel Foucault', *Eighteenth-Century Studies*, VI (1972–3), 238–56 (chap. 3 above).

4 Kuhn, *Scientific Revolutions*, 10: 'In this essay, "normal science" means research firmly based upon one or more past scientific achievements that some particular scientific community ackowledges for a time as supplying the foundation for its further practice'.

5 *The Enlightenment: an Interpretation*, II: *The Science of Freedom* (New York, 1969), 167–215.

6 See Alexander Koyre, *Newtonian Studies*, (Cambridge, 1965), 63–7, and *From the Closed World to the Infinite Universe* (Baltimore, 1957), 131–4, for analysis and discussion of Newton's reasons.

7 Towards Defining an Age of Sensibility', *English Literary History*, XXIII (1956), 144–52.

8 I do not consider the two identical, although they are obviously related in dozens of aspects, Historically and generally speaking sensibility was the larger of the two, touching almost every aspect of life; sentimentalism came later, especially in imaginative literature, and was the more religious, moral, literary, and far less aristocratic of the two; it was also the one that lent itself more readily to radical modifications and variations from an already blurred original. In every case the distinction is grey, never black or white. Some excellent philological explorations into these labels have already been undertaken: see E. Erametsa, *A Study of the Word 'Sentimental'*, (Helsinki, 1951), and R. F. Brissenden, ' "Sentiment": Some Uses of the Word in the Writings of David Hume', in R. F. Brissenden (ed.), *Studies in the Eighteenth Century: Papers Presented at the David Nicol Smith Memorial Seminar Canberra 1966* (Canberra, 1968) 89–106 and *Virtue in Distress* (London, 1974) part I, chap. ii: ' "Sentimentalism": an Attempt at Definition'.

9 *Pathologiae Cerebri* (1667), tr. Samuel Pordage as *An Essay of the Pathology of the Brain*, in *The Remaining Medical Works of Dr Thomas Willis* (1681); Willis's two other most important works are *Cerebri Anatome* (1664) and *De Anima Brutorum* (1672), the last also tr. by Pordage as *Two Discourses concerning the Soul of Brutes, which is that of the Vital and Sensitive Soul of Man* (1683).

10 'Suggestions Toward a Genealogy of the "Man of Feeling" ', in *The Idea of the Humanities* 2 vols. (Chicago, 1967), I, 188–213, originally published in *English Literary History*, I (1934), 205–30. Crane's exact words are (I, 190): 'If we wish to understand the origins and the widespread diffusion in the eighteenth century of the ideas which issued in the cult of sensibility, we must look, I believe, to a period considerably earlier than that in which Shaftesbury wrote and take into account the propaganda of a group of persons whose opportunities for moulding the thoughts of ordinary Englishmen were much greater than those of even the most aristocratic of deists.' Crane's intuition about a chronology 'earlier than that in which Shaftesbury wrote' is sound but his reasons are altogether unacceptable. He maintains that sensibility was 'not a philosophy which the eighteenth century *could have* derived full fledged from ancient or Renaissance tradition. It was something new in the world – a doctrine, or rather a complex of doctrines, which a hundred years before 1750 would have been frowned upon, had it

ever been presented to them, by representatives of every school of ethical or religious thought' (I, 189–90, italics mine). Benevolence and related ideas of 'doing good' almost certainly *could* have developed before 1750, or 1660, or (for that matter) 1640, for they are everywhere present in the Bible, and in medieval and Renaissance Christian ethical teaching. But a theory to explain the self-conscious personality could not have derived from earlier times (earlier, that is, than the Restoration) because there was no scientific model for it. *'Sensibility'* used more narrowly, as a term to connote self-consciousness and self-awareness, has a history different from Crane's umbrella term (although my usage is not altogether unrelated to his). This is the sense in which many eighteenth-century writers, especially scientists, employed it, and it is the sense in which I use it.

11 Frye writes: 'I do not care about terminology, only about appreciation for an extraordinarily interesting period of English literature, and the first stage in renewing that appreciation seems to me the gaining of a clear sense of what it is in itself; and 'Contemporary poetry is still deeply concerned with the problems and techniques of the age of sensibility, and while the latter's resemblance to our time is not a merit itself, it is a logical enough reason for re-examining it with fresh eyes'. These two sentences appear in *English Literary History*, XXIII (1956), 145, 152. As Frye indicates, he is uninterested in the label – as I am – but concerned with literary techniques and strategies, especially the sense of time held by authors 1750–1800 and their Longinian view of literature as 'a process' culminating in various calculated, emotional responses.

12 Galen's enormous influence on the history of medicine is a subject in itself, especially the manner by which some (but not all) of his physiological doctrines remained virtually intact during the seventeenth and eighteenth centuries. Of unusual interest to my thesis are the following: R. B. Onians, *The Origins of European Thought about the Body*, 2nd ed (Cambridge, 1954); Erich Voegelin, *Anamnesis* (Munich, 1966), K. E. Rothschun, *Physiologie: der Wandel ihrer Konzepte* (Munich, 1968); Peter H. Niebyl, 'Galen, Van Helmont, and Blood Letting', in Allen G. Debus, (ed.) *Science, Medicine and Society in the Renaissance*, 2 vols. (New York, 1972), II, 13–23; F. N. L. Poynter, *The History and Philosophy of Knowledge of the Brain and its Funtions: an Anglo-American Symposium*, (Oxford, 1958; rev. ed. 1972) F. Solmsen's study of physiological theories prevalent in the time of Plato makes it evident at least by implication that Galenic concepts would have been sufficiently 'open-ended' to create interest; but whether they deflected enough men to be 'paradigmatic' in Kuhn's sense I cannot say. See 'Tissues and the Soul', *Philosophical Review*, LIX (1950), 435–68.

13 Kuhn's phrase for the scientific community that becomes deflected after a paradigmatic work (10).

14 See *The History and Philosophy of Knowledge of the Brain*, especially three papers in the Third Session: Walter Pagel, 'Medieval and Renaissance Contributions to Knowledge of the Brain and its Functions', 95–114; Walther Riese, 'Descartes's Ideas of Brain Function', 115–34; W. P. D. Wightman, 'Wars of Ideas in Neurological Science – from Willis to Bichat and from Locke to Condillac', 135–48.

15 In *English Literary History*, I, 205–30.

16 In L. G. Stevenson and R. P. Multhauf, (ed.), *Medicine, Science, and Culture* (Baltimore, 1968), 135. Clarke rightly notes two exceptions: 'But there were two investigations in the eighteenth century, the results of which were readily available to all, which pointed to the future. In 1717 Leeuwenhoek saw and illustrated the single myelinated nerve fiber, the center of which (the axis cylinder or axon) he took to be hollow . . . Of greater significance, however, was the second discovery, made by Fontana in 1779 . . . Again, this was the myelinated axon of today, but Fontana's work seems to have had little immediate effect, probably because of the suspicion engendered by most eighteenth-century microscopic investigations.' My own research on nerves and animal spirits corroborates Clarke's findings: I have found no evidence that the discoveries of Leeuwenhoek and Fontana were acknowledged, understood, or digested. This

development is not surprising in view of the fact that Leeuwenhock himself never realised what he had observed.

17 Clarke, *Medicine, Science, and Culture*, 123–41, has performed the research and settled the matter once and for all. His statement (124) about scientific models in physiology is revealing and germane to the rise of 'sensibility' as a serious subject for scientific concern: 'In general, the customary sequence of events during the accumulation of knowledge regarding a part of the animal or human body is that its morphology is established first of all: *thereafter its phsyiology can be investigated*. This has been true with structures like the heart, but in the case of nerves the advancement has been more complicated because of the greater complexity of nervous tissue and organs. Here, during the seventeenth and eighteenth centuries speculation predominated in respect to both form and function. It is probable that the ancients, having accepted the suggestion that the nerve acted by means of a substance passing through it, *also had to postulate a hollowness or porosity* so that this *would be possible*. Structure was therefore *determined* by the demands of function' (italics mine). But Willis's paradigmatic works created a revolution in science in that he made it *possible* – in Clark's sense – to explore the physiology of nerves in the first place. Until the seat of voluntary and involuntary motion was limited to the cerebrum and cerebellum and their network of surrounding nerves, speculation about Clarke's 'form' (i.e. morphology) was necessarily erratic and uncontrollable.

18 Especially in *Pathologiae Cerebri* and *De Anima Brutorum*. Almost every modern historian of physiology has spoken about Willis with wonder and awe, e.g. Sir Michael Foster, *Lectures on the History of Physiology during the Sixteenth, Seventeenth and Eighteenth Centuries* (Cambridge, 1901; repr. with an intro. by C. D. O'Malley, New York, 1970) 269; 'Though Malpighi . . . devoted much attention to the histology of the nervous system, we find in his writings very little concerning its function . . . One man alone perhaps during this century stands out prominently for his labours on the structure and functions of the brain, namely Thomas Willis'. One of Willis's most thorough biographers, Dr Hansruedi Isler (*Thomas Willis* (Stuttgart, 1965); tr. by the author, 1968, New York and London), maintains that 'Willis' achievements in neuroanatomy and neurophysiology comprise the first useful theory of brain localization of pshychic and vegetative functions as well as the first interpretation of nerve action as an energetic process. His new concept of nerve action led him to the idea – and the term – of reflex action, whereas his localization theory gave rise to the development of experimental physiology of the central nervous system. In order to complete his account of the nervous system Willis described the bulk of the nervous and psychic diseases: the three books he published from 1667 to 1672 contain *the most complete text of neuropsychiatry since Greek antiquity*. Most later interpretations of psychophysical relationships have been influenced by his ideas, either directly or indirectly' (x; italics mine). John F. Fulton, surely the most distinguished twentieth-century historian of neurophysiology, considers the cornerstones of modern neurology to be based on six books by Willis (1664), Whytt (1751), Magendie (1882), Hitzig (1874), Ferrier (1876), and Sherrington (1906) (*Physiology of the Nervous System*, 2nd ed (1943), 163). Fulton, while recognising some of the important discoveries of Robert Whytt, considers him relatively unimportant in the line of revolutionary theories about brain localisation like those of Willis: 'In his memorable *Cerebri anatome*, published in 1664, Thomas Willis, suggested that the cerebrum presided over voluntary motions and that the cerebellum governed involuntary movements'. Willis had noted that 'when the cerebellum was manipulated in a living animal the heart stopped, and if the cerebellum was removed the animal died. Suggestive indeed was the idea that the cerebellum facilitated involuntary action . . . There was little further advance until 1809 . . .' (*Physiology of the Nervous System*, 463). Kenneth Dewhurst, another biographer of Willis, has also stressed Willis's revolutionary role in the development of modern science: see *Thomas Willis as a Physician* (Los Angeles, 1964). In two other important works, he demonstrates Willis's profound influence on Locke: *John Locke, 1632–1704, Physician and Philosopher: a Medical Biography* (1963), and 'An Oxford

Medical Quartet – Sydenham, Willis, Locke, and Lower', *British Medical Journal*, II (1963), 857–80. R. K. French (*Robert Whytt, The Soul, and Medicine* (1969) 134) is right to note that 'Towards the end of the century opinion inclined away from placing mental functions in structures within the brain, and many, agreeing with Steno that Willis had been too speculative, favoured a more general placing of the soul in the substance of the brain'. Nicolaus Steno's *Discours . . . sur l'anatomie du cerveau* (Paris, 1669) and Humphrey Ridley's *The Anatomy of the Brain* (1695) were among these works. But *all* these books were answers to Willis and merely attest to his 'paradigmatic' ability to deflect, as Kuhn says, 'succeeding generations of practitioners'.

19 While there is a great deal of evidence pointing to Willis's influence on Locke in the *Essay* (see, e.g., Isler, *Thomas Willis*, 176–81, in which Isler traces many Lockan passages to Willis), there is less known about his influence on later physiologists. To propound that Whytt and Haller were perfectly well aware of his theories about voluntary and involuntary motions, and all the replies, rebuttals and disagreements regarding his all-important 'intercostal' nerve, is to indulge in simplicity about the history of science: one might as well set out to prove that Pope had heard of Milton (see R. K. French, *Robert Whytt*, 32ff.). The response of vitalists and animists equally demonstrates clear knowledge (even if it is not always unequivocally stated) of every aspect of Willis's brain theory. See H. Driesch, 'Georg Ernest Stahl (1660–1734)', in *The History and Theory of Vitalism*, tr. C. K. Ogden (1914), 30–6; George Canguilhem, *La Formation du concept de reflexe* (Paris, 1955); L. J. Rather, 'Stahl's Psychological Physiology', *Bulletin of the History of Medicine*, XXXV (1961, 37–49).

20 Anna L. Barbauld (ed.), *The Correspondence of Samuel Richardson*, 6 vols. (1804), iv, 30.

21 *The Rise of The Novel* (Berkeley, 1957), 184.

22 For the most exhaustive survey of the controversy, see R. K. French, 'The Controversy with Haller: Sense and Sensibility', in *Robert Whytt*, 63–76.

23 The passage is found in George Cheyne, M.D., *The English Malady*, 2 vols. (1733), I, 71.

24 One can test the hypothesis by consulting scientific works written in the 1650s, especially by Hobbes and some of the early Cambridge Platonists; nowhere is the brain invoked in this manner before 1664, the date of publication of Willis's *Cerebri Anatome*.

25 A list like this perhaps raises questions about Defoe and Fielding: were they not exposed to the same ideas as Richardson? Were their nerves any less sensible? Yes, Fielding received similar exposure – everyone did – but his physiology, the era of Mrs Donnellan would have argued, was much less exquisite than Richardson's. The truth is of course more elaborate than this but, however crude, her answer is an approximation, and we see it splendidly mirrored in Johnson's estimate of Fielding as a 'barren rascal'.

26 *Humphry Clinker* (1771); J. Melford to Sir Watkin Phillips, 18 April.

27 In *Collected Works*, ed. Arthur Friedman, 5 vols (Oxford, 1966), IV, 29.

28 Such is Bloom's theory in *The Visionary Company: a Reading of English Romantic Poetry* (New York, 1961; rev. and enl. ed. 1971). Bloom, taking his cue from Northrop Frye, titles his first chapter 'The Heritage of Sensibility'.

F

6

Threshold and explanation: social anthropology and the critic of literature in the age of post-disciplines

During my first year in Cambridge, England (1979–80) critical discussion in the college (i.e., local knowledge) was centred on a few specific books written in English: Lawrence Stone's The Family, Sex and Marriage in England: 1500–1700; *as well as E. P. Thompson's* Albion's Fatal Tree: Crime and Society in 18th Century England; Whigs and Hunters: the Origin of the Black Act; *and* The Poverty of Theory and Other Essays, *all of which had recently been published. The last book made a particularly strong impression on me, especially its comforting assurance that critique and metacritique were not dishonourable even if they were often communicated in a pungent and polemical tone. In Thompson's memorable words: '. . . theory cannot be developed or tested without critique, and critique must involve the direct identification of alternative positions in a polemical manner. If one cares about ideas, it is difficult to write about error (or imputed error) without a certain sharpness of tone. I hope that I have always argued with reasons' (404). Thompson's* Writing by Candlelight *appeared in the spring of 1980, as I was leaving England. I read it at once, and was further startled by its brutal frankness about the modern university and its chaotic research agendas in an age of post-disciplines.*

This is the kind of discourse we need for eighteenth-century studies, I thought: writing that was unabashedly frank by reflecting on its ideological and epistemological imperatives, yet which inexorably re-contextualised the author – the speaking voice – by placing him or her in the centre of the arena rather than on the periphery. Yet in North America we were still getting effete, vestigial New Criticism, where hordes of instructors and assistant professors hoping for tenure continued to churn out yet another book providing 'new readings' of five essential poems, plays, or novels.

Under the spell of these authors – Stone to Thompson – I composed this essay, which Ian Watt asked me to prepare as a plenary session address to be delivered before the International Association of University Professors of English, convening in Aberdeen in the summer of 1980. A year later I published it in a journal in Texas called The Eighteenth Century: Theory and Interpretation, *XXII (spring 1981), 127–52. When it went into galley proof, there was some difference of opinion about the appropriateness of the running heads: 'social anthropology and literature'. Some of my colleagues privately expressed to me their concern that I would be ridiculed for advocating the cloacal stuff of social history and social anthropology after two generations of a succession of 'new criticisms' had refined the tastes and sensibilities of the modern academy. I allowed the runners to stand, as I did the four archetypes identified for analysis: widows, whores, bachelors, and homosexuals. It was still not quite proper to name these figures in polite discourse, much less so to discuss their structures of kinship among eighteenth-century scholars who had not problematised them to any significant degree, unless it were under the aegis of irony, metaphor, or some other rhetorical trick. Little did I realise that all this would soon change – explode – as sex, race, and gender carried the day in the postmodernist 1980s, especially within the walls of the contemporary university, where such diverse methods as Lacanianism, semiotics, and New Historicism, all privileged just these types of marginal and problematic figures. At the time of composition the essay seemed bold – in conception as well as execution; it now strikes me as too tame and actually lacking much of the reflectiveness for which I was then searching.*

I begin with an autobiographical disclosure by Foucault:

> If one poses, for a science such as theoretical physics or organic chemistry, the problem of its relations with the political and economic structure of society, doesn't one pose a problem which is too complicated? Isn't the threshold of possible explanation placed too high? If, on the other hand, one takes a knowledge [*savoir*] such as psychiatry, won't the question be much easier to resolve, since psychiatry has a low epistemological profile, and since psychiatric practice is tied to a whole series of institutions, immediate economic exigencies and urgent political pressures for social regulation? Cannot the interrelation of effects of knowledge and power be more securely grasped in the case of a science as 'doubtful' as psychiatry? It is this same question that I wanted to pose, in *The Birth of the Clinic* apropos of medicine: it certainly has a much stronger scientific structure than psychiatry, but it is also very deeply involved in the social structures. What 'threw me off' a bit at the time was the fact that the question which I posed did not at all interest those to whom I posed it. They considered it a problem without political importance and without epistemological nobility.[1]

Those who are opposed on principle to all varieties of structuralism will naturally dismiss this plea for the elevation of threshold on grounds that it has been made by an admittedly brilliant if besotted madman who insists on demonstrating his distaste for traditional literary criticism by the continual dissolution of authors and texts in his own writings – in *Madness and Civilization, The Birth of the Clinic, The Order of Things, The Archaeology of Knowledge, Discipline and Punish*, and now in *The History of Sexuality* – in favour of philosophical theory which discounts practical criticism *à la* I. A. Richards. For such opponents of Foucault and structuralism – the two are not, of course, synonymous but I am considering them synonymous here for the sake of convenience – the fact that Foucault's question about threshold and explanation 'did not at all interest those to whom I posed it', and the further historical fact that in 1967 his colleagues in France deemed his question 'a problem without political importance and without epistemological nobility', is neither here nor there but is merely irrelevant. These enemies of structuralism dismiss the question, and if they could they would ban Foucault's books. Friends of Eliot and enemies of Foucault (and the pollution he represents), they dangerously reduce the scope of possible approaches to one contrary-state of Eliot versus Foucault without asking themselves what contribution Eliot ever made to the understanding or appreciation of eighteenth-century English literature, or interrogating whether the eighteenth century itself would have placed 'Taste' so far above 'Ideas' in its chain of intellectual being. Nevertheless, Foucault has again and again shown himself to be the *only* thinker since 1960 capable of redeeming eighteenth-century imaginative literature from the prison house in which it continues to remain confined. If this vast body of supposedly great imaginative literature is divided according to the language in which it was written – French, English, German, etc. – and the country where it is being studied, even graver consequences obtain. In Britain the study of eighteenth-century English literature is practically non-existent; it seems to have been given up even in Oxbridge, usually the last stronghold of tradition. In France and Germany the literature is also dead and the few scholar–critics who continue to read and lecture on it concede in private that they do so under duress and out of guilt: usually to fulfil a requirement such as the degree *docteur ès lettres* in order to remain in the academic profession, though they are no sooner validated than they cease reading and lecturing on it and defect to the modern period. Only in North America is this literature still creatively read and studied. Yet we study it surrounded, as it were, by 'danger signs'. For one thing, academic America is a vast continent and those who apply themselves to this field have no sway or influence; for another, the students we can hope to engage are constantly disappearing and time is running out, though few of us will admit it. Despite the beginning of a new decade we – those of us in American who teach this literature – are actually worse off than we were in 1951 or 1961. I venture to affirm that the 1970s have shown and the 1980s may confirm the inability of contemporary higher criticism altogether. Sterne is the only exception and even he lags behind the front rank of authors of whom almost all lived after 1800. The reasons for this failure are not mysterious: eighteenth-century British literature considered as a whole represents certain empirical beliefs and moral values in which a very large segment of the contemporary literate world is uninterested and to which it does not want to be converted. Notions of right reason, rule and authority; ideas about the polite ego and the rightfully-extended self; strains of entrenched piety and inflexibility hierarchy, to say nothing about rules of conduct as well as rules for writing – are nothing for which our fellow readers are pining in an age such as ours in which the obscure, the exotic, the unseen, the forbidden, the vicarious, the transformed, the irrational are far more sought after in literature. Even critics who profess to care about the 'great tradition' of English literature from Beowulf to Virginia Woolf seem to be much too preoccupied with other urgent business to take time out to read and write about some of our distinguished writers, though they churn out books and monographs about twentieth-century authors.[2]

Yet while these higher critics, by which I do not mean solely academic critics, have turned to other periods, critic-scholars interested in the eighteenth century have not gone to sleep. It may be impossible to generalise adequately and fairly about their writings during the last two decades, but one thing is clear: if the New Criticism and Aristotelianism (or Chicagoism) were the two rival pillars of the 1950s, a house torn assunder by W. K. Wimsatt and R. S. Crane both of whom wrote extensively about the eighteenth century, the house of the 1970s was far more peaceful and enjoyed a pluralism capable of including as partners textual exegesis, critical biography, the history of ideas, structuralism, metacriticism, and many other varieties. One partner in the 1970s was the social anthropology of literature, by which I do not mean social history which is but one branch. Essentially interdisciplinary, social anthropology places the text and the '*con*-text' – the context – on almost equal footing and thereby deeply appeals to the relativistic mood and egalitarian trends of our times. For some academic scholars and literary critics the appeal of social anthropology is its exoticism: it indulges a romantic wish that may enable us to salvage literary studies from their doldrums and thereby – as Beckett might have said – 'to go on', to regenerate ourselves and to continue to attract new students. Therefore, the externality and interdisciplinarity of a socio-anthropological approach are not its only merits: it is also pedagogically useful. By encompassing the visual arts and the social sciences, as well as the psychology and philosophy of the age – its entire *Gestalt* – social anthropology enlarges the role of literary critics from that of narrowly conceived philological and exegetical concerns. The socio-anthropological critic asks questions with a high 'threshold', which is why he profoundly disturbs more traditional scholars and often elicits their contempt. Because this threshold of possible questions and adequate answers is pitched so high, the social-anthropologist critic–scholar often attempts to exceed the boundaries of rhetorical ploy and narrative ambivalence. Ronald Paulson was satisfied at the start of this career to write about irony in *A Tale of a Tub*; his latest book, *Popular and Polite Art in the Age of Hogarth and Fielding* (1979), enlists no single author, major or minor, as its ostensible subject or hero but expounds instead on jokes, lies, card games, arcane medicines, cartoons and caricatures – crudely speaking the cookies, coconuts, candy-bars, popcorn, and peanuts of Georgian popular culture. It is emphatically and unequivocally a work in the mold of social anthropology. Likewise the recent sociological works by Pat Rogers ('The Writer and Society', in *The Context of English Litera-*

ture, 1978) and Lawrence Stone (*The Family, Sex and Marriage in England: 1500–1800*, 1977): these books represent more than Michel Foucault's 'disappearance of the subject'; they demonstrate a new threshold of analysis and an enlarged range of interests.

. Also, the social anthropologist knows, whether he contains his understanding or broadcasts its, that ultimately one's critical vocabulary is everything; but he does not permit this knowledge to reduce the level of his threshold of explanation or to cast his net over a narrow domain. He himself – whether Ronald Paulson, Lawrence Stone, or Pat Rogers – is a critic and a scholar, that is, an elitist thinker with vast knowledge; but he wants to penetrate beyond the eternal ambiguity of words to the ordinary people and ordinary things of the eighteenth century. In a sense he is tired of 'great authors' and 'traditional readings' and 'definitive biographies'. He doesn't really want to write another book about irony in *A Tale of a Tub* or another biography of Hogarth, so he 'saves literature' by saving himself from the onerous chore, and by so doing somehow persuades himself that he – whether a Paulson or a Stone – is a part of that 'culture-of-the-whole' about which he writes, knowing of course that he is a somewhat solitary professor confined to his ivy tower and grove. There is of course much more than this to say about the approach I am rather crudely calling socioanthropological, but it would be false and misleading to suggest that there is already a 'school' by this name. There is no such thing. What exists is a handful of scholar–critics here and there, among whom I suppose I count myself, writing about eighteenth-century literature and history in this vein. Yet the rise of such students has not been determined merely by the limitations of practical criticism but also as a consequence of the infinite cultural richness of British life between Dryden and Wordsworth. Nor is social anthropology in vogue as a consequence of default: because it has replaced a primary English literature less than great. Surely English literature from Dryden and Pope to Collins and Blake – still eighteenth-century men – has nothing whatsoever to be ashamed of. If higher criticism today feels unattracted to it, this may be a critical rather than a literary failure. The rapid change in the genres in the eighteenth century is one clue about the strengths of social anthropology: genres do not alter themselves, or alter as a mere consequence of internal energies; society exerts terrific pressures on the genres with which the 'practical critic' often poorly copes. That society – not only the world of Anne and the Georges but the grass-roots world as well – has yet to be understood. As the late Professor John Butt reportedly commented to friends while writing his *Oxford History of English Literature*, 'we have not even begun to ask the right questions yet', and he may have been right.

Finally, social anthropology quietly but proudly contends that there is more to the past than rhetorical analysis. It nowhere diminishes rhetoric, nor does it extol certain texts merely for the sake of performing rhetorical pyrotechniques. It interprets, studies, 'reads' texts – but it does not exclude whole classes of texts judged by some not to have enduring literary merit. Nor does it favour any methodology: it welcomes internalist as well as externalist approaches, structuralism as well as practical applied criticism. One strength of social anthropology is that it is among the most pluralistic of methodologies in a contemporary intellectual milieu that itself is radically pluralistic. And social anthropology – unlike traditional historicism especially that historicism which wants to preserve the status quo – usually concerns itself with the common man; thus it consults archives, counts wills, studies folk traditions while embracing the new methodologies of the social sciences: psychoanalysis of many varieties – not merely Freudianism, Jungianism or Lacanianism; sociology – especially the sociology of the arts; and, of course, politics and economics. The social anthropologist is also far less insular, geographically speaking, than many applied critics: he sees beyond national boundaries, reaps the methodological benefits of many countries, not just of his own. And he does not abjure an approach or method of interpretation merely because it is literally foreign: as the British renounce French methods as the French renounce the British, the Americans the French, the French the American, and so forth. Rather, he searches for methods with high thresholds. Therefore, if the work of the French *Annales* School writers – to give but one example – is unmistakable by virtue of a pro-Marxist bent and a proclivity towards reliance on post-Freudian psychoanalysis, if North American writing in this historical mode virtually omits the politics and psychoanalysis of the historian, the writings of contemporary social anthropologists who study our eighteenth century nevertheless enjoy a tie even stronger than these: namely the interpretability of territories extending beyond the domain of written texts, certainly beyond a monolithic and unequivocally prescribed body of primary texts. Moreover, the social anthropologist admires literary style and rhetorical polish but does not strive for it as an end in itself any more than he strives for interdisciplinarity. Nor does he resemble Arthur Koestler's scientific 'sleepwalkers' who cannot sleep because they are troubled by inner demons crying out to be vindicated.[3] The social anthropologist has ceased to hear (if ever he heard at all) the shrill cries of the Leavisites about 'a great tradition'. E. P. Thompson's words, a manifesto, resound instead: 'Collectively we command no funds, control no appointments, prescribe no examinations . . . What provokes in them [our opponents] this paranoia, I suppose, is the indecency of our lack of deference, in continuing to write despite the decision that we do not exist.'[4] This self-serving rhetoric of alleged persecution is, to be sure, more frenetic on British soil than in continental North America because, geographically speaking, Britain is so small. In the vast expanses of North-

American academia the social anthropologists are swallowed up: it is not, alas, as Thompson affirms, that 'we do not exist' but rather that it makes no difference here *whether* we exist or not, but all this digression, though necessary, is a prelude towards understanding that the social anthropologist wants to interpret 'ordinary people' as well as set texts. He concerns himself as much with the sociology of the Black Act as with Pope's imagined Windsor Forest where the 'Blacks' committed most of their perfidy, with Tyburn and the Fleet as with *Moll Flanders*, with domestic proposal scenes as with *Clarissa* or *Pride and Prejudice*, and with the mundane life of Grub Street as well as with the visionary *Dunciad*.

But the social anthropologist should not be viewed as a fringe scholar – as someone for ever on the margins of discourse. When he does interpret literary texts, he is often more penetrating than the New Critical vestiges; and the insight provided by his 'marginalities' is often worth a dozen reworked traditional readings. He gets a handle on texts by studying the facts and mythologies of ordinary people. He may be a new type of mandarin himself; but when engaged in the critical act, his conscious ruling passion is illumination of just the ordinary 'things of this world'.[5] As such, the social anthropologist enjoys no pride in custodianship. He is not a preserver but a pioneer: he researches, is forever opening avenues of approach, takes immense intellectual risks, connects disparate realms, but does not protect privileged territory or guard the past from rash impostors who may violate it. In time he realises that there is a political ideology connected to his practice as a social anthropologist. But the realisation, at least in America, is still an awakening. Perhaps it will mature in the 1980s.

To document some of these above developments I have selected four texts, each demonstrating a particular aspect of the social anthropologist's approach. In two cases – the middle two – work has already begun, and although I suggest further avenues for exploration a start has been made. In some ways the first and last texts are problematic, and I suggest how these 'texts' can be illuminated and enriched by such an external approach.

WIDOWS: *Tristram Shandy*

Because Sterne has been the only author of the period seriously to engage the attention of contemporary criticism, it may be appropriate to look at *Tristram Shandy* – not the whole novel but one of its characters, the Widow Wadman. I select her because she seems such an obvious 'type' – the lascivious widow – and because Sterne's recent critics have said so little about her. She has actually never come into her own as a major (that is to say engaging or prepossessing) figure; she has captured our attention – the argument goes – only to the degree that she illustrates, as a foil, Uncle

Toby's ingrained sentimentalism and profound benevolence. From the time of Scott and Thackeray to the present day, critics have neglected her perhaps as a consequence of her characterisational clarity, perhaps because she represents something not fit for polite conversation; yet she is certainly the antagonist of volumes eight and nine. Our era, professing to celebrate the emancipation of Every Man, may be on the verge of finding significance in her plight as we recommend her for 'Widow's Liberation', but some of her judges have been less kind. Melvyn New says more than most critics: 'While Toby tries to conduct an affair of the heart, the widow Wadman is busy conducting an affair of the groin.'[6]

Successful it may be, but not because Wadman is in the tradition of the Wishforts and Loveits. Elsewhere New comments that 'the Widow is "a daughter of *Eve*", "*a perfect woman*", a human being with merely the flesh that man is heir to; the flesh that the sentimentalist would like to ignore, and indeed does ignore'.[7] At least from the time of Chaucer, the widow was viewed as a lecherous predator, if not identical with the 'old whore' type then a sister of hers.[8] Granted that certain legal rights were withheld from married women, she was at once freer to indulge her carnality and to do so with economic impunity; she could control her own money and her former husband's, as well as that of future ones, which her unmarried sisters could not. The widow retained this image of unquenched lechery throughout the Middle Ages and Renaissance, giving rise to a literature in which she always played the same stereotypical role: as one who is now bereft of the sexual pleasures of marriage; who has the money to pay, if necessary, for her pecadillo; who is robust and ruddy, not yet ready for the sexual grave, let alone the real one. By the Restoration there is evidence that the widow has learned to see herself for what she is and has begun to reform herself somewhat. This is why Congreve could depict his Wishfort so ruthlessly: had the real Wishforts in 1700 been as naive about their lechery as the crude old hag they saw on the stage, they would have been far more incensed than we know they were. Even so, some were offended by Congreve's widow – who continued to draw the loudest applause – mistaking genial satire and hyperbolic rhetoric for outright savagery. But the widow in the Restoration and eighteenth century continued to enjoy her right to manage her dead husband's bank accounts, the only female type so privileged. On just this point rests the tangled plot and secret of the two widows, Wishfort and Fainall, in Congreve's play.

But Sterne's Widow Wadman is an altogether different configuration. Obviously cast in the tradition of the lecherous bloodsucking widow, she is less crude and harmful than the Wishforts and Loveits. She has patiently waited 'for eleven years', and although admittedly far more interested in Toby's groin than Trim's knee, underneath she has been conducting an affair of the heart after all. Though 'she kicked the pin out of her fingers' and 'stood . . . harnassed and caparisoned at all points', though always ready to light Toby's candle on fire and follow 'his fingers and knees and eyes', though possessed of 'venereal eyes' and called a 'daughter of *Eve*' more than once, the Widow's heart is the part most affected after all. This is why Sterne is sexually and geographically so meticulous in the inserted tale (IX, 4–10) about 'the Jew's widow at Lisbon'. The debates and controversies over the 1755 earthquake at Lisbon – just a few years before Sterne composed *Tristram Shandy* – left some believing that it was the European capital of degeneracy. In Lisbon Trim's brother Tom had been 'smote' by her 'eyes' just as Toby has been by the Widow Wadman's. Here, too, the 'Jew widow' is portrayed within an assumed knowledge of the lecherous widow type. But with a difference: a Jewess, she is greedy as well as wealthy and lecherous. Her husband has left her 'in possession of a rousing trade' (IX, 5) – a sausage shop where she acts as a wonderful master to male apprentices, explaining the method of (the pun is of course intended) 'making them' (IX, 7): 'First, by taking hold of the ring of the sausage while she stroked the forced meat down with her hand – then by cutting the strings into proper lengths, and holding them across her mouth . . . and so on from little to more, till at last he adventured to tie the sausage himself, while she held the snout' (IX, 7). While she held the snout she discoursed, Tom recounted to Trim, about sausages 'a little gayly – as, "With what skins – and if they never burst – Whether the largest were not the best" ' (IX, 7). Although we do not hear the entire tale of this concupiscent Jewish widow, Sterne assures us that 'it went on – and on – it had episodes in it – it came back, and went on – and on again; there was no end of it' (IX, 10).

Sterne inserted it into the longer account of the Widow Wadman's 'love' for purposes of clear contrast. Whereas the Jewess is pre-eminently after lucre and bawdy, the Widow Wadman, though she also flirts bawdily, has a heart. The Jewess's husband 'had the ill luck to die of a strangury' (IX, 5) – a sure clue that she had sexually worn out his organ[9] – whereas Wadman's husband died of natural causes clearly not originating in the pelvic cavity. Sterne ends his account of the Jewish widow by withholding from the lascivious reader the bawdiest (and very lengthy) 'episodes'. All we know for certain – so carnal is the story – is Tristram's verbal ejaculation ' – G – help my father! he pish'd fifty times at every new attitude . . .' (IX, 10). 'She has a thousand virtues, *Trim!*' (IX, 31), cries Uncle Toby a few paragraphs before the novel closes, persuaded of 'the compassionate turn and singular humanity of her character' (IX, 31). It is true, her campaign has been conducted in the name of the groin but her obsession with the flesh is only skin deep. Seated on Sterne's inimitable 'sopha' in the parlour, Uncle Toby offers to let Mrs Wadman 'lay [her] finger upon the place' (IX, 20); but the lady, though in love, will not. She knows how high the stakes are. Thus 'I will not touch it, however, quoth Mrs. *Wadman* to herself', to which Sterne comments, 'This requires a second translation: – it shews what little knowledge is got by mere words.' Indeed it does and Uncle Toby has ultimately not mistaken her 'accent of humanity' (IX, 26). Though Mrs. Wadman 'went round about *Namur* to get at my uncle *Toby's* groin (IX, 26), she is, as Toby notices, a tender and loving 'sister' to him, one who wants marriage not an affair. Walter's diatribe (IX, 32) to the effect that the 'devil' is in widows 'and that the whole of the [Wadman] affair was lust' is only partly accurate: *sentiment* alone can finely discriminate between bawds like the Jewish widow and 'humanists' like Mrs Wadman; and the telling distinction shows the clarifications of a socioanthropological reading.

The social anthropologists have not as yet isolated the widow in eighteenth-century literature as a type. When they do, they will naturally cast Mrs Wadman as one of their heroes and convey more finely discriminated estimates of her place in the European tradition of the widow. They will be intrigued by Sterne's use of language in the two volumes (8 and 9) in which Mrs. Wadman's affair of 'the groin and the heart' carries the narrative forward, and they will see how he has assumed a tradition that is now practically lost to us. 'The knee is such a distance from the main body,' Corporal Trim observes in desperation, 'whereas the groin . . . is upon the very *curtin* of the *place*' (IX, 31). The succession of this passage and 'My uncle *Toby* gave a long whistle' is precisely what makes the texture of Sterne's narrative so original. The key and pitch of the whistle is everything – as consequential for the acute reader as the silences and omissions between interlocutions – and the social anthropologist does not omit these; he augments them by development of a social milieu, and he gives us a picture of the widow that is more precisely focused than anything we have ever had. Surely the Widow Wadman does not deserve any of the charges a modern might make against her – charges of lechery, melancholy, eccentricity, and greed – who is unaware that her distance from these qualities, almost always found in widows, is precisely what distinguishes her. The social anthropologist realises the strange paradoxes of the widow's world, he can unlock some of her secrets, and he agrees when Edmund Wilson writes to Dorothy Walsh admonishing her for the false Arnoldian belief that life and literature exist worlds apart. Wilson quietly inquires, 'But isn't literature simply *a part of life*, as much as conversation?'[10] In a word, Wilson, like the social anthropologists, is probably right about the limits of rhetorical criticism.

My second text is *Pamela*. Now if there is one type Pamela is *not*, it is
that of the whore: but the most recent research on young servant girls
offers an interesting context in which to reconsider the ambiguities of
Pamela's character.[11] Moreover, if Lawrence Stone's discoveries in *The
Family, Sex and Marriage in England 1500–1800* (a work of eight hundred
pages covering three centuries that will require years, perhaps decades,
before its contents are digested) are to be credited, then Pamela is such an
exception to the rule that modern criticism may have altogether misgauged
her degree of heroism. Stone's approach to sex, marriage, and the family
is almost clinical. He gathers statistics, turns demographer, uses display
charts, contructs graphs, measures curves, weighs evidence, counts pro-
teins that reach the brain, construes sex in nutritional terms. In this sense
he goes far beyond anything that Needham and Utter, or George Sherburn
and Christopher Hill – historians who have written about this problem –
ever dreamed of.[12] He also removes himself as far away from a moral or
religious position as Leavis had come close. His categories are modern:
'the nuclear family', 'the demographic facts', 'the companionate marriage',
'mating arrangements'. He is a Masters and Johnson of the eighteenth
century who documents what he propounds. Even a quick browse
through this goldmine of information never before collected lends an
impression that nothing has escaped his eye, not even the number of times
males went down on their left knees as opposed to right knees when
proposing. Nor does Stone steer clear of sexual evidence when he finds
it, including the *per diem* average and median number of contacts. If he
could, Stone would compile the angle of the pelvic thrust of every
eighteenth-century *liaison dangereuse*. Stone on Boswell's 'Gentlemanly
Sexual Behaviour' is as well documented as the best legal brief, with
positively nothing left to the imagination, not even the accoutrements of
Boswell's 'very large member',[13] though Stone's own wit occasionally
intrudes and peppers a narrative that otherwise could have been solemn.

Stone is even better than this on servant girls and whores. He shows
how easily the one could degenerate into the other, how servants became
a part of the household more often than not to be sexually abused by their
masters. The risk was pregnancy in pre-contraceptive days: if the female
domestic servant became pregnant she was dismissed, not because of any
value placed on virginity but rather as a consequence of her inability to
work. The masters were ruthless in dismissing the girls, their wives
equally vicious and often jealous. As Stone says, 'without protection from
parents, kin, neighbours, ministers or local opinion, these girls were
easy victims of seduction',[14] yet 'it remained true that the largest single
occupation for single women was in domestic service'.[15] Of the teenage

girls who made 'declarations of pregnancy', Stone discovers that half had been impregnated by their masters.[16] And a large majority of girls 'alleged that they had had a promise of marriage which was later repudiated'. What then is poor Pamela to do when Mr. B. begins his advances? By the time Stone has surveyed 'plebian sexual behaviour', it is clear that Pamela is not enjoying an increased libidinal drive owing to improved nutrition and health. 'There is no sign of any improvement in health . . . and no evidence of increased calorie intake *per capita*, so that the possibility of an increase in libidinal drive after 1660 remains no more than an unproven and unprovable hypothesis.'[17]

If the remarkably high number of impregnated female domestic servants was not owing to biological conditions, neither did it derive solely from economic developments. As Stone shows, rampant cultural secularisation and disintegration of the family induced 'a shift in the consciousness of young unmarried women from the poorest classes'.[18] But the shift was owing to female emancipation rather than to economic conditions which have been the traditional explanation: emancipation from parents, the church, the parish, 'even . . . from deference to their social superiors'. Teenage women from the bottom of the social scale began to float to an unprecendented degree. Nor was their floating confined to the country and towns. Stone provides hard evidence to show that between 1700 and 1750 there occurred in England a vast expansion of domestic service. Country girls were lured to the cities or, like Pamela, lured further afield into the countryside without any protection. Moreover, the institution of marriage had sunk into disrepute in almost every respect except the economic one; and all types of men, especially the masters of houses, would daily make promises they could easily repudiate.

What does all this do for literary criticism of *Pamela*? It suggests that cultures change, and that the change direly jeopardises the status of the work of art; it suggests, moreover, that the historical approach is the only means by which to restore that work of art to its deserved place, to justify it to moderns, to explain how and why it deserves mention in the first place. When Stone writes that 'one has to steel oneself to read such boring, moralistic and sentimental contemporary best-sellers as Richardson's *Pamela*',[19] he means at the present time, *today*. And contemporary experience bears out the candid contention (the last student I had who actually read and professed to love the novel was an ageing nun in one of the Los Angeles convents). But Pamela's plight – her whole situation – must have seemed remarkably fresh, if familiar, to the first readers of *Pamela*. We no longer look at the first critics of *Pamela* – except for Fielding – but even they noticed her radical difference: they instantly recognised Richardson's sociological triumph and Pamela's difference from other domestic servants, although they could not see the whole picture of the times as well as we can. Though the daughter of a poor farmer, Pamela's mother has educated her. She is therefore equipped, unlike her colleagues, to be Mr B's wife, although, as Stone notes, she is 'hopelessly unfitted for her probable future of household drudgery among her "milkmaid companions" '.[20] When Stone documents the remarkable sexual modesty of the whole lower-middle class, and shows how it did not extend to the superior classes – *pace* Lady Booby! – one realises how very different our responses to Richardson are from those who read *Pamela* in 1742, or, again, from those who read the novel *c*. 1800 when Richardson was considered an evil author unfit for innocent females.[21]

BACHELORS: *The Correspondence of Pope*

My third and fourth texts focus on men as opposed to women. The third taken from George Sherburn's *Correspondence of Alexander Pope* (5 vols., Oxford, 1956), is epistolary and boasts such professions of 'love' and 'devotion' as these:

> In real truth, I have felt my soul peevish ever since with all about me, from a warm uneasy desire after you. I am gone out of myself to no purpose, and cannot catch you. (II, 388).

> I cannot express the warmth, with which I wish you all things, and myself you. Indeed you are engraved elsewhere than on the cups you sent me. (II, 388).

> It is a perfect trouble to me to write to you, and your kind letter left for me . . . affected me so much, that it made me like a girl, I can't tell what to say to you; I only feel . . . that 'tis almost as good to be hated, as to be loved. (II, 447)

> I may say you have used me more cruelly than you have done any other man; you have made it more impossible for me to live at ease without you. (II, 387)

These emotional outpourings were answered by replies almost as passionate and ebullient:

> I can only swear that you have taught me to dream, which I had not done in twelve years. (II, 393)

> I love and esteem you for reasons that most others have little to do with, and would be the same although you had never touched a pen, further than with writing to me. (II, 384)

These are not the private cries and whispers of man to woman, of the fashionable Lady Booby to her young bucks and Joeys, or even of Clarissa Harlowe to her confidante Anna Howe. They are the romantic interchanges of Pope and Swift, of which there are dozens of other examples in the extant correspondence: to Swift, to Caryll, to Bolingbroke, to Gay. They do not emanate from a 'romance' or novel but from the everyday life of these men, both of whom were, so far as is known, bachelors. They reveal the warmest language of the heart and a vocabulary and rhetoric so emotionally charged and romantically loaded that most readers and scholars have overlooked it in sheer bewilderment. John Trimble displays courage and brilliance in a recent Berkeley doctoral dissertation when he argues that Maynard Mack has misgauged the quantum of energy in Pope's letters to his male friends.[22] Mack had written that no matter who the addressee of a Popean letter might be, the 'real substance is almost always the substance of a love letter, if that term may still be used today *without sexual or romantic implications*'.[23] Trimble, in a psychobiographical study of Pope, concludes that Mack 'is very discerning, though I doubt the appropriateness of trying to dispel all such implications [because] it is beyond question that most of the ordinary outlets for libidinous energy were denied him, and it is also beyond question that that energy demanded expression in some guise'.[24]

Unlike Trimble, one does best not to circumvent the issue at stake – Pope's personality – and hide under a cover of polite 'sexual tendency'. I do not believe that anyone who has scrupulously studied Pope's life could honestly believe that he possessed more than the barest minimum of latent homosexual tendencies. A homosexual Pope simply is not found. But as even Housman – whose daily personality was as restrained as Pope's was impassioned – noticed, Pope possessed a 'sincere inward ardour' coupled with a passionately romantic nature. This is why the starvation of Pope's heart by women was such a blow to him all his life, and why he sublimated – why he *had* to sublimate – his keen libidinous drives. Fortunately for Pope there existed a circle of males, including Caryll and Swift and Gay, with whom he could express his romantic sexual nature without fear of rejection. Indeed, as we have seen, they often reciprocated the warmth, though not so passionate themselves as was Pope. But such sincerity expressed in love letters a century or two earlier – say in 1520 or 1620 – would have been unthinkable. Granting that Pope-the-man would probably have been as naturally and erotically passionate no matter when he lived, had he been born much earlier it is unlikely that he would have discovered so many other bachelors who, although probably predominantly heterosexual, would have been capable and willing to accept his continuous declarations of love and loyalty. How different would the course of eighteenth-century English literature have been had Pope not found these other homoerotic men, not have been able to release his repressed sexual energy through them, and as a consequence not have been well enough to write great poetry – for surely healthy psyches are capable of creating more everlasting art than sick, repressed psyches. Why then was there a ready and willing circle of male bachelors around 1720 whereas there certainly was not around 1620?

Here, again, the work of scholars whom I crudely call social anthropologists sheds some light, because it raises the threshold of explanation, though it does not answer all the questions. Lawrence Stone has provided one important clue about the rise of the bachelor as an eighteenth-century type:

> In the late seventeenth and eighteenth centuries, there was a distinct trend towards bachelordom among owners of medium to large country houses in three sample countries. The cause of this is a mystery, although some may have been homosexual and now more willing to admit their deviation in the more tolerant atmosphere of the eighteenth century . . . The result was that the proportion of sons . . . who were still unmarried at fifty from the late seventeenth to the early eighteenth centuries was between one in four and one in six of the whole.[25]

Stone's logic is sensible: primogeniture was centuries old by the eighteenth century; the eldest son had been inheriting for a long time; younger sons had gotten little, if anything, for centuries; why should younger sons suddenly refuse to marry? This is the question; it is not easy to answer it, for any adequate reply requires a sharp distinction between homosexual and heterosexual bachelors. I shall say more about homosexuality in a moment, but the statistics for eighteenth-century bachelordom produced by Stone are remarkably high. Those for previous centuries were much lower – so much lower that it would be astonishing if the eighteenth century itself did not realise what was occurring. Of course it did; in fact it thought that the proportion of bachelors was much higher than it actually was and that it spelled doom. This is why there is such a torrent of abuse of bachelors in the literature, some of it satirically pungent. This is why the *Spectator* creates Will Wimble, the bachelor younger brother of a baronet, who is bred to no business and born to no estate'.[26] And this is why Steele lashes out against bachelors under the *nom de plume* of Rachel Welladay, who recounts how Augustus separated the married equestrians from the single and told the latter 'that their Lives and Actions had been so peculiar, that he knew not by what name to call 'em; not by that of Men, for they perform'd nothing that was manly; not by Citizens, for the City might perish notwithstanding their Care; nor by that of *Romans*, for they design'd to extirpate the *Roman* Name'.[27] Rachel Welladay wants 'Mr Spectator' to conduct a survey of the number of bachelors, whose number, she says, will horrify this 'particular Age' and cause it to 'amend itself'.[28] This is also why Congreve can make bachelor types – Hartwell, Vainlove, Wittol – the basic theme of his comedy of manners in *The Old Bachelor*. And this is why Defoe writes tract after tract complaining about the growing number of spinsters and prostitutes, and why Churchill the poet will declaim, like Juvenal, in *The Times*, much later on, that the whole of England consists of nothing but the 'slaves of SODOM'. All was owing to an actual growth in the numbers of bachelors and to a common perception that this increase was far greater than it actually was. When one adds the also increasing tribe of lecherous widows to the numbers of spinsters and prostitutes, it becomes evident that no eighteenth-century bachelor in his right mind, no matter how deformed or impecunious, ever had to marry for sex. That was his last reason – and Widow Wadman's last reason too!

Stone is perplexed by the sudden rise of bachelordom because he does not find it limited to younger sons. Given the ready availability of sex and the high number of willing women from *all* the social classes – here one thinks of *Tom Jones* – we would expect younger sons not to marry and eldest sons to marry. But the demographic facts show that the eldest sons were also remaining unmarried. Their new bachelordom contributes to the sudden statistical rise of a social class or type. These eldest sons inherit, become men of means, can readily afford to marry, but do not. Now at this point literary biography offers some clues, though probably not enough. It has long been observed – by Turberville and J. H. Plumb and other social historians of the age – that there are more bachelors among eighteenth-century writers than in any other period: Pope, Swift, Gay – the basic core of the Scriblerians; Blackmore, Prior, Thomson, Gray, Walpole, Collins, Goldsmith, Cowper, Shenstone – the best mid-century poets; Reynolds, Gibbon, Thomas Warton, and many other first- and second-class didactic writers; Hume, one of the most powerful and influential minds of the century; even a large number of the distinguished scientists, Newton included, and musicians such as Handel. Commentators have mentioned the fact and then quietly dropped the matter.[29] Considering how very little is known about what we would call an eighteenth-century sociology, it is probably premature to construct anything more than tentative reasons. Yet it is curious, in the light of Stone's demographic facts, to notice in our catalogue of bachelors that over fifty per cent are either siblingless children – as was Pope – or eldest brothers. This fact in itself is of course without significance in view of the randomness of the catalogue, but is there any reason to believe that a more extensive sample would produce different results?[30] It is also important to notice that over fifty per cent of those in the catalogue of bachelors were either sickly children or suffered lonely and miserable childhoods in which they were shipped off to a benevolent aunt or uncle. There seems to be no connection between social class and bachelordom in this sample: almost as many bachelors come from the lower class as from the upper, and only in a few cases (such as Pope's) does the presence of a widowed mother relying on her son for companionship and protection make any difference whatsoever. It is true that in some of these cases dire and extreme circumstances bear on the writer's celibacy: as I have suggested, medical infirmity, a dependent and ailing parent, dedication to one's calling as a writer and the desire not to be distracted, and, of course, homosexuality. But seventeenth-century writers who married were also dedicated and sick and also had ailing parents. There must then be elements unique to the eighteenth century, as Stone suggests, and it is necessary to discover precisely what they might be if we wish to understand this period.

All these contexts, it seems to me, ought to alter our sense of the bachelor Scriblerians, and particularly of the Pope–Swift correspondence. Ultimately it is altogether inadequate to notice, as James Winn has,[31] that Pope wrote in one voice to women and in another to men, or to postulate, as Archibald Elias has, that because Pope planned eventually to publish his letters to Swift that both men engaged in 'a routine of mutual deference, usually on high-minded topics like friendship, benevolence, or philosophy'.[32] This is being suspicious to a paranoid degree, and it falsifies Pope the man. To reduce Pope's repeated professions of love and loyalty to his male friends to mere self-aggrandisement and cant, to platitudes to please posterity, betrays Pope in the cheapest way. Pope did care about fame and the future, and did write within a tradition of letter writing (using Voiture and others as models), but he also revealed himself to men in ways rarely found in his letters to women. This is why his collected correspondence takes one further into the psycho-social sexual pathology of the times – especially so far as bachelors are concerned – than any other literary correspondence. These letters are not always amorous confessions, which often prove less substantial than intellectual disclosures, but deep self-revelations – in Pope's metaphor, disclosures made by looking through 'a Window in the bosom, to render the Soul of Man visible'.[33] That students of Pope should turn away from the nature of Pope's sexuality is not a question that need concern us here. But the variety of his male ties, however homoerotic, and the further fact that friendships tend to develop for Pope only when the other male is capable of reciprocating in however small measure some of the impassioned ardour, requires a type of analysis and level of threshold which I believe Stone and others are beginning to provide, although it is ultimately our task as literary scholars to make use of this research in order to comprehend why bachelordom and friendship are integrally related in the eighteenth century.

HOMOSEXUALS: *Roderick Random*

This brings me to my last text, *Roderick Random*. It is not hard to see why some of Pope's biographers have been suspicious and even paranoid about his male ties. If they have not said so in print or possessed Stone's demographic knowledge, they cannot help but have known how many of the major and minor authors – as we have already said – were bachelors. Of these several were apparently homosexual: Gray, Walpole, Beckford, Lord Hervey; others, like Newton, Handel, Gay, are questionable: and while one is constrained here to be speculative, one can at least say that the heterosexuality of these men has never been fully established. In Pope's case, as is well known, there is an extraordinary medical condition as well as a possible anatomical impediment of the genitals;[34] but it has never been ascertained to what degree this may have interfered with active or passive sexual performance. If indeed the eighteenth century is 'an Age of Bachelors' with the heterosexuality of so many celebrated men in doubt, the next logical question concerns Pope's own heterosexuality, and this topic has reduced, and continues to reduce, many of his biographers to nervous anxiety. My last subject is not homoeroticism but homosexuality – not *à la Don Juan* the logical extension of bachelorhood but as a consequence of the sociological decline of the family, the increase of leisure, and the weakening of the Church. Here *Roderick Random* is selected for containing the most unabashed portrait of flagrant homosexuals in any eighteenth-century English novel.

In view of the relevance of homosexuality to late twentieth-century Western culture, it is not surprising to discover more social anthropologists working on the subject than other topics I have discussed.[35] The important scholars are Lawrence Stone in the book already discussed, Randolph Trumbach in *The Egalitarian Family*, Michel Foucault in the first volume of his history of sexuality, and a massive doctoral dissertation about homosexuality and the drama being completed at the University of California by Terrence Johnson.[36] Because the subject is politically and emotionally charged there is no agreement among these students about the sharp rise in eighteenth-century homosexuality. Thus Stone's 'demographic facts' are transformed into 'persecuted political victims' by Foucault. Yet these social anthropologists agree on one thing: the relatively sudden increase of the phenomenon. Stone has succinctly epitomised the state of affairs:

> Homosexuality was apparently becoming more common, or at any rate more open, among the upper classes . . . By the early eighteenth century, homosexual clubs existed for the upper classes in London, and through the century there were well-known wealthy deviants, like William Beckford . . . It also seems possible that the higher proportion of the social

elite were indeed homosexuals. What is certain is that male homosexuality
was practised and talked about more openly in the eighteenth century than
at any previous time.[37]

Whether the 'increase' was in absolute or relative numbers or rather
an increase merely of talk is unknown, but there can be no doubt about
the negative reception of its apparent spread,[38] and the general sense then
held that it was on the increase. Nevertheless, my purpose here is neither
to document the social anthropologists' recent researches or to contextualise the 'politics of sexuality' – Kate Millett's wonderfully loaded and
ambiguous phrase – as it applies to homosexuality in the eighteenth century. I am much more interested in asking some basic questions about its
relation to our literature: first and foremost whether it sheds any genuine
light on this body of literature – that is, anything we would not or could
not have known about the literature without comprehending it; second,
whether in our literary criticism we can profitably use the now documented fact that by 1700, and certainly by 1750, there was a whole new
homosexual underworld in England comprised of men's clubs, pubs, and
tea rooms as well as a fashionable homosexual *beau monde* in which upper-
class homosexuals dined together and economically benefited one another;
and lastly, what light, if any, this research sheds on the bachelor authors
– the Popes, the Grays, the Walpoles, the Beckfords – so prominently
celibate.

Now this is precisely the point at which the threshold I mentioned
before differs between the traditional literary scholar and the one with
social or sociological interests. The traditionalist – if I may dare to apply
these inadequate labels – stops at the point of acknowledgement that
Smollett felt his times to be degenerate, just as 'Estimate Brown' and
those vociferous in the controversies about the Lisbon earthquake believed
the times to be degenerate. For whatever unannounced reason, those
satisfied by a low threshold of explanation do not notice that the image
of the homosexual appears in every one of Smollett's early works, in both
poetic satires of 1747, in *The Regicide* in which 'foul effeminacy' is judged
a cause of political decline, and, of course, in the masterful multiple
portraits in *Roderick Random*. To propose, then, that what is diagnostic in
the early Smollett, and especially in *Roderick Random*, is that the effeminate
hero has now (in the 1740s and 1750s) become a social type to be satirised,
is unacceptable. The scholar who contends, unlike Stone and Trumbach
and company, that around 1750 there is nothing new about homosexuality
in England does not know whereof he speaks and subscribes to a flawed
social history of England. He may point to 1600 and Marlowe and Shakespeare and Marston and James I and minor Caroline and Jacobean plays
permeated with subtle asides about 'another sex of mankind', and to the

flood of poems after 1689 satirising William as a homosexual and his favourite Dutch guards as his catamites; but he has failed to grasp the impact of the social anthropologists' new discoveries that 'what is certain is that male homosexuality was practised and talked about more openly in the eighteenth century' than at any previous time in history.

Some of us may not like what this implies about the eighteenth century, or what Stephen Marcus may have called 'the *other* eighteenth century', but Stone and Trumbach have the facts to prove the change. For good reason, then, Smollett turned away from 'the fumbler' of Restoration comedy to depict the new 'effeminate hero' who urgently required delineation precisely because he was such a realistic copy. The Restoration world of Rochester's *Sodom* may have been morally as reprehensible to Smollett as the mid eighteenth century, but now there was a new dimension: what was contained in courts and salons was now being practised everywhere, even on the open oceans on Her Majesty's ships! How then can homosexuality fail to be a crucial issue for Smollett the moralist? Almost nothing, in Smollett's mind, could exaggerate its urgency; and this is why he loses no opportunity to introduce the homosexual type proliferating everywhere in his society. It will not do to argue that the whole point of the urgency of homosexuality is a trumped-up issue because Smollett's contemporaries did not comment about the subject and satirise to the extent he has. They do comment, they do satirise – although there isn't time to present the evidence here – though often they remain silent because the subject is impolite, not to say heinous and forbidden. But Smollett was not the eighteenth-century Laurel and Hardy of homosexuality; he was not attempting what *La Cage aux folles* has tried to successfully in our time: to neutralise a painful subject by trivialising it. Smollett's confrontations with homosexuality produce anything but laughter in the reader; because Smollett intentionally and sometimes mercilessly withholds every trace of humanity in his homosexuals, he generally elicits only responses of revulsion and condemnation; and because of this lack of levity I suspect – although I have no evidence – that his diagnosis of the homosexual menace resulted from real encounter rather than from any idealistic or pious position he may have held as a moral arbiter of his age. Smollett *was* outrageous within the historical contexts of Georgian civilisation: his outrage is in large part a reflection of the disgust also felt by his contemporaries. But as I have said elsewhere, it will not do to subdue Smollett's voice and make it conform to our notions of the 'polite and refined literature' of the eighteenth century. Smollett *is* raw; he thinks rawly; he sees some of the rawest sociological types in his society, and is willing to lay them low – no pun intended – in his writings because he believed they are unparalleled social menaces.

Roderick Random, the novel, supports this contention. This is Roderick's account of his adventures in London and at sea as a surgeon's mate. Roderick encounters no fewer than four overt homosexuals among the twenty-odd male figures with whom he interacts – a very large ratio when judged by any standards. Two of these Roderick meets at sea and two in London, suggesting the pervasiveness of the type. On board Roderick discovers the homosexual Captain Whiffle and his surgeon Mr Simper. In London, Roderick encounters Lord Strutwell and a physician named Dr Wagtail. 'Whiffle, Simper, Strutwell, Wagtail' – these Jonsonian humour characters are revealed by their names. But there is something else to notice too. Not all four are effeminate: if the surgeon Simper is flamboyantly effeminate, and if Whiffle paints and powders, Strutwell is masculine and typically aristocratic. He plays the role of the leisurely earl so well that the naive Roderick does not immediately catch on, this despite 'frequent squeezes of the hand', 'a singular complacency in his countenance', and 'a tender embrace' (chap. 51).[39] Smollett did not automatically associate homosexuality with effeminacy. Lord Strutwell is a type for Smollett – that of the corrupt and debauched aristocrat – but the same cannot be said of Wagtail, an ostentatious and epicene homosexual physician whom Smollett wants to ridicule, or of the homosexual couple, Whiffle and Simper, who are not only effeminate and inseparable – 'a cabin was made for him [Simper] contiguous to the state-room where Whiffle slept' (chap. 25) – but who provoke Roderick's personal rage to a dangerous limit.[40]

Smollett also invokes homosexual characters (four out of about twenty) to serve within his works as a kind of extended metaphor for the extreme corruption he sees everywhere about him. This is made plain by Strutwell's set speech to Roderick in the lord's *boudoir* (chap. 51).[41] But Smollett's metaphor for social corruption is interesting not only because it is a metaphor – something substituting for something else though charged with its own rich local suggestiveness – but also because Smollett 'reads' his whole culture and interprets it through the eyes of the metaphor. Homosexual allusions and echoes are everywhere in the novel; the reader who knows what's going on may try to escape them but cannot. Of discussions about the autobiographical elements in *Roderick Random* there will be no end, but one thing is clear: the young novelist who writes so passionately in his first novel about homosexuality, who views homosexuality above *all* other vices as the truest index of the pulse of the times, must have known whereof he spoke. The young Scot, Tobias Smollett, came to London at eighteen, without two farthings in his pocket, without connections and with an unmistakable brogue: although no one can prove or disprove the contention, it is inconceivable that Smollett was not propositioned occasionally. As Smollett himself intimates in his early poetic satires,[42] corruption has progressed so far that the only road to fame in England (as opposed to his purer native Scotland) is by means of the sodomite's bed. Smollett's image of the homosexual, like Sterne's of the widow, is intriguing because of its extremism. As Terrence Johnson has noticed, 'the charge of sodomite was an extreme form of ridicule beyond which one could not go'.[43] If homosexuality is the worst crime of all, and if it is as prevalent as Smollett charges, then the age must be very corrupt and depraved indeed. Today we may have serious doubts about interpreting the degree of corruption in a given society by its quantum of overt homosexual activity, especially after Margaret Mead and other cultural anthropologists have discovered it to be such a universal form of behaviour in primitive tribes; but Smollett had no difficulty doing exactly that.[44] For Smollett and his contemporaries (including Churchill) homosexuality was a *topos*: a place from which to measure their own emotions of rage and disgust. From these extreme emotions they proceeded to construct satiric vehicles, such as *Roderick Random*, containing a typology of homosexual figures. But it would be false to contend that these homosexual types are monolithic and conform to the stereotype of earlier ages: effeminate, soft, weak, emasculated. By Smollett's time the homosexual figure in imaginative literature is various, and it makes sense to talk about a broad spectrum. The great touchstone of Smollett's *Roderick Random*, then, is not that the novel offers any clue about Smollett's own sexuality. Smollett may have been entirely heterosexual, or he may have felt homosexual urges: one can never be sure. But there is no doubt about the rage Smollett felt when contemplating the new homosexual condition in England. To Smollett it was living proof that times had never been so degenerate.

CONCLUSION

My conclusion is that any hostility or scepticism felt towards the social anthropologist is necessarily both healthy and unhealthy. Widows, whores, bachelors, homosexuals: the crucial types in the eighteenth century are not necessarily the crucial types today, yet it is valuable to measure the differences in so far as they help us to understand eighteenth-century texts. The socio-anthropological approach thrives on sound historical knowledge, on documented fact; and it attempts to shatter the notion that literary criticism should leave social and intellectual history alone because every literary critic subscribes to a different historicity. Would any of us argue, by the same faulty logic, that literary scholarship should omit criticism because every scholar subscribes to a different type of criticism? Naturally I want to maintain a certain degree of scepticism about critical tides of taste, but if one consequence of our new awareness of the social backgrounds of eighteenth-century literature is to make our own criticism socially more relevant – by comparison of our own age with theirs – then I see nothing wrong with this. And there is one other thing: by dwelling on the strengths of such an externalist approach I do not mean to dissolve the great differences among the writers treated here. They are very different sensibilities: my discussion of the margins and backgrounds of these texts hopes to bring the literature into better focus, not merely to reduce these writers to the cloacal stuff of social history. Why, then, should I want to bother? Perhaps to change the minds of those who have now neglected the eighteenth century for over two decades on grounds that it is not, as Northrop Frye argued only twenty years ago, 'an extraordinarily interesting period of English literature'.[45]

NOTES

An earlier version of this paper was delivered in August 1980 before the International Association of University Professors of English in Aberdeen, Scotland. I am grateful to Professor Ian Watt of Stanford University for reading multiple versions of the paper and for plentiful harsh criticism that compelled me to understand the consequences and implications of my discussion. I must also thank Professors Pat Rogers (Bristol), Maren-Sofie Røstvig (Oslo), and Irene Simon (Liège) for commenting on the IAUPE version.

1 Michel Foucault, 'Truth and Power: an Interview with Alessandro Fontano and Pasquale Pasquino', in Meaghan Morris (ed.), *Michel Foucault: Power, Truth, Strategy* (Sydney, 1979), 29–30.

2 Part of the problem is that traditional practical criticism (Richards, *et al.*) is not faring well on either side of the Atlantic and that the best known structuralists, especially Derrida, Barthes and Lacan, do not read or write about English literature, although they pronounce on American authors such as Poe.

3 Arthur Koestler, *The Sleepwalkers* (1959).

4 E. P. Thompson, *Whigs and Hunters: the Origin of the Black Act* (1975; Peregrine edition, 1977), 311.

5 The phrase derives from Richard Wilbur's 1956 collection of poems, *Things of this World*, in *The Poems of Richard Wilbur* (New York, 1963).

6 Melvyn New, *Laurence Sterne as Satirist: a Reading of Tristram Shandy* (Gainesville, 1969), 194–195.

7 *Ibid.*, 197.

8 This point is made by Robert S. Haller in 'The Old Whore and Medieval Thought', a dissertation discussed by D. W. Robertson in *A Preface to Chaucer* (Princeton, 1962), 330–1. The literary and cultural history of the widow remains to be delineated. At least from the Middle Ages to the late eighteenth century, she is the emblem of lust and greed. By the Restoration she seems to have hardened into a figure of incontinence, and authors rarely feel the need to justify their harsh treatment of her: even the plays of George Chapman (*The Widow's Tears*) and Thomas Middleton (*The Widow*) present her as lusting after men, having been accustomed to regular intercourse during marriage, and, later on, the plays of Aphra Behn, Thomas Betterton (especially *The Amorous Widow, or, the Wanton Wife*), Thomas Shadwell (*A True Widow: a Comedy*), John Motley (*The Widow Bewitch'd*), William Kenrick (*The Widow'd Wife: a Comedy*), and many others assume such a type as an easy target for ridicule. In the Clark Library of the University of California at Los Angeles is an interesting pamphlet by Mrs Alice Hayes that sheds light on the subject: entitled *A Legacy, or Widow's Mite* (1740), it is an account of the religious conversion to Quakerism (Freud might have said the religious sublimation) of a widow who cannot contain her sexual desire. In part III of

Female Policy Detected (7th ed., 1761), Ned Ward, author of the *London Spy*, portrays a lusting widow in 'A True Character of a Virtuous Woman, or Wife Indeed. With a Poetical Description of a Maid, Wife, and Widow', 80 ff. Still another literary representation of the lusting widow is found in Victor Benjamin's scandalous novel *The Widow of the Wood* (1755), which apparently so enraged Sir William Wolseley, one of the husbands of the notorious widow, that he went about the country buying up and burning every copy he could discover. There was a 'Widows Coffee-House' in London by the early 1730s, in Devereau Court across from the Temple and on the site of the present Essex Street, although very little is known about its social function (see Brian Lillywhite, *London Coffee Houses* (1963), 746); but it may have been a meeting ground for fortune seekers and incontinent widows. After 1790 the lusty widow is sentimentalised and begins to figure as a pitiful character-type overburdened with misery and woe; see, for example, James Rodwell, *The Young Widow: a Comic Piece* (1800). The widow's sexuality is curiously not discussed in such recent books as P. M. Spacks, *The Female Imagination* (New York, 1976).

9 The contemporary medical literature is clear on this point. See, for example, *The Female Physician, Containing All the Diseases Incident to that Sex*, in *Virgins, Wives and Widows* (1724), 93: 'Widows should take care lest by their repeated demands upon the Man, they weigh him with the fatal *Strangury* through over use', and a generation earlier, John Pechey's *A General Treatise of the Diseases of Maids, Bigbellied Women . . . and Widows*, (1696) who makes the same point on 245–6.

10 Edmund Wilson to Dorothy Walsh, 10 September 1969, in Edmund Wilson, *Letters on Literature and Politics 1912–1972* (New York, 1977), 703.

11 Recent discussion includes the biographers of Richardson (Ben Kimpel and Duncan Eaves), Ian Watt, Leslie Fiedler, Morris Golden, Elizabeth Bergen Brophy, and A. O. J. Cockshut. Much less has been written about the eighteenth-century whore, in any of the varieties in which she appears, than one would think. It is a subject basically neglected by historians who have difficulty discovering the necessary evidence, and by literary critics who do not consider it a polite subject. A certain amount of information is found in David Foxon's *Libertine Literature in England, 1660–1745* (1964), but this information is bibliographical rather than interpretative. Also useful is Douglas Hay (ed.), *Albion's Fatal Tree* (1975), especially the chapters dealing with the undergrowth of crime and corruption. But even in these works the whore is only one figure among a company of dark silhouettes, and her plight seems never to be openly discussed or penetratingly evaluated.

12 See George Sherburn, 'Fielding's Social Outlook', *Philological Quarterly* xxxv (1956), 1–23; and Christopher Hill, 'Clarissa Harlowe and her Times', *Essays in Criticism* v (1955), 315–340.

13 *The Family, Sex and Marriage* (1977), 574.

14 *Ibid.*, 642.

15 *Ibid.*, 646.

16 *Ibid.*, 642. These statistics apply to France, but Stone comments (p. 642). 'There is no reason to believe that the records for the town of Nantes, which have been analysed in detail, would not also apply to England. The witnesses were mostly country girls in their early twenties from very poor homes, who had allowed themselves to be seduced, either by men of their own class . . . or by their masters.'

17 *Ibid.*, 643.

18 *Ibid.*

19 *Ibid.*, 238.

20 *Ibid.*, 349.

21 Stone traces the evidence from 1780 to the early Victorian period on pp. 675–6.

22 See John Trimble, 'The Psychological Landscape of Pope's Life and Art' (Ph.D diss., University of California at Berkeley, 1971), 53–67.

23 Quoted in Trimble, 61.

24 *Ibid.*, 58.

25 *The Family, Sex and Marriage*, 43–4 and 377.

26 Joseph Addison, *Spectator* 108, 4 July 1711, Donald Bond (ed.), *The Spectator*, 5 vols. (Oxford, 1965), I, 446–9.

27 Richard Steele, *Spectator* 528, 5 November 1712, *ibid.*, IV, 383.

28 *Ibid.*, 528. The social history of the bachelor in England is complicated and seems to depend upon the political exigency of the moment. During the Restoration and eighteenth century he is the beneficiary of a cultural fantasy about his sexual freedom and libertinism, and he often lives up to his image as a perpetual rake and inveterate hedonist. This collective fantasy about the male bachelor is used as the basis for justification of a single life and, conversely, for the miseries of a married life, an ongoing debate that further secularises the bachelor into the type of an antireligious and unrelenting hedonist. It is precisely these debates and this image of the bachelor that inspires the anonymous author of a series of tracts in the British Museum bound together under the title *Tracts on Matrimony 1701–1709*: these include *The Bachelor's Banquet*, a series of poems romanticising the pleasure and carefree life of bachelors, especially in *The Bachelor's and Maid's Answer to the Fifteen Comforts of Matrimony* (which contains, incidentally, a long section, pp. 4–5, on the new prevalence of 'Sodom' in London). Prose fictions such as *The Bachelor of Salamanca* (London, 1737–9), originally written in French by Le Sage, were no doubt read by the middle class as the literature of fantasy and escape. Here the bachelor hero, Don Cherubin de la Ronda, travels far and wide, courts wealthy widows and pining mistresses, and gads about from one court intrigue to another. This same fantasy about the carefree bachelor is evident in *The Bachelor's Estimate of the Expences of a Married Life*, which reached a seventh edition by 1761 and twenty-first by 1784. But by mid-century, criticism of the bachelor was growing and altering the fantasy, as is evident in some of the ephemeral literature of the 1750s and 1760s, perhaps nowhere more clearly described than in Goldsmith's twenty-eighth letter of *The Citizen of the World* on the great numbers of old maids and old bachelors in London and the causes for this increase. Although the narrator, Lien Chi Altangi, is ironic and sarcastic, a passage such as this one makes little sense if understood as mere ironic commentary: 'I behold an old batchelor in the most contemptible light, as an animal that lives upon the common stock without contributing his share: he is a beast of prey, and the laws should make use of as many stratagems and as much force to drive the reluctant savage into the toils, as the Indians when they hunt the rhinoceros.' See the A. Friedman (ed.), *Collected Works of Oliver Goldsmith*, 5 vols (Oxford, 1966) II, 121. Letter 72 dealing with the Marriage Act also condemns bachelors. Also of interest to the typology of bachelorhood after mid-century are the anonymous volume *The Bachelor: Select Essays* (1772) and Cruikshank's pictorial 'progress' entitled *The Bachelors Own Book: or, the Progress of Mr Lambkin (Gent.) in the Pursuit of Pleasure and Amusement* (1844). Pope's very unusual correspondence – considered as a single text – is enriched when placed against this social background.

29 See, for example, M. Dorothy George, 'London and the Life of the Town', in A. S. Turberville (ed.), *Johnson's England*, 2 vols. (Oxford, 1933), I, 164.

30 And even if he did, which I rather doubt, would it change our estimate of the bachelorhood of eighteenth-century writers? The pattern I discern leads to no immediate conclusions: among the bachelors Gay, Cowper, and Shenstone were eldest brothers; Walpole, Hume, and Warton were youngest brothers; Thomson, Goldsmith, Reynolds, and William Law were middle children; and Swift, Pope, Prior, Gray, Collins, and Gibbon were siblingless children.

31 See James Winn, *A Window in the Bosom: the Letters of Alexander Pope* (Hamden, 1977),

where the quotation cited below appears on p. 233: and Archibald Elias, 'Jonathan Swift and Letter-Writing' (Ph.D. diss., Yale University, 1973), 197.

32 Quoted in Winn, *Window in the Bosom*, 233.

33 The phrase is from the opening sentence of Pope's letter of 12 December 1718 to Jervas: 'The old project of a Window in the bosom, to render the Soul of Man visible, is what every honest friend has manifold reason to wish for.'

34 See Marjorie Hope Nicolson and G. S. Rousseau, 'A Medical Case History of Alexander Pope', in *This Long Disease, My Life', Alexander Pope and the Sciences* (Princeton, 1968), 7–82; and Maynard Mack, 'Pope: the Shape of the Man in his Work', *The Yale Review* LXVII (1978), 495–6.

35 See L. Stone, n. 13 above: Randolph Trumbach, *The Rise of the Egalitarian Family: Aristocratic Kinship and Domestic Relations in Eighteenth-Century England* (New York, 1978); Michel Foucault, *Histoire de la sexualité*, I: *La Volonté de savoir* (Paris, 1976), translated from the French by Robert Hurley as *The History of Sexuality, Volume One: an Introduction* (1978), the first volume of an announced six-volume series. Neither the definitive cultural nor literary history of the homosexual in England has been written. There is not even a cursory bibliography of works dealing with the figure of the homosexual, or a list of court cases that illuminates his legal history from the Middle Ages. Important work bearing upon my discussion of the eighteenth century include (listed without place in chronological order): Ned Ward, *The History of the London Clubs* (1709); Thomas Bray, *For God or Satan* (1709); an anonymous homosexual novel set in the court of William III, *Love-Letters Between a Certain Late Nobleman and the Famous Mr. Wilson* (1723); two anonymous pamphlets: *Hell upon Earth; or the Town in an Uproar* (1729) and *A Ramble through London* (1738); an anonymous pamphlet in the Bodleian Library recounting recent homosexual scandals at All Souls College: *College Wit Sharpened, or a Head of a College with a Sting in the Tail* (1739); John Brown, *An Estimate of the Manners and Principles of the Times* (1757), 67–8 and 186; 'The Pretty Gentlemen' in the anonymous very popular *Fugitive Pieces, on Various Subjects* (1761), I, 195–221. Terrence Johnson's study referred to below in n. 36 will study this literary image in much greater detail than I have space for here and will demonstrate how English drama from the Restoration to the late eighteenth century continued to use the homosexual figure for its own largely negative purposes. Valuable information is also found in two recent articles: M. McIntosh, 'The Homosexual Role', *Social Problems* XVI (1968), 185–97 and R. Trumbach, 'London's Sodomites: Homosexual Behavior and Western Culture in the Eighteenth Century', *Journal of Social History* (1977), XI, 1–33; and in H. Montgomery Hyde's book, *The Love that Dared not Speak its Name* (Boston, 1970).

36 Terence Johnson, 'Homosexuality in the Restoration and Eighteenth-Century Drama', (doctoral dissertation in progress at the University of California at Los Angeles): the main focus here is on the drama.

37 See Stone, *The Family, Sex and Marriage* 541–2.

38 *Ibid.*, 541. Stone is right to discuss *both* the negativity of response and the widely held belief that homosexuality was rapidly increasing, though he is naturally unable to support either contention with statistics and is prudent to state: 'Whether or not the practice *was* on the increase must remain a far more open question' (542, italics mine).

39 Not even the most modern editors of *Roderick Random* have commented on this chapter composed of exclusive homosexual scenes. The only comments (and they are brief comments) I have seen are by P.-G. Boucé in the Oxford English Novels Series; see *The Adventures of Roderick Random* (Oxford, 1979), 471. Churchill's *The Times* has also been overlooked, and the reader of the notes to this poem in the Clarendon Press edition of *The Poetical Works of Charles Churchill* (Oxford, 1956) edited by Douglas Grant, goes away wondering how Churchill can have believed that every Englishman other than himself was 'a slave of SODOM'.

40 Virtually nothing has been written on the sexual relations encouraged by close sleeping

quarters in the British navy of this period and the tyranny of autonomous homosexual and heterosexual captains. This omission arises primarily from the delicate nature of the subject: for the type of cover-up of the subject I notice here and an example of the nonsense perpetrated about Smollett's harsh criticism of sex life at sea, see N. C. Starr, 'Smollett's Sailors', *The American Neptune* (1972) XXXII 81–99; and, more generally, Christopher Lloyd and Jack L. S. Coulter, *Medicine and the Navy 1220–1900*, 4 vols. (Edinburgh, 1961).

41 Roderick learns nothing from his repeated encounters with homosexual men, neither to recognise them or to predict their advances and subsequent actions. This lack of learning isolates an area in which criticism of the text greatly benefits from the isolation of character types by social anthropologists and demonstrates that it is unwarranted to call *Roderick Random* a *Bildungsroman*, or novel of learning. There is, of course, a further problem here: at the chronological moment that Smollett writes, the homosexual type is growing unrecognisable and becoming increasingly disguised. By Roderick's repeated naivety Smollett may therefore wish to suggest the new protean disguises of homosexual behaviour. It is hard to be confident about this last point, especially in that Smollett is the only major novelist of the time who is obsessed with homosexuality.

42 Especially the attacks on homosexuals who are named in the poetic sequence *Advice* and *Reproof* (1746–7); in these satires the homosexual also functions as a metaphor for extreme corruption.

43 See Johnson, 'Homosexuality in the Restoration and Eighteenth-Century Drama', introduction.

44 Satirists and other commentators from Ned Ward at the beginning of the century to Charles Churchill, Thomas Rowlandson, and George Cruikshank later on did the very same thing. The difference in Smollett is that he *internalises* the image of corruption (i.e. the homosexual) and lays all blame on it for his own personal failure, whereas Churchill and others are satisfied to ridicule the homosexual type without personalising it to this severe degree. Compare, in this sense, the harsh tone of Smollett's verse satire (see n. 42) and Chruchill's tone in *The Times* (1764) ll. 285–96.

45 'Towards Defining an Age of Sensibility', in James L. Clifford (ed.), *Eighteenth-Century English Literature*, (New York, 1959), 312.

7

New Historical injunctions

I wrote this essay in 1986 when the New Historicism had just appeared on the scene. Although the debate then focused on the ability of the New Historicism to revive historicism in the wake of its massive losses to structuralism and deconstructionism, two aspects of the debate struck me as very odd: first, that those who claimed to be practising the New Historicism were focusing on such small segments and minute historical units – small topoi within the categories of power and authority – that the history they claimed to be reinvigorating was not actually being restored by that route at all, but was instead generating another version of history almost as impoverished as that of the nonreferential schools; secondly, that the New Historicism was not being discussed concretely in relation to the academic disciplines and post-disciplines. There was no discussion – for example – of the recent fate of the disciplines of history, literature, and their combined literary history.

The latter point seemed the more important to me, particularly because of the challenges deconstructionism had hurled in the face of all referential methodologies, and in view of the nature of academic migration (or the lack of it) in America and Europe. I tried to indicate in the essay that it was not accidental that a revived historicism would claim to be flourishing just at the moment when it was clear that the post-disciplines had replaced the disciplines, and when the hegemony of the great universities had finally been called into doubt and genuine talent was being scattered widely over many universities throughout North America and Europe.

It is easy to forget that some critics acquired four or five critical idioms in just a few decades – Hillis Miller: traditional literary history, New Critical formalism, Pouletean phenomenology, Derridean deconstruction, and whatever the idiom at Irvine will be – each idiomatic shift often coinciding with migration from one university to another. Others learned one or merely absorbed the idiom of their teachers in graduate school, who had absorbed theirs. But it isn't profitable to generalise about everyone; everyone has taken different routes. For understanding to obtain, the critic's background must be reconstructed: education, migrations, the idioms learned, their type and number, and the precise circumstances and conditions of acquisition. An extraordianry sense of power derived from this diversity of idioms among those conversant in them, but it is hard to identify the source of this power. Did power reside in the proliferation of 'critics' all suddenly migrating and identifying themselves as 'theorists', or were the critics already powerful because they represented genuinely new breeds communicating in idioms few could understand (i.e., mumbo-jumbo)? Given our proximity to the development, it is hard to know, yet this sudden proliferation of the *number of idioms* in critical theory was the real revolution, the true pluralism, whose history will be narrated many times in centuries to come.

More locally, the resistance to theory among some of our (especially patriarchal) colleagues in the eighteenth century has been both healthy and unhealthy. A healthy reticence in that critical theory is now clearly a full-time vocation: those who arm themselves to the teeth with it usually have no time for anything else, least of all the empirical eighteenth century and its primary literature. But unhealthy resistance in that it gradually became apparent during the sixties that all sorts of first principles and basic assumptions were never going to be addressed by those who were, irrefutably but not self-reflectively, consummate scholar–critics, and that the question would not be put unless some major discontinuity occurred. Critical theory, viewed on the broad canvas of intellectual activities then pursued, became the forum for that disruption. And if the candles of poststructuralism and deconstruction now begin to flicker, weakened by an inability to answer hard questions about their relation to historical and philosophical referentiality (as seems evident to some shrewd observers), their shadows will nevertheless linger over us for a long time.

Today, the issue about theory in relation to eighteenth-century studies is not primarily one of acceptance or rejection, co-operation or resistance, or the precise degree of entrenchment in certain geographical locales, but the moral, ethical, and referential dimensions of theory. Acceptance or rejection (though never so monolithically antithetical as this), like the biographical backgrounds of individual critics, has its own exigencies and histories. Indeed, the history of the enclaves of critical theory and their degree of entrenchment are chapters to be documented; already there are competing versions of the state of affairs in the 1960s that could have precipitated such dislocation.

Our essential tension today regards the status of *value* in theory in relation to *value* in empirical approaches to eighteenth-century studies and the sense we harbour of the *value* of each in relation to our complex lives as civilians, teachers, scholars, critics (old or new), and – of course – professionals with a career (and a salary) to protect. Everyone sensible concurs that Derrida and de Man, Foucault and Barthes, Lévi-Strauss and Geertz, Bakhtin and Bachelard, to say nothing of the best of the recent feminists and Marxists, generated a great deal of thought about language and society that was both original and useful; everyone concedes that some of their followers on both sides of the ocean formulated important ideas as well. And everyone knows that Habermas and Gadamer (to name but two thinkers) made valuable contributions to the discussion about history in relation to the interpretation of texts, and about discourse in relation to hermeneutics, as well as recognising that their theory can usefully be applied to research and writing about the eighteenth century without polluting the entire field. But even a novitiate senses that Derrida and de Man harboured a defective sense of referentiality, and that their philosophical systems (to the degree that they were self-contained philosophical systems) were nevertheless useful no matter how seriously marred by this flaw. Anyone who has seriously read Foucault recognises how readily his critical theory lends itself to applications in synchronic projects, especially in the social sciences – hence Foucault's implicit historicity within an ingrained, almost Nietzchean, anti-empiricism that was fundamentally ahistorical. Continuing in this vein, one could anatomise the whole pantheon of contemporary theory – from Adorno to Saussure, Deleuze to Lévi-Strauss, Derrida to Todorov – according to the strengths of each (more or less philosophical) system and demonstrate how it could be usefully applied to a particular branch of eighteenth-century studies.

But it has been less clear whether the *application* of one or another of these theoretical systems – here it matters, of course, *which* system – would advance or impede *empirical* studies of the eighteenth-century. Empiricism remains the sore spot: evidence, grounds for evidence and proof, methods of logic and reason its open wounds. In some instances – for example, Foucault in the domain of madness and asylums during the Enlightenment – application clearly enriches the whole field. Can anyone today *imagine* the history of madness *sans* Foucault? In other fundamentally ahistorical territories – Derrida and de Man on the rhetorics of certain writers of the Enlightenment (i.e., Rousseau) – it has been less apparent what the theoretical value is or could be.

This ingrained ahistoricity of the theorists and its implications for referentiality pierce to one crux of the matter. If the application of Derrida or de Man to a single text could explain better that work or that author's art, I think we would agree that the theoretical importation had been worthwhile, i.e., valuable. We would not then disparage its theoretical status or ridicule those who violate the laws of empiricism to apply it, under certain conditions applying it as interdisciplinarians. It is only when the application fails to reveal anything new, anything we could not have known without it or when it fraudulently masquerades as something that it clearly is not, that frustration and despair set in.

Despair rather than terror because the notion of *the terror of theory* is an irresponsibly hysterical attitude not altogether different from the hysteria of medieval scholars who claimed to have been 'terrified' (*pavor terrificus*) by the universalist–nominalist controversies then raging. The notion entertained by many ultraempirical historians that theory represents miasma – an abomination that pollutes – is not merely uninformed, but even superstitious and ultimately demonic. Theory possesses this negatively sublime power for these empiricists because of their terrific fear that they will no longer recognise the eighteenth century. Yet if they would merely demythologise the theoretical realm, and scrutinise it sufficiently to discover its cracks and holes, its nitty-gritty (which even the best theoretical methods and systems reveal), it would prove less terrifying. But some of our (again generally patriarchal and often anti-Foucaldian) colleagues, proclaiming to act with a spirit of extreme empiricism and nominalism, have actually shut their minds to theory before even surmising what it entails and what its natural limitations are. This is a pity because theory can, upon occasion, be useful. In my own case, I cannot imagine having done some of my work without having read all of Foucault and much of Bachelard, Bakhtin, Feyerabend, and Kuhn.

Others purport that theory is waning as a 'new' historicism replaces it, an historicism allegedly grounded in Foucault and the best roots of the social sciences: the new anthropology, psychology, sociology, all of which are necessarily language-bound, time and space oriented, empirical, nominalistic, referential. And the 'new' Foucaldian historicism is touted by some as healthy because it, unlike its Derridean and de Manian predecessors, promises to be fundamentally *contextual*: grounded in the time, place, and life of the maker of the object (thereby reinvigorating the recently much abused genre of biography), as well as aware of the complex ways that meaning and value remain *prior* to the formal, artificial languages inscribed in it – that is to say fundamentally *historical* by concerning itself with explanations of the way the present came to be the way it is.

Construed in this way – as the inevitable response to a flawed poststructuralism and deconstruction – the New Historicism is a positive force, especially when it emphasises that the *words* of a culture (not merely eighteenth-century culture) are but a *portion* of its truths and lies, and that imaginative literature is a symbolic rather than literal expression of a people. But here the deconstructionists also erred. To their detriment they never bothered to enquire why the French Revolution, for example, was not a phenomenon of the Middle Ages and the Holocaust of the Renaissance. Some deconstructionists gleefully obliterated history altogether, claiming that their method was a criticism of *criticism* not a method of application, pronouncing in their works as if the historical Holocaust (again for example) had never *occurred*, and perilously suggesting that 'the event' (any event, small or large, insignificant or consequential) was itself another 'interpretation' – but an interpretation of *what?* This question, especially its consequences for literary criticism, they did not pursue, but now that they have been held to account, they are apologetic for their radical privileging of language among the diverse expressions of any culture. The New Historicism, in contrast, will presumably take some of its profoundest cues from Foucault and the anthropologists rather than from the deconstructionists, and will enrich eighteenth-century studies by expanding the kinds of questions that can be asked (even without the New Historicism, think of what Foucault has *already* done for the history of Enlightenment sexuality, Bachelard for studies of the scientific imagination between Boyle and Laplace, and Bakhtin for Terry Castle's civilisation of masquerade). I cannot imagine anyone seriously opposing the new historicims, except to interrogate (quite justifiably) the precise versions of its claim to novelty.

Yet some of the most vocal champions for new historicism have been neo-Marxists of one or another variety who thus far have been unwilling (for whatever personal motives) to make explicit the relation of their public ideology as the espousers of a theoretical neo-Marxism to their equally public role as teachers, scholars, and citizens paid to impart learning and instil cultural broad values to students in a capitalist society (I assume that America is not yet a Marxist country).

Some observers of the new historicism allege that this strategy is calculated and that the new historicism remains the façade of a subversive socialist programme. I doubt it, but what is a 'capitalist' country anyway? If anything, a free zone where all ideas can be articulated, if not accommodated, despite the knowledge that Marxism (classical or derivative) will *lose out* in the end. If history represents the ongoing discourses of the *present*, then the New Historicism must be a boon in so far as it will permit us to test our ideas about the eighteenth century (its intellectual ferment as well as the ideas of its individual figures) against this continuing dialogue about the present.

The New Historicism, viewed in this dialectical sense of mediating between a past and present (i.e., the eighteenth and twentieth centuries), is already more enriched than the neutrally logocentric and intentionally unreferential Derrideanism of the seventies, and potentially more useful for those who care about previous societies and their achievements. Not merely advantageous because it will restore history to eighteenth-century studies (and not merely the old empirical history of the philologists but a reinvigorated cultural and transdisciplinary history that has a much higher threshold of explanation), but also useful as a consequence of its endorsement of the social sciences, which the formalists despised yet which has continued to enrich our field for decades. Think of the excellent work of a broad range of feminists whose methods are grounded in the social sciences and of those who write about childhood and death in the Enlightenment. History, the story of how the present got to be the way it is, can never – fortunately – be obliterated or entirely suppressed, not even by the fiercest opponents of referentiality; so the urgent issue continues to be whether the methods of the new historicists, whose work thus far has been heavily grounded in the assumptions of the social sciences, will be subverted, or tyrannised over, by personal motives driving them to crave the kind of professional power held by the theorists in the 1970s. Less cumbersomely put, whether the New Historicism will become the programme, as New Criticism and deconstruction once were, of tyrannical academic authority for those who espoused and practised it best.

It is unlikely. The monopoly of distinguished scholar–critics concentrated in a handful of universities on the East Coast (the good old days of Sherburn, Brower, Bate; Wimsatt, Osborn, Mack; Nicolson, Clifford, Landa) has come to an end, and there is no possibility of a return to this pattern of the monopolistic past. This guaranteed and widespread distribution of talent bodes well for eighteenth-century studies. There isn't space to develop the point about the all-important gap between intention and espousal but if there were, it would be patent that nothing less is at stake here than the function of, and the roles played by, intellectuals in contemporary capitalistic Western societies (here again is the dialectical sense of a mediation between the eighteenth century and our own). This gap is not a subject about which anyone has pronounced – not even the sociologists – with any degree of learning or authority. And even now it remains unclear what impact, if any, the intellectuals of America (almost all of whom are based in research institutes and universities) are having on our society, although they continue to write and speak as if they wielded the last sword of influence.

But the gap between personal motive and public espousal, as Foucault would have been the first to emphasise, needs to be addressed. An example from contemporary neo-Marxist theory suggests why. If the abundant Marxist theory generated in Western countries during the last forty years has made anything plain, it is that Marxism (of whatever variety) possesses no programmatic means, let alone adequate theoretical methods, of dealing with the crucial matter of gender relations, not even theoretical gender distinctions. No satisfactory explanations have emerged from the Marxists except banal ones grounded in notions of a preordained natural order that arranges relations between the genders in certain hierarchical and patriarchal ways.

Almost everything of substance on the subject has come from the *non*-Marxist anthropologists. Consequently, the neo-Marxist account of the history of sexuality and sexual relations in Western civilisation is even more defective (based as it necessarily is on these assumptions about gender), resorting to monolithically dyadic explanations of authority and

submission, tyranny and freedom, church and state. Despite this historio-
graphical fact, a number of Continental and North-American neo-Marxists (the British generally disdain theory) have generated their own theories
of sexuality as if Westernised neo-Marxism had adequately coped with
these matters and (more deviously on the part of those who pretend that
Marxism has the answers) posited adequate, if not healthy, solutions.
Nothing could be further from the truth. The most profound gender
studies and histories of sexuality have not issued forth from the espousers
of Marxist methodologies, unless by the label 'Marxist' one designates
(that old saw again!) *anyone interested in history and class structure*, in which
case the label loses all meaning and force. Are *all* historians interested in
gender and class structure Marxists merely by virtue of their interest?

My conviction remains, then, what it has been for some time and
develops from a sense of what the life of the mind ought to be in a
democratic country that is necessarily pluralised. To encourage the learning of new critical idioms, which is tantamount to being *pro theory*; to
encourage the New Historicism (i.e., based on the social sciences rather
than on political history), which can only invigorate eighteenth-century
studies; and to continue to make a case for broad contexts rather than
narrow disciplinary ones: all this in order to promote deeper understanding
of the epoch of choice rather than repetitive rehashing of the same literary
author or work over and over again, which will permit, in time, new
types of questions to be asked and new kinds of explanations to be offered
through higher thresholds of discussion.

But *all three at once*,[1] for one without the other plunges us further
back than we were before the dissemination of theory. I see no contradiction whatever in this position. To be *for* theory does not automatically
necessitate that one is antiempirical or antihistorical, and those who believe
that it does entail contradiction have not looked in the mirror. And vice
versa: those who are *for* history (old or new) need not be against theory;
I can think of some fine eighteenth-century scholars who blend history
and theory well. Indeed, this commensurability of theory and history
defines and forms the heart of my own pluralism, which I see as intellectually defensible and morally democratic. Those who don't should demonstrate why they are incompatible or should explain – at the least – their
own anxiety about the perceived incompatibility. It is easy, of course, for
the Old Fogeys to pooh-pooh theory as irrelevant, illogical, and illegit-
imate and to deride theorists as radicals, liberals, Whigs, and Marxists,
New Lefters, upstarts, and Class-of-'68-ers; easy to deconstruct the deconstructionists and debunk other poststructuralists by leveling them (with
the sword of Swiftian irony) to laughing stocks. Yet it is a futile activity
that ultimately gets us nowhere, except to reassert the status quo of the
Old Fogeys of the early 1960s. Those who crave a return to 'those good

old days' unpolluted by theory and theorists are welcome to do so. Yet as one who *was* a Class-of-'68-er, who lived through the revolution, so to speak, and who vividly remembers what life was like under the tyranny of the Old Fogeys' regime, when all sorts of topics could not be explored because there existed no methods by which to approach them and when all manner of questions could not dare to be asked because they were neither politic nor polite (such as the autonomy of *all* past individuals, not merely the Dukes and Duchesses of Marlborough but the Martin Guerres and the Charlotte Charkes) – I personally will pause before regressing to Old Fogey Land. Some of the theory of the last decade, I concede, *has* been tantamount to nonsense, but it has been, in a way, meaningful nonsense: a phase through which contemporary thought has had to pass, and it did some good. Yet to pretend, now that we are reaping so much of its good (as well as its bad), that *all* theory (not merely the Northrop Fryes but the structuralists and poststructuralists) has polluted us without recollecting the way it reinvigorated scholarship in general, and the eighteenth century in particular, is sheer folly.

To continue: I would rather never have to *choose between* theory and history ('*Wit* and *Judgement* often are at strife . . .') because I see them as complementary rather than opposed categories. But if I were *compelled* to make a choice, under duress I would select the latter, especially for pedagogical reasons. For no matter how important theory is, how valid its claims, history logically supersedes it: especially the referentiality and contextuality that give eighteenth-century literature so much of its meaning. If history cannot be restored to theory as the mutual companion it deserves to be, then the heteroglossia of pluralism will terrifically isolate readers and writers, teachers and students, colleagues and colleagues, who will no longer be able to communicate because they have divested themselves of their most precious common heritage: the past.

In the end it would be pathetic for us to be teachers in a milieu in which students no longer commanded any primary familiarity with the past, not even a rudimentary understanding of the reasons why the English, French, American, Dutch, German, and Russian revolutions developed when they did. Still more pathetic to attempt to educate students who have inferred from their mentors that the Holocaust could just as well have been a development of the Enlightenment as of the mid twentieth century, or that the idea of progress could have been the credo of the Middle Ages as well as of the eighteenth century. Santayana, perhaps remembering Johnson, described the pathos better than anyone in his famous passage about those who have never learned history remaining children forever and children of a lesser god. Children who are enslaved to the present because they know nothing about the past.

NOTE

1 See G. S. Rousseau. 'Ephebi, Epigoni, and Fornacalia: Some Meditations on the Contemporary Historiography of the Eighteenth Century'. *The Eighteenth Century*, xx (1979), 203–26 (*Enlightenment Borders*, chap. 3) and 'Threshold and Explanation: the Social Anthropologist and the Critic of Eighteenth-Century Literature', *The Eighteenth Century*, xxii (1981), 127–52 (chap. 6 above).

8

The debate about the New Historicism and the history of science

In 1985 the Thames Polytechnic in London celebrated the tenth anniversary of the launching of its in-house journal Literature and History produced by its own students. Its editors invited me to contribute, which I happily did, as I thought it rare for such a new school to sustain a decade of scholarship of this quality.

I decided to have another go at the historiography of sensibility, following up on the points I had developed in Australia (chap. 5). This time my post-disciplinary cultural anthropology paced the material differently. By focusing on two important previous versions of sensibility – those of the eminent North American eighteenth-century scholars Donald Greene and Jean Hagstrum – I sought to demonstrate to what perilous detriment the discourses of empiricism, especially science, medicine, and the technologies of cultural production in the Enlightenment, had been entirely omitted from the debate. Hagstrum had not even mentioned science or the scientists.

Both Greene and Hagstrum were offended. Greene, the doyen of Johnson scholars, claimed to be pro-science – a veritable empiricist in the tradition of Samuel Johnson – and performed the work of an exegete; he wrote copious notes in the margins of the published essay and returned his copy to me. These were permeated with ironic aspersions insisting he was an empiricist but that science had nothing to do with the development of sensibility. Hagstrum, for his part, was even more offended but refused to reply personally or discuss the issue publicly.

The historiography of sensibility, it seems to me, still remains in a pre-Bakhtinian state: the victim of those dialogic spaces between disciplinary and post-disciplinary discourse. Its current students would learn much from Foucault's Discipline and Punish, if they would read this work as a metaphor for our own contemporary academic disciplines as houses of confinement built in the eighteenth century and designed to punish post-disciplinary inquiries – such as sensibility – which stray from the old nineteenth-century evolutionary categories, at the same time legitimating those that do not. The diachronic rise of sensibility cannot be explained merely in the light of theology; its dispersed Enlightenment cults require much more than an account of local sentimentalism. The postmodernist discourse of sensibility must be revised if its claim that it can explain anything is to be valid.

Only when the great maladies of the Enlightenment are properly addressed – hysteria, hypochondria, melancholy: all those medical and psychiatric conditions afflicting the nerves which the Enlightenment appropriated to itself – will we understand how important science was for the genesis of the ethics and sentimental cults of sensibility.

An editor of *Literature and History* has expressed five serious 'limitations' and 'failings' of the journal (anniversary issue, XI:I (spring 1985), 9). These include 'too little genuine debate', a sense that 'the nineteenth-century novel is the only form of literature', and a British 'insularity of coverage' that 'remains deplorable'. My discussion of a set of specific problems in the literary history of the European Enlightenment aims to ameliorate this state of affairs, as well as address an interdisciplinary topic. But my treatment here remains a discussion and nothing more than a discussion; as such, it necessarily uses sharp tones and occasionally abrupt transitions since theory cannot be generated or tested without a certain amount of sharpness. Furthermore, the literature and history I deal with is that of the Restoration and eighteenth century; the nineteenth does not even enter into the debate, except in the obvious sense that all of us thinking and writing about literature and history today owe much to the nineteenth century for the formation of our critical intelligence. Finally, I am American by birth as well as education, and although I have had two stints as a visiting professor at Cambridge University, in no sense whatever can I be considered British. The editor's fourth caveat – that the journal has had 'plenty of critical theory but only . . . a limited amount of literary history' – touches a delicate nerve on both our parts, I suspect. *Quant à moi*, although I have admired the journal's courage from the start, I must nevertheless concur with the editor's view about the imbalance of theory and literary history. By addressing an aspect of this particular imbalance in my own work, I have realised to what degree my discussion here is generated in an attempt to move toward a more coherent theory of literary history: one that does not wilfully ignore the crucial domains of science and medicine in its programme. My own realisation is partly historical. If the last decade's wars over critical pluralism make anything clear, it is this: that literary history, as it had been traditionally practised before the 1970s, now appears old-fashioned and out of vogue to a whole generation of Anglo-American literary critics because it has not sufficiently examined its own critical premises. These fundamental assumptions are being re-examined in various quarters. But surely the time is also ripe to search for a new, coherent, enriched literary history that does not obliterate history altogether, or reduce to ashes the basic blocks of culture: government, economics, the arts, the sciences, medicine. My discussion here is generated in this hope, and in the wish that others may be willing to address the imbalance in their own work.

Of the scholars whose work is discussed below, all are well known and prominent in their field. Two of these, Professors Donald Greene and Jean Hagstrum, are particularly prominent and have been remarkably influential in the development of eighteenth-century studies since World War Two. Greene has dominated studies of Samuel Johnson and preserved the value of traditional approaches to literary history, while Hagstrum has performed pioneering work in the development of the 'sister-arts' and has contributed to the rise of literature and painting as a valid field of inquiry.

When I was in graduate school at Princeton in the 1960s, we read their articles and books for rare insight and sustained illumination. Later on, in the 1970s, Greene took on R. S. Crane about 'the genealogy of the man of feeling' (see the discussion below), in debates that were so widely known that my research students referred to Greene's position as the Gospel according to Greene. In academic circles in America where interest in eighteenth-century studies was high, it was generally believed that Greene had said the last word in the debate with Crane. But all the scholars named below are, or were (Crane is dead), authoritative figures who have dedicated themselves to teaching and studying the eighteenth century in which they are so erudite; nothing I say below can, or ought to, detract from eminence which was established long ago.

Nevertheless, it seems to me that they, like so many other humanistic scholars of their generation, share an ingrained resistance to science and the history of sciences. I do not mean that they devalue theoretical or applied science in their daily life; for example, that they avoid telephones, calculators, computers. But they intentionally diminish the role science played in the history of human culture, and take less account of it in their scholarship than is historically accurate or ideologically healthy. This state of affairs may have been otherwise if the Middle Ages had been the chronological period in which they worked, although even then, as historians of science continue to demonstrate, science was important. But science was crucial to almost every aspect of daily life in the eighteenth-century, and it is inconceivable to think that any author who wrote then, or any problem related to that period, could be studied apart from deep understanding of the Lockian, Newtonian and many other types of science and medicine then developing, being tested, and popularised.

The ensuing discussion is made with these distinctions and caveats in mind. I raise these matters because they are crucial for the relations of history and literature, more generally for the interpretations of cultures, not as a result of the particularity of the below *dramatis personae*; and I certainly intend no attack *ad homine*. I respect the work of these scholars too much to contemplate, let alone execute, such a programme. But I do believe that now is the time to redress the balance and bring science into the eighteenth-century cultural debate, as it were, to the degree it properly deserves.

THRESHOLD

In any discussion of an interdisciplinary nature such as this one clearly professes to be – literature *and* psychology or psychology *in* literature – great care ought to be taken to ensure a high threshold of discussion, a healthy self-consciousness about the types of questions being asked, and a clear sense of precisely what one hopes ultimately to explain.

By *threshold* I refer to the opposite of the reductive approach; but I do not call for an indiscriminate pluralism that transforms such abundance of cause and effect into a Boolean algebra with which no one can cope.[1] That is, a pluralism of causes that renders all resulting explanations literal non-sense. By *high threshold* I do not beg for discussion that resembles William James's conception of an infant's idea of the universe as 'one big, booming, blooming, buzzing Confusion'.[2] Ours is an age of theory, of course, and theory breeds indiscriminate pluralism, so much so that many academic scholars, eager to tell the *whole truth* and nothing but the *whole truth*, live in daily dread of being called reductionistic – the opposite of indiscriminately pluralistic. In pleading for *high threshold* I do not seek to abandon integrated and refined interpretations. On the contrary, I consider these essential; but it is equally crucial to recognise from the outset the kinds of questions one is asking and what one hopes to explain by posing the problem (i.e. framing it, contextualising it, relating it, etc.) in this and no other way. My discussion stands or falls on this proviso; and no matter how persuasive my argument is about the role of psychology *in* eighteenth-century literature, ultimately *threshold* determines what I can hope to explain. These caveats are not, therefore, gratuitous morsels of introduction.

Having said this, I must iterate that I am, of course, a twentieth-century commentator addressing an allegedly eighteenth-century problem, and even if I wanted to shed myself of twentieth-century biases I could not. For example, I approach the whole domain of *psychology* without asking what the word means – hardly a state of affairs that would have obtained in Swift's day or Pope's.[3] And I, like most of my contemporaries, possess a more or less clear sense of the subdivisions of psychology into psychiatry, medicine, neurology, physiology, clinical theory, the social sciences, etc. as well as – in the other half of the relationship: literature – a sense of the flow of English literature after 1800: neither can have been the case for a Swift or Pope. The question about the *interrelations* of psychology *and* literature before 1800, or about psychology *in* literature before 1800, therefore cannot be so simple as it appears, especially if I enquire, briskly and pointedly, what can I hope to explain by relating them in the first place? Do I mean, what would Swift have said of the 'and' or the 'in' relation? That is, surely, a very different thing from what

I would say about it, being neither an Anglican churchman nor the victim of continuous professional disappointment and, moreover, bearing as I do a different attitude to the domains of religion and science.[4] If I speculate about Locke's response to the 'and' or the 'in' relation, it becomes clear that his attitude must have differed from Swift's for reasons also involving religion and science. And this would have differed again from what a Coleridge or a Hegel or a Freud would, and indeed did, say about this very pregnant relation (the 'and' or 'in') that has continued to intrigue as well as baffle good minds for over two centuries.

I tried to cope with these problems in *The Ferment of Knowledge.*[5] Asked to explain what the eighteenth-century equivalent of our modern psychology was, I attempted to demonstrate that there was *no* easy equivalent; that in my research I had found more difference than similarity. The word psychology existed, of course, as did conscious and unconscious, and even consciousness and unconsciousness,[6] but their meanings and uses differed so greatly from ours that it makes little sense merely to perform a 'translation'. I also paused for a long time about the title of my section. I could not call it 'the theological view of man' because this heading omits the natural history of the subject: man viewed as a natural creature apart from his theological being. I could not entitle it 'the many eighteenth-century thinkers, in his economic, social, anthropological, societal and historical condition, a context much broader than the one I was willing to adopt and, moreover, a context requiring a threshold pitched even more highly than the already stratospheric one I had invoked. I did not dare call the section 'psychiatry' for obvious reasons: because the term suggests therapies of treatment and presupposes that the whole class of mankind studied is deranged or close to it – this caveat apart from the glaring fact that the eighteenth-century concepts of psychiatry, to the extent that there existed a theoretical underpinning to its various therapies, possesses none of the conditions modern psychiatrists consider necessary (not merely optional) to any theory, or science, or psychiatry. For similar reasons I did not title the section 'physiology'. Eighteenth-century physiological theory commented at great length on abnormal psychic states but I did·not wish to lend an impression that the only 'psychology' I was discussing lay in the domain of abnormal types. 'Philosophy' may have been a better title than all these, but it omits a vast body of scientific literature then influential on psychological theory: even Locke was a trained scientist tutored at Oxford for years by the greatest physiologist of the day and became a practising physician who could not have written the *Essay Concerning Human Understanding* if he had not first studied the new medicine.[7] Finally I settled on 'psychology' and realised that there would be controversy no matter which of these labels I chose.[8]

Of one thing I was certain: whatever 'psychological' theory was in the eighteenth century; however 'pure' its theoretical underpinnings may have been, it had nevertheless been influenced by social and political considerations; so much so that it would be folly to discuss psychology in the broad sense in which I had defined it without taking account of these contributory factors. In every psychological institution I had surveyed – in the social history of madhouses (public and private), in the development of concepts of abnormal mental states, in the notion of mental health held by philosophers and theologians – it was patent that there had never been such a thing as a 'purely *scientific* theory' of the human psyche; moreover, that eighteenth-century psychological *knowledge* (knowledge on the limited but widespread popular misconception that science is ultimately nothing but knowledge) – knowledge about the human mind was so various, just as it is today, as to render the idea of 'psychology *in* the eighteenth-century' – as if there had been only *one* psychology – a futile subject unless one were willing to grapple with its types. It would be silly as well as false, that is, to isolate just *one* type of psychological knowledge and call it representative of the whole eighteenth century.

I had also come to realise the strengths and weaknesses of the lexical approach. Intensive study of individual key words *à la* C. S. Lewis and William Empson[9] – words such as conscious, unconscious, consciousness, unconsciousness, memory, attention, imagination – might produce subtle shades of meaning and indicate change but it would not account for the deeper reasons initiating the changes. For these deep-layer causes one would have to look beyond the lexical approach, valuable though its results are. Furthermore, the lexical approach permits the student of vocabulary to weave his fantasy with seeming impunity and without an attentive ear to great cultural transformation. Our trust is placed in him, although his results may be nothing more than the product of imagination. Trained as a literary critic, I had of course realised what a powerful tool the lexical approach could become, but I also recognised its limitations, its potential for abuse, and concurred with Samuel Johnson who must also have sensed its limitations when he pronounced that 'Language is only the instrument of science and words are but the signs of ideas'.[10] A grasp of psychology *in* the eighteenth century based on the *OED* would, for example, be disastrously defective even before it was launched. It is naturally a comforting thought to know that professors of English are usually adept at the lexical approach; but it will not do, alas, to persuade sophisticated cultural historians who look further afield than merely to words used in *limited contexts* and without attention to competing discourse. Over thirty years ago Erik Erametsa published a lexical *Study of the Word Sentimental* (1951) that isolated five major changes, but he never bothered to ask himself what *caused* the word to change in the first place. Today such a study is considered old-fashioned and inadequate precisely because of its refusal to consider linguistic exclusive of *non*literary agents as possible sources of protean change. Its threshold is pitched altogether too low.

'SENSIBILITY' AS CASE STUDY; GREENE AND HAGSTRUM

Surely Donald Greene's approach to sentimentalism in 'Latitudinarianism and Sensibility'[11] – ostensibly a reply to R. S. Crane – reveals a higher threshold and explains more than Erametsa and similar types of lexical students. Greene did not aim to *explain* the semantic bases of sensibility – others had tried and failed; nor did he try to chart *à la* Ian Watt 'the rise of the sensibility movement' – he made it perfectly clear that he doubted if it ever existed; but he noticed that Crane had not asked a crucial question about the genealogy of the man of feeling: the question of origins. Crane argued that the sermons of the Restoration and early eighteenth century offered worshippers a *new* type of latitudinarianism based on ideas of doing good and acting benevolently, but he failed, according to Greene, to realise that these very same ideas had been promoted in sermons and other religious writings long before the Restoration. In Greene's words, these tenets 'had been held and preached from the time of the Reformation and earlier'.[12]

So much for Crane's theory of cause and effect, but the argument about *sensibility* can hardly be put to rest here for two big questions intrinsically related to psychology *in* literature must still be put. First, when did these ideas of benevolence begin to reach large numbers of British worshippers, and, secondly, why did the English literature we now call – *faute de mieux* – 'sentimental' develop them from the earlier eighteenth century onward and not prior? Greene's position is unequivocal. 'If there is any causal connection', he writes, 'between those tenets [of benevolence] and the presence of "sensibility" or "sentimentalism" in literature – a large "if" – then we should expect to find it in literature long before the eighteenth century'.[13] Greene contends that we do, although he does not specify whether it begins – moving backwards – in Cromwellian days, Elizabethan times, medieval days, or possibly Roman or Greek. More importantly, Greene argues that even if 'it could somehow be established statistically that there was an unusual upsurge in the amount of sentimental literature appearing in England in the mid eighteenth century, *a hypothesis that would account for it more plausibly than Crane's* [this is the crucial phrase] would be the growth of a much larger and less discriminating reading public than in the past'.[14]

Now the notion of an expanding (middle-class?) reading public as *the* cause of sentimentalism is certainly a possible explanation but is surely not the *only* one. Indirectly, Kuhn and Feyerabend offer two competing theories that deserve to be considered despite their (the theories') limitations.[15] The Kuhnian theory or paradigm, as by now almost everyone knows, is that scientific thought and the 'paradigms' [i.e. books] that are its results are largely responsible for creating the world view of a given age. According to Feyerabend, scientific thought plays a part in the creation of that worldview, but not a greater role than philosophy, the arts, and all other types of thinking. Kuhn and Feyerabend share one thing: both agree that there is a great deal more in common between, for example, Sophoclean narrative and the philosophy of ancient Greece *vis-à-vis* the nature of man, than there is in common between this narrative and philosophy and the narrative *of other ages*. The 'other ages' is the crux of the matter, for the theory is ultimately an historical one that uses the social sciences in an essential way. Whatever their differences, Kuhn and Feyerabend stand or fall on this point about commonality with other ages.

The implication of both hypotheses for sensibility is that something ought to have happened *just before*, or *shortly before*, it begins to appear in the sentimental English literature we all read and teach. Whatever it was, it cannot have occurred *after* sensibility flowered in literature. Likewise, if Kuhn and Feyerabend are right, it cannot have developed *so long ago* – Rome, the Middle Ages, Scholasticism – as to separate it from its proximate worldview. The whole thrust of Kuhn and Feyerabend, social scientists charging themselves to explain large cultural shifts (i.e. world views), is that great historical *dis*continuities occur when relatively proximate causes stop having their customary effects. Stated otherwise, a map of culture that *includes* the scientific and the artistic domain – that is, a map which embraces *everything* – must be made before one can hope to explain great cultural differences. Science cannot be omitted under any circumstance at any time. And it is more probable, Kuhn and Feyerabend argue, that explanations have as much in common across discourse lines, as explanations within the same discourse have across epochal and cultural boundaries. Today, almost every historically-minded social scientist who is worth anything stakes his whole life on this last point about boundary lines. Narrow literary exegetes are among the few types who have held out.[16]

In just this mood Robert Brissenden wrote *Virtue in Distress*, a study of the European sentimental movement.[17] He used the lexical approach as one tool: he found the scientific (Kuhn) and artistic (Feberabend) world view even more productive for understanding the essential nature of sentimental man. He recreated 'sensible man' and showed how novelists drew on empirical theories of him. He limited himself to novels but he did not argue that sensibility or sentimentalism was restricted to the novel: he knew perfectly well how many poems in the eighteenth century invoke the muse Sensibility for their inspiration and how many plays depict a sentimental ethic. Had Brissenden been better read in the history of the science, he may have followed Kuhn more rigidly and may have argued that 'sensible man' – the man of feeling – required a *specific* scientific legacy before he could develop. But he did not and therefore pitched his explanation lower than Kuhn and most social scientists would consider acceptable. All Brissenden had to rely on was Crane's influential essay; he did not have the advantage of Greene's corrective reply and, now, Hagstrum's *Sex and Sensibility*.[18]

Hagstrum's book also focuses on sensibility, as its title suggests,[19] and adopts a chronological approach as indicated by its subtitle: a study 'from Milton to Mozart'. It is a brilliant book, as I have commented elsewhere,[20] in its sweep and in the narrow explication of individual works; equally brilliant for its inclusion of 'painters of sensibility' who, according to Hagstrum, embraced similar ideals to the writers'. Brissenden reviewed the book and said as much but claimed to be disappointed because Hagstrum 'omitted Diderot and Haller' – the whole empirical map of sensibility that constituted proof that it had existed in the first place.[21] Neither Brissenden nor Hagstrum doubted that there had been a 'sentimental movement' – a rise of sensibility – in the eighteenth century; their only difference regarded *what* it was, *when* it started, and *why* it got going. Brissenden, moreover, did not criticise Hagstrum for deficiencies in the history of empiricism or the history of science; rather he was asking for two things he found sorely lacking in the book: (1) some consideration of the Kuhnian paradigm, especially since Hagstrum had relied on the books of Lawrence Stone and was not wholly ignorant of the work of 'outsiders';[22] (2) clear reasons why we should believe that sensibility *begins* with Milton and more or less *ends* – presumably ends, if the subtitle designates anything – with Mozart. If Hagstrum's reply were that Milton and Mozart were *arbitrary* choices, then the theoretical foundation of the book, surely, would be called into question: why write a book about 'sensibility' with Milton as its 'pioneer' – its founder – if Milton had been all along an *arbitrary* choice? Brissenden's essential question thus amounts to this: if Milton is not arbitrary, then who is? And if Milton is merely a convenient starting place to write a book about the Restoration and eighteenth century, then why go to such trouble to argue that he really was the *founder* of something called 'sensibility'?

AUGUSTINIANISM AND SENSIBILITY: LITERATURE AND PSYCHOLOGY

A response to these questions is crucial – by Hagstrum and anyone else who cares about the matter – because the mind/body problem necessarily lies at the centre of all discussions about 'sensibility'. To know what a modern or contemporary scholar believes about sensibility, one must learn first what he or she thinks of the history of the mind/body dichotomy. All else follows from it; the sense of the nature of man, the way that nature changes and why it succumbs to change. In this connection it is crucial to note that the best historians of philosophy do *not* believe it is an 'ancient problem'.[23] Plato and Aristotle of course pronounced at many junctures about mind and body, but Descartes and Locke formulated the problem in a new way that bore little resemblance to anything in ancient philosophy. There must be agreement about this point if progress is to be made, nor ought it to be treated cavalierly as if it were some minor impediment. Moreover, Husserl laid the Cartesian–Lockian view to sleep on the other side, at the end of the nineteenth century, and ever since then it has been viewed as a pseudo-scientific, or quasi-scientific, matter.[24] For forty years Suzanne Langer, the distinguished philosopher, has been writing a multi-volume essay on precisely this issue; the last volume reads as if it were a treatise in advanced neurophysiology and confirms the point about the mind/body problem in the aftermath of Husserl.[25] But the Cartesian–Lockian view of the mind/body problem as the ultimate dualism was not the only model of man *c.* 1700. As Donald Greene has argued[26] – rightly in my view – it vied with an older Augustinian version in which monistic man is seen as a fallen creature prone to the easy elevation of his own pride, a psychological predisposition often causing him to endorse the wrong values and having rather little to do with the enigmatic mind/body problem. After 1700, as even Greene concedes, the Augustinian view lost force, although it hardly became extinct. In Greene's words: 'The history of belief in the Augustinian view of human nature in England after the early eighteenth century becomes more complicated, with theologians like the Reverend Samuel Clarke and Bishop Joseph Butler introducing considerations apparently deriving from Greek and Cartesian philosophy . . .'[27]

The empirical competitors of the Augustinian view are central to any discussion of psychology and literature *in* the eighteenth century, as well as crucial to the genesis of sensibility. Descartes jolted the whole edifice of Augustinianism by a radical dualism that eventually changed older concepts of 'selfhood'. Locke challenged selfhood even more radically when he cast memory as the centrepiece of personal identity. It may be true, as Greene suggests,[28] that 'the standard authors' of English literature derived these views more than they endorsed them; but it is an incontrovertible fact of literary history that whether or not they endorsed them, they were shaken by these empirical views; and it is therefore silly to argue that they passively 'derived' them without re-examining the whole foundation of their supposed Augustinian world view. Why else would the poet of *An Essay on Man* have been so troubled that the traditional hierarchies of the 'Great Chain of Being' were in disarray? *Gulliver's Travels* and *The Dunciad*, moreover, are practically the direct expression of extreme psychological anxiety in their authors over the new empirical (i.e. psychological) concepts of man: there is no passive derivation evident in these works.[29] Yet it is as false to contend that the Lockian view of man prevailed over the Augustinian: surely each survived in different corners and in many cases at least there was a blend, or synthesis, of the two. For Pope and Swift, no matter how good as writers, were but two voices in a century of hundreds; and the greatest distortions occur if one myopically views all thought through their eyes. Still, one thing is clear: virtually *all* the eighteenth-century writers we now label 'sentimental' – Steele, Richardson, Sterne, Smollett, almost the whole French Englightenment, certainly Diderot and his seminal *Rêve de d'Alembert*, the von Haller who was a splendid poet and who founded Europe's most distinguished school of new science based on 'sensibility' – confronted rather than derived the Lockian and post-Lockian view while retaining or abjuring the Augustinian.

Perhaps Locke-the-man captures the point. According to his biographers he himself was a Sunday Christian, but presumably he believed sufficiently in his own hypothesis about the nature of man to subscribe to it.[30] Are we then to conclude that he was a Christian 'emotionally' and Lockian 'intellectually'? Or a Lockian for six days a week and Augustinian on the Sabbath? Greene contends that man had 'been sentimentalised' long before 1700.[31] This may be true but there cannot have been an empirical, or scientific, explanation of sentimentalism – the precise reasons for his sympathy, his degree of sensitivity, genius, intuition, reason, imagination, memory, benevolence and caring, his whole moral sense – before the empirical revolution of Descartes and, more relevantly, Locke. The reason is simply that the empirical (i.e. scientific) explanation of sentimentalism, of the man of feeling, requires some sophisticated physiology.[32] The sixteenth century had been a golden age of anatomy (Vesalius *et al.*) but its physiology was primitive. Descartes, Willis (Locke's teacher), and Locke himself, changed all that, causing modern historians of science to label the seventeenth century 'the revolutionary period of physiology'. This process whereby science infiltrates a worldview has been Kuhn's theory all along. But Hagstrum either has not bothered to look into the empirical tradition or does not believe it can affect his own map of sensibility.

What is the Hagstrum map? It is the view that sensibility arises when heterosexual relations are idealised. Hagstrum's hypothesis is that Milton is crucial to the genesis of sensibility (note: *before* Crane's benevolent sermons) because he broke away from the Augustinian tradition. 'That [Augustinian] tradition', Hagstrum writes, 'tended to subordinate, even to denigrate woman, who was considered sometimes a sink of loathsome sensuality . . . an intellectual nonentity'.[33] Hagstrum repeats the point in case it is overlooked: 'Against that [Augustinian] tradition Milton's portrayal of marriage as a joyous heterosexual friendship constitutes one of the most eloquent protests in Christian history'.[34] Yet again for emphasis: 'What I [Hagstrum] have said of Milton so far clearly places him in the camp of the Moderns, not the Ancients . . .'.[35] Hagstrum nowhere in his book (*Sex and Sensibility*) mentions Greene's directly relevant 'Augustinianism and Empiricism' although he refers on several occasions to Greene's rejoinder to Crane.[36] Yet Hagstrum seems unaware that the matter of 'Augustinianism and Empiricism' touches more fundamentally on his own map of sensibility:

(1) Sensibility is inevitably tied to sex and its idealisation.
(2) Milton embodies the connection and espoused it *long before* Locke.
(3) Milton leads to Dryden – a 'pioneer' in sex and sensibility – and to the standard authors of English literature who will also espouse it.
(4) Milton endowed sensibility to English literature, and it passed from him to the Restoration dramatists, the early novelists, Richardson, Rousseau, Sterne, Gothic writers, and even Jane Austen.

But what happened to Greene's 'large "if" '? Greene, it will be recalled, had doubted there ever was such a thing as sensibility and argued that if it existed at all 'a hypothesis that would account for it more plausibly than Crane's would be the growth of a much larger and less discriminating reading public than in the past'.[37] Is one to assume then that this 'growth' and 'less discriminating reading public' developed in the middle of the *seventeenth* century rather than the eighteenth, thereby permitting Milton conveniently to draw upon it for his apparent sensibility, or is the Hagstrum thesis incompatible with Greene's?

Whether incompatible or not, clearly Hagstrum has abandoned Kuhn and Feyerabend before he ever heard of them – and Greene too – for science (empiricism) does not exist in this map of sensibility and Milton does not need a Descartes or Locke in order 'to revolt'.[38] Moreover, Milton's 'eloquent protest' against traditional Christianity is attributable in Hagstrum's view to his personality or temperament but not to any external factors in his, or any relatively proximate, social milieu; certainly not to any new reading public, in Greene's thinking the only single factor that could have caused a sentimental movement.[39] But notice that Hagstrum's map of sensibility in our period also invalidates Greene's Augustinian view of human nature. Greene had clearly stated his position: 'To Boas's list of English writers . . . who *professed orthodox Christian belief* [italics mine] could be added Dryden, Defoe, Steele, Young, Smart, Richardson, Fielding, Sterne, Cowper, Crabbe, and a host of lesser figures'.[40] Presumably Milton too? But one cannot have Milton, or for that matter Richardson or Sterne, *both* ways: as a rebellious anti-Augustinian protestor (Hagstrum) and as an orthodox Christian embracing established doctrine. Milton is either an orthodox Christian or he is not – or is orthodox Christianity such an ambiguous and slippery matter that any 'standard author' can be called orthodox or unorthodox or blended: a hybrid?

Likewise Richardson. Richardson-the-man certainly went to church on a Sunday, professed to believe, used orthodox Christian teachings as the basis of his writing and never revolted against Augustinian ethics, but the author of *Clarissa Harlowe* cannot have been an entirely believing Augustinian-type Christian. He is too voyeuristic and obsessed with sexual matters for that. Perhaps, as Hagstrum suggests,[41] Mark Rose neatly hit the matter on the head when commenting that 'Augustine, Paul's spiritual heir, was fated to struggle with a nature unusually passionate, and, having triumphed over his body, he bequeathed to Christianity a rather vicious portrait of his defeated enemy [body lust]'.[42] This *aperçu* serves rather well as a gloss on the imagination that invented Clarissa Harlowe. But intellectual historians who must deal with causes and worldviews must be more literal than Mark Rose. An orthodox Christian either follows some ethic close to Augustine's and triumphs over his own body – and for imaginative writers like Pope or Richardson the implication presumably includes triumphing over their Eloisas and Clarissas – or doesn't triumph, in which case the writer may be given many labels but not called 'Augustinian'. The young Berkeley who wrote in a notebook that 'Sensual Pleasure is the Summum Bonum . . . the great principle of Morality',[43] may have been, as Greene contends,[44] a 'devout Christian' (a label perhaps capable of as many interpretations as are Augustan or neo-Augustan), but surely he cannot have been 'Augustinian' unless some very extraordinary qualifications are placed on this term.

KUHN, FEYERABEND . . . THEORY

There isn't space to continue with other matters related to 'the rise of sensibility' or, in textual terms, 'discourses writ against the spleen' as Sterne says,[45] but even in this brief discussion it should be patent that psychology and literature *in* the eighteenth century is not a simple matter unless one wishes 'to play it safe' (i.e. avoid the whole issue or pretend it doesn't exist). No chronological survey *à la* Boring's standard *Historical Survey of Experimental Psychology* is going to be of much use:[46] it may trace psychological thinkers and theories from antiquity to the present time but it won't settle the above matters and probably won't shed terrific light on such matters as consciousness, personal identity or the sensibility movement unless some of the concerns of threshold I have mentioned are quickly yoked to it. Kuhn's approach offers much more. It helps to know, for example, that the sixteenth century witnessed a veritable revolution in anatomy, the seventeenth in physiology, and the eighteenth in psychology. It helps even the student of the decline of European Augustinianism to know precisely what the foe, empiricism, was accomplishing in the three hundred years between 1400 and 1700.[47] Even so, it helps more to know whether the perpetrator of these empirical revolutions – whether a Vesalius, a Bacon, a Descartes, a Locke or a Hume – was an Augustinian or an empiricist or an Augustinian *manqué*, or whether an ancient or a modern, and little light about the matter will be shed before then. For psychology *and* literature, as well as psychology *in* literature, requires more knowledge than information about isolated theories of memory, imagination, consciousness, personal identity, the self, the other, etc., which exist in some form or shape in all periods. Hypothesis about all these topics with the possible exception of personal identity had been generated in the Ancient world.[48] There was nothing new to Bacon about a psychological theory of imagination unless the specific elements of that theory were even *less* Augustinian than the elements implicated in his theory;[49] and the single hypothesis in psychology that *was* new – Locke's personal identity – was endorsed or rejected in the early eighteenth century, as Christopher Fox has now shown,[50] more or less according to one's larger belief about the nature of man. It is impossible to imagine an 'Augustinian Hume' but even if he had been less sceptical than he was, he still would have rejected the idea of personal identity on purely empirical grounds: so far had his scientific method progressed.

All I have argued is, of course, irrelevant and gratuitous if *formal proof* is required that individual writers owned certain books, actually read them, notated them, commented upon them and referred to them by verse and chapter. No such documentation exists for more writers in the eighteenth century, nor should it be implied that the consequence of this lack of formal proof is that just the opposite of what I have been arguing is true. For writers in all times absorb much more information and material than they can possibly have read, and it is foolish to argue that they did not 'feel the sway' of the new empiricism just because they had not actually read book upon book. My argument about *threshold* is thus not fatally imperiled by the absence of proof in many cases. But it is endangered by those contemporary critics and scholars – some of whom work in the eighteenth century – who continue to believe that we can do our work in psychology *and* literature, or in psychology *in* literature, without worrying about the focus of the map, or worldview, before us; and even more urgently endangered by those critics who think that none of the above has any direct relation to English literature and who will continue blithely composing still another 'reading' of *Macflecnoe* or *Tom Jones*. They have yet to learn that context is everything.

NOTES

1 For discussion of the 'reductive fallacy' and 'the fallacy of indiscriminate pluralism' see David Hackett Fischer, *Historians' Fallacies: Toward a Logic of Historical Thought* (1971), 172–7.

2 William James, *Psychology* (Cleveland, 1948), 16.

3 Thomas Willis, the noted physiologist of the Restoration, uses the terms 'psychalogia' and 'psyche-logia' to refer to discourse about the *psyche* in his medical works of the 1660s and 1670s and Thomas Pordage, his English translator in the 1680s, translates the term as 'psyche-logia' or 'discourse of the mind': see the preface to *Pathologiae Cerebri* (1667) and *De Anima Brutorum* (1672), translated by Pordage as *An Essay on the Pathology of the Brain* (1683) and *Two Discourses concerning the Soul of Brutes, which is that of the Vital and Sensitive Soul of Man* (1683). But it is not at all clear whether empirical thinkers in the Restoration understood 'psyche-logia' to mean 'discourse about the psyche' in any way similar to our current usage of the term psychology. There cannot be any doubt, however, that writers such as Swift and Pope were perfectly aware of an old medical tradition that had discussed 'psycheologia' or 'the physick of the soul'. See Pope's own annotation to *The Dunciad*, (A), 81–2: 'The *Caliph. Omar I*, having conquer'd *Aegypt*, caus'd his General to burn the *Ptolomean* library, on the gates of which was this inscription, *Medicina Animae, The Physick of the Soul*'.

4 The last matter is the most crucial in the series, i.e. religion *and* science. Ever since Romantic thinkers rebelled against both mechanism and empiricism, religion and science construed as separate domains have been much *further apart* than they were in the eighteenth century, and it is almost impossible for most contemporary intellectual historians, as well as literary historians, to imagine that religion and science could still have been wedded as recently as the eighteenth century. But the fact is that there was little contradiction then between religion and science, a state of affairs that permitted a Newton, for example, to devote himself to both areas without worrying about 'the two cultures' of C. P. Snow and F. R. Leavis. Much of the basis of religious and empirical thought is misunderstood unless this precise relationship is perfectly well focused.

5 G. S. Rousseau and Roy Porter (eds.), *The Ferment of Knowledge: Studies in the Historiography of Eighteenth-Century Science* (Cambridge, 1980). Robert Weyant has produced a review of my chapter in the *Journal of the History of the Behavioural Sciences* (spring 1983), 226–33, which discusses the complex problems of contextualising the history of psychology in the eighteenth century; not surprisingly, though, he demonstrates how much resistance there remains to the point made in note 4 above about religion *and* science when he states (p. 226): 'that as the first thoroughly secular and sceptical century . . . [the eighteenth century] marks the real beginning of the modern era and thus deserves more serious study than it has received'. But the eighteenth century was hardly 'thoroughly secular and sceptical'.

6 For discussion of the use of these terms in the eighteenth century see: F. H. Lapointe, 'Who Originated the term Psychology?' *Journal of the History of the Behavioural Sciences*, VIII (1972), 328–35 and 'The Origin and Evolution of the Term Psychology', *American Psychologist*, xxv (1970), 640–5; L. L. Whyte, *The Unconscious before Freud* (New York, 1960); E. L. Margetts, 'The Concept of the Unconscious in the History of Medical Psychology', *Psychiatric Quarterly*, XXVIII (1953), 115–38; and J. Yo Hon, *Thinking Matter* (1983) and *Perceptual Acquaintance from Descartes to Reid* (1984).

7 Almost every recent Lockian – Cranston, Yolton, Dewhurst, Colie, Ashcraft *et al.* –

has made the same point. See especially K. Dewhurst, *John Locke, 1632–1704, Physician and Philosopher: a Medical Biography* (1963) and – for Willis's influence on Locke's philosophic thought – H. Isler, *Thomas Willis* (Stuttgart, 1965).

8 And there is going to be. See, for example, G. Cantor, 'The Eighteenth-Century Problem' (a twenty-page review essay of *The Ferment of Knowledge*), *History of Science*, xx (1982), 44–63, who writes: 'G. S. Rousseau's contribution [on psychology] . . . while contributing a wealth of erudication, is less substantial in content. One problem is the essay's topic, 'psychology', which does not correspond to any clearly-defined subject in the eighteenth century' (p. 49). Psychology may not 'correspond' to a 'clearly-defined subject' taught in schools and universities but there was plenty of writing, discourse and discussion about 'psychealogia'. At least from the time of Thomas Willis in the 1670s, treatise upon treatise showed that 'the psyche' lay at the centre of its focus, and – somewhat less capable of proof or demonstration – any beginning student of the period and its primary literature knows that psychological situations form the basis of much of its didactic prose; for example, George Cheyne, *The English Malady: or, a Treatise of Nervous Diseases of All Kinds* (1733), and Z. Mayne, *An Essay on . . . Consciousness* (1728).

9 C. S. Lewis, *Studies in Words* (Cambridge, 1967); William Empson, *The Study of Complex Words* (1951).

10 Preface to *A Dictionary of the English Language* (1755).

11 Donald Greene, 'Latitudinarianism and Sensibility: the Genealogy of the "Man of Feeling" Reconsidered', *Modern Philology*, LXXV (1977), 159–83, hereafter referred to as Greene, *LS*.

12 Greene, *LS*, 180.

13 Greene, *LS*, 180.

14 Greene, *LS*, 180.

15 See Paul Feyerabend, *Against Method: Outline of an Anarchist Theory of Method* (Atlantic Highlands, 1975), and Thomas Kuhn, *The Structure of Scientific Revolutions*, 2nd ed. rev. and enl. (Chicago, 1970).

16 The reasons for this complex development involving the academic profession of literature in universities and competition from other developing twentieth-century subjects – especially the social sciences – is nothing that can be studied here for lack of space; nevertheless, the matter is not so simple as dividing up the universe of literary scholars into 'historians' and 'critics'; for many scholars according to this dual nomenclature derive their knowledge of the all-important 'historical contexts' from secondary sources, and the issue in contextual writing therefore centers on issues of *'whose* contexts has the scholar adopted'? This contextualism is, in a sense, the issue raised by Feyerabend and Kuhn, and is also the crucial issue in my test case about sensibility. .

17 R. F. Brissenden, *Virtue in Distress: Studies in the Novel of Sentiment from Richardson to Sade* (1974). Brissenden's mood is captured in his 'attempt at definition' in the long opening chapter. He writes (pp. 11–12): 'Scholars and historians of ideas are reluctant to confront directly the question of what is or what was *meant* by sentimentalism and sensibility . . . But no matter what may have happened to [the term] "romanticism", the same fate will not, I think, overtake "sentimentalism": despite the industry of the scholar, it is not likely to be defined out of existence'. Contemporary students of the period who doubt the currency of its usage should merely consult the PMLA Program (Nov. 1982), e.g. seminar 434, 'Landscape in an Age of Sensibility'.

18 Greene, *LS*, 180, writes of *Virtue in Distress*: 'from one recent book, whose author's *purely critical work* merits praise . . .' [italics mine]. Greene presumably insinuates that the *theoretical* portions of the book – those not dealing with individual texts – are less excellent: perhaps Brissenden's adoption of the notion sensibility and sentimentalism, or his decision to write a whole book about a 'movement' or 'ethic' which, according

to Greene, never existed. On the other hand it is possible that Greene's objection centres on Brissenden's reliance on the Crane hypothesis.

19 Jean Hagstrum, *Sex and Sensibility: Ideal and Erotic Love from Milton to Mozart* (Chicago, 1980).

20 See G. S. Rousseau, 'The Perfect Blendship', *The American Scholar*, L (autumn 1981), 552–5.

21 'Its [the book's] limitation is a failure to do more than gesture at the philosophical and scientific aspects of sentiment and sensibility in the eighteenth century. One can sympathise with the author's wish to impose some bounds on his material – and it must be admitted that a great virtue of the book is the clarity of its shape and structure – but he cannot pass over Diderot, for instance, quite so cavalierly, or fail to notice a figure so seminal as Albrecht von Haller.' See R. Brissenden, *The Scriblerian*, XV (autumn 1982) 49.

22 Hagstrum's index contains twenty references to the work of Lawrence Stone from p. 1 to p. 275, i.e. spanning the largest part of the book, yet listed is only one reference to Descartes, one to Locke, one to Newton, and none to Berkeley. I do not produce these entries to criticise Hagstrum's use of primary sources – although one could inquire into his contextualism and ask how it it possible to write about sensibility without making greater use of the deists and empiricists of the early eighteenth century; rather, I cite these figures because Hagstrum is a universalist, unlike the nominalistic Greene, and believes that it *is* possible to generalise about the relation of intellectual ideas and the uses made of them in primary literature. In a nutshell: if Hagstrum is willing to refer to Stone's social history twenty times over a range covering pp. 1–275 why is he unwilling, as Brissenden has noticed, to neglect the entire philosophical and scientific tradition?

23 See Wallace I. Matson, 'Why Isn't the Mind–Body Problem Ancient'? in H. Feigl (ed.), *Mind, Matter, and Method* (Minneapolis, 1966), 92–102, whose conclusion is this (p. 92): 'Any teaching assistant can set up the mind–body problem so that any freshman will be genuinely worried about it. Yet none of the ancients ever dreamed of it, not even the author of *De Anima* [Aristotle]'. Many other contributors to this philosophical study of the mind–body problem, including Feyerabend who wishes to enlarge the role of Locke, are in agreement with Matson.

24 See Edmund Husserl, *The Crisis of European Sciences and Transcendental Phenomenology*, trans. with an intro. by David Carr (Evanston, 1970).

25 Suzanne Langer, *Mind: an Essay on Human Feeling*, 2 vols. (Baltimore, 1967–). See especially her discussion of consciousness and the unconscious in biological and neuro-physiological terms in II 272ff.

26 See D. J. Greene, 'Augustinianism and Empiricism: a Note on Eighteenth-Century English Intellectual History', *Eighteenth-Century Studies*, I (autumn 1967), 33–68, here-after cited as Greene, *AE*.

27 Greene, *AE*, 48.

28 Greene, *AE*, 39–40.

29 W. B. Carnochan has argued in the longest chapter of *Lemuel Gulliver's Mirror for Man* (Berkeley and Los Angeles, 1968), 116–65, that Swift was practically obsessed with Locke's empirical philosophy in the Fourth Voyage of *Gulliver's Travels*; but Carnochan was unable 'to prove' that the Swift of *Gulliver's Travels* either endorsed or ridiculed Locke's psychology in the *Essay* and, as a consequence, Carnochan's heuristic argument was not constructed as seriously as it ought to have been. But whether or not Swift was endorsing Locke, Swift surely was not 'passively deriving' Locke's theories or 'passively' responding to them. Carnochan's argument is worthy of re-examination: 'Locke's view that we cannot know more than the nominal essence of man is not merely part of the intellectual climate that brings forth the *Travels* but, somehow, a specific incentive to their satire' (p. 130).

30 What can Donald Greene mean by arguing in *AE*, 39, that Locke 'was a devout Christian'? Where is any documentation or evidence for this belief? Greene presumably relies on Locke's last biographer, Maurice Cranston, who asserts, again without evidence, in *John Locke: a Biography* (1957), 148, that Locke was a traditional Christian; but it isn't even possible to determine which parish Locke frequented, let alone to know how often he went there and what he heard. If Donald Greene means to suggest by the phrase 'devout Christian' that Locke was a 'devout Anglican' then the evidence does not bear out the contention; for the Locke who wrote at least three essays on toleration and who pleaded for toleration in religion in *The Reasonableness of Christianity* (1690) may have been a practising Christian of some type – independent? – latitudinarian? – but he cannot have been any sort of *traditional* Anglican. The notion, finally, of an 'Augustinian Locke', however loosely defined, adds up to little and cannot be supported: Locke's attacks on Catholicism, on the Trinity, and on almost everything Augustine came to symbolise in the second half of the seventeenth century, virtually rule out the possibility. Richard Ashcraft's belief that Locke was not 'a devout Christian' but a loose type of independent thinker in the manner of John Owen, the Oxford Puritan divine, and James Ferguson, some of Locke's closest associates at the time he was forming his ideas for the *Essay*, may be closer to the truth: see R. Ashcraft, 'John Locke: the Two Treatises and the Exclusion Crisis', in R. Vosper (ed.), *John Locke* (Los Angeles, 1980), 27–144, and *John Locke* (Princeton, 1985).

31 Greene, *LS*, 160.

32 I attempted to explain some of the reasons in 'Science and the Discovery of the Imagination in Enlightened England', *Eighteenth-Century Studies*, III (autumn 1969), 108–35 and 'Nerves, Spirits and Fibres: Towards Defining the Origins of Sensibility', in *Studies in the Eighteenth-Century III: Papers Presented at the Third David Nichol Smith Seminar, Canberra 1973* (Canberra, 1976), 137–58, reprinted in A. Giannitrepanni (ed.), *The Blue Guitar* (Rome, 1976) 'with a new postscript 1975', pp. 125–56. (chap 5 above). Further reasons are offered in T. S. Hall, *Ideas of Life and Matter*, 2 vols. (Chicago, 1969) and in the various writings of the historian of science Theodore Brown which deal with philosophical shifts from mechanism to vitalism in the period 1650–1750. The point is that whereas anatomy studies organs in *static* conditions, physiology traces the connections of these organs and bodily systems *in process* and can therefore accomplish what anatomy positively cannot. Sentimental man thriving on a nervous system that functioned according to clearly ordained mechanical laws based on nervous sensibility could not be explained until physiology had developed as a subject and, after it developed *c*. 1600–60, until it adopted some sophisticated mechanical vocabulary. Some of the proof of this development lies in the great imaginative literature of the eighteenth century. For example, *Tristram Shandy* is replete – not with *anatomical* but with *physiological* imagery, a web of images crucial for understanding of the essential sentimental intentions of the book, as several critics have noted; see, for example, James Rodgers, ' "Life" in the Novel: *Tristram Shandy* and Some Aspects of Eighteenth-Century Physiology', *Eighteenth-Century Life*, 1 (October 1980), 1–20 based on his 1978 doctoral dissertation completed at the University of East Anglia on the same subject. But the imagery is not random or merely based, as D. W. Jefferson suggested many years ago in an essay on Sterne and 'the traditions of learned wit', on previous 'schools of learning'. There is a clear reason why *physiology* rather than any number of other empirical domains and images drawn from its vocabulary play such a central role in the language of *Tristram Shandy*; they have to do with the empirical understanding of the nature of sentimental man himself. This is the point which Brissenden's caveat hoped to make, in the review cited above (see n. 21) and the terrain about which Hagstrum either has not bothered to inform himself or which he believes is irrelevant to his map of sensibility.

33 Hagstrum, *Sex and Sensibility*, 30.

34 *Ibid.*, 31.

35 *Ibid.*, 34.

36 *Sex and Sensibility* contains three references to Donald Greene: one to an article by Greene dealing with Swift's scatological imagery, two to the 'polemic' discussed above and cited as *LS*. Again, I do not cite these entries to fault Hagstrum's scholarship, which I consider otherwise admirable, but rather to observe that footnotes are the single best guidepost to an historian's contextualism and, furthermore, to his or her map of intellectual movements and currents within a given period.

37 See Greene, *LS*, 180. Greene's caveat about Crane's hypothesis is supported (180, n. 64) by the following statement: 'This theory is discussed in Q. D. Leavis, *Fiction and the Reading Public* (London, 1932); and Leo Lowenthal, *Literature, Popular Culture, and Society* (Palo Alto, Calif., 1961), esp. chap. 3 (with Marjorie Fiske).' But most eighteenth-century scholars today would not be happy to take the late Mrs Leavis's word for the existence or disappearance of a movement (i.e. sensibility) that was literary *in part only*, and Leo Lowenthal, contrary to the suggestion implicit in Greene's note, does not have any *theory* about the relationship of sentimental man and the reading public in the eighteenth century, although the relationship is certainly worthy of pursuit. Lowenthal discusses sentimentalism in five brief paragraphs (83–5) and only this statement can be construed as a 'theory' or 'hypothesis' involving the spread of sensibility: 'Because of the improbable nature of the seventeenth- and early eighteenth-century romance, and perhaps also because it had been read by fewer people than was the novel of sentiment, few before the middle of the century had been concerned about the effect of fiction on the reader' (84). Lowenthal's comments (84, n. 91) about 'the prevailingly sentimental tone of the novels of this period' owing to the efforts of women authors is also germane but will hardly account, as Brissenden had suggested in *Virtue in Distress* (11–19), for a set of terms and concepts 'used by the eighteenth century itself'.

38 The terminology is Hagstrum's; see *Sex and Sensibility*, 31 and 34: 'Against the [Augustinian] tradition Milton's portrayal of marriage . . . constitutes one of the most eloquent protests in Christian history . . .' Hagstrum also comments (34) in this context that for Milton 'body and soul are inseparable' and that 'this union elevates the sexual'. Nevertheless, Hagstrum's implication is that the monistic Milton did not need 'to revolt' against a dualistic Descartes for empirical developments have little or no influence in this map of sensibility.

39 Not even Leo Lowenthal (see Greene, *LS*, 180, n. 64) has argued for a new reading public in the *seventeenth* century, nor am I aware of any modern sociologist who has.

40 See Greene, *AE*, 39.

41 See Hagstrum, *Sex and Sensibility*, 30, n. 13.

42 Mark Rose, *Heroic Love: Studies in Sidney and Spenser* (Cambridge, 1968), 7.

43 Luce and Jessop (ed.), *The Works of George Berkeley*, 1 (Philosophical Commentaries, No. 769).

44 See Greene, *AE*, 59.

45 In *Tristram Shandy* and as had Swift before Sterne in *A Tale of a Tub*. Actually there is a long tradition of imaginative writing 'against the spleen' that is both *medical* and *non*-medical, i.e. medical as well as polemical, and which includes a broad repertoire of works *contra* enthusiasm *c.* 1700. This discourse intensified in the Restoration period often in strict medical contexts (e.g. medical commentaries on hypochondria and melancholy); but it also grew in *non*-medical writing *vis-à-vis* the social analysis of enthusiasm and is found in much religious, social, and political debate of the time. This existence of a tradition going back at least to Burton accounts for the large number of references and allusions to hypochondria and melancholia in the early eighteenth century that are polemical *rather than* strictly medical. Hypochondria and melancholy were convenient metaphors – in the loosest and most promiscuous sense – to invoke in polemical arguments against ranters and enthusiasts of all types. *A Tale of a Tub* was squarely written in this tradition, as was Mandeville's *Treatise of the Hypochondriack and Hysterick Passions* (1711) which, like the *Tale*, calls itself 'a treatise

writ against the spleen'; and possibly even *The Fable of the Bees* (1714), which may be viewed as 'medicine' for persons suffering from hypochondriacal afflictions, ought to be viewed within this specific type of discourse as it was intended, according to Mandeville, to cure persons who were 'distempering the body politic'. After Swift and Mandeville many writers (including Sterne) invoked the loose metaphor of melancholy and the discourse of hypochondria for polemical reasons and for literary rather than socially diagnostic purposes. But my larger point is that the discourse of sensibility functions in a somewhat similar way and that it is impossible to understand the rise of this discourse, in the first place, without having reconstructed a broad seventeenth-century context that *includes* medical and scientific (i.e. empirical) writings.

46 Nor such of his works as *A History of Experimental Psychology* (New York, 1929) and *Sensation and Perception in the History of Experimental Psychology* (New York, 1942) because of their narrow context and lack of historical understanding. Boring, a leading historian of psychology *c*. 1920–50, wrote in the school of Wundt and Titchener, nineteenth-century German scientists who invoked history not as 'truth' but as 'background' and, moreover, as background for particular nationalistic purposes.

47 Greene's discussion in *AE* gives the impression that the foe – empiricism – accomplished rather little before 1660 and the founding of the Royal Society but this was not the case, as many historians of science have now shown; see Robert Mandrou, *From Humanism to Science 1480–1700*, trans. B. Pearce (1978), originally published in French as *Des humanistes aux hommes de science: xvie–xviie siècles* (Paris, 1973), and R. Hooykaas, *Humanisme, science et réforme* (Leyden, 1958).

48 As is demonstrated by an excellent anthology of modern essays edited by John Perry and entitled *Personal Identity* (Berkeley and Los Angeles, 1975).

49 See Karl. B. Wallace, *Francis Bacon on the Nature of Man: the Faculties of Man's Soul: Understanding, Reason, Imagination, Memory, Will and Appetite* (Urbana, 1967), who traces the medieval and Renaissance heritage of each of these 'faculties' in Bacon's psychology. Wallace's caveat in the introduction is worth citing as a comment on my own endeavour in this case study of literature and psychology: 'The period [1600–1700], which for my ends includes the ideas of John Locke, did not use the term psychology. Instead, as a rough equivalent, men spoke of the nature of man or man's soul. Although [my] study can be considered a small chapter in the history of psychology, I have avoided for the most part the terms and vocabulary that later became the special property of psychology, and have preferred the language of the period' (pp. 2–3).

50 See C. Fox, 'Locke and the Scriblerians: the Discussion of Identity in Early Eighteenth-Century England', *Eighteenth-Century Studies*, XVI (autumn 1982) 1–25.

9

Madame Chimpanzee

While serving as the Clark Library Professor at UCLA in 1985–6 I discovered in that library's collection an anonymous tract about a chimpanzee called An Essay towards the Character of the Late Chimpanzee *published anonymously in 1739.*

Its strange genre and mysterious, elusive contents intrigued me. Today, the creatures closest to us on the 'great chain of being' fascinate us as much as they did our Enlightenment predecessors, who viewed them with even more bewilderment. I set myself the task of decoding the tract. The complex reasons for its genesis also represented the challenges of practice – historical, anthropological, rhetorical – for which I knew much of my theory had been generated. I spent many weeks during that academic year as a combination detective and field anthropologist attempting to crack the riddle of the Madame Chimp. The results are here; I still think they are entirely correct.

A few years ago the Clark Library in Los Angeles acquired an anonymous thirty-one page prose satire titled *An Essay towards the Character of the late Chimpanzee Who died Feb. 23, 1738–9*, published in March 1739 by 'L. Gilliver and J. Clarke at Homer's-Head in Fleetstreet'. Lamenting that no 'able Pen . . . hath yet' undertaken to draw the character of 'the late incomparable *Chimpanzee*', the author humbly proposes to make a 'faint Essay' at the task himself. As any contemporary reader would have recognised immediately, the title and the mock panegyric that follows it are at once an allusion to a chimpanzee that had recently been shown in London and a parody of Alured Clarke's *An Essay towards the Character of Her late majesty Caroline*, published a year earlier. While the satire is aimed at a broad range of targets, its comic force derives from the parodic substitution of the chimpanzee for the Queen of England.

The conceit was outrageous enough to serve the author's satiric purposes. Yet in the context of eighteenth-century thought, and more particularly of the events of the preceding few months, it was not as purely fanciful as the modern reader might assume. In portraying the chimpanzee as a lady of high rank and endowing her with the learning and refined sensibilities that Clarke had attributed to Queen Caroline, the satirist took his hint from the extraordinary history of the chimp's five-month stay in London. Since much of the comic effect of the piece depends on the readers' familiarity with the ground of factual details and scientific theory that the satirist plays upon, the first part of this article will focus on the story of Madame Chimpanzee, as the Earl of Egmont claimed she was called. The second part will turn to the satire.

British interest in chimpanzees, or 'orang-utans', dates at least from the early years of the Restoration, when Pepys viewed a 'strange creature' brought from Africa, 'a monster,' he was persuaded, 'got of a man and she-baboone'. But it was Dr Edward Tyson, at the end of the century, who laid the empirical foundations for the fascination with chimpanzees that explains the phenomenon of Madame C (and that continues to the present day). Tyson, an English anatomist and physician, was the first to dissect a chimpanzee. He published the results of his study in *Orang-Outang, sive Homo Sylvestris . . .* (1699), a comparative anatomy that firmly established this animal just below man in the Great Chain of Being. Tyson's seminal work not only captured the attention of many naturalists but stimulated popular interest in these creatures that resembled man in so many ways.

Though Tyson himself carefully maintained the distinction between man and ape, it tended to become blurred in the work of some of his eighteenth-century successors. Linnaeus, in 1736, classified the chimpanzee as a species of man, and Lord Monboddo placed both within the same species, arguing that the chimp was more advanced than certain primitive humans. As part of the attempt to define the relation between man and ape, there was considerable debate throughout the period over the ape's capacity for reason and speech, with learned arguments offered on both sides of the question.

Extant records do not disclose whether any chimpanzees were brought to England in the earlier decades of the eighteenth century, but the sensation created by the arrival of the chimp in September 1738 suggests that none had been on public view, at least, for many years. During the last weeks of September, every London newspaper reported on the event. Under the dateline 'Thurs. 21' the *London Magazine*, for example, announced:

> A most surprising Creature is brought over in the *Speaker*, just arrived from *Carolina*, that was taken in a Wood at *Guinea*; it is a Female about four Foot high, shaped in every Part like a Woman excepting its Head, which nearly resembles the Ape: She walks upright naturally, sits down to her food, which is chiefly Greens, and feeds herself with her Hands as a human Creature. She is very fond of a Boy on board, and is observed always

sorrowful at his Absence. She is cloathed with a thin Silk Vestment, and shows a great Discontent at the opening her Gown to discover her Sex. She is the Female of the Creature, which the *Angolans* call Chimpanzee, or the Mockman.

Although later commentators were to dispute this report of her height, remembering her as having stood two feet, four inches, all the accounts, early and late, were in essential agreement that the chimp was a prodigy. The *London Post and General Advertiser* proclaimed her 'perhaps the greatest Curiosity in the known World'. The *Weekly Miscellany* of 22 September further reported: 'She is so great a Rarity, that 250 Guineas' – then a vast sum – 'was offered for her in the Country.'

Evidently this offer was rejected, for a few days later the *Daily Post* informed the public that the chimpanzee could 'be seen at Randall's Coffee-house against the General Post-Office in Lombard Street'. Randall's at that time functioned as a meeting place for persons interested in natural history – if not quite an indoor zoo, then a place where the primary attraction was exotic animals that could be seen on display for a small fee. All autumn the proprietor of Randall's, or more likely the owner of the chimp (they were apparently not the same person), levied a shilling's admission on those wishing to view this 'greatest Curiosity in the known World', just as the trustees of Bethlehem Hospital, in nearby Moor Fields, charged visitors a shilling to view the lunatics.

Among the first to visit Randall's was Sir Hans Sloane, the president of the Royal Society and one of the most respected naturalists in England, who pronounced himself 'extremely well pleas'd' with the chimp and 'allow[ed] it to come the nearest to the Human Species of any Creature.' Sloane's opinion, according to an advertisement that first appeared in the *Daily Post* of 13 October, was universally shared: 'the great Numbers of the Nobility and Gentry, who daily resort' hither have expressed the ·utmost 'Satisfaction . . . in the Behaviour' of the 'wonderful Creature'. Precisely how great the numbers were is nowhere reported, but they included some of the most distinguished personages in the kingdom: by early December the Duke and Duchess of Montague, the Duke of Rox-burgh and his son Lord Beaumont, the dukes of Marlborough, Albemarle, and Richmond, and such foreign dignitaries as the Sardinian and French ambassadors had all made the pilgrimage to Randall's. Although the chimp's promoters chose to focus on the nobility and gentry for advertis-ing purposes, presumably such of the ordinary London citizenry as could spare a shilling helped to swell the crowds.

Stories of the chimpanzee's almost human sensitivity and intelligence soon began to appear regularly in the newspapers. A letter from an alleged 'Stranger', for example, which appeared in the *Daily Post* of 26 October,

describes a curious event he had witnessed while at Randall's. A woman
and her infant were in the audience. Several men present asked the woman
to put her baby down, to observe what the chimp would do. When the
mother did so, according to the letter, the chimp set down 'a Cup of
Tea . . . and an Apple', and then, displaying even greater delicacy and
refinement, 'with both Hands clasped round the Child's Neck, embraced
and kissed it, to the great Surprize of all the Gentlemen and Ladies then
in Company'. Another letter, from one 'Publicus', tells a similar kind of
tale, but with an amusing twist which suggests that the chimp's promoters
encountered a good deal of initial scepticism:

> Imagining I should find the extraordinary Accounts which have been so
> frequently set forth in the News Papers, of the Creature call'd a *Champanzie*
> to be nothing but Puff and Stratagem, to draw in the Multitude, . . . I
> could not prevail on myself, (tho' I had the greatest Inclination) to go see
> it. But on Saturday last I . . . did go as, I then thought, to throw away a
> Shilling, and took the Dusk of the Evening, when I might not be seen,
> imagining I should be accosted with nothing but the Sight of a Monkey.
> But at my Entrance into the Room I found the Creature . . . walking erect
> as a young Child, and following the Master about; . . . I was fill'd with
> Surprize to find it so near Humane, and on my asking what Food they gave
> her, she immediately rose from a Chair she was sitting in, as if she knew
> what I said, and brought from another part of the Room a Loaf of Bread
> in one Hand, and a Knife in the other, and gave them to a Person to cut
> her a Piece, which she both took and eat, in so decent a manner, that I
> confess my Surprize was so much increas'd, that I could not help thinking
> it was my Duty to recommend it in this manner to the Publick; especially
> as I had in some measure injur'd the Proprietor of her, and had prevented
> several Gentlemen and Ladies of my Acquaintance from going to see it . . .

Whether or not one, or even both, of these letters were 'Puff and Strat-
agem, to draw in the Multitude', they and others like them are clearly
based on specific incidents and no doubt accurately reflect the reaction of
the audience. Never having seen a creature like the chimp before and
perhaps, like Publicus, expecting deception, spectators were so startled by
her humanlike behaviour that they were ready to attribute human
emotions and human intelligence to her as well.

The temptation to carry the possibilities to their logical end was
irresistible. The Earl of Egmont concludes a diary entry detailing his
observation of the chimpanzee's behaviour and appearance with the comment: 'Sir Hans Sloan says she has all the parts of speech in her, which is
as much as to say she is made to speak, which, whenever it happens,
may, I suppose, be followed by school instruction; and who knows but
she may become as famous a wit and writer as Madame Dacier.' As the
stories of the chimp's 'humanity' proliferated, so too did this mocking

(but perhaps only partly mocking) impulse to write about her – and to treat her – as if she were indeed human. The events of the last few months of her life take a grotesquely comic turn that leads straight to *An Essay*.

Near the end of November, not long after Publicus's letter appeared, the *Daily Post* announced that the chimp 'hath sat for her Picture', which 'is most beautifully and justly engraved on a Copper-Plate, by the known great Artist Mr. G. *Scotin*, from a Drawing which was taken naked from the Life, by the celebrated Mr. Gravelot'. The plate was inscribed to Sir Hans Sloane, obviously an attempt to authenticate the enterprise with the stamp of the Royal Society. Within two weeks prints were being sold all over town by the 'Booksellers of London and Westminster', and they continued to appear in various sizes and visual forms through the following winter.

Whether the print scheme reflected some falling off of business at Randall's, an attempt to shore up profits, is not clear, but two days before Christmas, ostensibly 'at the Desire of several Persons of Quality', the chimp was removed 'to Mr. Leflour's, at the White Peruke, next Door to the King's Sadler at Charing-Cross'. The White Peruke was a small coffee-house in St Martin's Lane, where the cost of housing, feeding, and displaying the chimp was probably higher than at Randall's; but her new home had the advantage of lying further to the west, in proximity to the town houses surrounding Leicester Fields, the present-day Leicester Square. It was apparently at the White Peruke that the chimp was first christened Madame (or Mademoiselle) Chimpanzee. As befitted one that had moved up in society, Madame was given a new wardrobe: 'She is now entirely dress'd', the *Daily Post* reported, 'after the newest Fashion *A-la-mode a Paris*, which is a great Advantage to the natural Parts she is endowed with.' Among the many titled visitors who paid court to Madame in her new quarters during the next two months, royalty itself was represented, in the person of the Prince of Wales.

On 15 February the newspapers reported that she had 'grown full two inches' and interpreted this growth as proof 'of her being very young' upon arrival in London the previous September. These accounts put her current age at fifteen months; Ephraim Chambers later reported in his *Cyclopaedia* that she was about twenty months. Whatever her age, on Friday 23 February 1739, just five months after her arrival, she suddenly died at the White Peruke. The cause, according to the *Universal Spectator*, was 'an intermitting Fever', and there is some evidence that she had been sick periodically since early November.

A more professional opinion on Madame's fatal illness was soon forthcoming. On the 24 February an autopsy was performed 'in the Presence of Sir Hans Sloane . . . and Mr. [John] Ranby, Surgeon to his Majesty's Household'. They adjudicated, with all the solemnity usually reserved for their distinguished human patients, that death was caused by 'the extravagant Quantity of the fluid Part of its Sustenance' (Madame was widely reported to be addicted to tea), 'and that it was attended with a confirmed Jaundice'. Jaundice then carried the connotation of hepatic poisoning, as it does now, and it was much more common in an age unable to preserve perishable food well. These same authorities also formally pronounced her (what everyone was by now convinced of in any case) 'perfectly of a human Specie'.

The *Universal Spectator*, in reporting the death of Madame C, had observed that the owner suffered a considerable financial loss, 'as she was a kind of an Estate to him'. Nevertheless, he contrived to salvage something from the ruin by putting her body on public display. If we can believe the account in the *London Evening Post* of 28 February, this final spectacle was a worthy climax to the history of her stay in London:

> Preparations are making at the White Peruke at Charing-Cross, for laying in State the African Lady Mademoiselle *Chimpanzee*, . . . which we hear is to be in the manner of the *Angolans* (the place of her Birth) the Inhabitants of that Country being noted in History, for many Centuries, for their extraordinary Pomp, Magnificence and Care which they shew to their deceased Friends, which Custom still subsists amongst them; and as this Lady hath had so much respect shewn to her by the most eminent Quality and Virtuosi when alive, 'tis to be hoped that the manner in which she will there lie, will be a pleasing Sight to the most Polite of both Sexes, and . . . great Care will be taken to Blazon her Arms, so as not to exceed the Bounds of proper Heraldry. . . . There are two Males of the same Species will attend her Corpse, in proper Attitudes, which are suppos'd to be her Elder and Younger Brothers, but both died in their Voyage hither.

The papers do not divulge her burial place, but it may be that a special site was chosen to perpetuate her memory.

Just over a month later, on 29 March 1730, the *London Evening Post* announced the publication of *An Essay towards the Character of the late Chimpanzee*. It was a small step for Madame from her apartment at the White Peruke to the pages of *An Essay*. As everybody who was anybody had observed and commented upon her, so, it appears, had she observed them, and she was not backward about voicing her opinions through the satirist.

The piece was obviously dashed off, but what it lacks in finish, it makes up for in comic imagination. To my knowledge, *An Essay* is the only literary work to exploit the satiric possibilities of Madame Chimpanzee's stay in London and the scientific speculations on her capacity to speak and reason. Taking as his premise that the chimpanzee belongs to the same species as the fashionable women of London, the author gives his satire an ingenious political turn by using Alured Clarke's much-maligned panegyric, *An Essay Towards the Character of Her late Majesty Caroline*, as a framework.

For opponents of the court and Whig ministry, Clarke, a court chaplain who had risen rapidly in the church through the queen's influence, had come to typify the venal clergy who gained preferment through flattery. He owed this distinction to his panegyric, an adulatory account of the queen that was, in essence, an impassioned defence of her character and policies against those who had attacked both. What particularly outraged the opposition was Clarke's plea at the end that, out of respect to the unparalleled virtues of the late queen, all loyal Britons should support the king and his chief minister, Sir Robert Walpole; to do otherwise, he implied, was treasonable.

Though all three editions of the work appeared before the end of January 1738, the attacks on it continued through that year and into the next. Ostensibly, Clarke himself was the target, though the ministerial *Gazetteer* may have been right in suggesting that he was merely a blind for an assault on the Crown. To the usual charge that he was a 'spiritual Sycophant' who had sold his pen for preferment (Pope refers to him as 'The Priest whose Flattery be-dropt the Crown'), the opposition newspaper the *Craftsman* on 5 and 12 August added a rather curious new one: that he had plagiarised his essay from Bishop Gilbert Burnet's panegyric on Queen Mary (1695). Paul Whitehead gave fresh currency to both charges by attacking Clarke in his notorious political satire *Manners*, published in February 1739, a few weeks before the essay on the chimpanzee was composed. Thus, when the panegyrist of Madame Chimpanzee defends his purity of motive by pointing out 'that she never had it in her Power to *prefer* any one, or has left behind her one Relation that is able to pay for the Panegyrick' and adds that, had he sought reward, he would 'as is common in these Cases, have borrowed from another Character', he expects his readers to catch the allusion, although Clarke is never mentioned.

Instead of attacking Clarke head-on, as Whitehead and others had done, the satirist pays him the compliment of imitation. He assumes Clarke's high-minded pose as an 'impartial Writer', motivated only by a desire to perpetuate 'the Memory of one so justly admired,' and proceeds to flatter outrageously. He appeals for confirmation of his account, as Clarke had, to 'all who knew her Virtues and were Eye-Witnesses of the Truth of what is here related', and proceeds to borrow liberally 'from another Character': he takes over such of Clarke's topics as suit his purpose, attributes several of Caroline's virtues to the chimpanzee, echoes phrases, and occasionally paraphrases whole passages. Here, for example, are Clarke and the mock-panegyrist, respectively, on Caroline's/Madame C's place in history:

> And as I can only pretend to draw the outlines of a character . . . I hope it will be a means of encouraging some able pen to raise a Monument to her glory . . . that will survive the injuries of time, and grow stronger with years, when the infamous libels of the present age, with all their mean and wicked Authors shall have perished together.

> From these faint Outlines it will be easily presum'd what a Figure she will make in History, when her Character shall be drawn by some able Historian; when she shall be plac'd out of the Reach of Envy or Party Rage: and her Memory be transmitted down to latest Posterity.

The borrowings, of course, irresistibly pull Caroline into the satire along with her panegyrist. The immediate target is the social-political world of early 1739, not the dead queen. But Caroline had helped to shape this world, particularly through her unfailing support of Walpole, and the opposition hadn't forgiven her. By implicitly associating her with a chimpanzee, the satirist leaves no doubt of his contempt. Although Caroline cannot be identified in any consistent way with the 'excellent Person' of the mock-panegyric, she remains a kind of background presence, tempting the reader to apply apparently general satiric points to her whenever they seem to fit.

In the fashionable world of *An Essay* the chimpanzee takes over Caroline's role as the 'Standard of genteel Breeding'. The term applies in two senses. The chimp is both a model for and a model of contemporary Georgian society, depending on how the details are viewed. Taken (when they can be) as literal references to the animal at the White Peruke, they present the chimp in exemplary contrast to the 'Quality' that flocked to see her: In keeping with her needs, she occupied small quarters, ate temperately, and had only one person to take care of her. She was friendly to everyone, regardless of social status. She never attended a play or masquerade (she 'was an utter Stranger to Concealments of any Kind') nor ever 'play'd at Cards'. And 'she was never heard to utter one Word of Slander; – she never invented a Lie, or improv'd one . . . nor once express'd a Desire to be acquainted with other People's Affairs'.

The satire, however, works in another (and more amusing) direction at the same time, and the details take on a different colour. The chimpanzee of the panegyric is not portrayed as an animal: 'as my Brethren do take the Freedom to make Gods of Men,' the panegyrist explains with another oblique glance at Clarke, 'I may, without Offence, make a Man of a Monkey'. By describing the chimp in terms of human society, attributing opinions and motives to her, and making her a rational creature who not only talks but reads and writes, he transforms her into a representative of Georgian society, 'the Standard of genteel Breeding' in an ironic sense. Not that the panegyrist intends any irony by flattering Madame into humanity. He simply wants to set 'Things in the best Light'. In his zeal, he eventually loses sight of the chimp altogether, and the satire works only at the second level.

He is constrained to admit at the outset that he can discover nothing about Madame's background ('Not one of the Family to be found in the whole Herald's Office'), though he is sure 'from her Appearance and Carriage, she must have been of a Gentleman's Family', probably a foreigner of some sort. So Madame, viewed in terms of the polite world, was a social upstart, like many others who had risen to prominence under Walpole.

Other aspects of her character and the world around her begin to suggest themselves as the panegyrist describes the innocuous details of the chimp's life at the White Peruke in social terms and amplifies them with whatever gossip happens this way. The boy who took care of her becomes a 'Servant . . . whom she us'd as a Valet de Chambre; which, to some Persons, is an infallible Proof of her being of *French* Extraction'. Her owner becomes the 'Gentleman always with her; whom some Ladies (to prevent any Reflections) call'd her Uncle: But I [says the panegyrist] can assure them he was no Relation; but only her Steward.' Her affectionate nature is translated into a preference for the company of men, whom she freely allowed 'those little Arts of toying and kissing' but had no intention of marrying. The admission price, 'the voluntary Subscriptions of the Nobility, Gentry, and Others', provided her with a 'very genteel Maintenance.' There is also a rumour, indignantly denied but perpetuated in the denial, that the excessive fluids that led to Madame's death were not tea but liquor; and one Doctor Urine, rejecting both hypotheses, hints darkly that she succumbed to the pox.

If Madame's morals come under a cloud of suspicion by the time the panegyrist is through, so does the sincerity of her opinions. In evidence of her 'Publick Spirit', for example, the panegyrist assures us that

> she had the Interest of this Nation so particularly at Heart, that, in order to encourage the Manufacture, she never would (as I was told by her Mantua-maker) wear any Thing for under Garments but Woollen. – And she had such Regard for the poor People of *Ireland*, that she declar'd her upper Garment (which was a kind of Robe de Chambre) should be made of nothing but *Irish* Linnen. – Had her Complexion permitted her to have worn an Head-Dress, the Cambrick Manufacture would have found no Encouragement from her; and she has often said it, that had she an hundred Children, provided their Complexions would bear it, they should every one wear Muslin.

Madame's professions of public spirit are in the right place. By the late 1730s, the steady decline of home manufacture of clothing had contributed to an economically disastrous imbalance of trade; high unemployment and wage reductions had led to the destructive weavers' riots of December 1738, and increasing numbers of clothiers, unable to compete on the domestic or foreign market, were forced out of business. The fashionable world, with its rage for all things French, was held primarily responsible. For months the newspapers had been urging women to show their patriotism by buying English woollen and Irish linen goods and substituting muslin for the fashionable cambrics imported from France. If largely ineffectual, the propaganda was insistent enough that there was no doubt a good deal of lip-service paid to the principle. When we recall that at the White Peruke Madame Chimpanzee was 'entirely dress'd after the newest Fashion *A-La-Mode a Paris*', it is hard to take seriously her professed concern for the 'poor People of *Ireland*' (shades of Caroline's encounter with Swift in 1726) or her protestation that, complexion permitting, she and all her hypothetical children would certainly wear muslin.

The panegyrist, of course, sees no hypocrisy here or in her other pronouncements, but even he has to confess that she had one 'little Failure': 'Alass! she had no Religion!' The question of religion troubles him as it had troubled Alured Clarke. Clarke had been at great pains to show that Caroline was 'a sincere Christian, a zealous Protestant, a real Friend to the Church, of *England*' to counteract persistent rumours that she had refused the last sacrament and was, at heart, a deist, which, in the eyes of orthodoxy, was tantamount to saying that she had no religion. Madame's panegyrist, however, is 'determin'd to tell the Truth, nor attribute *that* to her of which she had not the least Notion'.

As he amplifies on the subject, the parallel with the queen becomes clearer. Although he has told us earlier that (like Caroline) Madame 'thought it a very great Reflection on a Rational Creature to spend her Time in Dress, and to neglect the Cultivation of her Mind', her studies were obviously misdirected. As 'Her Well-wishers observ'd with Concern', she favoured 'the Conversation of Deists and Free-thinkers'. She avidly read every deistical book she could get her hands on and was especially impressed by Matthew Tindal's *Christianity as old as the Creation*, which set out to show that the Christian revelation was superfluous; 'but, by Mistake, [her steward] brought a Book wrote by a certain Dean; which she no sooner had read but tore into a Thousand Pieces'. The 'certain Dean' is presumably Swift, whose high-church, Tory views would have been anathema to a deist like Madame, as they were to Caroline, but which of his books had aroused Madame to such fury isn't clear. While the apologist can't quite bring himself to condone her lack of religious principles, he excuses it as best he can by pointing out that 'in this she imitated the Example of Most Persons of Rank and Condition'. Besides, 'If she had no Religion, she had an excellent Taste, which made her make a much better Figure in the World'.

From Madame's religion the panegyrist moves finally to her politics, and her character is fully explained: 'She was a Whig, – and carried her Notions higher than any Woman was ever known to do.' Forgetting that he has praised her for her even temper, the panegyrist now tells us that, in political disputes with her Tory steward, 'She was very violent and sanguine,' to the detriment of her complexion. Such was her party zeal that she took up her pen in behalf of Walpole's most unpopular policies:

> I . . . was well assur'd, she wrote several Papers in the *Gazetteer*. – Some will not scruple to say she had a Salary for writing: I cannot aver the Truth of that; but 'tis agreed on all Hands, that some of the best Letters in that Paper are hers. There was an unfinish'd Pamphlet found in her Study, in Vindication of the Convention; which has been since compleated and publish'd by one of her particular Friends.

The pamphlet attributed by the panegyrist to Madame Chimpanzee (and by modern scholars to Walpole's brother Horatio), *The Convention Vindicated*, was published anonymously on 28 February 1739 as part of a campaign to win parliamentary ratification of the treaty with Spain signed at the Convention of the Pardo in January. This treaty, which sought to negotiate a settlement of longstanding trade disputes, was widely perceived, even by many within Walpole's own party, as a sellout of British interests and British honour, and it precipitated a crisis that nearly brought the ministry down. Madame Chimpanzee's faithful support of Walpole at this critical juncture would have gratified the likes of Alured Clarke; to the great majority of Englishmen, who demanded (and eventually got) an 'honourable' war, it would have seemed an act of perfidy.

In singing the praises of Madame Chimpanzee, the panegyrist reveals a different character from what he intends – the 'Example to all Womankind' is a creature of dubious morals, hypocritical, irreligious, a devotee of the cult of taste, a bluestocking with an unbecoming predilection for political and theological dispute, and a writer in the service of Walpole. The beast has degenerated into a feministic Court Whig.

Whether *An Essay* had any following in its own time I don't know. There was apparently no second edition, and I haven't discovered any contemporary references to it. Perhaps it was too comical in its approach to appeal at a time when satires like Whitehead's *Manners*, angry frontal onslaughts against individuals barely masked under initials, had become the favoured weapon against Walpole and the Court Whigs. But *An Essay*, with its clever blend of literary and scientific parody, can still afford amusement, while the minor satires that more accurately reflected the 'party rage' of the period are now virtually unreadable.

10

An anthropology of mind and body in the Enlightenment

One of the responsibilities of the Clark Professor is to select a subject for the annual Clark Library lecture series and to assume editorial responsibility for publication of the addresses. The series is normally devoted to a topic intrinsic to the diachronic period of the seventeenth and eighteenth centuries. In my year as Clark Professor I chose the subject of mind and body in the Enlightenment. Foucault was to have opened the series as the first speaker, but his death in June 1985 pre-empted the possibility, and the tone of the series was therefore somewhat different from what it would otherwise have been. The lectures were published in a volume entitled The Languages of Psyche: Mind and Body in Enlightenment Thought *(University of California Press, 1990).*

This essay located mind and body in their long European tradition and was written with Roy Porter, with whom I had been collaborating for ten years. It is an attempt to construct a 'natural history of mind and body', without displaying too much concern for the post-Nietzschean destiny of this often ill-fated dualism. On another level, it also continued my own dream of a social anthropology of mind and body that would bridge the age-old dualism by bringing together seemingly disparate discourses: medical, scientific, historical, literary, philosophical. This was a tall order in a post-disciplinary age.

By now – the fin dé siècle of our own century – it has become evident to me how ideological all these discourses were in their own time. (i.e., during the Enlightenment), and how ideological the diverse metacritiques about them remain today. No matter how pernicious and tyrannical the tropes of this most pervasive of all the dualisms in history had been, it seemed useful to produce a map of its peculiar diachronic and synchronic history.

The mind–body problem has long taxed Western thought. *The Languages of Psyche: Mind and Body in Enlightenment Thought* is not, however, another contribution to the philosophical argument about mind–body relations *per se*.[1] Rather, the common endeavour uniting these essays amounts to something different, the desire to explore the *problem* of the mind–body problem. In their different ways, all the authors investigate why it has been the case (and still is) that conceptualising consciousness, the human body, and the interactions between the two, has proved so confusing, contentious, and inconclusive – or, as we might put it, has acted as the grit in the oyster that has produced pearls of thought. Furthermore, the volume as a whole has the wider purpose of taking that mind–body dichotomy which has been such a familiar feature of the great philosophies and locating it within its wider contexts – contexts of rhetoric, fiction, and ideology, of imagination and symbolism, science and religion, contexts of groups and gender, power and politics. To speak of the mind–body problem as if it were a timeless abstraction, a *topos* for unlimited discussion by countless symposia down the ages, would be to perpetuate mystifications. It must itself be problematised – theorised – in relation to history, language and culture. And here, the first thing to notice – a bizarre fact – is the paucity of synthetic historical writing upon this profound issue.[2]

If we acknowledge a certain plausibility to Alfred North Whitehead's celebrated dictum that all subsequent philosophy is a series of footnotes to Plato, we might be especially disposed to the view that the mind–body problem is amongst the most ancient and thorny – yet fundamental and inescapable – in the Western intellectual tradition. For the predication of such differences was one of Plato's prime strategies. In attempting to demonstrate against sophists and sceptics that humans could achieve a true understanding of the world, Plato developed rhetorical ploys which postulated dichotomies between (on the one hand) what are deemed merely fleeting appearances or shadows, and (on the other) what are to be discovered as eternal, immutable realities. Such binary opposites are respectively construed in terms of the contrast between the merely mundane and the truly immaterial; and these in turn are shown to find their essential expressions on the one side in corporeality and on the other in consciousness. The construction of such a programmatically dualistic ontology provides the framework for epistemology, as for Plato, the only authentic knowledge – not to be confused with subjective 'belief' or 'opinion' – is that which transcends the senses, those deceptive windows on to the world of appearances. But it is equally the basis for a moral theory, as dozens of philosophers have shown: knowing the good is the necessary and sufficient condition for choosing it, and right conduct constitutes the reign of reason over the tumult of blind bodily appetites.

The Homeric writings are innocent of any such clear-cut abstract division between a unitary incorporeal principle called mind or soul, and the body as such. So too the majority of the pre-Socratic philosophers. But 'Enter Plato', as Gouldner put it, and the terms were set for philosophy.[3] And, as Whitehead intimated, the formulations of post-Platonic philosophies can be represented as repeatedly ringing the changes upon such foundational propositions. Admittedly, as early as Aristotle, there was dissent from Plato's postulation of Ideas, or ideal forms, as the eternal verities indexed in the empyrean; yet in practice the Aristotelian corpus

212 Enlightenment crossings: anthropological

affirmed the equally comprehensive sovereignty of mind over matter in the natural order of things, which found expression – ethical, sexual, social and political – in his images of the good man (the gender is significant) and his superior status within the hierarchies of the family, economy, polity, and cosmos. And in their varied ways, most other influential philosophies of antiquity corroborated the elemental Platonic interpretation of the order of existence as organised through hierarchical dichotomies which dignified the immaterial over the physical, and, specifically, mind over the flesh that was so patently the seedbed of mutability and the harbinger of death. Through its aspirations to 'apathy' – and, if necessary, in the final analysis, suicide – Stoicism aimed to reduce the body to its proper insignificance, thereby liberating the mind for its nobler offices. Neo-Platonists in the Renaissance and later, with their doctrines of love for higher, celestial beings, likewise envisaged the soul soaring upwards, in an affirmation of what we might almost call the incredible lightness of being.

Moreover, the rational expression of the Christian gospel, drawing freely upon Platonic formulae, was to recuperate the radical ontological duality between mind and gross matter in its assertion that 'in the beginning was the Word'. (Here, of course, are the origins of the logocentrism that proves so problematic to our contemporaries.) Various sects of early Christians, from Gnostics to Manichaeans, took the dualistic disposition to extremes, by mapping the categories of good and evil precisely on to mind and body respectively, and urging modes of living – e.g., asceticism or antinomianism – designed to deny the demands of the body in ways yet more drastic than ever the Stoics credited.[4]

There is no need to provide a detailed route-map through the history of Western thought, charting the course taken by such dualistic ontologies of mind over matter, mind over body, ever since antiquity gave it its philosophical, and Christianity its theological, expression, and Thomist scholasticism synthesised the two. Influential Renaissance teachings on the nature of man and his place in nature – in particular, those of Ficino and Pico – articulated Christian versions of neo-Platonic idealism;[5] Christian Stoicism was soon to have its day. And Descartes's celebrated 'proof' of the mind–body polarity – under God, all creation was gross *res extensa* with the sole exception of the human *cogito* – confirmed the priority and superiority of mind with a logical *éclat* unmatched since Anselm, while providing a vindication of dualism both deriving from, and, simultaneously, legitimating, the 'new science' of matter in motion governed by the laws of mechanics. Furthermore – and crucially for the future – Descartes contended that it was upon such championship of the autonomy, independence, immateriality and freedom of *res cogitans*, the human consciousness, that all other tenents fundamental to the well-being of that thinking subject depended: man's guarantees of the existence and attributes of God, the reality of cosmic order and justice, the regularities and fitnesses of Creation.

Micro- and macrocosmic thinking, ingrained as part of the medieval habit of mind, found itself reinvigorated by the Cartesian dualism. Whether this was owing primarily to religious or to secular developments, or again to the challenge given to the 'old philosophy' by the 'new science', continues to be the subject of fierce controversy among a wide variety of historians on many continents. But the progress of micro–macrocosmic analogies itself is unassailable. For the Malebranchians and Leibnizians, Wolffians and Scottish 'common-sense' philosophers who manned the arts faculties of eighteenth-century universities, instructing youth in right thinking, the analogy of nature underlined the affinities between the divine mind and the human, each unthinkable except as reflecting the complementary Other. From the latter half of the seventeenth century, it is true, rationalist and positivist currents in the European temper grew increasingly sceptical as to the existence of an array of non-material entities: fairies, goblins and ghosts, devils and wood demons, the powers of astrology, witchcraft and magic, the hermetic 'world soul', and perhaps even Satan and Hell themselves – all as part of that demystifying tide which Max Weber felicitously dubbed the 'disenchantment of the world'.[6] Yet subtle arguments were advanced to prove that such a salutary liquidation of false animism and anthropomorphism served but to corroborate non-material reality where it truly existed: in the divine mind and the human. For many eighteenth-century natural philosophers and natural theologians, the more the physical universe was drained by the 'mechanisation of the world picture' of any intrinsic will, activity, and teleology, the more patent were the proofs of a mind outside, which had created, sustained and continued to see that all was good.[7]

It would be a gross mistake, however, to imply that Christian casuistries alone perpetuated canonical restatements of the mastery of mind over body. The very soul of the epistemology and poetics of a Romanticism in revolt against the allegedly materialistic attitudes and aesthetics of the eighteenth century was the championship of mental powers, most commonly finding expression through the idea of the holiness of imagination and the transcendency of genius. Genius and imagination, no matter how designated, had been among the commonest themes of the rational Enlightenment: the basis of its developing discourse of aesthetics; the salt of its political theory, as Locke and Burke showed; even the ideological underpinning of its 'scientific manifestos'. Later on, contemporary philosophical idealism in the form of Hegel-on-horseback likewise interpreted the dynamics of world history as the process whereby *Geist*, or spirit, realised itself in the world, spiralling dialectically upwards to achieve ever higher planes of self-consciousness. And we must never minimise the idealist thrust of the developmental philosophies so popular in the nineteenth-century *fin-de-siècle* era – from Bosanquet and Balfour to Bergson, and influenced by Hegelianism no less than by the *Origin of Species* – which represented the destiny of the cosmos and of its noblest expression, man, as the progressive evolution of higher forms of being out of lower, and in particular the ascent of man from protoplasmic slime to the Victorian mind.[9]

Given this philosophical paean down the millenia affirming the majesty of mind, it is little wonder that so many of the issues which modern philosophy inherited hinged upon mapping out the relationships between thinking and being, mind and brain, will and desire, or (on the one hand) inner motive, intention and impulse, and (on the other) physical action. In one sense at least, Whitehead was a true child of his time. Twentieth-century philosophers such as G. E. Moore still puzzled over the same sorts of questions Socrates posed, wondering what the shadows flickering on the cave walls really represented, and pondering whether moral truths exist within the realm of the objectively knowable. Not only that, but the kinds of words, categories and *exampla* in circulation to resolve such issues have continued – for better or worse – to be ones familiarised by Plato, Locke or Dewey.[10]

To its credit, recent philosophy has urged the folly of expecting to find solutions to these ancestral problems through honing yet more sophisticated variants upon the formulae traded by post-Cartesian rationalism or Anglo-Saxon empiricism. A few more refinements to utilitarianism or the latest model in associationism will not get us any further than will laboratory experiments in search of the true successor to the pineal gland. And when Richard Rorty pronounces the death of philosophy in his latest *tour de force*,[11] one wonders to what degree the age-old dualism as conspired to cause it. Rorty, like Philippa Foot, suggests that philosophers had just as well throw down their hands – perhaps even do better by denying the dualism of mind and body altogether. It may be, as Rorty maintains, that, philosophically speaking, 'there is no mind–body problem',[12] and that as a consequence Rorty is entitled, as a professional philosopher, to cast aspersions on, even to crack grammatical jokes about, all those who believe there is. For this reason, Rorty believes that 'we are not entitled to begin talking about the mind and body problem, or about the possible identity of necessary non-identity of mental and physical states, without first asking what we mean by "mental" '.[13] And as a direct consequence of his aim to shatter Cartesian dualism and the philosophies that built on its dualisms all the way up to Kant, Rorty can announce his own aim in *Philosophy and the Mirror of Nature* as being one 'to undermine the reader's confidence in the 'mind' as something about which one should have a 'philosophical' view, in 'knowledge' as something about which there ought to be a 'theory' and which has 'foundations', and in 'philosophy' as it has been conceived since Kant'.[14]

Above all, new bearings in philosophy – Wittgenstein proved a seminal impulse for many, phenomenology for others – have reoriented attention, away from the traditional envisaging of emotions, desires, intentions, states of mind, acts of will, etc., as 'things', inner natural objects with a place within some conceptual geography of the self, the causal connections between which it is our duty to discover by introspection and thought experiments. Such a reified view of being, thinking, and acting – a Marxist critic might say it is no more than is to be expected within commodity capitalism – has sustained devastating attack, and modern cross-currents in philosophy have been claiming that we should rather attend to the meanings of our moral languages understood as systems of public utterance. Thereby we might escape from the sterilities of a figural mechanics of the mind which, as Alasdair Macintyre has emphasised, and as Rorty has now demonstrated, threatened to drag moral philosophy down into a morass, and address ourselves afresh to more urgent questions of value and choice.[15]

Comparable processes of revaluation have also transformed literary theory. In England, Victorian criticism (itself sometimes proudly hitched to the wagon of associationist psychophysiology) commonly believed its mission was to judge novelists and playwrights for psychological realism: were their *dramatis personae* credible doubles of real people? Somewhat later, various schools of criticism, enthused by Freudian dogmas, went one stage further, and took characters out of fiction and set them on the couch, attempting to probe into their psyches (how well was their unconscious motivation grasped?) and into the unconscious of their authors (how were their fictions projections of their neuroses?). Today's criticism has discredited such preoccupations with the physical presence and the psychic potential of characters as banal, as but another form of literal-minded reification. For many theorists today, especially the feminists, the task of dissecting the body of the text is coeval with that of the body of women, while the traditional notion of the authorial mind as creator – a notion reaching its apogee in Romanticism – has yielded to a fascination with genre, rhetoric, and language as the informing structures.[16]

We may applaud the transcendence – in philosophy, in criticism, and elsewhere – of crude mechanical models of the operations of thinking and feeling, willing, and acting. This is not, however, to imply that the interplay of consciousness and society, of nerves and human nature, has somehow lost its meaning or relevance. Far from it. For it is important, now more than ever, to be able to think decisively about the ramifications of mind and body, their respective resonances, and their intersections, because the practical implications are so critical.

For ours is a material culture which is rapidly replacing the received metaphors which help us understand – or, arguably, mystify – the workings of minds and bodies. Deploying such models is nothing new. To conceptualise the mind, suggested Plato, think of the state; the understanding begins as a blank sheet of paper, argued Locke (for Tristram Shandy, by contrast, its objective correlative was a stick of sealing wax). Above all, during the last few centuries, the proliferation of machinery – watches, steam engines, and the like – has provided models for the functions of corporeal bodies and the processes of the understanding – the image of thinking as a mill, grinding out truths, was especially powerful.

Indeed, as Otto Mayr has remarked, particular forms of technology may even determine – or, at least, shape – distinctive ways of viewing the mind itself.[17] Clockwork mechanisms as found in watches yield images of man, individual and social, as uniformly and predictably obeying the pulse of centrally driven systems. Such a behaviourist image of man-the-machine, Mayr suggests, was particularly prominent in the propaganda of *ancien-régime* absolutism (and we may add, in images of factory discipline in the philosophy of manufactures). In Britain, the more complex regulatory equipment of the steam engine, with its fly wheels and contrapunctal rhythms, perhaps offered a rather different metaphor of man: that of checks and balances, counterpoised within a more decentralised and self-regulating whole, suggestive perhaps of a kind of individuality in tune with the English ideology. And, more recently, in the aftermath of late nineteenth-century positivism, neurobiology and neurophysiology have become persuaded that mind is brain, and that brain is an entirely mechanical, machine-like instrument whose operations are barely understood because of the vastness of its complexity.[18] In this sense, the human brain is more complex than the largest computer.[19] This radical mechanism, shunning any traces of vestigial vitalism (of the old Bergsonian or Drieschian varieties), forms the unarticulated basis of practically all laboratory biology and physiology today, yet its roots, *vis-à-vis* mind and body, extend at least as far back as the eighteenth-century Enlightenment. In a sense, then, mechanism, at least viewed within its mind–body context, has come full-circle back to its Cartesian, and somewhat post-Cartesian model.[20]

Mechanical models – realised in Vaucansonian automata – were obviously integral to Cartesian formulations of man as an intricate piece of mechanism yoked, however mysteriously, to an undetermined mind – the whole amounting to the notorious 'ghost in the machine'.[21] Such Cartesian mechanical metaphors – widely condemned by Romantics old and new for their supposedly disembodying and alienating implications[22] – were commonly drawn upon, with rather conservative intent, to reinforce the age-old belief that *homo rationalis* was destined, from above, to govern those below.

But there are also significant differences between these old Romantic views and our world of artificial intelligence and cognition theory. The material analogues in vogue today, by contrast, are arguably far more challenging and less flattering to entrenched human senses of self. Ever since Norbert Wiener and Alan Turing, cybernetics, systems analysis, and the computer revolution have been changing our understanding of the transformative potentialities of machines. If the Babbagian computer was merely a device to be intelligently programmed 'from above', the computers of today and tomorrow have intelligence programmed into them, and they possess the capacity to learn, modify their behaviour, and 'think' creatively – in a sense, to evolve. The more the notion of 'machines that think' becomes realised, the more urgent will be the task of clarifying in precisely which ways we believe their feedback circuits differ from ours; or perhaps we will have to say, the ways in which those alien, artificial intelligences believe our calculating operations differ from *theirs!* Human—robot interactions, once the amusing speculations of science fiction, may ironically become the facet of the mind–body problem most critical to that twenty-first century which is but a decade away. What is it, if anything, that gives us a 'self', a personality, entitling us to rights and duties in a society denying these to artificial intelligence? Today, as in the seventeenth and eighteenth centuries, the philosophers, especially philosophers of mind, speak out on these vital subjects. John Searle and many others regard 'free will' – the traditional predicate of autonomous mind – as an unsatisfactory and obsolete answer.[23]

If airing such issues may still seem frivolous or futuristic, it can hardly be fanciful to focus attention upon the transformations that living bodies and personalities are nowadays undergoing. Spare-part surgery became a *fait accompli* long before philosophers had solved its moral and legal dilemmas. Surgeons have implanted the kidneys, hearts, lungs of other humans, and even other primates. Surely such developments (it might have been thought) must have caused intense anxiety for identity in a culture which still speaks – if metaphorically – of the heart as the hub of passion and integrity, and the brain as the seat of reason and control. But it hardly seems to have proved so. Should we conclude that we are all Cartesians or Platonists – or maybe even Christians – enough to regard the bits and pieces of the body as no more than necessary but contingent appendages to whatever we decide it is that does define our unique essence? One wonders (sceptically) whether we would feel as nonchalant about brain transplants. Are we sufficiently confident in our dualism to believe that acquiring another's brain would not make us another person, or, indeed, a centaur-like monster? Contemporary philosophers such as Thomas Nagel think not,[24] and Philippa Foot reminds us to what degree Enlightenment philosophers such as Locke and Hume pondered these matters, albeit in a different key.

And, more perplexing, perhaps, because more imminent, what of the implantation of fragments of brains, or elements of the central nervous system? Would these involve dislocations of identity? – the equivalent perhaps to the caricaturists' macabre vision of the Day of Judgement when the bodies of those dissected by anatomists and dismembered in war arise, yet with their parts grotesquely muddled and misassembled. Here we seem to be on terrain already laid bare by current practices within psychological medicine. In the psychiatric hospital, advances in neuropsychiatry enable us, through drugs and surgery alike, radically to transform the behaviour and moods of the disturbed, so that we colloquially say that they have turned into 'another', indeed, a 'new' person. Can somatic interventions thus make a whole new self? Because the patients involved are 'psycho-pathological' cases, to which regular public legal constraints may not apply – or because, to put it crudely, such developments have been largely pioneered in the back wards, out of sight and out of mind – the dystopian implications of such medically-induced personality transformations do not always receive full attention.[25]

Yet our dramatically increased capacity to wreak such changes, to make 'new men' of old, is obviously a matter of great moment for the natural history of the somatic–psychic interface. The ethical and legal ramifications are obviously epochal – although, law courts in their own fashion currently tend to handle such issues on an *ad hoc*, case-by-case basis, often hearing the authority of biology in the distant background. The widening horizons of genetic engineering, reproductive technology, and gender-change operations raise parallel issues as to wherein the unique – and permanent? – human personality should be deemed to reside: is it in genetic material which is essentially somatic, in particular organs, or in an experiential *je ne sais quois* such as memory? (It may be one thing for the law, another for morality, and something different for the people themselves.)

Finally, though certainly not least, all these issues have been sharpened by our new technologies for managing death. Until quite recently, death was defined by some palpable and natural organic termination: the heart stopped beating, the breath of life expired. Even among the more superstitious and mystical, the 'will to live' (life force?) was translated into organic dysfunction or disease. Medical technology, however, has marched on, from iron lungs to resuscitators and respirators. The implicit

Cartesian in us can happily accept that a person remains alive even after the cessation of spontaneous body activity such as the heartbeat. But does that not leave us with no unambiguous index of death at all? – or, indeed, signs of life? (Are some people simply more dead, or more alive, than others?) Medical attention has, of course, switched to the conception of 'brain death' – which itself implicitly trades upon the humanist assumption that what finally defines mortal man is consciousness, while also embodying the more specifically modern faith that, while mind may still be more than brain, the needles registering presence of electrical impulses in the cortex betoken that the mind is still 'alive'. The paradoxical outcome of this eminently 'humane' chain of reasoning is that we nowadays aggressively keep 'alive' those in whom none of the indices of consciousness recognisable to the 'naked eye' survive.[26]

The argument so far has accentuated two points (the second developed below). First, the question about how we envisage the two-way traffic between mind and body is of fundamental concern for us today as well as for diverse cultural historians concerned with the diachronic past. It determines matters of grave import – ethical, legal, social, political, personal, sexual. The intricacies of exchange between consciousness and its embodiments are not gymnastic exercises designed to tone up mental athletes for the philosophers' Olympics, but are integral to everyone's intimate sense of what being human is and ought to be. Mental and physical interaction is a subject extending far beyond the historian's workshop or the philosopher's purview.[27] Idiomatic expressions – being somebody or nobody, or a nobody, being in or out of one's mind – prove the point beyond a shadow of doubt.

Thus our understanding, private and public, of mind and body has always been deeply important – for the law of slavery no less than for the salvation of souls. Yet it is crucial that we avoid the trap of hypostacising 'the mind–body problem' as if it were timeless and changeless, one of the 'perennial questions' of the master philosophers – indeed, itself a veritable Platonic form, immemorially inscribed in the ether. Even in specific terrains, history – social and political, religious and economic – has taken its toll. For one thing, as already suggested, the dilemmas involving disputed readings of psyche/soma relations, and the terms in which discussion has been conducted, have been radically transformed over the centuries.[28]

At one time, to take an example, proof of the existence of a consciousness seemingly independent of this mortal coil counted because it seemed confirmation of a soul destined, as was hoped, for a glorious immortality; nowadays, by contrast, many defend autonomy of the mind against scientistic reductionisms precisely because no such heavenly bliss after death can be expected. Early eighteenth-century thinkers were not confronted with organ transplants as problems for practical ethics. They did, however, puzzle themselves, at least mock seriously, about the status of Siamese twins: one body, two heads – but how many souls did such monsters have?[29] Other philosophers and projectors of the time asked what a 'soul' was anyway. Did all moving creatures possess one? When was soul acquired? Did it make any sense to ponder a cat's soul or a cow's? Could a black African be said to have the same soul as a white? (Blake's 'little black boy' in *Innocence* was born 'in the southern wild' and is black: 'but oh', he pleads, 'my soul is white'.) These and other similar questions were asked under as many agendas as there were philosophers. The notion of multiple 'personality', of course, came much later, once the techniques of hypnotism and dynamic psychiatry had revealed the disturbing presence of a plurality of apparently hermetically-sealed chambers of the consciousness (*cogito ergo sumus*, as it were).[30] In other words, concepts such as 'soul' and 'personality' must be handled with care, paying due respect to their resonances in context over time.

Second – and this is the key contention – it would be a mistake to speak of the mind–body problem as if it were an conundrum that had always existed. Mind–body relations became pressing in the guise of the mind–body *problem* only rather recently, and in response to specific cultural configurations. Above all, it was the eighteenth century (to deploy that diachronological expression somewhat elastically) and the intellectual movement we term the Enlightenment, which problematised this feature of the human condition. How was this so?

As indicated above, mainline philosophical currents from the Greeks onwards adumbrated a mythic conceptual geography which, in its value hierarchy, elevated the ideal above the material, the changeless over the mutable, the perfect over the processual, the mental over the physical, the free over the determined, and superimposed each pair upon the others. Demonstrating such an order of things could not, it is true, be achieved without some ingenuity and acumen. After all, the existence of the eternal form of a table, or the survival of the soul beyond the body, are not ideas predicated upon immediate objects of sense experience.

Nor could such a metaphysic be established without intellectual aplomb. Aristotle's polished conceptualisation of nature, for instance, is a far cry from the messy chaos of contrary motions and kaleidoscopic multiplicity of shapes which greets the innocent eye.[31] Christian apologetics in particular had to overcome what *prima facie* appear to be profound internal tensions, not to say contradictions, in its theology. The Christian faith, zealous in its denigration of the (original) sinfulness of the flesh, set particular value upon the immortal destiny of a unique, personal soul (an element absent, in different ways and for distinct reasons, from both neo-Platonism and Judaism). Yet at the same time, and no less uniquely, the

Scriptures revealed that embodied man was made in God's image, that God's own Son was made flesh, and that His incarnation, crucifixion and resurrection were typologically prophetic of a universal resurrection of the flesh at the impending Last Judgement. Few creeds made so much of the other-worldly, but none so honoured the flesh. This particular tension lay at the root of Augustine's ambivalence, forming the substratum of his ethics and epistemology, as well as his troubled view of mind in relation to body.[32] And those Christian exegetes and scholiasts who followed in Augustine's steps commented upon the paradox of flesh and fleshless within a single credo.

Thus the articulation of orthodox Christian theology might well be read as a heroic holding operation, attempting to harmonise the most unlikely partners. Through the Middle Ages and in to early modern times, churchmen battled against the flesh, extolling asceticism, mortification, and spirituality, while believers were almost ghoulishly fascinated by the seemingly incorruptible tissues, freshly spurting blood and weeping tears of long-dead saints, and awaiting the resurrection of the body in expectation of a very palpable orgy of bliss in heaven.[33] The endlessly controversial status of the eucharist – did the sacrament truly mean consuming the blood and body of the Saviour? or was it essentially an intellectual *aide memoir* of Christ's passion and atonement? – perfectly captures the essential tension between the spirit and incarnation within Christianity.

Nor was the triumph of the 'mind over body' metaphysic achieved without opposition. After all, antiquity itself had its atomists and materialists – Democritus, Diogenes, Epicurus, Leucippus, Lucretius – who in their distinct ways discarded the radical dualism of matter and spirit, denied the primacy of spirit, and proposed versions of monistic materialism which reduced the so-called nobler attributes to particles in motion and to the promptings of the flesh under what Bentham much later called the 'sovereign masters, of pleasure and pain'. The history of orthodox theology from Aquinas onwards amounted to a war of words: a logomachy waged on behalf of what Ralph Cudworth, the late seventeenth-century Platonist, was tellingly to call the *True Intellectual System of the Universe*, against advancing armies of alleged atomists, eternalists, mortalists, materialists, naturalists, atheists and all their tribe of Machiavellian, Hobbist and Spinozist fellow-travellers, who were all supposedly engaged in hierarchy-collapsing subversion, intellectual, religious, political and moral.[34]

Many have doubted whether these levelling metaphysical marauders were in fact real (or at least, numerous) – or were rather, as might be said, *ideal*, or ideal types – demonic bogeymen invented to shore up orthodoxy. They have doubted with good reason. Research is uncovering a larger presence of sturdy grass-roots materialism – as exemplified by

Menocchio the Friulian Miller, with his cosmology of cheese and worms – than once was suspected.[35]

Yet, after every qualification, it is clear that the overarching hierarchical philosophy of the mind–body duo became definitive for official ideologies in a European socio-political order which was itself massively and systematically hierarchical.[36] Often articulated through correspondences between the bodies terraqueous, politic, and natural, the mind–body pairing was congruent with, and supported by, comprehensive theories of cosmic order which attributed to every last entity of Creation its own unique niche on that scale of beings stretching from the lowest manifestation of inanimate nature up to nature's God. On this great chain, the material was set beneath the ideal, and man was 'the great amphibian', pivotal between the two.[37]

This bonding of mind and body was, moreover, all of a piece – as hinted above – with a divine universe, presided over by a numinous celestial wisdom. Were mind not lord over matter – were the relations between man's soul, consciousness, and will on the one side, and his guts and tissues on the other truly baffling and ambiguous, would that not have been a scandal in a cosmos created and ruled by a transcendent mind, pure being? Only what one might call perversely heterodox believers, with theologico–political fish of their own to fry, would contend that the doctrines of immaterial minds and souls so cardinal to Christian orthodoxy were downright heresies. Lies, moreover, even inimical to the Gospel, and, by contrast, promoting a deterministic philosophical materialism as their pristine faith.

There was, of course, abundant scope within Christian belief for heresy, and much of that was radical. Yet most rebel creeds involved attacks upon the banausic 'knife-and-fork' materialism of paunchy prelates and the espousal, from Luther through to the New Light and the First Church of Christ Scientist, of more intensely spiritual outlooks than established churches with their feet on the ground of Rome or Canterbury allowed. Many of the most exciting, modernising philosophical movements in the sixteenth and seventeenth centuries aimed to slough off what were seen as the excessively materialist Aristotelian components of scholasticism, replacing them with the more idealistic doctrines of neo-Platonism and neo-Pythagoreanism and dozens of grass-roots varieties of the two. Reijer Hooykaas, the contemporary Dutch historian of science, has suggestively drawn attention to the congruence between the protestant God and the transcendental voluntarism of the 'new philosophy'.[38] It is a similitude – or at least a convergence – that needs to be weighted in all our discussion of the mind–body relationship in modern times.

Hence the first comprehensive and sustained questioning of mind–body dualism, and the wider cosmology of which it was emblem and authorisation, came with the Enlightenment.[39] The relationship was eventually analysed, explored, questioned, contested, and radically reformulated – a great intellectual wave sweeping over Western Europe from the middle of the seventeenth century onwards. The terms of the debate were fierce, as could be (in the cases of scientists and divines) the stakes. Indeed some even rejected root-and-branch its very terms. There was no single line of attack, and certainly no uniform outcome. It was a dialogical undertaking – in Bakhtin's sense – whose grandness could only be gleaned in the architectural magnificence of its details; in the case at hand in the ramifications and implications of the debate that seemed to touch on every single subject under the sun. But in a multitude of ways, what hitherto had been taken as a fact of life – albeit not without its difficulties and unrelenting tensions – became deeply problematic to many and repugnant to some.

In certain respects the fabric came apart at the seams not because of ideological animus or ulterior political motives, but because inquiry inevitably uncovered loose threads begging to be pulled. Essentially internal investigations in science and scholarship, new discoveries and technical advances, all served inevitably – though not uncontroversially – to modify the mental map. Anatomy was one of these fields. Ever since the Renaissance endeavours of Vesalius, Falloppio and others, the forging of more sophisticated techniques of *post mortem* dissection as part of the rise of anatomy teaching stimulated intense curiosity about the relationship between structure and function, normalcy and pathology, the living body and the corpse on the slab.

As well as investigating muscles, bones and, most celebratedly, the vascular system, seventeenth-century anatomy devoted fertile attention to the nerves. These nerves became the European sportime of anatomists and physiologists, whose narrative discourses reveal to what degree the nerves also engaged the imagination, and often, the genius, of these scientists. The pathways between nerve endings, the central nervous system conducted along the spine, and the distinct chambers of the brain were finely traced, above all by the English physician and scientist, Thomas Willis, with a precision vastly outstripping Galen's pioneering investigations. Such work invited inferences not merely about the role of the brain as the receptor of nervous stimuli from the senses and the transmitter of motor signals but about the localised functions of the distinct brain structures: cerebrum, cerebellum, etc. The logic of anatomical investigation was offering every encouragement, not merely to the general intuition that the brain was connected with thinking, but to the more radical prospect that specific pieces of grey matter governed identifiable facets of sensation, ideation, and behaviour.[40]

There was of course nothing new in a broad, essentially mechanistic, 'medical materialism' – the perception of every doctor (indeed, every patient) that physical states affect·consciousness; such views were of a piece with the most orthodox humoralism. What *was* new, and challenging about Willis's 'neurologia' and 'psyche-ologia' was that it pinned down the mind remarkably – even uncomfortably – close to the brain. In making these observations, Willis had no grander axe to grind. Blamelessly orthodox in his Anglicanism and a true-blue royalist in politics, he was no *protophilosophe*. Even his use of language – a prose style that was closer to Bacon than to the more baroque Sir Thomas Browne and Thomas Burnet of his time – was remarkably conventional and augured for scientific style the plain prose advocated by Thomas Sprat's *History of the Royal Society*.[41] But his own work, and later investigations by others such as Albrecht von Haller (the Swiss Enlightenment physiologist) into the nervous system, and its functions of irritation and excitability, were easily appropriated by those whose vision of a 'science of man' (to complement and complete the 'science of nature' which had been so successfully pursued in the seventeenth century) was intended as a weapon of war against the entrenched cosmology, theology and politics.

This is no place to retell the tale of the Enlightenment, or even of the role of scientific materialism within it.[42] As Peter Gay has emphasised, however, we must never forget that the sharpest intellects of the generations from the late seventeenth century forward were primed to be systematically critical of old orthodoxies, and eager to map out new-found worlds, cognitive as well as physical. The voyages of discovery, the philological criticism pioneered by Renaissance humanists, the dazzling techniques of historical inquiry, and the new science accelerating from Galileo to Newton all joined forces to question traditional authorities as graven in the authority of books, including the Book of God's Word and delivered in the *ipse dixits* of the ancients and the entrenched hand-me-down orthodoxies of metaphysics, scholasticism, and custom. To set human understanding on a sure footing, searching inquiries had to be initiated into man's nature, and his place within the entire living system, into his natural faculties, propensities and endowments, his history, his social ties, his prospects. And if the proper study of mankind was man, as the great poet had pronounced, such knowledge (it was claimed) patently could not be plucked down from abstract eternal fitnesses or looked up in books, but had to be grounded upon first-hand facts, derived from observation and experiment, subject to the searing sunlight of criticism.[43] Yet few pursuits in the history of science in the modern age invigorated empiricism more so than the dilemma of mind and body. It was a dualism almost guaranteed to elicit the latest empirical strain in every man (and woman).

The mobilisation of such programmes – Hume spoke for his age in expressing his aspiration to become the Newton of the moral sciences – broke down, or at least left uncertain and indeterminate, that overarching structure of analogies and correlations between the microcosm of man and the macrocosm of the universe which had been the guarantor of traditional epistemologies. This was the larger 'breaking of the circle', about which the late Marjorie Hope Nicolson has written so eloquently,[44] but the collapse was felt as much in the domain of mind and body as in the organic and inorganic sciences. Indeed, Hume's sceptical *Dialogues of Natural Religion* questioned the very possibility that man could attain to any determinate understanding of his (teleological) station within the cosmos, or any grasp of the meaning of the universe, just as his radical moral philosophy appeared to deny that the order of the natural world could provide the basis for an ethical code by which to live.[45]

Hence in a multitude of ways, Enlightenment inquirers convinced themselves that the highest priority for a true understanding of man – to serve as the basis for the critique and reform of society – must be (to use Hume's terms) an *Inquiry into Human Nature*. This was an endeavour conducted in a variety of fields or disciplines – we may anachronistically call them politics, religion, aesthetics, psychology, anthropology, history, and so forth – by the distinguished succession of thinkers from Bayle and Locke, through Montesquieu, Voltaire, Hume, and La Mettrie, and on to Helvetius, Diderot, d'Holbach, Rousseau, Lessing and Herder, to say nothing of innumerable lesser figures. Their outlooks were often remarkably diverse, as they debated and disagreed on levels extending beyond methodological and clerical ones. Also, their vantages differed in accordance with national and regional cultures and changed over time.[46] Yet when viewed as a whole, the movement served to destroy the traditional notion – the creed of Milton, Pascal, Racine, and Bossuet – that man had been placed in a divinely ordered universe as a unique compound of immaterial and immortal soul and mundane, mortal body, as Sir Thomas Browne's 'great amphibian':[47]

> to call ourselves a Microcosm, or little World, I though it onely a pleasant trope of Rhetorick, till my neer judgement and second thoughts told me there was a real truth therein. For first we are a rude mass, and in the rank of creatures which onely are, and have a dull kind of being, not yet priviledged with life, or preferred to sense or reason; next we live the life of Plants, the life of Animals, the life of Men, and at last the life of Spirits, running on in one mysterious nature those five kinds of existences, which comprehend the creatures, not onely of the World, but of the Universe. Thus is Man that great and true *Amphibium*, whose nature is desposed to live, not onely like other creatures in divers elements, but in divided and distinguished worlds: for though there be but one to sense, there are two to reason, the one visible, the other invisible.

Many *philosophes*, sketching in what was often called a 'natural history' of man, believed it was imperative to treat man less as a fixed and final object of creation, an 'Adam', than as the product of time, circumstances, and milieu – the creature of education (as Locke, Condillac and Helvetius especially stressed),[48] of climate and physical environment (Montesquieu) of physical evolution (Buffon, Erasmus Darwin and Lamarck)[49] or of history (Vico, Boulanger, Ferguson, Miller, Herder).[50] Man's physique and consciousness were both the result of processes of natural and social advancement from savagery to civilisation, from rudeness to refinement – or, as some saw it, possibly the result of a deterioration from some pristine golden age through to latter-day decadence. In the process of such dynamic interaction with the environment, of learning and adaptation, body and awareness had endlessly, indefinitely interacted. Consciousness (both individual and collective) developed out of the senses, and the senses themselves – whether considered in terms of the individual adult maturing from infancy or the collective psycho-history of the species – had equally been the product of dynamic processes of refinement, atunement, or possibly, enfeeblement.[51]

Nevertheless, it would be grossly misleading to imply that Enlightenment thought was programmatically atheistic or revolutionary, or even optimistic about the prospects of radical praxis.[52] Diderot's dialogues hardly share the practical confidence of Lenin's tone: *What is to be done?;* the conclusions of *Candide* and *Rasselas* are conclusive within an intentional inconclusivity; and so self-conscious a work of advanced thought as *Tristram Shandy* is ultimately an elegy – an *English* elegy – to inaction. Yet the Enlightenment advanced visions of man's life that saw his essence lying in change, process, transformation, becoming – anything but a fixed point on an inflexible scale. Man had less of a nature than a history, or rather his history was his nature. He was made by the sum of all the determining forces; but out of the resources of his milieu man also made himself – and through the dynamic dialectic of habit and education, constantly remade himself over and again. And this was a process, as Diderot emphasised so clearly, long before Marx, in which material circumstances shaped consciousness even as consciousness itself changed material circumstances. Thinking was thus an expression of being, and self was a creature of experience. A radical prospect – indeed, a daunting one, when a Laurence Sterne (whose hero tells us, deferring to Locke, that a man's mind is a veritable history book), goes on to have his hero asked 'Who are you?', to which his only response is 'Don't puzzle me'.[53]

Man was thus a creature less of fixed being than of becoming. Lockians denied he was born naturally endowed with a full complement of innate ideas and moral understanding. Experience was all, and experience was derived from the senses and was mediated by the highly somatic mechanisms of pleasure and pain. Thus, a tacit materialism was seeping in through the cracks, as is illustrated by Locke's canny acknowledgement that there was nothing incompatible with the divine creation in the possibility of 'thinking matter' – though it was not a notion he expressly espoused.[54] Yet the radical transformation of mind–body concepts had less to do with doctrinaire materialism than with the softening-up process whereby man's faculties, traditionally taken as 'given', such as the will, or the understanding conceived as the 'candle of the Lord',[55] as a divinely endowed 'ratio recta', were subjected to intense scrutiny – one might almost say 'deconstructed' – their operations itemised, part by part and one by one, and the contingencies and vagaries of consciousness thereby accentuated.

Thus the various forms of utilitarianism attempted, in the name of scientificity, to reduce the exercise of moral judgement to sets of component decisions taken in a lawlike way on the basis of the operation of the mechanisms of desire and aversion. Likewise, epistemological associationism pictorialised the processes whereby edifices of knowledge were built up out of the primitive building bricks of sense impressions.[56] As Locke's revolutionary *Essay Concerning Human Understanding* shows, associationism was not necessarily committed to a materialist physiology; yet, as in Hartley's subsequent system, it often was. As Foucault (in such well-known books as *Madness and Civilization* and *Discipline and Punish*) and other scholars have noted, underlying theory and practice in such eighteenth-century endeavours as child-rearing, pedagogy – not least instruction for the deaf and blind – and penology was the radical new model of a will which was neither free nor instinctually wicked but malleable, and available for conditioning in a controlling environment. These developments assumed an understanding for simpler concepts – attention, learning languages verbal and symbolic, reading – which have yet to be fully studied.[57] Even so, by the middle of the eighteenth century it was perfectly clear to those who entered into such physiological and psychological discussion that consciousness, like memory and desire, was not an activity that could profitably be discussed without full recourse to both mind and body.

Such developments had many faces. Reflecting widespread contemporary excitement, many of our historians have enthused over the Enlightenment 'discovery' of man, and its formulation of new, scientific and secular concepts of the personality and identity; of the birth of self-awareness and the exhilarating odyssey of individualism and of the growing importance of the notion of *Bildung*, with its proclamation, paralleling the Kantian *'sapere aude'*, of *'esse aude'*, dare to be, or to become, asserting the true emancipation of mankind from ancient, self-imposed, fetters. At the end of this avenue lies the declaration of the rights of man: startlingly secular, individualist, utilitarian.[58] And from these natural rights – natural because they derive from man's anatomy and physiology, his or her body as much as any other consideration – follows the modern state with its peculiar blend of democratic liberty and social control.

Or one could speak in more pessimistic tones of the dissolution of traditional stable senses of self, soul, and of social obligation in that welter of indulgent narcissism and moral solipsism encouraged by the fashionable new sensibility and the utilitarian hedonic calculus. The erosion of that value hierarchy which the mind/body template had inexorably under-written was (in this reading) that highroad to nihilism trodden by none other than that hero of the late Enlightenment, the Marquis de Sade.[59]

Or, as a third possibility, one might eschew premature judgments between optimistic and pessimistic readings, the visions of self-emanci-pation and self-imprisonment, and rather preserve a studied ambivalence, echoing the open questions of Diderot's final drama, *Est-il bon? Est-il méchant?* Whichever line is taken, what seems beyond dispute is the upshot of the Enlightenment conviction that to know the world it was vital first to know the knower; to look within man himself to grasp his faculties, dispositions, and potentialities was a radical uncertainty about the bound-aries of body, the status of consciousness, and the interplay between the two. Whether viewed dialectically, as Kant and Blake would, or more simply as contrary states of body and mind, interplay required consultation of *both*. One without the other – say mind without body, or body without consciousness – entailed an epistemological, even ontological, impossi-bility. A constituted anomaly whose just proportions could only be set straight by consultation of the Other. In this radical inclusivity lay much of the elusive originality of Enlightenment thinking on mind and body, whether viewed in its English, French, German, or along any other national lines.[60]

Above all, the Enlightenment did actually generate, almost for the first time in Western culture, a thoroughgoing materialist strand, which was generally – though not necessarily, as the cases of Hartley and Priestley amply testify – associated with a strident religious freethinking verging on atheism: true materialism would expose theistic idealism as false con-sciousness. This was an agenda whose vitality remains to be explored and measured for the latter part of the eighteenth century. Taking up sugges-tions such as Locke's hints of the possibility of 'thinking matter', the suggestion was widely investigated and disseminated – it is bandied about as a shocking commonplace by Diderot – that mind might be fully and entirely comprehended by the activities of the brain, nerves and juices, and that thought was nothing but the secretion of the brain just as bile was the secretion of the stomach. From the middle of the eighteenth century, this materialist agenda became privileged. La Mettrie first comprehensively spelt out a materialism applied to man in *L'Homme Machine*, D'Holbach expounded a totally materialistic vision of the cosmos in his *Système de la Nature*, and the Ideologues later systematised a functionalist philosophy of thinking, in which they emphasised that the phenomena of consciousness were purely the products of the fine-tuned organisation of matter.[61] It may appear an odd position: this radical materialist notion of consciousness and ideation. Yet it was widely explored and – what is more – continues to find staunch champions among the élite of our contemporary neurobiological and neurophysiological establishment who continue to insist that brain is matter, thought brain, and (as John Keats, the young doctor-poet, might have remarked) that this is all we need to know. To be sure, the sociobiologists and environmentalists have countered this extreme materialist position, but the results are still out, and it would be imprudent and premature to believe that one or another position lies close to any agreed-upon truth. This fierce ambiguity underlies some of (but not all) the eternal fascination of mind and body.

In the eighteenth century materialist outlooks appeared in many other guises too, such as Erasmus Darwin's pioneering version of biological evolutionism. This version envisaged the evolution of all forms of organic activity out of the first living filament, driven by an urge to aspire to higher levels of sensory enjoyment. The inherent drives of wriggling matter eventually blossomed forth in the human consciousness.[62] This Darwinian position was highly influential on early Romantic thinkers, in England and on the Continent, who derived much of their sense of mind and body from Darwin's materialist biology, perhaps even more so than from the great philosophical tradition from Hobbes and Locke to Kant and the Germans.

It is no accident that Darwin – like La Mettrie, Hartley, Cabanis, and literally dozens of others who would figure into a detailed study of mind and body – was a physician. For the most powerful, yet profoundly ambiguous, toehold for a mode of materialism within traditional European thought had been the discourse of medicine – a discourse as vast as it was diverse. Doctors had long enjoyed a notoriety for what we might call their professional materialism, alongside their proverbial (if probably unjustified) reputation for atheism. Traditional humoral medicine was materialist through and through, if we mean by that that it acknowledged – as must any medicine worth its salt – the central role of psychosomatic and somatopsychic activities in determining health and disease. No doctor or patient earnestly examining the parameters of sickness could seriously question that physical disorders – or indeed medical drugs – affected mental states, or, vice versa, that physical health depended to no mean degree upon emotional disposition, states of mind, and so forth. The placebo effect was highly familiar to doctors attuned to the magic of sympathy and the strength of imagination in governing matters of health.[63] Medicine was permitted this potentially threatening perspective, in part because the needs of practice required it, and, far more so, because, dealing definitionally with pathological states, with the diseased individual, the ground-rules governing normal human values were obviously suspended. One might incidentally compare the licence granted the satirist or carica-turist to imply that his target was none other than an insect, a wild beast or a machine. Such 'medicinal' satire did not derogate from the dignity of human nature precisely because it exposed the sickness of those who truly threatened it.[64]

Further more, despite an older and erroneous historiography, Car-tesian philosophy no more undermined the traditional psychosomatic medical perspective than the 'scientific revolution' of the seventeenth cen-tury destroyed humoral medicine (although, as we have seen, a new emphasis upon the key role played by the nervous system is everywhere evident).[65] It is hardly surprising in such circumstances that medicine (broadly understood) proved one of the key sites for the further elucidation of the seemingly infinitely complex and shifting relations between con-sciousness and corporeality.

It is widely argued these days, in part following Foucault, that the age of reason could not tolerate 'unreason' and had to sequestrate and silence it in the 'great confinement'; and that, by consequence, eighteenth-century therapeutics for the mad fell back more heavily upon mechanical and medical means to restrain the body.[66] This marginalisation of the Enlightenment doctors was almost unprecedented – it is said – in Western Civilisation. But this interpretation is far too simplistic a reading, and demonstrates the point by using students' medical dissertations, which have rarely been consulted. The 'mad doctors' assessed by our best his-torians of medicine fully understood the importance of mental and emotional precipitants of the sicknesses of their charges, just as they intertwined medical and moral treatments in their often highly original therapeutics. Medical concepts, centred upon the mediating role of the nerves, and psycho-physiological categories, such as the idea of the pas-sions of the soul and their pathology, effectively established the interlink-age. The result was a more elaborate and psychopathological medical theory (collectively, that is) than we have recognised: one taking account of dreams and visions, nightmares and hallucinations, fantasies and phan-tasmagorias – an entire underworld of dark subconscious passions often sinking the patient in a sea of mental conflict. The nerves could not be forgotten, of course, prime movers that they were. Yet even they were only a part of the evidence heard by the Enlightenment physician, who also listened to the cries and whispers of the spectral, night-time world of his patients.[67]

Doctors and laymen were equally aware that the organism possessed a rather mysterious and often mocking wisdom of its own. Both the clergyman-novelist, Laurence Sterne, and the physician-novelist, Tobias Smollett – each suffering from a consumption he clearly knew would prove fatal and cause early death – expressed in their writings the perception that states of health and disease were not gross matters of mechanism, nor entirely under the,control of imperious reason. Each recognised that his best hope for health depended deeply upon the animated expression of his own personality in action,[68] in motion, in the velocity of change. *Au fond*, it was a recipe for health lying proximate to our twentieth-cent, ry holistic views that celebrate the unity of mind and body, the constant occupation of the imagination, and motion, or exercise, elevated to new degrees of sophistication.

Medicine, with, as we have seen, its materialist undertow, diagnoses sickness and proffers remedy. As Peter Gay has pointed out, the *philosophes* adored the picturing of themselves as physicians to a priest-ridden, poverty-stricken *ancien régime* they regarded as sick, materially, intellectually, and spiritually.[69] Indeed, they diagnosed such traditional theological and metaphysical conceptions as the absolute mind–matter, or mind–body dualisms, or the disembodied soul, or the dogmatic espousal of free will, and its correlate, sinfulness, as themselves symptoms of mental folly or even derangement. Such 'fictions' became the targets of those unmasking campaigns for disillusionment and demystification that animated much of the best Enlightenment criticism.

Thus *philosophes* made free with attacking forms of consciousness as diseased, as the expressions of psychopathology. Metaphysical dogmatising, system-building, religious ravings and speaking in tongues – these (critics argued) were not rational minds at work, but the shriekings of the sick and suffering. 'The corruption of the senses is the generation of the spirit', Swift sardonically remarked, in a materialising formulation that any competent *philosophe* might have appropriated.[70] Likewise, Enlightenment pundits enjoyed representing supposed proofs of 'free consciousness', as quintessential expressions of *false* consciousness, analogous to nightmares, ghosts, spectres, incubi and succubi; the entire range of sonambulism or mesmeric phenomena thus offered manna to satirists. 'The sleep of reason produces monsters', judged Goya, for whom so much official culture betrayed an ingrained psychopathology.[71] We should see to what degree this was a psychopathology widely disseminated throughout the various layers and segments of Enlightenment culture; medically generated, perhaps, but also widespread elsewhere, having filtered down to many parts of society.

In Enlightenment knockabout histories, entire disciplines such as scholastic metaphysics or dogmatic theology were relegated to the status of mere delusion, mental aberrations, or at best products of a species in its immaturity, a stage in the progress from mental infancy up to modern maturity. Thus idealism was exposed to the whiplash of criticism as the archetype of false consciousness. Formulating theories of 'fictions' was integral to the endeavours of reformers such as Bentham. He represented the very idea of the immortal soul as the fabrication of vested interests, above all the clergy, eager to indoctrinate the masses with beliefs that magnified their own authority, and, more broadly, systematically promoting a self-serving 'fiction' of the superiority of the spiritual over the physical, head over hand, priesthood over people. For radical *philosophes*, the very notions of God, Satan, and all other non-material powers were phantoms of priestcraft, fabricated to keep the people in their place. Yet the line from Hartley (who was also a physician) to Priestley, and then Priestley to Bentham, has not been studied in this light: as a discourse of radical will, part mind, part body, and thoroughly soaked in the elaborate medico-philosophical labyrinth of the time.

More comprehensively, and even constructively, such diagnoses of the psychopathology of the *ancien régime* were incorporated into a systematic socio-historical critique through the programme of the *Ideologues*, notably Cabanis.[72] For these intellectuals living in times of revolutionary social change, expressions of thought were to be treated as one of many products of the integrated, unified human organism. Such unity may have been more imagined than scientifically demonstrable, and it also happened to follow in the footsteps of the giant waves of vitalism sweeping over late Enlightenment thought.[73] But the idea of a complex organic form as the basis of a unified human organism was so strong that it invigorated this research programme continuously, especially in France and in centres of learning where French influence carried sway. It was thus axiomatic for them – within the mind–body context – that consciousness could not be regarded on its own terms but had to be understood as complementing the thinker, whose ideas were to be read as functional to his interests. In thus developing the notion of 'ideology' into an analytic weapon – the weapon that was eventually transformed through the breakdown of other vital connections into nineteenth-century sociology and twentieth-century sociology of knowledge – the *Ideologues* proved astute commentators upon their own times.

For they – and others besides them – were perceiving that traditional doctrines of consciousness were obsolete; in this sense, traditional concepts of the old mind–body dualism being just as out-of-date. It was no longer plausible to maintain that the order of things, natural and social, was to correspond to truths, revealed in Scripture, enshrined by the Church, and expounded by right reason. Such prescriptive visions had to yield to analytic accounts that acknowledged and explained the socio-historical fact that information, ideas, images, public opinion, and propaganda – in short, ideology – were increasingly playing a crucial, indeed, a dominant, role in ordering and managing society,[74] so magisterial was the authority of knowledge in the High Enlightenment. The very power of the *philosophes*, the spread of books and the press (the fourth estate), was making Swift's dictum that 'the pen is mightier than the sword' prove prophetic, and confirming Hume's view that mankind is governed, *au fond*, by 'opinion'. Wishful thinking aside, it was hardly fortuitous that it was the *philosophes* who made such observations, because in their war to displace priests and official propagandists as the mouthpieces of society, they became masters of the media of an increasingly opinion-conscious society.

Yet here lies a profound paradox which may stand as the summation of that multitude of ironies which sprang out of the mind–body dialectic. Enlightenment thinking, as we have suggested, was profoundly critical of the theologic – metaphysical myth of the autonomy of mind and its correlate, free will. Such fictions sanctioned priestcraft, superstition and hellfire. *Philosophes* anatomised such absurdities, and their wider practical manifestations – the irrationalities of credulity, faith, devotion, magic, spells, folklore and faith-healing.[75] Yet the whole body of such beliefs and practises proved amazingly resilient. Explaining the acceptance and continuing purchase of such nonsense presented no small problems, especially for reformers desperately trying to convince themselves and the world that mankind was growing ever wiser in what Paine called the Age of Reason. Worse still, progressives had to face the embarrassing fact that many such absurd beliefs and practices appeared to be efficacious. Old charms and new Mesmerism might be stuff and nonsense, silly mumbo-jumbo from the viewpoint of Newtonian science; yet both seemed to possess curative properties, and to exercise strange 'occult' powers, if only because of the deviousness of the human imagination.[76] Might not human nature and the human mind then also harbour dark mysteries? Mysteries impenetrable to any science, Newtonian or even more advanced? Impenetrable for ever?

An ominous cloud hovered over the Enlightenment: the fear that, for all their faith in the progress of humanity, all their secular evangelising, all their optimistic demythologising crusades, the human animal himself might not prove fit for the programmes of education, organisation and consciousness-raising the *philosophes* were mobilising. Might there be some secret soul within? Some metaphysical *je ne sais quoi* no microscope could ever detect? For the Voltaire of *Candide*, as well as the Johnson of *Rasselas*, man seemed only to have the definitive capacity for making himself miserable. For the Diderot of *Rameau's Nephew*, man was all antitheses (perhaps like Pope's vile Sporus), a chameleon, a monster even. And the Shandy males (in what remains one of the most highly genderised 'cock and bull' stories in any language) argued themselves into incapacity. The culture of sensibility thus seemed to entrap itself in a maze of contradictions, and not least, as that famous, if corpulent, 'nerve doctor', George Cheyne, contended, long before Freud, the pursuit of civilisation brought only the discontents of the 'English Malady'.[77] All these ironies were encapsulated in that archetypal Enlightenment disorder, hypochondria,[78] melancholy, hysteria, low spirits – depression. Call it by any other name, wax sceptical even, it remained psychological misery none the less.

Stated otherwise, the eighteenth century which aimed to erect a Newtonian moral science, discover the laws of thinking and action, and generate social technologies to pave the way for progress, increasingly stumbled upon hidden depths within the human animal that hindered organised improvement. The boundless and wilful anarch, the imagination, was one such sphere. Enlightenment writers continually expressed their anxieties at what Samuel Johnson called 'the hunger of imagination', that power of wishing or fantasising which captivated the consciousness and paralysed the will, driving individuals into dreamworlds of delusion and flights of phantasmagoria. Imagination – and worse still, fancy – had disturbingly ambiguous resonances.[79]

Not least, growing fears were expressed that exercise of imagination entailed the direst practical consequences for both genders. A growing literature laid bare the dangers of fantasy-induced nymphomania in young women, and, above all, masturbation in both sexes.[80] Earlier ages had construed masturbation as a relatively harmless physical abuse, in response to ordinary genital irritation. Enlightenment doctors such as Samuel Tissot, however, reconceptualised onanism not as physically stimulated but as the product of a warping of the mind, overheated by diseased imagination. As such it was more perilous. Indeed, because imagination was so central, onanism was far more dangerous than mere fornication, more habit-forming, more corrupting of the fabric of character, and ultimately deleterious in its long-term effects.

In other fields too, Enlightenment writers grew preoccupied with the evil consequences of vices which they saw as stemming from mental habits. Excessive drinking paradoxically ceased to be regarded as a vice of excess, with essentially physical *sequelae*, and increasingly was diagnosed as the expression of mental disorder. Narcotic-taking was also seen in a similar light to drunkenness. Coleridge presents the paradox of a thinker whose Romantic commitments made him unfold a heroic vision of the transcendental independent mental faculties of reason and imagination but whose everyday addiction to opium – he called it a *'free-agency-annihilating*

Poison' – illustrates both the practical reality of growing addiction to narcotics, and its recognition as a disease of the mind. Yet Coleridge was the prophet of mental autonomy who enslaved himself. In his *View of the Nervous Temperament*, delivered almost at the graveside of the Enlightenment, the British physician Thomas Trotter exposed the modern philosophy of desire – classically expressed in the terms of utilitarianism – as the pathogenic agent perverting civilisation into a drug culture, a mocking materialisation of that scientific vision of mechanical man, subject to the laws of cause and effect, so dear to the Enlightenment.[81]

Thus, in one of the great ironies of history, that 'mind' which the Enlightenment set out to expose as a 'fiction' fought back and reasserted itself, in surprising and troublesome fashions. For one thing, its pathological face was revealing itself. For late eighteenth-century medicine was coming to recognise that lunacy was not just seated in the blood, nerves, or brain, but was an authentically *mental* disorder, requiring to be treated with 'moral' means (the limitations of such methods would not become apparent until rather later).[82] For another, mind went underground. As Ellenberger and Whyte have shown, the notion of the 'unconscious' was taking on an at least inchoate existence in the age of sensibility, coming out in the culture of Romanticism. The Age of Reason closed, so to speak, with increasing, if grudging, homage to its opposite.[83]

Profound currents of Enlightenment thought, we have argued, set about challenging the sovereignty of mind, because it regarded that sovereignty, in its traditional hierarchico-theological forms, as objectively reactionary and ideologically subservient to tyrannies, personal, social, and political. Mind–body dualism was an instrument of power. Progressives such as Condorcet aimed to undermine such traditions by insisting that consciousness was merely an expression of body-based impressions and sensations.[84] Yet across the spectrum of experience the result was not as expected. For one thing, Romanticism emerged – eventually throughout Europe – as a triumphant vindication of mental individuality, an irreducible integrity, a celebration of uniqueness. And at the same time a mocking deviousness of the will asserted its resistance, manifest in its extreme form as mental morbidity, or what Freud honoured as the psycho-neuroses. These twin developments might respectively be represented as, on the one hand the naturalisation of theism, and, on the other, the survival of satanic possession.

Together they paradoxically combined to ensure the endurance of the age old dualism. Throughout the nineteenth century – long after one can validly conjure up Enlightenment debates of any type – fierce challenges to mind were made. These came not only from expected quarters – in the name of credos and cults, the Church at large, all the arts – but also from such newly developing academic subjects as anthropology, sociology, psychology, and, in some ways most crucially, from the newly privileged discourse of psychiatry. Body and consciousness played elusive roles in this nineteenth-century evolution of an old relationship: by now a worn-out dialectic, even a reciprocity. Too amorphous to be pinned down or pegged to anything concrete in an age of incremental positivism, consciousness was still viewed either in its mental or physical states, but rarely as the expression of a holistic unit called man or woman. Those who persistently pleaded for body tended to enforce the dualism, in its rhetorical antithesis more forcefully than anywhere else.

Thus minds and bodies were assured a legacy as individual entities, even by those whose unequivocal aim in the nineteenth century, and afterwards, was to quash its durability. As the nineteenth century wore on, ever persuaded that its scientific discoveries were new and complacent in the belief that its predecessor (the century of Enlightenment) had uncovered nothing worthy of preservation, its discourses of mind and body became politically more explosive than they had been. Paradoxically again, the dialogue acquired a type of collective authority that enfranchised, even guaranteed, the survival of the already age-old dualism.

Looking back from the vantage of our century, one can predict that such a sensitised view of mind and body will result in impasse. Indeed, as the nineteenth century wore out, it became practically impossible to become dialogical about mind and body in any open-ended sense (here Bakhtin was the great exception). If mind was construed as Self, and body as Other – a fair construction considering the degree to which man's rationality was celebrated in the long nineteenth century – one sees why neutral debates could not be held about the mind–body relationship which were incorporative, recuperative, or homogenising of the Other. By the turn of the twentieth century, the desire to understand otherness – whether mind *or* body – was no longer ideologically or even politically acceptable, except as small waves and insignificant currents in an ocean of selfhood. The mainstream remained divided, as laboratory dualists and philosophical monists, for example, worked independently of the Other. Our dominant late twentieth-century attitude to mind and body, in contrast, has entailed something of a denouement: less polarised, less dialogical, a topic less urgent even among those who plead for integration, as entire segments of civilised society concede that they are entrapped in the dualism while hoping to escape from it, or dismiss its existence, altogether.

NOTES

1 Rigorous study of the mind–body relationship construed in the philosophical sense begins as a subset of the philosophy of mind in the nineteenth century, and a case can be made that there are traces of it evident in eighteenth-century rational thought. By the time the journal *Mind: a Quarterly Review of Psychology and Philosophy* was launched

in England in 1876, the mind–body relationship was a widely-discussed philosophical topic and a valid field of serious inquiry, as is evident, for example, in books written by diverse types of authors. See, for example, the philosopher George Moore's *The Use of the Body in Relation to the Mind* (1847), Benjamin Collins Brodie's *Mind and Matter* (New York, 1857), and the famous British psychiatrist, Henry Maudsley's medico-philosophical study of *Body and Mind* (1873).

By the turn of the twentieth century, discussions of mind/body continued to flourish in the major European and American schools of philosophy, as can be seen in the tradition from Wittgenstein to Gilbert Ryle and A. J. Ayer, and in such works as the well-known philosopher C. D. Broad's *The Mind and its Place in Nature* (1925). More recently, see R. W. Rieber (ed.), *Body and Mind: Past, Present and Future* (New York, 1980); Neil Bruce Lubow, *The Mind–Body Identity Theory* (Oxford, 1974); Michael E. Levin, *Metaphysics and the Mind–Body Problem* (New York, 1979); and Norman Malcolm, *Problems of Mind: Descartes to Wittgenstein* (New York, 1971); authors writing on the relationship from different perspectives and for different diachronic periods. The literature is vast and continues to produce scholarship, as can be surmised from the entry on 'Mind and Body' in the recently published *Oxford Companion to the Mind*, edited by R. L. Gregory (Oxford, 1987), 204.

2 The historiography of the mind–body relationship extends, of course, as far back as the Greeks and demonstrates a long tradition of speculation, so abundant that it would be foolish to attempt to provide any sense of its breadth in the space of a note. But we want to comment on the main curves of the heritage of mind and body, especially by noticing the supremacy of mind over body throughout the Christian tradition, and the reinforcement of this hierarchy in the aftermath of Cartesian dualism. Both mind and body received a great deal of attention in the Enlightenment, and it is one of the purposes of this book to annotate this relationship in a variety of discourses, more fully than the matter has been studied before. There is also a large literature, scientific and mystical, secular and religious, in the seventeenth and eighteenth centuries, that treats of the mind's control over the body or the converse: see for instance the Paracelsian physician Van Helmont: *The Spirit of Diseases, or Diseases of the Spirit . . . wherein it is shewed how much the Mind Influenceth the Body in Causing and Curing Diseases* (1694). Other works attempted to demarcate the boundaries of mind and body, such as John Petvin's *Letters Concerning Mind* (1750); John Richardson's (of Newtent) *Thoughts upon Thinking, or a New Theory of the Human Mind: Wherein a Physical Rationale of the Formation of our Ideas, the Passions, Dreaming and every Faculty of the Soul is Attempted upon Principles Entirely New* (1755); and John Rotherham's *On the Distinction between the Soul and the Body* [1760], a philosophical treatise aiming to differentiate the realms of mind from soul. Still other discourses, often medical dissertations writing with an eye on Hobbes's *De Corpore* (1655), actually aimed to anatomise the soul as distinct from the brain in strictly mechanical terms; see, for example, Johann Ambrosius Hillig, *Anatomie der Seelen* (Leipzig, 1737). In all these diverse discourses, the dualism of mind and body was so firmly ingrained by the mid eighteenth century that compendiums such as the following continued to be issued: [anon.], *A View of Human Nature: Or Select Histories, Giving an Account of Persons, who have been Most Eminently Distinguish'd by their Virtues or Vices, their Perfections or Defects, Either of Body or Mind . . . the Whole Collected from the Best Authors in Various Languages . . .* (1750).

More recently, in the Romantic period, there was realignment of the dualism often in favour of the body, as J. H. Hagstrum has noted in *The Romantic Body: Love and Sexuality in Keats, Wordsworth and Blake* (Knoxville, 1985). In our century, the discussion has proliferated in a number of directions. On the one hand, there is a vast psychoanalytic and psychohistorical literature that we do not specifically engage in this volume, but whose tenets can be grasped, if controversially, in Norman O. Brown's *Life and Against Death: The Psychoanalytical Meaning of History* (1957), a classic expression of the Freudian viewpoint; and in Leo Bersani's *The Freudian Body: Psychoanalysis and Art* (New York, 1985). On the other, the philosophy of mind within the academic study of philosophy has continued to privilege mind over body. But there is now also a tradition of revaluation that (at least nominally) attempts to view the mind–body relationship neutrally, giving each component allegedly equal treatment no matter which diachronic period is being studied, and still other critiques that view body in relations to society, as for instance, in A. W. H. Adkins, *From the Many to the One: a study of Personality and Views of Human Nature in the Context of Ancient Greek Society, Values and Beliefs* (1970), and in Bryan Turner's *The Body and Society* (Oxford, 1984). Francis Barker's *The Tremulous Private Body: Essays on Subjection* (New York, 1984), represents the deconstruction of the body according to the lines of modern literary theory.

Other, more diverse, studies pursuing literary, artistic, political and even semiotic relationships include: David Armstrong, *Political Anatomy of the Body* (Cambridge, 1983); Leonard Barkan, *Nature's Work of Art: the Human Body as Image of the World* (New Haven, 1975); *Body, Mind and Death*, readings selected, edited and furnished with an introductory essay by Anthony Flew (New York, 1964); J. D. Bernal, *The World, the Flesh and the Devil: an Inquiry into the Future of the Three Enemies of the Rational Soul* (1970); Robert E. French, *The Geometry of Vision and the Mind–Body Problem* (New York, 1972); Jonathan Miller, *The Body in Question* (1978); Gabriel Josipovici, *Writing and the Body* (Brighton, 1982); for a literary interpretation, see M. S. Kearns, *Metaphors of Mind in Fiction and Psychology* (Lexington, 1987). Rebecca Goldstein, British novelist, has written a novel about the dualism entitled *The Mind–Body Problem* (1985).

During this decade there has been a proliferation of studies of the body in respect of gender, as in: Sandra M. Gilbert and Susan Gubarr, *The Madwoman in the Attic: the Woman Writer and the Nineteenth Century Literary Imagination* (New Haven, 1979); *idem, No Man's Land: the Place of the Woman Writer in the Twentieth Century* (New Haven and London, 1988); Susan Rubin Suleiman (ed.), *The Female Body in Western Culture: Contemporary Perspectives* (Cambridge, 1985); Catherine Gallagher and Thomas Laqueur (eds.), *The Making of the Modern Body* (Berkeley and Los Angeles; 1986); Elaine Scarry, *The Body in Pain: the Making and Unmaking of the World* (Cambridge, 1984). The full range of studies of the body in our time will become apparent when Dr Ivan Illich's comprehensive bibliography of 'The Body in the Twentieth Century' appears.

3 Alvin Gouldner, *Enter Plato: Classical Greece and the Origins of Social Theory* (New York, 1965) emphasises how Plato makes a break with earlier thought traditions. A good introduction to Plato's strategies is offered by G. M. A. Grube, *Plato's Thought* (Indianapolis; 1980). Popper's attack upon Plato is worth remembering in this context: Karl Popper, *The Open Society and its Enemies* (1945). See also Bennett Simon, *Mind and Madness in Ancient Greece* (Ithaca, 1978).

4 F. Bottomley, *Attitudes to the Body in Western Christendom* (1979); Peter Brown, *The Body and Society: Men, Women and Sexual Renunciation in Early Christianity* (New York, 1988).

5 Valuable here are Paul Kristeller, *Renaissance Thought* (New York, 1961); Charles Schmitt and Quentin Skinner (eds.), *The Cambridge History of Renaissance Philosophy* (Cambridge, 1988).

6 See the argument in R. D. Stock, *The Holy and the Daemonic from Sir Thomas Browne to William Blake* (Princeton, 1982).

7 For the relations of God and Nature see Amos Funkenstein, *Theology and the Scientific Imagination from the Middle Ages to the Seventeenth Century* (Princeton, 1986).

8 Illuminating on the philosophy of imaginative genius are J. Engell, *The Creative Imagination* (Cambridge, 1981); P. A. Cantor, *Creature and Creator. Myth-making and English Romanticism* (Cambridge, 1984); and, more generally, G. S. Rousseau, 'Science and the Discovery of the Imagination in Enlightenment England', *Eighteenth-Century Studies*, III (1969), 108–35 and E. Tuveson, *The Imagination as a Means of Grace* (Berkeley, 1960).

9 See Peter Bowler, *The Eclipse of Darwinism* (Baltimore, University Press, 1983).

10 See J. Passmore, *A Hundred years of Philosophy* (New York, 1966).

11 Richard Rorty, *Philosophy and the Mirror of Nature* (Princeton, 1980).

12 *Ibid.*, 7. Rorty's fervour to smash dualism is everywhere apparent. For example, in this same introductory section entitled 'Invention of the Mind', Rorty writes: 'at this point we might want to say that we have dissolved the mind–body problem' (32), and a few sentences later, on the same page, 'the mind–body problem, we can now say, was merely a result of Locke's unfortunate mistake about how words get meaning, combined with his and Plato's muddled attempt to talk about adjectives as if they were nouns'.

13 *Ibid.*, 32. Rorty continues this passage by derogating the grand aims of contemporary professional philosophy: 'I would hope further to have incited the suspicion that our so-called intuition about what is mental may be merely our readiness to fall in with a specifically philosophical language game.' Here Rorty's polemical pronoun ('our') shrewdly hovers between professional philosophers on the one hand and interested amateurs who have thought about the dualism of mind–body on the other.

14 *Ibid.*, 7. The implication would seem to be equally true for the 'body'. But historically speaking, there have been three species of books about body, all of which have produced a large number of metacritiques in the last century: (1) those written by philosophers of mind with an interest to keep the dualism (Rorty would say 'philosophical language game') alive by diminishing the importance of body when considered in its physiological, or neurophysiological, state; (2) those by scientists (anatomists, physiologists, neurophysiologists, and other empirical laboratory experimenters) often concerned to demonstrate that the dilemmas called linguistic by the philosophers are actually as yet unexplored neurophsiological mysteries related to the workings of the central nervous system; and (3) those by a broad range of historians and other cultural commentators interested in the social dimensions of the mind–body problem when considered with respect to individuals or societies viewed collectively.

15 Alasdair Macintyre, *After Virtue* (Notre Dame, 1984).

16 In the process, the human body is abandoned, and discourses consulting the human *form* rather than 'the body as text' or 'the body as trope' become increasingly rare. Amongst them see John Blacking, *The Anthropology of the Body* (1977); Julia L. Epstein, 'Writing the Unspeakable: Fanny Burney's Mastectomy and the Fictive Body', *Representations* (fall 1986), 131–66; Robert N. Essick, 'How Blake's Body Means', in Nelson Hilton and Thomas A. Vogel (eds.), *Unnam'd Forms: Blake and Textuality* (Berkeley and Los Angeles, 1986). The more usual approach applies the paradigm 'read the body – read the text', as if to equate the two through a metonymy, and as discovered in so many (often excellent) works of contemporary feminism (see those mentioned in n. 2 above). But these trends appear to be absent, or at least minimal, in contemporary philosophy; see, for example, Mark Johnson, *The Body in the Mind: the Bodily Basis of Meaning, Imagination and Reason* (Chicago, 1987). Further reasons for this recent development, viewed within the context of literary theory, are provided in H. Aram Veeser (ed.), *The New Historicism* (1989).

17 O. Mayr, *Authority, Liberty and Automatic Machines in Early Modern Europe* (Baltimore, 1986); L. Mumford, *The Condition of Man* (1944); *idem, Technics and Civilization* (New York, 1963).

18 For the reciprocity of mind and brain, see Patricia S. Churchland, *Neurophilosophy: Toward a Unified Science of the Mind/Brain* (Cambridge, 1986); John Eccles, *The Neurophysiological Basis of Mind* (Oxford, 1953); *idem, Brain and Human Behavior* (New York, 1972); *idem, The Understanding of the Brain* (New York, 1973); Marc Jeannerod, *The Brain Machine: the Development of Neurophysiological Thought* (Cambridge, 1985); Morton F. Reiser, *Mind, Brain Body: Toward a Convergence of Psychoanalysis and Neurobiology* (New York, 1984); Fred A. Wolf, *The Body Quantum: the Physics of the Human Body* (1987). Arguing against the radical mechanism of these positions is Herbert Weiner, M.D., 'Some Comments on the Transduction of Experience by the Brain: Implications for our understanding of the relationship of mind to body', *Psychiatric*

Medicine, XXXIV (1972), 355–80. For the shrewd input of a Nobel Laureate in physics on the question of material reciprocity, see E. P. Wigner, Emeritus Professor of Physics at Princeton University, 'Remarks on the Mind–Body Question', in I. J. Good (ed.), *The Scientist Speculates – an Anthology of Partly Baked Ideas* (New York, 1962), 284–302.

19 Victor Weisskopf, *Knowledge and Wonder: the Natural World as Man Knows It* (Cambridge, 1979), 244.

20 The endurance of these Cartesian models, from Descartes to the present, in regard to the mind–body dualism, as well as in such disparate academic territories as linguistics, medicine, and psychology, is discussed in William Barrett, *Death of the Soul: from Descartes to the Computer* (New York, 1986); Richard B. Carter, *Descartes' Medical Philosophy: the Organic Solution to the Mind–Body Problem* (Baltimore, 1983); Harry M. Bracken (ed.), *Mind and Language: Essays on Descarates and Chomsky* (Dordrecht, 1984); Marjorie Grene, *Interpretations of Life and Mind: Essays around the Problem of Reduction* (1971); and *idem, Descartes* (Brighton, 1985); Kenneth Dewhurst and Nigel Reeves (eds.), *Friedrich Schiller: Medicine, Psychology and Literature* (Berkeley and Los Angeles, 1978); E. H. Lenneberg, *Biological Foundations of Language* (New York, 1967); Amelie Oksenburg Rorty, *Essays on Descartes' Meditations* (Berkeley and Los Angeles, 1986); Margaret D. Wilson, *Descartes* (1978); Albert G. A. Balz, *Descartes and the Modern Mind* (New Haven, 1952). Some of these topics are anticipated in René Descartes, *Lettres de Mr Descartes: ou sont traites les plus belles questions de la morale, physique, medecine & les mathematiques* (Paris, 1666–7).

21 For this Cartesian legacy, see Aram Vartanian, *Diderot and Descartes: a Study of Scientific Naturalism in the Enlightenment* (Princeton, 1953); and see, of course, Arthur Koestler, *The Ghost in the Machine* (1976).

22 For modern critics of the supposedly dire consequences of Cartesian dualism, see F. Capra, *The Turning Point: Science, Society and the Rising Culture* (New York, 1982); M. Berman, *The Re-enchantment of the World* (1982).

23 John Searle, *Mind, Brains and Science* (Cambridge, 1984). Modern neurosurgeons have made useful contributions to this subject, especially within the contexts of the complex way in which the brain processes language in relation to a perceived external reality and to the role of the will within this reality, a subject of immense concern to poststructuralist theory, especially Derridean and post-Derridean deconstructionism. Among these Fred Plum, M.D., has been especially eloquent; see, for example, F. Plum (ed.), *Language, Communication and the Brain* (New York, 1988); G. Globus (ed.), *Consciousness and The Brain* (New York, 1976).

24 Thomas Nagel, *Mortal Questions* (Cambridge, 1979); *idem, The View from Nowhere* (New York, 1986).

25 For criticism of invasions of the rights of mental patients, see T. Szasz, *The Myth of Mental Illness* (New York, 1961). See also T. Szasz, *Pain and Pleasure: a Study of Bodily Feelings* (1957).

26 On the modern medicalisation of death see R. Lamerton, *The Care of the Dying* (Harmondsworth, 1980).

27 Despite the unassailability of the crucial function they play there. For example, the late American philosopher Susanne Langer devoted her entire professional career to the interaction of mental and physical phenomena in an attempt to generate an aesthetics based on the link.

28 Cf. W. I. Matson, 'Why Isn't the Mind–Body Problem Ancient?', in P. K. Feyerabend and G. Maxwell (eds.), *Mind, Matter, and Method* (Minneapolis, 1966). This matter of origins viewed within the context of the seventeenth- and eighteenth-century debates is discussed by Douglas Odegard in 'Locke and Mind–Body Dualism', *Philosophy*, XLV (1970), 87–105, and Hilary Putnam in 'How Old is the Mind?', in Richard Caplan (ed.), *Exploring the Concept of Mind* (Iowa City, 1986).

29 See C. Kerby-Miller (ed.), *Memoirs of the Extraordinary Life, Works and Discoveries of Martinus Scriblerus* (New York, 1966), for the sad story of Indamira and Lindamora.

30 See S. P. Fullinwider, *Technologies of the Finite* (Westpoint, 1982).

31 Michael V. Wedlin, *Mind and the Imagination in Aristotle* (New Haven, 1989).

32 For Augustine on mind and body see F. Bottomley, *Attitudes to the Body in Western Christendom* (1979), and Jean H. Hagstrum, *The Romantic Body* (Knoxville, 1985), chap. 2.

33 Such paradoxes are brilliantly illuminated in P. Camporesi, *The Incorruptible Flesh: Bodily Mutation and Mortification in Religion and Folklore* (Cambridge, 1988); see also *idem, Bread of Dreams: Food and Fantasy in Early Modern Europe* (Cambridge 1988); *idem, The Body in the Cosmos: Natural Symbols in Medieval and Early Modern Italy* (Cambridge, 1989).

34 See Amos Funkenstein, *Theology and the Scientific Imagination from the Middle Ages to the Seventeenth Century* (Princeton, 1986).

35 E. Le Roy Ladurie, *Montaillou* (New York, 1979); Carlo Ginzburg, *The Cheese and the Worms* (New York, 1982). For the culture of 'plebeian' materialism, see M. Bakhtin, *Rabelais and his World*, tr. H. Iswolsky (Cambridge, 1968); Peter Stallybrass and Allon White, *The Politics and Poetics of Transgression* (London, 1986).

36 L. Barkan, *Nature's Work of Art: the Human Body as Image of the World* (New Haven, 1975).

37 A. O. Lovejoy, *The Great Chain of Being* (Cambridge, 1936) remains the classic discussion of the meanings of hierarchical metaphysics.

38 R. Hooykaas, *Religion and the Rise of Modern Science* (Edinburgh, 1972). Illuminating also are I. Couliano, *Eros et magie a la Renaissance* (Paris, 1984), and W. Leiss, *The Domination of Nature* (New York, 1972); and, for the long-term retreat of the 'animist' world view, E. B. Tylor's anthropological classic, *Primitive Culture* (1871).

39 Ernst Cassirer, *The Philosophy of the Enlightenment* (Boston, 1964) remains the most penetrating account of the metaphysics of the Enlightenment. S. C. Brown (ed.), *Philosophers of the Enlightenment* (Brighton, 1979) contains valuable discussions of *philosophes* from Locke to Kant.

40 For Willis see also Hansruedi Isler, *Thomas Willis, 1621–1685, Doctor and Scientist* (New York, 1968); and on the nerves, J. Spillane, *The Doctrine of the Nerves* (1981); G. S. Rousseau, 'Nerves, Spirits, and Fibres: Towards Defining the Origins of Sensibility; with a Postscript', *The Blue Guitar*, II (1976), 125–53 (chap. 5 above); *idem*, 'Psychology', in G. S. Rousseau and Roy Porter (eds.), *The Ferment of Knowledge* (Cambridge, 1980), 143–210 (chap. 4 above).

41 There is no study of Thomas Willis's prose style, certainly no exploration approaching the work that has been completed for Sprat, Thomas Burnet and other early prominent members of the Royal Society. For the debates over rhetoric and science within the Royal Society at this time see Brian Vickers, *In Defence of Rhetoric* (Oxford and New York, 1988); *idem* (ed.), *Occult and Scientific Mentalities in the Renaissance* (Cambridge, 1984); also useful for the linguistic milieu of all those post-Cartesian figures is *Rhetoric and the Pursuit of Truth: Language Change in the Seventeenth and Eighteenth Centuries: Papers read at a Clark Library seminar 8 March 1980*, by Brian Vickers and Nancy S. Struever (Los Angeles, 1985); and Hans Arsleff, *From Locke to Saussure: Essays on the Study of Language and Intellectual History* (Minneapolis, 1982).

42 For admirable introductions, see Peter Gay, *The Enlightenment: an Interpretation*, 2 vols. (New York, 1966–9); Norman Hampson, *The Enlightenment* (Harmondsworth, 1968).

43 Paul Hazard, *The European Mind, 1680–1715* (Cleveland, 1963), and *idem, European Thought in the Eighteenth Century: from Montesquieu to Lessing* (Cleveland, 1963) capture, in vivid language, the effervescence of intellectual transformation produced by the new

science, scholarship and geographical discoveries. See also, R. F. Jones, *Ancients and Moderns: a Study of the Background of the Battle of the Books* (St Louis, 1936).

44 See M. H. Nicolson, *The Breaking of the Circle Squares in the Effect of the 'New Science' upon Seventeenth-Century Poetry*, rev. ed. (New York, 1960).

45 See David Hume, *Dialogues Concerning Natural Religion*, ed. by N. Kemp-Smith (New York, 1948).

46 A point argued in Roy Porter and Mikulas Teich (eds.), *The Enlightenment in National Context* (Cambridge, 1981).

47 Geoffrey Keynes (ed.), *The Complete Works of Sir Thomas Browne*, 6 vols. (1928–31), I, 47 (section 34). Browne, like Willis, conducted a thriving medical practice all his life, but the intersection of his literature and medicine, especially viewed within the medico-linguistic realm, or in relation to mind–body dualism, has not been explored. Such fine books as Thomas N. Corns's *The Development of Milton's Prose Style* (Oxford, 1982) discuss baroque English style in the age of Browne but omit these seminal scientific figures.

48 See, for instance, D. W. Smith, *Helvetius: a Study in Persecution* (Oxford, 1965), a fine account of the pioneering utilitarian.

49 For the history of man set in the context of vibrant ideas of life see Jacques Roger, *Les Sciences de la vie dans la pensée française au XVIII siècle* (Paris, 1963).

50 For Enlightenment conjectural histories of man see Gladys Bryson, *Man and Society: the Scottish Inquiry of the Eighteenth Century* (Princeton, 1945); J. H. Brumfitt, *Voltaire, Historian* (Oxford, 1958); P. Rossi, *The Dark Abyss of Time: the History of the Earth and the History of Nations from Hooke to Vico* (Chicago, 1984).

51 For ideas of the malleability of man see J. Passmore, *The Perfectibility of Man* (1972).

52 See Henry Vyverberg, *Historical Pessimism in the French Enlightenment* (Cambridge, 1958).

53 Laurence Sterne, *The Life and Opinions of Tristram Shandy*, ed. C. Ricks (Harmondsworth, 1967).

54 John Yolton, *John Locke and the Way of Ideas* (New York, 1956); idem, *Thinking Matter: Materialism in Eighteenth Century Britain* (Minneapolis, 1983); idem, *Perceptual Acquaintance from Descartes to Reid* (Minneapolis, 1984).

55 The favourite Cambridge Platonist image; see Rosalie Colie, *Light and Enlightenment* (Cambridge, 1957).

56 Perhaps the finest discussion of the rise of such mechanistic imagery of thinking remains Elie Halévy, *The Growth of Philosophic Radicalism* (1928).

57 Attention, learning to read, and language theory as it reflected the relation of words to things were subjects of supreme significance throughout the Enlightenment, and those who wrote on these subjects – from whatever vantage – inevitably found themselves commenting upon mind and body. Among these, for example, were such diverse thinkers as the Swiss classicist Samuel Werenfels, the opponent of false sublimity and author of *A Discourse of Logomachys, or Controversies about Words, so Common among Learned Men. To which is Added, A Dissertation Concerning Meteors of Stile, or False Sublimity* (1711); the English philologist, James Harris, the author of the 1756 *Hermes* (reprint, Menston, 1968), from whose work the passage in our epigraph is taken; the illustrious French philosopher–social-commentator, Condorcet, in his *Progress of the Human Mind* (see the edition by Stuart Hampshire *et al.* (1955)); and Charles Bonnet, the Swiss naturalist whose psychology of mind and body formed the basis of his very interesting theories of attention and learning. For Bonnet, see *Considerations sur les corps organisés, ou l'on traite de leur dévélopment, de leur reproduction, &c., ou l'on a rassemble en abrège tour ce que l'histoire naturelle offre de plus certain & de plus interessan sur ce sujet* (2nd ed., Amsterdam, 1768); idem, *Essai analytique sur les facultés de l'âme* (reprint, New York: Olms, 1973); idem, *Essai de psychologie* (reprint, New York, 1978), as well as

Lorin Anderson, *Charles Bonnet and the Order of the Known* (Dordrecht, 1982); G. Murphy, in *Psychological Thought from Pythagoras to Freud* (New York, 1968), does not identify 'attention' as a valid category until the nineteenth century, but it was surely a crucial category in the eighteeth-century Enlightenment.

58 For the eighteenth century as an era of the achievement of self-identity see S. D. Cox, *'The Stranger Within Thee': The Concept of self in late Eighteenth Century Literature* (Pittsburgh, 1980); J. O. Lyons, *The Invention of the Self* (Carbondale, 1978); P. M. Spacks, *Imagining a Self* (Cambridge, 1976); J. N. Morris, *Versions of the Self* (New York, 1966); for philosophical background see H. E. Allison, 'Locke's theory of personal identity: a re-examination', in I. C. Tifton (ed.), *Locke on Human Understanding: Selected Essays* (Oxford, 1977), 105–22.

59 Lester G. Crocker, *An Age of Crisis: Man and World in Eighteenth-Century France* (Baltimore, 1959); *idem, Nature and Culture: Ethical Thought in the French Enlightenment* (Baltimore, 1963). Crocker highlights the dilemmas produced by Enlightenment naturalism, subjectivism, and relativism.

60 See Peter Gay, *The Enlightenment: an Interpretation*, 2 vols. (New York, 1966–9); and Roy Porter and Mikulas Teich (eds.), *The Enlightenment in National Context* (Cambridge, 1981).

61 For Enlightenment historical and critical exposes of religion as false consciousness, see Frank E. Manuel, *The Eighteenth Century Confronts the Gods* (New York, 1967); R. Knox, *Enthusiasm* (1950); B. R. Kreisler, *Miracles, Convulsions and Ecclesiastical Politics in Early Eighteenth-century Paris* (Princeton, 1978); G. Rosen, 'Enthusiasm: "a dark lanthorn of the spirit" ', *Bulletin of the History of Medicine*, XLII (1958), 393–421; H. Schwartz, *Knaves, Fools, Madmen, and that Subtile Effluvium: a Study of the Opposition to the French Prophets in England, 1706–1710* (Gainesville, 1978). For materialism, see in particular Margaret C. Jacob, *The Radical Enlightenment: Pantheists, Freemasons and Republicans* (1981); A. C. Kors, *D'Holbach's Circle: an Enlightenment in Paris* (Princeton, 1977).

62 Maureen MacNeil, *Under the Banner of Science: Erasmus Darwin and his Age* (Manchester, 1987); D. King-Hele, *Erasmus Darwin and the Romantic Poets* (New York, 1986), for this theory of consciousness amongst Romantic literati.

63 For explication see L. S. King, 'The Power of the Imagination', in *The Philosophy of Medicine: the Early Eighteenth Century* (Cambridge, 1978), chap. 7; Owsei Temkin, *Galenism: the Rise and Decline of a Medical Philosophy* (Ithaca, 1973); and more broadly, *idem*, 'Health and Disease', in P. P. Wiener *et al.* (eds.), *Dictionary of the History of Ideas*, II (New York, 1973), 395–407.

64 But it did not call into question the semiology of disease and the role of imagination within this semiotic system of medical diagnosis. Also, satires on the imagination in the period reflected the intersection of these two realms: medical and literary – in such works, for example, as (in England) Dr Malcolm Flemyng's *Neuropathia* (1747), and (in Italy), the polymathic Lodovico Antonio Muratori's book on imagination, human health, and dreams (1747). For medical satire, see M. H. Nicolson and G. S. Rousseau, *'This Long Disease, my Life': Alexander Pope and the Sciences* (Princeton, 1968), but there remains no in-depth study of the medicalisation of the imagination in the Enlightenment, as G. S. Rousseau noted two decades ago in 'Science and the Discovery of the Imagination in Enlightened England', *Eighteenth-Century Studies*, III (1969), 108–35.

65 Modern critiques of Cartesian dualism stress the continuing degree of psychosomatic interplay, even in the discussion of brutes, for which see L. Cohen Rosenfeld, *From Beast-machine to Man-machine: The Theme of Animal Soul in French Letters from Descartes to La Mettrie* (New York, 1940). See also T. Brown, 'Descartes, Dualism and Psychosomatic Medicine', in W. F. Bynum, Roy Porter and Michael Shepherd (eds.), *The Anatomy of Madness*, 2 vols. (1985), II, 40–62; Sylvana Tomaselli, 'Descartes, Locke and the mind/body Dualism', *History of Science* XXII (1984), 185–205; R. B. Carter, *Descartes' Medical Philosophy* (Baltimore, 1983); L. J. Rather, *Mind and Body in Eighteenth-*

Century Medicine (Berkeley, 1965: *idem*, 'Old and New Views of the Emotions and Bodily Changes', *Clio Medica*, 1 (1965), 1–25. A contrary interpretation is to be found in P. Lain Entralgo, *Mind and Body: Psychosomatic Pathology: a Short History of the Evolution of Medical Thought* (1955).

66 See classically M. Foucault, *Madness and Civilization*. Similar views are to be found in the Frankfurt School interpretation of the Enlightenment, as in, for example, Theodor W. Adorno and Max Horkheimer, *Dialectic of Enlightenment* (New York, 1972).

67 This spectorial nighttime world is just beginning to receive attention, although no one has written so lucidly about it as Luyendijk-Elshout in *The Languages of Psyche;* see Terry Castle, 'Phantasmagoria', *Critical Inquiry*, xv (1988), 32–49. M. Kiessling's valuable study *The Incubus in English Literature: Provenance and Progeny* (Washington, 1977) treats the literary dimension without consulting its medical underbelly.

68 See D. Furst, 'Sterne and Physick: Images of Health and Disease in *Tristram Shandy*' (Ph.D. diss., Columbia University, 1974); J. Rodgers, 'Ideas of life in *Tristram Shandy:* Contemporary medicine' (Ph.D. diss., University of East Anglia, 1978); A. Cash, *Laurence Sterne: the Early and Middle years* (1976); and for Smollett, G. S. Rousseau, *Tobias Smollett: Essays of Two Decades* (Edinburgh, 1982).

69 See P. Gay, 'The Enlightenment as Medicine and as Cure', in W. H. Barber (ed.), *The Age of Enlightenment: Studies Presented to Theodore Besterman* (Edinburgh, 1967), 375–86.

70 J. Swift, *A Tale of a Tub and Other Satires*, ed. K. Williams (Everyman ed., 1975), 191–4.

71 Ronald Paulson, *Representations of Revolution, 1789–1820* (New Haven, 1983).

72 Sergio Moravia, *Il pensiero degli ideologues* (Firenze, 1974); M. Staum, *Cabanis: Enlightenment and Medical Philosophy in the French Revolution* (Princeton, 1980).

73 The classic statement is, of course, by Jacques Roger, *Les Sciences de la vie* (Paris, 1963), but Bakhtin has added to the discussion in his 1926 statement about the 'dialogism of vitalism' in which both Enlightenment mechanists and vitalists are seen as more entrenched in 'the Other' than has been acknowledged; see Michael Bakhtin, 'Sovremennyi Vitalizm [Contemporary Vitalism]' in *Chelovek i Priroda*, 1 (1926), 9–23, 33–42, and G. S. Rousseau's analysis of this work in relation to the traditions of Enlightenment vitalism: 'Bakhtin and Enlightenment: an Essay on Vitalism for our Times', in F. Burwick *et al.* (eds.), *Modernism and the Traditions of Vitalism* (New York, 1990). For vitalism as it impinges on the mind–body question, see the now classic early twentieth-century statement by Hans Driesch, *The History and Theory of Vitalism* (1914); and *idem, Mind and Boy*, trans. Theodore Besterman (New York, 1927). The role of vitalism in relation to mind and body was widely studied in the eighteenth century in medical dissertations, especially in middle European universities, and in relation to Stahl's animism, Barthez's vitalism (discussed in Rousseau above), and, most fully, by the German psychologist Ferdinand Carus in his *Geschichte der Psychologie* (Halle, 1795).

74 See Raymond Williams, *The Long Revolution* (1961); Elizabeth Eisenstein, 'On Revolution and the Printed Word', in Roy Porter and Mikulas Teich (eds.), *Revolution in History* (Cambridge, 1986), 186–205; Robert Darnton, *The Business of Enlightenment: a Publishing History of the Encyclopédie, 1775–1800* (Cambridge, 1979); *idem, The Literary Underground of the Old Regime* (Cambridge, 1982).

75 See K. Thomas, *Religion and the Decline of Magic* (Harmondsworth, 1973); and also H. Leventhal, *In the Shadow of the Enlightenment: Occultism and Renaissance Science in Eighteenth-Century America* (New York, 1976).

76 On Mesmerism and similar sympathetic powers see W. Falconer, *A Dissertation on the Influence of the Passions Upon Disorders of the Body* (1788); John Haygarth, *Of the Imagination, as a Cause and as a Cure of Disorders of the Body* (Bath, 1800); and, amongst modern scholarship, R. Darnton, *Mesmerism and the end of the Enlightenment in France* (Cambridge, 1968); Jonathan Miller, 'Mesmerism', *The Listener*, 22 Nov. 1973, 685–90:

Roy Porter, 'Under the Influence: Mesmerism in England', *History Today* (Sept. 1985), 22–9.

77 On sensibility see Erik Erametsa, *A Study of the Word 'Sentimental' and of Other Linguistic Characteristics of Eighteenth-Century Sentimentalism in England* (Helsinki, 1951); Janet Todd, *Sensibility: an Introduction* (1986); L. Bredvold, *The Natural History of Sensibility* (Detroit, 1962); more broadly cultural are S. Moravia, 'The Enlightenment and the sciences of man', *History of Science*, XVIII (1980), 247–68; *idem*, 'From "Homme machine" to "Homme sensible": Changing eighteenth-century models of Man's Image', *Journal of the History of Ideas*, XXXIX (1978), 45–60; K. Figlio, 'Theories of perception and the physiology of mind in the late eighteenth century', *History of Science*, XIII (1975), 177–212; and on the positioning of the 'English Malady', as Cheyne christened the peculiar nature of English melancholy within the wider history of mental illness, see Stanley W. Jackson, *Melancholia and Depression From Hippocratic Times to Modern Times* (New Haven, 1986).

78 See E. Fischer-Homberger, 'Hypochondriasis of the eighteenth century, neurosis of the present century', *Bulletin of the History of Medicine*, XLVI (1972), 391–401. For the politics of hypochondria in Britain see Roy Porter, 'The Rage of Party: a Glorious Revolution in English Psychiatry?' *Medical History*, XXIX (1983), 35–50; and much other recent scholarship devoted to the medical career of Dr George Cheyne.

79 For the ambushes of imagination, see S. Cunningham, 'Bedlam and Parnassus: Eighteenth-century Reflections', in B. Harris (ed.), *Eighteenth-Century Studies*, XXIV (1971), 36–55; Roy Porter, 'The Hunger of Imagination: Approaching Samuel Johnson's Melancholy', in W. F. Bynun, Roy Porter and Michael Shepherd (eds.), *The Anatomy of Madness*, 2 vols. (1985), I, 63–88.

80 G. S. Rousseau, 'Nymphomania, Bienville and the Rise of Erotic Sensibility', in P.-G. Boucé (ed.), *Sexuality in Eighteenth-Century Britain* (Manchester, 1982), 95–120 (*Perilous Enlightenment*, chap. 2); Roy Porter, 'Love, Sex and Madness in Eighteenth Century England', *Social Research*, LIII (1986), 211–42. And for masturbation, see P.-G. Boucé, 'Les Jeux interdits de l'imaginaire: onanism et culpabilisation sexuelle au XVIIIe siècle', in J. Ceard (ed.), *La Folie et le corps* (Paris, 1985), 223–43; E. H. Hare, 'Masturbatory Insanity: the History of an Idea', *Journal of Mental Science*, CVIII (1962), 1–25; R. H. MacDonald, 'The Frightful Consequences of Onanism', *Journal of the History of Ideas*, XXVIII (1967), 323–41; J. Stengers and A. Van Neck, *Histoire d'une grande peur: la masturbation* (Brussels, 1984); L. J. Jordanova, 'The Popularisation of Medicine: Tissot on Onanism', *Textual Practice*, 1 (1987), 68–80; and for a wider vision of bourgeois culture as leading to a masturbatory privatisation of the body, F. Barker, *The Tremulous Private Body* (New York, 1984).

81 See Roy Porter (ed.), 'Introduction' to *Thomas Trotter, an Essay, Medical, philosophical and Chemical on Drunkenness* (1988; 1st ed. 1804). See also *idem*, 'The Drinking Man's Disease: the Prehistory of Alcoholism in Georgian Britain', *British Journal of Addiction*, LXXX (1985), 384–96. For other paradoxes arising out of the mind–body problem and the emergence of ideology, see *idem, Mind Forg'd Manacles: a History of Madness from the Restoration to the Regency* (1987).

82 On moral therapy see A. Digby, *Madness, Morality and Medicine* (Cambridge, 1985); *idem*, 'Moral Treatment at the York Retreat', in W. F. Bynum, Roy Porter and Michael Shepherd (eds.), *The Anatomy of Madness*, 2 vols. (London, 1985), II, 52–72; W. F. Bynum, 'Rationales for therapy in British psychiatry 1780–1835', *Medical History*, XVIII (1974), 817–34.

83 L. L. Whyte, *The Unconscious Before Freud* (New York, 1962); H. P. Ellenberger, *The Discovery of the Unconscious: the History and Evolution of Dynamic Psychiatry* (New York, 1971).

84 K. M. Baker, *Condorcet: from Natural Philosophy to Social Mathematics* (Chicago, 1975), a fine study of the late Enlightenment's most important social scientist-*cum*-prophet.

Also relevant are R. V. Sampson, *Progress in the Age of Reason* (1956); and C. Vereker, *Eighteenth Century Optimism* (Liverpool, 1967).

INDEX

Goodwin, Philip, 85
  and *The Mystery of Dreams, Historically Discoursed* (1658), 85
Gouldner, Alvin, 211
Goya y Lucientes, Francisco José de, 231
Grange, Kathleen, 101
Gravelot, Hubert François Bourguignon D'Anville, engraver, 202
Gray, Thomas, 71, 127, 157, 159–60
Great Awakening, the, 97
Greece (or 'Greeks'), ancient, 67, 70, 93, 96, 185, 187, 220
  and philosophy, 187
Greene, Donald, 178–80, 184, 186–9
  and 'Augustinianism and Empiricism', 189
  and 'Latitudinarianism and Sensibility', 184
Grimm, Jakob Ludwig Karl, 46
Grossard, professor of medicine at Montpellier, 32, 35
Guattari, Felix, 102

Habermas, Jürgen, author of *Philosophical Discourse of Modernity* (1987), x, xii, 41, 171
  see also discourse therapy; Michel Foucault; rationalism
Hagstrum, Jean, 178–80, 186, 188–90
  and *Sex and Sensibility*, 186, 189
Haizmann, Christoph, 106
Haller, Albrecht von, Swiss physiologist and Enlightenment thinker, Professor of Medicine at University of Göttingen, 11, 29, 31, 126, 128–9, 131, 133–5, 186, 188, 224
Handel, George Frideric, 134, 157, 159
Harding, D. W., 42
Harley, E. H., 14–15
Hartley, David, 5, 11, 17, 68, 84–5, 135, 227–9, 232
  and sensationalism, 17
Harvey, Gideon, 89
Harvey, William, 2, 44, 48, 55, 79
  and *De Motu Cordis*, 129
Hasidism of the Baal-Shem Tov, the, 97
Haslam, John, 74
Hegel, Georg Wilhelm Friedrich, 41, 54, 103, 182, 214
  and Hegelianism, 214
Heinroth, 88
Heisenberg, Werner, 135
Helmont, Franciscus Mercurius van (1614–99), 131
Helvetius, Claude Adrien, 225–6
Henry, George W., 67

Herder, Johan Gottfried von, 225–6
Hervey, Lord John, 159
Heywood, Eliza, 100
  and *Life's Progress through the Passions*, 100
  and *Love in Excess*, 100
  and *The Secret History of the Present Intrigues of the Court at Caramania*, 100
Hill, Christopher, 97, 152
Hill, R. G., 68
  and *Lunacy, its Past and its Present* (1870), 68
historicism, xiii–xiv, 65–76, 169–77, 178–97
  and Foucault, 40–60
  and the history of science, 178–97
historiography, x–xiv, 40–60, 94, 169–77, 230–2
  see also anthropology; disciplines; history of science; psychology; psychiatry
history, x–xiv
  and the disciplines, xi–xiii
  of mind–body relations, 210–38
  of psychiatry, 84–96
  of psychology, 65–87
  of science, 178–97
  see also anthropology; Michel Foucault; historiography; New Historicism
History and Theory, the periodical, 67
history of science, xiii, 178–98, 224–7
  see also disciplines
Hobbes, Thomas, 3, 44, 84–5, 229
Hoffman, Friedrich, 29
Hogarth, William, 88, 134, 146
Holbach, Paul Henri Thiry, baron d', eighteenth-century philosopher and encyclopedist, 27, 225, 229
  and *Système de la Nature*, 229
Holland, 89, 99
Holocaust, the, 172, 176
Homer, 27
homosexuals, 159–63
  see also bachelors
Hooke, Robert, 4
Hooykaas, Reijer, 222
Hôtel-Dieu, 27
Housman, Alfred Edward, 155
Hughes, John, 10
Hume, David, 44, 68, 79, 123–4, 131, 135, 157, 191, 218, 225, 233
  and *Dialogues of Natural Religion*, 225
  and *Treatise of Human Nature*, 123
Hunter, Richard, 68, 88, 93, 101
  and *Three Hundred Years of Psychiatry 1535–1860* (1963), 68
Hunter, William, anatomist, 135
Husserl, Edmund, 187

Lewes, George Henry, 68
  and *The Biographical History of Philosophy
    from its Origin in Greece down to the
    Present Day* (1853), 68
Lewis, C. S., 183
linguistics, 46–8
Linnaeus, Karl, 44, 48, 199
  and bisexual classification, 49
  and taxonomy, 49
Literature and Science, 81
  see also Enlightenment Borders
Littre, Maximilien, 32
Locke, John, 2–4, 7–9, 11, 14, 17, 68, 79,
    82, 84–5, 123–6, 128, 131–3, 136, 182,
    187–9, 191, 213–14, 216, 218, 225–9
  and *An Essay Concerning Human
    Understanding*, 4, 123–6, 128, 131, 182,
    227
  and the *Essay* as discourse, 4, 5, 17
  and Blake's *Jerusalem*, 17
  and psychology, 5
  and the theory of association, 2, 17
London Magazine, 199
London Post and General Advertiser, The,
    200, 203
London School of Economics, 40
Lord Beaumont, 200
Lorry, Anne Charles, author of medical
    literature, 74
Lucretius, 41, 221
Luther, Martin, 222
Lyell, Sir Charles, 123
  and *Geology*, 123
Lyotard, Jean-François, xi

Macalpine, Ida, 68, 82, 93, 101
  and *Three hundred Years of Psychiatry
    1535–1860* (1963), 68
MacCabe, Colin, 61
Macflecnoe, 192
Macintyre, Alasdair, 215
Mack, Maynard, 174
Mackenzie, Henry, 71, 135–6
  and *The Man of Feeling*, 71
madness, 6–10, 14–17, 71–96, 234–6
  and asylums, 15–16, 87–96
  and Foucault, 55
  in history, 230–6, 245
  within mind–body relations, 230–45
  see also psychiatry; witchcraft
Magnus, Albertus, 49
Malebranche, Nicolas, 3, 7, 213
Malpighi, Marcello, 28–32, 35
Malthus, Thomas Robert, 52
Mandelbaum, Morris, 84
Mandeville, Bernard, 84, 87, 124

Mandrou, Robert, 66
Manichaeans, 212
Manley, Mary, 99
  and *The Adventures of Rivella*, 99
Marat, Jean Paul, 34, 124
  and *Philosophical Essay on Man* (London,
    1773), 34
Marcus, Stephen, 161
Margetts, E. L., 69
Marlborough, Duke of, 200
Marlowe, Christopher, 160
Marston, John, 160
Marx, Karl, 52, 226
Marxism, 172–5
Marxists, 72, 170, 173–5, 215
materialism, 13–23, 222–40
  medical, 224
  scientific, 224–31
  see also imagination; mechanism; vitalism
Mayr, Otto, 216
Mead, Margaret, xiii, 163
mechanism, 10–24, 29–35, 79–87, 127–32,
    217–44
  and anatomy, 28–36, 223–5
  and models, 7–22, 216
  and physiology, 2–24
  and Vaucansonian automata, 216–17
Meckel, Johann Friedrich (1724–74),
    professor of science in Berlin, 91–3
medicine, philosophy of, 82
  and Enlightenment, 40–60
  and imagination, 1–25
  and mind–body relation, 210–41
  and psychology, 61–120
  and racism, 26–37
  and satire, 230
  and sensibility, 122–41
Medmenham Monks, the 99
melancholy, 112
  see also hypochondria; hysteria;
    sensibility
memory, 211–42 passim
  see also imagination
Menocchio, the Friulian miller, 222
mental acts and states, 214–15
Merquior, J. G., 40
Merton, Professor Robert, 16, 42
Mesmerism, 233
Middle Ages, the, xi, 78, 149, 172, 176,
    180, 185, 221
Midriff, Dr John, 82, 89
Mill, John Stuart, 17
Miller, J. Hillis, 169
Miller, Perry, 94
  and *The New England Mind*, 94
Millet, Kate, 160